PROFESSIONALS IN DISTRESS

Issues, Syndromes, and Solutions in Psychology

Richard R. Kilburg
Peter E. Nathan
Richard W. Thoreson

Editors

Library of Congress Cataloging-in-Publication Data

Professionals in distress.

    1. Psychologists—Mental health. 2. Psychologists—
Job stress. I. Thoreson, Richard W. II. Kilburg,
Richard R., 1946–   III. Nathan, Peter E.
IV. American Psychological Association. [DNLM:
1. Job Satisfaction. 2. Psychology, Clinical.
3. Stress, Psychological. WM 172 P964]
RC451.4.P78P76 1986   616.85'21   85-18487
ISBN 0-912704-43-8 (pbk.)

Copies may be ordered from:
Order Department
P.O. Box 2710
Hyattsville, MD 20784

Published by the American Psychological Association, Inc.

1200 Seventeenth Street, N.W., Washington, DC 20036
Copyright © 1986 by the American Psychological Association.
Printed in the United States of America.

Contents

SECTION III: SOLUTIONS

INTRODUCTION

Richard R. Kilburg

he American Psychological Association (APA), the national professional association of psychologists in the United States, has been working on the issue of professionals in distress since 1980. More details on these efforts will be presented later in this introduction. One facet of the work on this problem involved the development of a proposal for a book dealing with the difficulties of professionals in distress from the perspective of psychology. The proposal was accepted by the APA Publications and Communications Board and work was begun in 1983. You now hold the results of that project in your hands—*Professionals in Distress: Issues, Syndromes, and Solutions in Psychology*.

This introduction presents a short history of psychology's efforts—as reflected in the activities of APA and of psychologists in general—to confront the issue of psychologists in distress and to place the development of this book in the context of these efforts. It also provides an overview of the three sections and 14 chapters that the book comprises.

A SHORT HISTORY OF PSYCHOLOGY'S EFFORTS

Founded in 1892 by a small group of university professors, the American Psychological Association (APA) has grown to become the largest organization of psychologists in the world. APA has a membership of more than 60,000, a full-time central office staff of approximately 350 people, and an annual budget in excess of 35 million dollars. The following description will not touch on the historical development of APA per se. More detailed treatment of this general topic is provided by Fernberger (1932; 1943) and Napoli (1975). Rather, it will provide a succinct summary of the specific activities that APA has undertaken on behalf of its distressed members.

APA is governed by a Council of Representatives, a group of approximately 120 individuals who are elected by the 42 divisions and 54 affiliated state and provincial associations that make up the major structural elements of the organization. The Council meets twice a year to consider policy issues and recommendations put forward by the Board and Committee structure of the

Association and by other parties. Kilburg and Pallak (1983) describe APA's governance structure and the elaborate process that has evolved in support of policy development.

As far as the editors and authors of this volume know, the first expression of concern about the problem of distressed psychologists was recorded in 1980. The Council met from August 31 to September 3, 1980, and Antoinette Appel introduced a resolution calling for the formation of a task force to address the issue of providing services to psychologists in distress. This motion was, in the normal course of Council business, referred to two of the major boards of the Association—the Board of Professional Affairs (BPA) and the Board of Social and Ethical Responsibility for Psychology (BSERP)—for their review and recommendations.

BPA has the responsibility for monitoring developments that are relevant to practice in psychology and for making policy recommendations to the Board of Directors and the Council. BSERP has similar duties in areas of social concern to the organization. Each of these boards, two of the nine major policy-recommending substructures of APA, has nine members and meets several times a year to deliberate on the issues in their areas of concern. BPA and BSERP reviewed the resolution in early October 1980. BSERP stated that it believed that the BPA was the appropriate body to develop a response on behalf of organized psychology. BPA requested staff to gather information on the incidence of these problems so that they could formulate a response that would emphasize educative and rehabilitative approaches rather than punitive measures.

At its meeting from February 6 to 8, 1981, the BPA voted to allocate one hour of its program time at the 1981 APA Convention to an open forum intended to gather information and other resources to begin to confront the issue of distressed psychologists. They also appointed three psychologists (the editors of this volume) as an ad hoc committee to organize the forum. The forum was held on Monday, August 24, 1981 at the convention. Well attended, this session developed many ideas about the problems that psychologists were having, generated a list of people who were interested in working on this issue, and identified four states in which organized efforts had already begun (Alabama, Arizona, California, and Georgia).

BPA received a set of recommendations generated by the conference organizers at its November 1981 meeting and moved to establish the Steering Committee on Distressed Psychologists whose primary job "will be to design and implement an organization to provide self-help and peer support services to members of APA who are in distress" (Nathan, Thoreson, & Kilburg, 1983). The Steering Committee met in January 1982 and developed a preliminary proposal to establish an organization to help distressed psychologists.

Initially called "Volunteers in Psychology," this nonprofit organization was to provide a range of services to psychologists in distress. At its spring 1982 meeting, the BPA concurred with the recommendations of its Steering Committee, but the proposal was routed through the rest of the APA governance structure for review and comment, as most major initiatives usually are. The majority of the groups that reviewed the recommendations were supportive of the idea that something should be done about the problems involved, but nearly all of them requested that additional information be gathered to document the need for such a program. The BPA then asked its Steering Committee to provide a more detailed proposal and to conduct a needs assessment. They asked the Committee to report to the BPA by fall 1983.

The Steering Committee met three times during 1983, conducted a survey, reviewed the literature, and drafted a more detailed set of proposals. The Committee found that there was a lack of reliable data concerning the numbers of professionals who were afflicted with difficulties such as alcoholism, drug addiction, mental and emotional disorders, and personal problems. The results of the survey suggested that there was a significant number of psychologists with such problems who were having difficulty resolving the issues on their own. In view of the efforts of other professions such as medicine, law, dentistry, and nursing to establish programs for their members, the Committee recommended that APA should develop a trial program to assist psychologists in distress and to collect more reliable information on the extent of the needs in the psychological community. Volunteers in Psychology, the program suggested to provide these services, was to be established for a three-year period. A separate nonprofit corporation, the organization would have its own governing board and be funded at approximately $131,000 total for the three-year period.

The Board of Professional Affairs responded well to the report and voted to forward it to the Council of Representatives with a recommendation that the report be circulated to APA governance and other interested organizations for review and comment. The Council concurred with this recommendation and approximately 2,000 copies were printed and disseminated. The Steering Committee met in April 1984 to review the responses and to draft its final report (Nathan, Thoreson, & Kilburg, 1984). Their report addressed the major issues raised by the critics of the project and identified several key issues that led to modifications in the recommendations. These included the need for confidentiality in the service system, clients' rights versus the right of the distressed psychologist to treatment, the need for more explicit criteria for program success and for a more detailed evaluation plan, the issue of people with problems not being identified and served, and, finally, the type of person the system would serve. The Committee increased the budget for the project to $173,400 and identified several legal issues for the BPA.

In recognition of the continued opposition to implement the proposed Volunteers in Psychology organization, the Committee also modified its recommendations to include an option that the formal Volunteers in Psychology operation not be established and that, instead, a small fund of $30,000, gathered from several sources, would be used to help several state psychological associations start small demonstration projects to serve their members. The BPA reviewed these revisions at their June 1984 meeting. They voted to request that APA's Board of Directors appoint a new, representative ad hoc committee to assist the states in establishing projects, that a fund of $30,000 be created from several sources to aid the states with the start-up costs for these projects, and that the goal of the initiative would be to create programs in two or three states in 1987.

The Board of Directors voted to circulate these proposals to the rest of the APA governance structure at their June 1984 meeting. A number of boards and committees in APA governance continued to react negatively to these recommendations. They questioned the credibility of the Steering Committee. The central issue was that these groups believed that the Committee needed to be broadly representative of the various elements in the association, if its recommendations were to be viewed as truly acceptable.

At its March 1985 meeting, the BPA reviewed these responses and voted to expand the membership of the Steering Committee to increase its representation of other constituencies in psychology. The BPA also directed the Committee to work with APA's Division of State Associations in developing a program for the 1985 APA Convention on the subject of the willingness and ability of state psychological associations to address the very difficult problems that some of their members were experiencing. The Committee met in May 1985 and decided that the primary responsibility for program design and implementation be given to state associations, with APA serving as a consultative resource. APA would serve as an information clearinghouse using Central Office staff in the Office of Professional Affairs. APA staff would also maintain a roster of psychologists who would provide pro bono consultation to states. The Committee also recommended that the Board appoint a Distressed Psychology Advisory Group of three members broadly representative of various constituencies in psychology and with experience in implementing such programs.

The Committee and the Division held a discussion of these recommendations at the convention. The participants concurred with the Committee and the recommendations were submitted to the BPA at its November 1985 meeting. BPA reviewed these proposals and voted to form the new advisory group. It is scheduled to meet in 1986 and to begin to work with states to develop programs for psychologists in distress. At this point, no other program funds have been allocated by APA.

The foregoing description provides an interesting view of just how difficult it can be for a national organization to respond to a problem that has broad implications for all of its members. Obtaining the support of all of the necessary groups so that something can be done is enormously time consuming. This is especially true when it is necessary to spend a substantial sum of money. Although APA has not provided any direct services to psychologists in distress, the activities undertaken thus far have had a broad impact on the field. The discussion that has occurred at the last five annual meetings and the various reports of the Steering Committee have served to raise the consciousness of the entire discipline about the plight of some of its members. In addition, "Psychologists Helping Psychologists," a new self-help group that focuses on individuals with alcohol and drug abuse problems, has become much more widely known and accepted in the field. This group now has a nationwide network of individuals who volunteer to counsel colleagues with these problems. Another result of this activity is that several other state associations have initiated efforts to reach out to distressed psychologists. Although the field appears to be moving at a glacial pace, in fact significant progress has been made in the last five years.

One other outcome of the work of the Steering Committee was the development of a proposal for a book focusing on the subject of psychologists in distress. In 1983 the Committee submitted this proposal to the APA Publications and Communications (P&C) Board, which enthusiastically endorsed the project. And the idea for this book, *Professionals in Distress,* became a working reality.

Initially, this volume had three purposes. First, it was to provide a comprehensive review of all of the relevant literature in the field on the subject of psychologists in distress. Second, it was to serve as a training manual for volunteers who were to work in the proposed organization to provide services to psychologists. And third, the volume would educate psychologists, the public, and other interested professionals about the state of psychology's knowledge in this area. As work on the service initiative continued, the editors pushed for completion of the book. Regardless of what happens at the national level to the various proposals to provide services to psychologists in distress, there is still a need to review the current state of knowledge in this area and to provide as much advice to the community as possible on how to manage these problems. After three years of continuous effort, the book is now finished. What follows is a brief preview of its contents.

AN OVERVIEW OF THIS BOOK

The Steering Committee discovered early on that information about professionals in distress was sparse, and what information was available was fragmented and unevenly distributed. Time pressures and lack of resources prohibited the Committee from preparing a comprehensive review on its own. Yet, the members of the group recognized the need for such a resource and believed that if the service program were established, adequate training would be required for the volunteers in the organization. In addition, the concern of the Committee extended to the families of those psychologists experiencing distress, to their colleagues, and to the general public, all of whom are directly affected by these problems. The Committee saw the need to pull the knowledge together into a central place and to highlight the gaps and implications for research, education, and practice in the field. As the group struggled with these various problems, it became clear that a single resource addressing all of these problems would be of great assistance to the field. The book was designed accordingly.

The first section of the volume introduces the problem and reviews the implications of the issues and knowledge presented in the book for the research and education communities in psychology. The second section presents comprehensive reviews of the literature available on the major dysfunctional syndromes that psychologists and other professionals experience. The final section provides specific advice to psychologists and other professionals, their families, and interested others about what can be done to assist people who have these problems. The material reflects the current state of empirical knowledge and actual practice.

In chapter 1, I present a profile of the typical distressed professional and discuss the origins of the problems experienced by professionals. In Chapter 2 Nathan pulls together the implications of this book for further research on this subject. It was clear from the start of the work of the Steering Committee that very little empirical work had been done on this specific topic. Although there was some relevant material in a number of areas that gave the Committee a reasonable basis for making recommendations, the central fact that critics of the proposals kept raising was that there was not a solid body of data to support the conclusions. It is hoped that the material in this book, together with the recommendations made by Nathan in this chapter will give the research community a set of ideas to pursue in their future work.

In chapter 3 Thoreson encourages the educational establishment to look at the ways in which they can better prepare their graduates to handle the stresses of professional life. It seems clear from the available evidence that more can be done in this area and that many of the people who leave school with adequate academic preparation are not prepared emotionally or socially to cope with the problems they encounter after training. Some specific suggestions are offered to programs that are concerned with doing a better job with their students.

Section 2, which deals with syndromes, begins with a chapter by Maslach, who provides a comprehensive overview of the research that has been done on stress. The material covers definitions of the appropriate terms, highlights the burnout and workaholic syndromes, and reviews several major issues arising out of the current research in this area. Maslach emphasizes the impact that stress-related disorders can have on the families of the victims and describes the various approaches to treating stress-prone individuals.

Thoreson and Skorina have integrated a remarkable amount of information about alcoholic professionals in chapter 5. They describe the difficulties experienced by these individuals and their families. Various models that are used in treatment and research are defined, and some solid advice for treating these problems is provided. They also describe a number of steps that the professions can take to be more supportive to their members who abuse alcohol.

In chapter 6 Millon, Millon, and Antoni review the rather sparse literature covering the incidence and prevalence of emotional and mental disorders among psychologists and other professionals. They conclude that there are not much data that indicate that psychologists suffer from these problems in any greater numbers than does the general population. They describe various factors in the training and work lives of psychologists that may make them susceptible to developing these disorders, and they outline the unique stressors that operate on psychologists in academic, human service, consultation, and administrative positions.

In chapter 7, Freudenberger covers the issue of alcohol and chemical abuse in the mental health professions. He describes the personality characteristics of abusing professionals and integrates this information with his wealth of knowledge about the burnout syndrome. The chapter contains a great deal of material about the various clinical problems that treating professionals are likely to encounter in working with people with these disorders.

Sexual abuse of clients is the most difficult issue facing the helping professions today. Brodsky provides an excellent discussion of this problem in chapter 8. Individuals who commit these acts frequently have remarkable difficulty seeing the damage that they inflict on their patients. Professional organizations have become increasingly concerned about this issue as the number of lawsuits has mushroomed and as the frequency of the abuse has been uncovered by researchers. Recommendations regarding the rehabilitation of these individuals and for prevention of the problems are also covered.

In chapter 9, which concludes the section on syndromes, Reaves gives an overview of the range of legal problems that sometimes confront professionals, covering civil, criminal, and licensure liabilities. Problems such as the duty to warn patients, families, and involved others of potential harm; revealing confidential information; sexual misconduct; and criminal fraud are highlighted. Reaves draws examples from actual cases to emphasize the serious nature of the difficulties that these legal problems sometimes entail.

Kaslow reviews the topic of the therapeutic management of distressed professionals in chapter 10, which begins the last section of the book—Solutions. The level of knowledge and sophistication of the individuals, along with certain personality characteristics, combine to produce some unique treatment issues for the mental health professionals who have the responsibility to care for them. Kaslow illustrates these conceptual issues with many clinical examples.

Chapter 11 provides an overview of the issues and difficulties confronted by professionals when they try to help their colleagues address problems they may be having. VandenBos and Duthie cover these issues in a sensitive fashion, allowing for the privacy of the afflicted individuals while simultaneously encouraging professionals to reach out to their friends and colleagues who may be experiencing difficulties. Several different approaches to confrontation are provided along with case examples that illustrate the problems and issues.

Most professionals who experience some problems have families who suffer along with them. In fact, it is the families of these distressed individuals who are often the first to spot the problem. In chapter 12, McCrady and Frankenstein comprehensively review the literature available on this issue and also provide a systematic approach that families can follow when they are confronted by a member who is distressed. They encourage the families to be involved in the treatment and rehabilitation of the person who has the problems.

In chapter 13, Cherniss and Dantzig address the issue of preventing these disorders. They review the major approaches to stress management developed for individuals. They address a variety of steps that organizations can take to reduce the stress levels under which their employees work. They encourage employers and colleagues to confront those people whom they believe to be suffering from any of the problems described in this book, and provide some advice for how the confrontation can be a productive one. The chapter emphasizes that there is a lot that can be done to prevent these disorders from happening in the first place and that employers have a responsibility to work toward reducing unnecessary stress in their working environments.

In chapter 14, Hall describes the regulatory organizations that have been developed in psychology and how they are brought to bear on the problem of psychologists who are in distress. The *Ethical Principles of Psychologists* (APA, 1981) state clearly that sexual exploitation of clients, substance abuse, deliberate fraud, and a wide variety of other behaviors are grounds for an investigation and possible disciplinary action if reported to the appropriate state on national ethics committees. In addition, the same violations of the Ethical

Principles can also lead to an investigation by the state licensing boards. If found guilty, psychologists can lose their licenses, be assigned to rehabilitative treatment, or be compelled to undergo additional education or supervision. In cases of criminal fraud, some psychologists have received prison terms. In medicine and nursing, prison sentences have been given to individuals who were found guilty of selling drugs. Hall provides an excellent analysis of these issues and makes recommendations about how to deal with state boards to professionals who may have such problems.

SUMMARY AND OBSERVATIONS

This book represents the best efforts made to date in the field of psychology to address the issues of distressed professionals. It summarizes the information that is currently available in a number of areas that are germane to these problems. There may be specific problems or issues that have been overlooked by the editors and authors, but, if gaps exist, they are purely accidental. The authors have labored for a long time to provide as comprehensive an overview as possible.

Some reviewers and readers may note that there is some redundancy among the chapters. The literature in this area is not very broad, and it was inevitable that some references would be used by more than one author. In addition, in the portions of the book dealing with legal and stress issues, a deliberate attempt was made to divide the material and the approaches, so that the chapters could be kept to a manageable length and the perspectives of several authors could be incorporated into the book. I believe that redundancy has been kept to a minimum, and that where it exists, it serves to enrich the reader by providing a new context to view the same material.

The terms *professional* and *psychologist* are sometimes used interchangeably in the book. Much of what can be said about psychologists is also true of other professionals: Most of the syndromes manifest themselves in a similar fashion, and the issues of confrontation and treatment are similar, particularly for the helping professions. I realize that there are aspects of distress that are unique to every field, but in this volume no effort has been made to address the specific issues for professions such as law, medicine, and nursing. The authors, however, have consulted many of the members of these other fields, and some of what is presented in this book reflects the constructive nature of contacts with these other professions. This book should serve to enliven the efforts of other professionals as well.

Finally, the reader may assume from reading the short history of APA's efforts on behalf of distressed psychologists that nothing has happened in the five years that the organization has been working on the problem. Although some people have criticized the slowness with which APA has acted, the fact remains that a considerable amount of education has gone on in these last five years. Programs have been started in a number of states, and some empirical research is now being conducted in departments of psychology. The editors of this book believe strongly that the pace of activity in this area will increase with the publication of this book and hope that the book provides a source of intellectual, professional, clinical, and personal stimulation for its readers.

References

American Psychological Association. (1981). Ethical principles of psychologists. *American Psychologist, 36*(6), 633–638.

Fernberger, S. W. (1932). The American Psychological Association: A historical summary. *Psychological Bulletin, 29*(1), 1–89.

Fernberger, S. W. (1943). The American Psychological Association 1892–1942. *Psychological Review, 50*(1), 33–60.

Kilburg, R. R., & Pallak, M. S. (1983). A professional's guide to the American Psychological Association. In B. D. Sales (Ed.), *The professional psychologist's handbook* (pp. 157–184). New York: Plenum Press.

Napoli, D. S. (1975). The architects of adjustment: The practice and professionalization of American psychology, 1920–1945. (Doctoral dissertation, University of California: Davis, 1975). *Dissertation Abstracts International, 36,* 12A. (University Microfilms No. AAD76-14224)

Nathan, P., Thoreson, R., & Kilburg, R. (1983). *Board of Professional Affairs Steering Committee on Distressed Psychologists: Draft report.* Washington, DC: American Psychological Association.

Nathan, P., Thoreson, R., & Kilburg, R. (1984). *Board of Professional Affairs Steering Committee on Distressed Psychologists: Final report.* Washington, DC: American Psychological Association.

SECTION I: ISSUES

THE DISTRESSED PROFESSIONAL: THE NATURE OF THE PROBLEM 1

Richard R. Kilburg

A TYPICAL DISTRESSED PROFESSIONAL

Floyd Benson gently closed the door to the garage and set his briefcase down in the hall. As he walked through the kitchen, he glanced at the clock on the stove. The cool green numbers flashed 2:30 a.m.

He stumbled a little as he passed the cabinet that held the liquor. Floyd was already quite drunk. He had been at a meeting earlier in the evening and had stopped off to have a few beers with some of his colleagues after the meeting had broken up. That was over four hours ago. He was glad that his wife and children were in bed. Not that they could tell that he was drunk—he held it rather well. It was better though that they did not see him go through the struggle that was now taking place.

Floyd knew that he had a drinking problem. He was trying to control it by using the best knowledge that his profession of psychology had at its command. However, he had passed his own self-imposed limit two hours ago and now faced a monumental decision in trying to go to bed without taking another drink.

He stood there for several minutes, frozen with guilt, anxiety, and indecision. Part of him knew that he was slipping out of control. It happened more often now. It was frightening when he thought of the full day of activities that lay ahead of him. That was less than four hours away. But, one more drink could not possibly hurt him now, so he reached into the cupboard and took out a glass. As he went to pour that drink, he heard his wife call downstairs to him, "Floyd, is that you?" Sighing audibly, Floyd put the glass and bottle away. "Yes, honey, I'll be up in a minute," he said. "Well, that settles the problem for this evening," he thought, as he climbed the stairs. But he shuddered inwardly as he realized that the war would start again as soon as he woke up in the morning.

Three hours after his head hit the pillow, the alarm began to shriek in his ear. Floyd chased after the off switch like a half-crazed lunatic. It was his sworn enemy, as it sat there indicting him for the sins he had committed just hours ago. He finally found the switch and struggled out of bed into the bathroom. His wife

Sue joined him shortly. "You were out late last night," she said. In no mood to banter, Floyd chopped off the conversation with a curt "So what?" Sue chose to ignore the comment and climbed into the shower.

Forty silent, tension-filled minutes later, they were joined in the dining room by their three children. The before-school ritual had begun. Floyd was still a little drunk from the night before and was beginning to be quite irritable. After his 7- and 8-year-old boys began arguing over which TV show they would watch after school, he screamed at them for being inconsiderate, selfish, and obnoxious. Hardly knowing what the words meant, the boys finished breakfast without saying another word.

After breakfast, Floyd's 11-year-old daughter was doing the dishes in the kitchen. She started to lobby her mother for a new pair of jeans for school. Sue responded, "I told you that we did not have the money to get new jeans this week." "But mom, all of the kids have the new jeans at school and I look like some hick wearing these!" Floyd heard this as he carried his coffee cup to the sink.

"Did you hear what your mother said?" he asked. "Yes I did, but she doesn't understand!" she replied. "No, it's you who doesn't understand. Nor do you respect anyone around here. And, if I hear one more word out of you, you're grounded for the weekend," he said in a threatening voice. "But that's not fair!" she yelled. "That's it! You're grounded," he screamed back and stomped out of the kitchen. "Mom," she cried as she burst into tears.

Floyd had the beginnings of a beautiful headache as he headed out the door for work. He ignored his wife who was signaling that she wanted to speak to him. "I'll see you tonight. I'm late," he yelled as he got into his car.

As he sat in traffic, he thought about the day that lay before him. A 90-minute class at 10:00 a.m. "I can do that blindfolded. Been teaching the same class for seven years," he thought. The meeting with the chairman of the department after lunch was a different thing. He knew that he was behind schedule on a critical project for the department. He had agreed to do the renewal application for one of their training grants and the material was due in just one week. He had done nothing so far, and he would need to tell the chairman something today. He was frightened by his inability to do this assignment. Until now, he had always been able to accomplish his tasks even if the work was sloppy at times.

He passed a series of restaurants and bars on the way into the faculty parking lot, feeling a strong urge to fortify himself for the class. He stopped himself from thinking any further about that by telling himself that he could have a drink at lunch. He made it through his class with a minor case of the shakes and went to lunch by himself. At his favorite restaurant, he ordered a double martini along with a beer and sandwich for lunch. After he drank the martini, his shakes disappeared and he began to feel like he could handle the meeting with the chairman.

A second martini after his sandwich convinced him that the meeting would be a breeze. He still had a full week to write the application. The chairman owed him many favors from the past, and there was the whole weekend to finish up what he could not get done this week.

He marched into the chairman's office with his head up. "George, I have a confession to make. I haven't made much progress on the grant because I've *been working on an article of my own. I've cleared it off my desk now and will devote all of this week to the grant application. We still have one full week to go before it is due, and you know that I can produce it in that much time," he said.*

"Floyd, the deadline was last week," George said quietly. "Don't you remember the conversation we had three weeks ago?" Floyd shook his head slowly as the truth began to sink in. He was in deeper trouble than he thought.

"Floyd, I told you, if I didn't have the draft in two days, I would do it myself. I submitted the grant last week, on time. I want to know what is wrong with you. Your work has begun to slip terribly lately. I'm worried about you. Almost every afternoon you come back from lunch smelling like a brewery, and today is no exception. I think you have a drinking problem, and you should get some help before it's too late."

Floyd stood up. "I don't need you to tell me my business, George. Doing that grant was your responsibility in the first place. All of us are tired of doing your work for you. You're the worst chairman this department has had in the 20 years that I've been here. I don't need to sit here and listen to this drivel from a person whose vitae is only half as long as mine." He turned and walked out without saying another word.

Floyd knew that because he was a tenured professor, George could not really hurt him. Still, the comment about the drinking problem had hit home. Perhaps he was not handling it as well as he thought. He had better be a little more careful at lunch. If George had noticed then others might have. It would not do to have the whole department talking about him.

Shaken up by the meeting with George, Floyd told the department secretary that he did not feel well and that he was going home. "And I will go home, after I stop off and have just one drink," he thought.

THE ORIGINS OF DISTRESS

Floyd Benson is a fictitious character, but he could be one of thousands of real psychologists with a drinking problem. Even more sadly, he could be one of hundreds of thousands of professionals in different fields in the United States with drinking or other personal problems.

With its increasing sophistication and demand for highly skilled people in a wide variety of technical areas, modern society has created a large population of well-educated, talented, and energetic professionals to meet its needs. Unfortunately, society and the organizations that employ and support professionals have been slow to realize that the pressures and pace of professional life take a toll on people that has staggering implications. Although resources to serve professionals who become distressed have improved remarkably in the past ten years, the knowledge base to support these services has been lacking in many ways. Not only has there been insufficient research done on the special nature of the problems facing professionals, but there has also been little, if any, information available on how to manage the problems of professionals once they are identified. This has been true in the field of psychology as well, despite the fact that many psychologists are themselves in the business of helping professionals who experience various forms of distress.

Most professionals begin their careers with little or no information about what they will really experience as practitioners or academicians in a particular field. Building on childhood and adolescent ambitions, they career from their years in undergraduate programs directly into their graduate training with little time for thought or preparation. The graduate years consist of anxiety-ridden rituals of hard work and dedication. There is practically no time to reflect on the wisdom of the commitment to join a particular profession, since all of the student's energy is taken up with the tasks of gaining entry in the first place. It is only years later, after graduating, passing the licensure examinations, and engaging in the first job or two in the field, that the average individual begins to recognize the tremendous effects that the decade of hard work has had on his or her life. Most individuals are able to cope effectively with the changes, the demands, and the very real problems. However, a significant number of the members of all professions are unable to adapt to the pressures, and they begin to experience major difficulties.

Society in general does not recognize these problems as being real or threatening in any meaningful way. After all, these individuals are frequently at or near the top of the monetary and social hierarchies. It is hard for someone who is struggling to pay rent to identify with well-paid professionals experiencing some personal distress. In fact, despite shared concerns and experiences, even colleagues in their own national organizations have difficulty recognizing the real problems that professionals have. And many of these problems stem from the nature of their work.

The Roles of Professionals

When the average person thinks about a professional, he or she usually has formed a global picture based on interaction with a particular professional person. Most of this interaction will have occurred in situations in which the professional delivered services to the person. Visits to the family physician, a psychologist, or a lawyer are familiar events to most people. What the average person does not see on these occasions is that the service delivery characteristics of professional life are only one part of a complex patchwork of roles that the average professional is called upon to play each day. Many professionals themselves do not experience these roles directly, as they rush from moment to moment trying to stay even with the rising tide of professional and personal demands.

Mintzberg (1973) presented an enriching view of ten managerial roles that the average professional manager employs in his or her daily activities. I have examined the work of psychologists based on these roles, demonstrating that most professionals employ them in their daily activities whether they work as an organization's employee or conduct their own practice (Kilburg, 1983).

The ten roles are divided into three groups: interpersonal roles, informational roles, and decisional roles. In the interpersonal category, the professional acts as a figurehead, leader, and liaison. In the informational category, the professional plays the roles of monitor, disseminator, and spokesperson. Finally, in the decisional category, the professional behaves as an entrepreneur, resource allocator, negotiator, and disturbance handler. Although Mintzberg's classification system was originally based on field studies done on top level executives working in organizations, their applicability to professionals working in other types of enterprises is readily apparent.

When they act in interpersonal roles, professionals are usually responding to the internal and external demands made by themselves or their parent institutions. They represent the organization to the outside world, serving as a symbol for those remaining on the job. They speak for and to their colleagues, sign contracts and enter into agreements, create the environment in which they and their colleagues work, hire and fire staff, train and motivate employees, and constantly tinker in ways that keep their organizations moving toward their goals. They also create networks of contacts that enable them to monitor the environments in which they and their organizations work. In this role as liaison, professionals try to open doors that bring in information, business opportunities, political contacts, and so forth. Professionals who perform interpersonal roles exercise a complex number of skills that are necessary to their continued growth and development. All professionals play these roles regardless of the type of job they hold or the setting in which they work.

In the informational category, when acting as monitors, disseminators, and spokespersons, professionals use the network of contacts that they establish in the interpersonal roles and employ other techniques to monitor their environments, collecting information relevant to their survival and that of their institutions. Bringing information that they acquire back to their parent organizations, professionals disseminate it to relevant members of the enterprise to keep them informed of developments that are germane to their work. When the organization needs to respond to the external world, professionals play the role of spokesperson to perform this task.

In the decisional roles, professionals create and protect the operations of their organizations. First, as entrepreneurs, they assess the opportunities available to them in the environment, deciding which ones are most advantageous and which problems are most threatening. They design strategies to address both types of issues and move to implement them as time and other resources allow. Second, as resource allocators, they are first and foremost the keepers of their own time. This most precious resource should be at the top of everyone's list for careful conservation. Beyond their own time, professionals manage finances, people, technologies, buildings and office space, and a variety of other resources as they pursue their goals. Third, as negotiators, they interact with many other people, trying to assure that they will be able to obtain the resources that they need in order to survive. In handling disturbances, they manage a myriad of conflicts and problems that arise daily and interfere with the operation of their organizations.

Adequate performance in this decisional tetrad is crucial to the continuing development of any professional. Yet, few, if any, professional educational programs prepare individuals to perform these roles. Usually, it is only in programs that formally train managers that some time is spent discussing such activities. Other professions turn their people loose without much thought about the complexity of the world that their graduates will face.

Lack of preparation in these areas frequently causes high levels of stress and failure for many professionals. How often do employers and colleagues recount sad stories over lunch or dinner about the brilliant new employee who was just fired because he or she failed in some nontechnical area of performance? Frequently, professionals do their technical jobs well; yet, they are not promoted because they do not manage their other roles well. Understanding how a professional becomes distressed depends upon employers and colleagues having an idea about the range of problems and issues that confront that professional in his or her life.

As I have described briefly, beyond these managerial tasks, professionals have specific responsibilities in the technical areas in which they were trained. Their preparation for these tasks takes several years of supervised graduate-level education. Additional expertise in specialty areas of practice sometimes takes even longer to acquire. Examples of this are readily apparent in the specialty areas of medicine, where certification exams frequently are not taken by physicians until they are in their late twenties or thirties. The fields of psychology and law are also becoming increasingly specialized, following the same general model of professional evolution as medicine.

Psychologists work in many different types of settings. Most frequently, they teach in universities and colleges; provide health and human services in hospitals, schools, mental health centers, private practices, and other organizations; consult with businesses, governments, and industries; and, increasingly, they manage these enterprises (Kilburg, 1984; Stapp & Fulcher, 1983). Each job a psychologist takes has a unique blend of responsibilities and duties, but similar pictures of numerous demands and resulting stress are seen.

Teaching, research, supervision, committee work, writing and editing, working in professional organizations, consulting, and playing a role in community relations are all part of the normal expected load of an academician. Yet, each of these tasks is a specialty area of practice in itself. Conceptual frameworks have been developed by specialists in these areas, and a significant amount of research has been done in many of them. Somehow, the average assistant professor is supposed to develop and maintain a high level of expertise in all of them, if he or she is to have even a chance to be promoted and to get tenure.

Someone who goes into a private practice or joins a health or human service agency as a service provider not only does evaluations, treats a wide variety of problems, and consults with colleagues on difficult cases, but he or she also serves on a number of institutional and professional committees; stays abreast of financial, legal, and regulatory developments relevant to the practice of psychology; keeps up with the literature in his or her chosen area of special expertise; and works in the community on a number of projects. Again, each of these technical roles has a knowledge base and a practice history that psychologists are expected to master. The pressures to perform well are extraordinary. Frequently, the lives of human beings depend upon the decisions and recommendations that these professionals make. Is it any wonder that they experience job-related stress that can lead to serious disturbance?

Similar pictures are seen in the professional lives of psychologists working in schools, government, business, and industry. The technical requirements for excellent performance are continuous and inordinately high. As with most professionals, the average psychologist does not have a lot of people looking over his or her shoulder inspecting the work. Nevertheless, the pressures are real and the results can be devastating, if they are not handled correctly.

The Characteristics of Professional Work

Mintzberg (1973) also explored the characteristics of the work of senior managers. He found six sets of attributes, in addition to those 10 roles, that are relevant to the performance of other professionals. These attributes include the quantity and pace of work, the pattern of activities, the relationship in the work between action and reflection, the use of different media, the relation to a number of contacts, and the interplay between rights and duties.

Graduate training prepares the fledgling professional for hard work. The classes, tests, competition, practicum requirements, and research demands all push the student to learn how to plan and use time and energy wisely. This grueling experience, however, is insufficient to alert most graduates to the pace and volume of activity with which their daily professional lives will burden them. Suffice it to say that the onslaught of publications that must be read—reports, letters, memos, research studies, and so on—seemingly endless meetings, appointments with clients, infinite variety of telephone calls, and constant demands of staff, all take their toll. On top of this kind of ceaselessly hectic barrage, the person also must take care of personal needs. If he or she has a family, family members too will ask for a reasonable amount of time and energy. This goes on every day for decades. How can any educational experience teach a person to manage something that will last for 40 years? It cannot. Living through it forces each person to adapt and to learn to cope.

Moreover, the work of professionals typically is brief, fragmented, and widely varied. There are few opportunities for the concentrated effort that graduate preparation entails. Each day, hour after hour, the clients coming in the door interrupt the telephone calls the psychologist is trying to answer. Having to attend a meeting after a client leaves means that the memo due the next day must be written at home in the evening. A serious emergency interrupts a meeting and must be handled immediately. This pattern requires the professional to diffuse his or her attention and energy in a net that catches all of the important and threatening events and allows potentially distracting trivia to pass through unnoticed. Having to function in this way is extraordinarily different from functioning as a student in lengthy classes, performing seemingly endless hours of reading, and writing the highly polished papers required in school. Learning how to attend to the fragmented activities and to make wise decisions in the face of conflicting or inadequate information, overlapping responsibilities, and high-pressure schedules is one of the most difficult tasks that confronts professionals.

Psychologists and other professionals today are faced with an interesting contradiction. There is more information available on more topics than ever before in history. Professionals have mountains of data available to assist them with the burdens of their work. Yet the evidence suggests that they do not carefully sift through all of the available information before they act. To be sure, there are exceptions to this. A lawyer preparing a key brief in a case, a researcher writing a grant proposal, a physician planning brain surgery on a patient, all take their time because the consequences of mistakes are enormous. However, in the daily routine, professionals show a preference for activity that brings them into contact with action and information that demand immediate response. As a result, although contemplative tasks are valued highly, there never seems to be any time for planning or evaluation. The immediacy of the live action requires attention. How do people who were excellent students turn themselves into action junkies and still avoid coping with stress? Most of them do not. They end up trying to adapt to the enormous pressures with the basic human skills that brought them through their training, and although many of them succeed, many fail.

While attending school, students develop intimate relationships with their books and their papers. They spend most of their time reading and writing. They become quite proficient at it, as well as at studying for and taking exams. Once they are out of school, they find themselves in a world gone mad with information. The sheer volume of written material is overwhelming. Even speed reading skills, honed ever so sharp in school, are insufficient to manage the requirements.

Furthermore, professionals find that reading is not nearly so important as their direct interactions with people. What happens in the consultation room with clients and in meeting rooms with colleagues is usually much more important than the information learned from reading a report or memo. The telephone has replaced the letter as the primary means of communication. Thus, in order to succeed, the average professional must develop a whole new repertoire of skills using these verbal media. Having to choose between the written and spoken word can have emotional consequences if the individual feels that he or she is not using time productively.

The effective professional maintains a strong network of contacts outside of his or her organization. This network brings in information, referrals, contracts, and other resources that are often critical to the success of an enterprise. In addition, these professionals must live between their superiors and subordinates and these outside relationships. A careful balancing act must be performed to ensure that everyone is properly informed about recent developments and that the professional knows what is happening that is crucial to the performance of his or her own tasks. Managing these relationships is time consuming and can be quite stressful.

As Mintzberg (1973) stated, professional work represents a blend of rights and duties. The individual has great latitude to make decisions in his or her area of expertise. Much of this latitude is confined to the initial decisions about what type of work to do and in which setting or organization to perform it. Some freedom is experienced in making long range or strategic decisions about what to do with time and other important resources. Once these decisions are made, however, the daily pounding described above takes over and forces the individual to respond to its demands. Subordinates, superiors, clients, colleagues, friends, and families all require the time, attention, and skills of the professional. For most people, these duties nicely balance the freedom experienced. For some, the constant demands that drain their resources generates a feeling that borders on panic.

Even the rewards received from working can generate stress. Usually, a nice compensation package, wonderful holidays, and a pleasant life style accompany a successful professional career. However, although careful management of financial resources can lead to the ability to provide for one's family and for the future, increased responsibility results, and inadequate manage-

PROFESSIONALS IN DISTRESS

ment can lead to increased pressure and stress. Financial demands mount even as the time and emotional resources required to meet them diminish.

Expectations From Colleagues, Consumers, Families, and Friends

As a professional, one receives the respect and admiration of those who share in and benefit from one's abilities. Earning and maintaining this respect, however, can be costly. Colleagues and consumers demand the best from professionals. Colleagues want the stimulation and support that comes from working with someone who is on top of every situation in the professional sense. They observe performances carefully, and although they may not perform a formal evaluation, they are constantly weighing how their fellow workers are doing. In large organizations, professionals frequently compete with each other for advancement, salary increases, and other benefits. The pressure of this competition can become crushing for individuals who do not want to, or cannot, handle the unrelenting pace and the constant comparison. Consumers, who are paying high fees for the services that they receive, expect and have every right to expect that the professional that they hire will be first rate in every phase of their chosen profession. The slightest variation from expected performance is frequently detected and often challenged. Although clients can be quite tolerant of errors and omissions, they can also resent such evidence of failure. They hold the power of the purse and do not pay when they are not satisfied.

In addition to these expectations, professionals must respond to their families' demands for time and attention. The chores of daily living must be accomplished. And, in a world where two-career marriages have become the norm, these requirements can become overwhelming. Poked, prodded, and pushed around at work, the tired professional arrives home wanting only to rest and recuperate for the next day's activities. There they frequently find an equally depleted spouse, a list of tasks to be completed before they can relax, and insufficient time to accomplish what needs to be done. And those who have children find that although they add richness to life, they add complexity as well. Their needs are very special, and they vary widely. Trying to stay in tune with them takes a lot of energy, and energy is what the distressed professional may lack most.

Friends are an important source of support and strength in this hectic world, but they also demand attention. People who have and maintain close friendships seem to manage stress better than those who do not. Scheduling time for these friends is crucial; time must be made because friends can often spell the difference between coping and failure, or illness and health for the individual professional. Yet, when even a simple act such as writing a letter can consume an hour or more from an overscheduled day, hurried lunches and an occasional weekend outing usually must suffice to develop and maintain these relationships.

Rewards and Frustrations in Psychology

The professional rewards and frustrations of psychologists vary depending on the area of the field in which they are employed. For academics, the grind of teaching, the pressure to produce publications and research, the mediocre salaries, and the demands of students and administrators combine to create a tension-filled environment. The relief seemingly obtained from long vacations is really an illusion, because of the time required to prepare for classes, write up research findings, and make applications for grants. For practitioners, the pressure of seeing clients hour after hour and dealing with human suffering first hand is enormous. Depending on whether the setting is public or private, the salaries can vary widely, and low salaries simply add to the burdens. For those in administrative positions, there are the constant worries about budgets, personnel, legal suits, program status, and personal position in the hierarchy. For all psychologists, the major issue is the lack of time to do everything that should be accomplished. The constant pressures to add activities loom larger as the individuals become better known and more accomplished. These problems are mirrored in practically every other profession as well.

On the positive side, the average psychologist enjoys a reasonable level of income, some degree of professional recognition, a personal sense of contributing actively to the solution of human problems, and the ability to watch themselves grow both personally and professionally. The nuances of these pleasures differ with the specific job focus of the individual psychologist. Academics are more likely to enjoy national recognition for their scientific work. Practitioners are more likely to have higher salaries and the satisfaction of watching their clients work through significant personal problems. Administrators have the gratification of seeing their organizations grow and change as they encounter the stresses in their environments. They all belong to and work in a field that they care deeply about and that continues to develop with each passing year. They mark their own progress along with that of psychology in general. This provides a deep and lasting source of nourishment to most of the members of the discipline. Again, these positive factors are replicated in almost every other known profession.

For most individuals, these rewards and frustrations balance each other fairly well. The psychologist learns that the world is not a perfect place and that there are difficult tasks that must be attended to if progress is to be made. It is only when the balance of positive and negative is tipped toward the negative that stress begins to mount steadily. The point at which this happens differs for each person. If the pressure becomes too great, something will give in the situation. The psychologist may decide to find a new job. His or her health might break down. Other significant problems may develop. Such situations are extremely worrisome, because no one believes that it could happen to them. Consequently, like all human beings, professionals tend to be unprepared to contend with problems when they do arise in the normal course of their lives.

Developmental Crises in the Lives of Professionals

Beginning with the application for training, individuals who seek careers in the mental health professions encounter a series of normal developmental crises that are part of everyone's life in these occupations. No one tells them that there will be crises to manage, no one trains them to cope with such difficulties, and no one points out that they will face a number of these problems as they move through their lives. The result is that professionals are just as surprised as everyone else when problems arise, just as unprepared to manage them, and suffer just as much in trying to resolve the issues. However, they believe that they should not be experiencing such difficulties, and that their talent and training should be up to the tasks of coping with any problem. For many of them, it is true that their training, talent, and skills enable them to overcome most problems. For others, however, this does not occur, and they enter into entanglements that they have difficulty resolving.

Many of these crises follow the normal life cycle of adult development. As outlined by Erikson (1963), Baltes and Brim (1979), and others, these events include separation from the family of origin, establishing oneself professionally, marriage, birth of children, job changes, deaths of loved ones, learning what one has become as an adult and how one may wish to change, coping with the process of aging, retirement, and eventually facing one's own death. Each crisis has its own peculiar characteristics, coming at unique times in the life of every individual.

Some of these events are not even experienced as crises by many individuals. They are simply normal life circumstances that must be handled in some way. Others experience the emotional and social turmoil more realistically, and they may even label the event as a crisis. They seem to manage these crises fairly smoothly, without major distress. For a minority of professionals, however, one or more of these crises can override their ability to cope. As they struggle to find methods to help them overcome the problems, they begin to experience symptoms of various types that reflect the stress that they are experiencing. For some, the symptoms are transitory, disappearing when the crisis is resolved. For many others, the symptoms may persist, becoming a maladaptive pattern of behavior that may itself reach crisis proportions.

There are subtle aspects to many of the life events facing professionals that are different than those confronted by other adults. Throughout the lives of these professional people, they have constantly worked to be the best. Virtually every day of their lives, they have competed academically, socially, and financially. They expect to win and to be first or near the top in everything that they do. The fabric of their personalities is woven from this competitive spirit.

Sooner or later, every one of these individuals must come to grips with their own limitations and their own mortality. For most of them, the process of learning about these limits is gradual. They have difficulty completing assignments in school, and perhaps they even do poorly in a course. They apply for internships or jobs that they want but do not receive. They find that a job that they had cherished from afar becomes a nightmare of stress, bitterness, and dissatisfaction. Even in jobs that they find satisfying, they may become bored, restless, or stale, looking for something else to do simply because of the discomfort that the routine tasks now generate. While these events are taking place, the individual is measuring his or her progress against that of peers and colleagues. The question that students begin to ask in the first days of formal education still haunts them as adult professionals: "Where am I in comparison to the others?" What they leave unstated is that they expect to be ahead of everyone. What is often unseen by themselves and others is the pain and destruction that frequently occur when the answer that they hear is, "I am behind where I think I should be."

There are several especially difficult times for professionals in their careers. Initially, most of the students that enter graduate training programs experience them as being overwhelming. The pace and volume of the work combine with the quality of the competition and the high expectations of faculty to generate a constant state of anxiety. Once the training tasks are mastered, the individual begins to think about the first steps along the road of their career—his or her first job, grants, licensure and certification examinations, and so forth. A significant amount of distress is experienced by many individuals in this phase of their development.

All of this occurs while the personality of the individual is in the final stages of consolidation. The identity that they pursue as a member of a particular profession becomes fused with the concept that they are forming of themselves as adults. For many of them, profession and self-concept become indistinguishable. They are as human beings what they have become as professionals. This works well as a psychological strategy as long as the professional identity is gratifying. When problems arise, however, those who are unable to see differences between themselves as people and as professionals can be in deep trouble. Such a lack of differentiation can create a dilemma at any point in someone's life.

At first, people take jobs to get some professional experience. Sometimes an individual settles into one position or company and never moves for the rest of his or her professional life. Most professionals move several times in their careers, because they seek advancement, stimulation, better pay or benefits, or a different climate. Whatever the reason, they move in an effort to make life better for themselves. Each decision to move requires a great deal of thought, preparation, and energy. Coping with new tasks, colleagues, and environments is both stimulating and difficult. Most often the change goes reasonably well, the person and the family settle down, and the crisis is short lived. Sometimes, however, the move is disastrous. The job is not what it seemed, the colleagues are not supportive, or the environment proves to be more hostile than was imagined. As a result, stress levels increase, and the individuals and their families must contemplate the necessity of making yet another move. Such periods are times of very high vulnerability for professionals as well as for their families.

Somewhere in the middle of professional careers a subtle change takes place. Professionals find that they no longer need to take jobs for the experience. At the same time, they have large investments in their families, in homes, and in the status quo. If boredom or staleness set in, they think hard about whether the upheaval that would be caused by changing jobs is worth the benefit to be obtained in improving their feelings about their careers. Whereas a decision to change brings with it all of the issues described above, a decision to stay in the existing situation can have its own unique challenges. Somehow, a person must find a way to recreate the position or the environment if he or she is to continue to feel good about the decision to stay. If the person cannot adjust, a sense of chronic dissatisfaction can arise, which in some people can lead to serious depression—even thoughts of suicide. This form of distress is a particular problem in the helping professions where the rate of suicide is higher than in most other segments of the population. More

PROFESSIONALS IN DISTRESS

common is the onset of the burnout syndrome described by Freudenberger and Richelson (1980) and others. Burnout has a wide variety of symptoms associated with it. Most frequently, it creates a sense of emotional and physical depletion that drains the victim of his or her ability and desire to cope with the events in daily life. Every professional is a candidate for burnout at some point in his or her career.

Usually, in their late forties or early fifties, most working people begin to think seriously about retirement. For many of them, this inevitably leads to a consideration of their accomplishments and of what they want to do during the last part of their working lives. If their lives have been full and satisfying to this point, they may feel that the range of their options is broad and that their problem is only choosing the activities that will prove to be most meaningful to them. If they feel that their achievements are less than satisfactory, then a sequence of problems can arise that can have dramatic consequences. The crisis that can occur originates with the professional's inner sense of devastation and pervasive dissatisfaction with the course of his or her life. In its worst form, these feelings create a state of overwhelming depression from which the individual finds it impossible to escape. The intensifying depression causes some to take their lives. Most frequently, it forces others into an adaptation to life that leaves them chronically impoverished in every conceivable way. They eventually escape into a bitter retreat from life, and frequently a premature death.

The Need for Assistance

Professionals can be their own worst enemies. Trained to be independent, creative, assertive, competitive, and hard driving, they do not readily acknowledge that they are in trouble or need assistance. More often, their combination of socialization and personality characteristics leads them to struggle on with a problem long after many other people would have at least sought consultation from family members or friends. Solitary battles are the most destructive for anyone because of the ease with which one loses perspective.

The 20-year conditioning process leading to the creation of a professional leaves the individual with virtually no psychological choice with regard to their identity. Whatever else they become, they must be a winner. To admit that they are having difficulties, that they cannot manage one or more aspects of their lives, that they have self doubts is tantamount to proclaiming that they have failed. Even if no other living soul discovers that they have sought assistance, professionals almost always need to confront this pervasive feeling that they have finished last in the race of life when they finally break down and see someone about their difficulties. It is ironic that this attitude is so widespread among people who, by and large, are trained to help others with their problems. The destruction that this unwillingness to seek assistance causes cannot be overestimated.

Clearly the road to professional and personal success is complicated and arduous. It is composed of many tests, tasks, and traps. Most of the people who choose to take the journey along this road are well equipped to handle whatever they encounter along the way. Despite the difficulties and the stress, they perform admirably and successfully. They achieve a comfortable life and a reasonable degree of personal and professional satisfaction. For some of those who take this road, however, life is not so good. In spite of the many ways in which they struggle to cope with the problems and to manage the stress, ultimately they fail in their effort to adapt. They become casualties in the superheated pursuit of excellence.

When this happens, it need not necessarily be a disaster for the individual or for their families. Frequently, potentially overwhelming problems that have developed can be addressed in a short time. The person can move on and once again function fully as a professional while feeling that they merely needed a brief respite, a pause to catch their mental and emotional breath before going on with life. Occasionally, major adjustments are required and the individual must be treated with more elaborate approaches. The exact nature of the treatment provided depends on what type of problem the individual is trying to overcome.

The most important thing for individual professionals and their national and state organizations to remember is that the majority of their colleagues and members who suffer from one of the array of problems that will be described in this book can be treated successfully and return to productive and satisfying work. As you, the reader, will see, the editors and authors of this volume believe strongly that these problems can and must be addressed both by the individuals with the problems and by the organizations that have been developed to support them.

References

Baltes, P. B., & Brim, O. G., Jr. (Eds.). (1979). *Life span development and behavior* (vol. 2). New York: Academic Press.

Erikson, E. H. (1963). *Childhood and society* (2nd ed.). New York: Norton.

Freudenberger, H. J., & Richelson, G. (1980). *Burn out: How to beat the high cost of success.* New York: Bantam Books.

Kilburg, R. R. (1983). The psychologist as a manager. In B. D. Sales (Ed.), *The professional psychologist's handbook* (pp. 495–537). New York: Plenum Press.

Kilburg, R. R. (1984). Psychologists in management: The unseen career path in psychology. *Professional Psychology: Research and Practice, 15*(5), 613–625.

Mintzberg, H. (1973). *The nature of managerial work.* New York: Harper & Row.

Stapp, J., & Fulcher, R. (1983). The employment of APA members: 1982. *American Psychologist, 38,* 1298–1320.

UNANSWERED QUESTIONS ABOUT DISTRESSED PROFESSIONALS 2

Peter E. Nathan

The growing conviction among professionals in recent years that impaired colleagues constitute a serious threat to themselves, their clients, and the professions of which they are members has led many professional groups to develop programs for impaired professionals (Bissell & Haberman, 1984; Dickason, 1981; Kay, 1980; Talbott, Richardson, & Atkins, 1977). By now, for example, formal programs for distressed health care professionals are operating at both the state and national levels for nurses, physicians, pharmacists, occupational therapists, chiropractors, social workers, and dentists. Psychologists have not yet established programs for impaired colleagues at either the state or the national level.

Unhappily, the perceived threat that distressed colleagues pose to their fellows has not been sufficient to generate research on issues that, if better understood, would undoubtedly aid efforts both to prevent and to treat impairment among professionals. It is the aim of this chapter to identify research lacunae of relevance to the treatment and prevention of impairment by professionals, primarily mental health professionals, and particularly psychologists.

DIFFERENTIATING DISTRESS AND IMPAIRMENT

At the outset, we admit to confusion over the phrases "distressed professional" and "impaired professional," although common convention has been to use the two interchangeably. Literally, the two phrases describe different people and different situations. The phrase "impaired professional" presumably refers to a professionally trained person whose professional work is impaired—interfered with—by something in the professional's behavior or environment. An impaired professional may or may not experience distress and may or may not believe him- or herself to be impaired. By contrast, the professional in distress is someone who feels distressed—who experiences the subjective sense that something is wrong—whether or not that feeling is associated with actual impairment in any area of life functioning including the professional. Although impairment is a frequent accompaniment of distress, it is not invariably a part of it.

The purview of this chapter—and the volume in which it appears—is both the professional in distress and the professional whose professional (and, likely, personal) functioning is impaired. Sometimes the two are one, sometimes they are not. A first order of business is research to indicate the relative frequency of subjective distress among professionals whose professional activities have begun to show deterioration, as well as of impairment in professional functioning among professionals beginning to experience subjective distress. Estimates of the interaction of these two variables have been made, but invariably by experienced clinicians whose estimates are simply educated guesses (e.g., Bissell). Empirically based research on the interaction of distress and impairment would be helpful, for example, in determining whether one or the other is more amenable to intervention, and whether intervention in one or the other instance is more likely to yield a successful outcome.

THE RESEARCH TO DATE

The scant research on distressed or impaired professionals reported to date has had little impact on the development of either prevention or treatment programs. Reasons include that what has been done has been both suspect on methodological grounds and basically irrelevant to the efforts of professional associations to develop programs for impaired members.

Research on impaired professionals to date has been of two kinds. First, there have been inquiries into the prevalence of distress and impairment among professionals (e.g., American Medical Association Council on Mental Health, 1973; Bissell, Fewell, & Jones, 1980; Bissell & Jones, 1976; Thoreson, 1984; Thoreson, Budd, & Krauskopf, in press). These studies have generally involved surveys, primarily by questionnaire, either of clinicians who have treated professionals in distress or of members of the professional group themselves, including both impaired and distressed professionals and those who have known such men and women. Several such studies of psychologists have been reported (e.g., Boyer, 1984; Laliotis & Grayson, 1985; Thoreson, Nathan, Skorina, & Kilburg, 1983; Thoreson & Skorina, 1986). Overall, these studies suggest that the prevalence of distress and impairment among professionals, including psychologists, is at least at the level of that in the general nonprofessional population.

Second, some treatment outcome research data on professionals have been reported. Studies generating such data are of two kinds. They might describe a particular treatment program designed for impaired, usually alcoholic, professionals of a specific kind, usually physicians, and report on their (usually impressive) success rates (e.g., Kay, 1980; Talbott et al., 1977; Vogtsberger, 1984). Or they might review outcomes of several treatment programs with important elements in common (for example, all might utilize the self-help approach to treatment) and attempt to generalize from them to other similar treatment programs for impaired professionals (e.g., Bissell & Haberman, 1984; Kliner, Spicer, & Barnett, 1980).

In both kinds of research, problems of external and internal validity, including inadequate sampling methods, small or restricted samples, experimenter bias, and inappropriate or inadequate data collection and analysis procedures, have prevented ready acceptance of their findings and conclusions (Nathan & Lansky, 1978).

One especially telling problem is that some of the research on distressed professionals has not been disinterested. That is, some discussions of research findings are clearly designed either to demonstrate the widespread nature of distress among professionals, largely to confirm that distress is a serious problem among professionals, or to prove how effective a particular treatment program designed for impaired professionals has been.

WHY DEVELOP PROGRAMS FOR IMPAIRED PROFESSIONALS?

What is the purpose of programs for impaired professionals? Without having data on the factors that have led various individuals and groups to develop prevention, early intervention, and treatment programs for impaired professionals, I suggest the following three primary reasons for developing such programs: (a) to enable impaired professionals to return to productive and useful work, (b) to protect an innocent public from exploitation or other harm at the hands of impaired professionals, and (c) to lessen or prevent damage to the reputation of the profession of which the distressed professional is a member.

I also presume, having no data to the contrary, that the eventual form that a program for impaired professionals takes depends, at least in part, on why it was established. If the program was developed to maximize the likelihood that the distressed professional will be able to return to his or her profession, the program will likely involve early case finding, extensive involvement by sympathetic fellow professionals, and assiduous avoidance of involvement with the state licensing authority. If, on the other hand, the program is designed to protect the public, the program might well be punitive and judgmental; literature describing the program might almost seem to go out of its way to make examples of impaired professionals in order to deter others from a similar professional path. And if the program is motivated by the desire to protect the profession against possible insult to its reputation and standing, little or nothing might ever be heard of the program, the numbers of professionals it has served, and reasons they have been served. Research on relations between a program's methods and its purposes would seem to be important, if only to permit future developers of programs to tailor them more accurately to the reasons for their initial development.

WHAT IS DISTRESS?

Most programs for impaired professionals focus either exclusively or primarily on alcohol- and drug-related problems (Bissell & Haberman, 1984). Two principal reasons are that (a) many of these programs are modeled after industrial alcoholism programs, and (b) alcohol and drugs are most often associated with problems that come to the attention of state licensing authorities (Isler, 1978; Medved, 1982; Skoler & Klein, 1979).

When programs for impaired professionals extend beyond alcohol and drug dependence, they tend to provide primarily for serious emotional and psychiatric disorders. An important research issue is the cost–benefit ratio of the various decisions that must be made on the focus and reach of programs for impaired professionals. A related issue is the prevalence of the several impairing conditions that might be handled in a comprehensive program. If, for example, 10 percent of the psychologists in the United States suffer from alcohol or drug dependence and half of them experience impairment of function from these conditions, then it is reasonable to develop programs for impaired psychologists that will accord these issues primacy (e.g., by ensuring that all program workers are trained to recognize and treat alcohol and drug problems). This precedence makes good sense, especially if no other impairing condition has the prevalence or impairment-causing capacity of alcohol or drug problems. By the same token, if it is determined that serious mental disorders burden 8 percent of American psychologists and impair half of them, it is also reasonable to structure programs for impaired psychologists that will facilitate recognition of and intervention in problems of emotional disorder. And thus could one rate the full range of other problems, including family disorder and abuse of clients, children, and spouses.

Unfortunately, data are lacking on the prevalence of disorders among psychologists, as are data on the extent to which each of these classes of disorders causes not only distress but impairment. In addition, data are needed on the success with which individuals suffering from each of these sources of impairment can be motivated to benefit from treatment—as well as the relative effectiveness of the treatments that can be offered them. There is little point in developing a program for persons who will not come to treatment or to undertake to treat conditions for which effective treatment does not exist.

WHO IS IN DISTRESS—AND HOW MANY?

Although much of the research on distressed professionals has sought to determine the true prevalence of distress and impairment among professionals, the key question remains unanswered. Are professionals—psychologists for example—in distress in the same proportion and to the same extent as the general population? Because methodologically adequate prevalence studies of distress and impairment among professionals have not yet been conducted, this important question remains open. And given the familiar difficulties of determining prevalence of mental disorder in substantial populations (Garfield, 1978), this basic research gap is unlikely to be filled soon.

What is required to determine true numbers and proportions of psychologists who are impaired, in distress, or both? The first requirement is to define the terms, the second is to create criteria for judging distress and impairment, and the third is to design a study whose methodologic soundness will enable confident generalization to the universe of psychologists.

Prevalence studies that use questionnaires or other self-report instruments are unlikely ever to yield sufficiently reliable information about the prevalence of distress, given the likelihood that the usual sampling methods will produce substantial numbers of respondents who are impaired but fail to recognize or acknowledge it. Accordingly, a sample of psychologists, stratified according to the variables associated with onset and maintenance of distress (for example, gender, age, highest degree, and subfield), would first have to be gathered. A structured interview would have to be designed to tap present and past psychopathology, perceived stress, and alcohol and drug use, along with level of family functioning and job satisfaction, and interviewers would have to be trained. Methods, procedures, and instruments from earlier large-scale studies of psychopathology in the general population (e.g., Srole, Langner, Michael, Opler, & Rennie, 1962) as well as from later studies of special clinical populations that utilized more sophisticated instruments (Othmer, Penick, & Powell, 1981; Robins, Helzer, Croughan, & Ratcliff, 1981) could be used. Unfortunately, studies of this kind are expensive. It is unlikely that funding will ever be found for a study whose sole purpose is to fine-tune a program to ameliorate the distress of a group of impaired professionals.

Are there less expensive, more realistic solutions to this problem? Not to my knowledge. The less expensive methods for assessing prevalence, most of which rely on self-report instruments or questionnaires, have already been tried. But because these methods require self-reports of psychopathology or second-hand observations of psychopathology in others, they do not yield accurate prevalence figures.

TREATMENT FOR PROFESSIONALS IN DISTRESS

Who Should Administrate Treatment Programs?

Assuming that the leaders of a professional association that is motivated to provide for members in distress have (a) defined the target sources of members' distress, (b) satisfied themselves that the prevalence of members' distress exceeds a threshold for action, and (c) concluded that intervention holds promise for success, their next step is to design a plan for reaching those in distress. This task is made more difficult by the likelihood that prevalence figures, if they exist, are probably not accurate.

A variety of options are open, in principle, to those responsible for programs for impaired professionals. To begin with, the national association can assume responsibility for administering the program, in which case the program can be administered by the central office, where central office staff are already on hand. This choice has the advantage of allowing central office staff to monitor all developments in the program. There are obvious cost savings in centralization, as well. Centralization, however, raises an important question: Can distressed professionals scattered throughout the country be reached best by a program designed and administered centrally, or are they more likely to agree to accept help offered by colleagues working and living nearby? Although outcome data on centralized versus decentralized programs do not exist, compelling data of a different kind are available. Most programs for impaired professionals are administered and run locally, by state, county, or local groups of professionals. Thus, decentralization is clearly the plan of choice for planners of distressed professionals' programs.

It may well be that such substantial differences exist nationwide in the nature and extent of problems that cause professionals' distress that local autonomy in the development of programs is essential. Decentralization may also be the consequence, in certain instances, of decisions by some professional associations (including the American Psychological Association) that they lack the financial resources or the mandate from their membership to run centralized programs for impaired professionals. In such instances, if programs are to exist, they will have to be organized locally.

What Kind of Treatment Should Be Developed?

The information gaps noted thus far are serious; even more serious are the lacunae in data on treatment for professionals. Should distressed professionals receive treatment especially tailored to their professional status? Which sources of distress should receive emphasis in the development of programs for distressed professionals? Who is best equipped to treat health care professionals—their colleagues, or other health care professionals? How should treatment programs for professionals be funded? What role, if any, should the state licensing authority have, and (a related question) what role, if any, should coercion play in a treatment program for impaired professionals? Finally, how should the cost-effectiveness of programs for distressed professionals be judged?

When the American Psychological Association (APA) began to consider developing a program for distressed psychologists, the Board of Professional Affairs requested membership response to the concept. One of the more common responses was that psychologists did not need to develop a program for impaired professionals because psychologists knew better than almost anyone else where and how to get help when they needed it. However, data indicate that this is not an accurate assertion. Reports by mental health professionals who have been distressed, and data attesting to high rates of suicide among psychotherapists, suggest that although mental health professionals, psychologists among them, may know where and how to help others, they cannot always help themselves.

A related question is whether treatment provided to mental health professionals, including psychologists, should be substantially different from treatment provided to others. Is there something about being a mental health professional that renders usual approaches to treating distressed professionals less effective? Does the psychologist know the "tricks of the trade" so well that different methods and approaches are required? Although data on this issue are lacking, decades of discussion and hundreds of articles on how to train therapists suggest that the process of treating mental health professionals proceeds in much the same way as treating any other intelligent, educated person who, by virtue of intelligence and education, emphasizes certain defenses in his or her efforts to deal with stress and conflict.

Which Problems Should Be Treated First?

When the APA Task Force on Distressed Psychologists asked for comment from constituent APA groups on its proposal for a decentralized program for distressed psychologists, several groups within APA objected to the plan first to seek out and aid psychologists suffering from alcohol or drug problems. These groups claimed that the problems about which they were most concerned, which included sexual abuse of clients and children and physical abuse of spouses and children, deserved attention before alcohol and drug problems. Their reasons were that physical and sexual abuse constitute a greater problem for society because they involve exploitation of innocent women and children but that alcohol and drug problems are self-inflicted and, hence, damaging only to the individual him- or herself. In response, the Task Force pointed to data that indicated the far greater numbers of psychologists in distress because of alcohol or drugs, the easier time workers would presumably have identifying and reaching alcohol and drug abusers because of the differences in stigma attached to dependency as opposed to sexual or physical abuse, and the fact that the alcoholism of a mental health professional affects family and practice as surely as it does the individual him- or herself.

How should the priorities for programs for distressed professionals, including distressed psychologists, be set? And what should those priorities be? Should alcohol and drugs be of first priority (as they are in most programs for distressed professionals), because alcohol- and drug-abusing professionals are most numerous? Or should those suffering from the serious mental disorders be accorded primacy, because they present with the worst prognosis and would likely be the most disabled? Or, finally, should those who sexually and physically exploit women and children be sought out first, because their behavior is most destructive to individuals who are least able to protect themselves?

Who Should Treat Professionals in Distress?

Another still unanswered question about the treatment of distressed professionals is whether they should be treated by their own colleagues. The question is especially germane to mental health professionals. Although it is easy enough to ensure that surgeons in distress are not treated by fellow surgeons, it is more difficult to refer a psychologist in distress to a nonpsychologist when a psychologist with special expertise in alcohol problems, depression, or marital discord is readily available.

Is a psychologist likely to be unduly critical of a colleague whose distress has led him or her to violate ethical standards? Or will the psychologist's professional identity permit more rapid development of a therapeutic relationship, without untoward attachments in either direction? A related issue is whether, in the case of alcohol or drug dependence, a recovering person—whether a fellow professional or not—is better able to provide help than a person who has not experienced alcohol or drug dependence. Most programs for distressed professionals, including those for distressed mental health professionals, do utilize recovering fellow professionals, because they are better able to identify with issues surrounding the dependency and its consequences. Yet there has never been a systematic effort to determine whether using recovering colleagues as alcoholism or drug counselors facilitates change in drinking behavior or drug use.

Is Coercion Necessary?

Many programs for distressed professionals have established a working relationship of one sort or another with the state licensing authority. Many people believe such a relationship to be necessary, because it allows the program to coerce reluctant program participants with the explicit or implicit threat of referral to the state board if he or she does not enter treatment. Professionals most extensively involved in programs for impaired professionals who have abused alcohol or drugs have noted that, without coercion, many professionals will not come to treatment (e.g., Talbott, 1982). Yet this widespread and influential belief has not yet been tested empirically.

A related question is whether an association alone can provide the coercion necessary to bring recalcitrant professionals into treatment. That is, if the program cannot refer impaired colleagues who refuse treatment to a state licensing authority but must simply rely on its own moral suasion or the threat of loss of membership, will it be less successful in inducing persons to enter treatment than associations that have the authority of a state licensing authority behind them?

How Is Cost-Effectiveness To Be Measured?

The proliferation of programs for distressed professionals, sponsored by national, regional, and local associations of professionals, attests to the widespread belief that these programs are cost-effective. Surprisingly, though, detailed empirical studies of the cost-effectiveness of such programs have not been reported.

One problem in designing a study to measure the cost-effectiveness of any program for distressed professionals is how to define the criteria by which to judge its effectiveness. Given the heterogeneous nature of the sources of distress that such a program must confront, it is not enough simply to define success by the number of persons abstinent from alcohol for a year or more, able to return to work after a depressive episode, or willing and able to stop abusing a spouse. Instead, a more uniform criterion measure seems preferable. Among the available options are (a) the percentage of professionals treated who have returned to their regular activities without restriction and have maintained themselves in full-time activity for an established period of time; (b) the net decrease in costs associated with disorders that typically increase hospitalization and insurance costs; (c) the decrease in absenteeism rate on the job, in number of clients seen, or in volume of work completed. Although other measures suggest themselves as well, including the number of spouses and children saved from abuse or the number of clients saved from sexual exploitation, these measures are clearly too specialized to have utility as overall measures of effectiveness.

How Can Professionals Be Mobilized To Develop Treatment Programs?

Given that there is opposition to developing programs for distressed professionals within some professional groups, for various reasons including cost, lack of perceived need, concern about public image, and disagreement over organization or focus, and given as well that many people believe that such programs have merit, how can the members of associations be mobilized to develop programs for their distressed colleagues?

As one of those involved in the still ongoing effort to develop a program for distressed psychologists for the American Psychological Association, I have given this particular issue a great deal of thought. Given my strong conviction that programs for distressed psychologists are in the best interests of the profession, the clients whom psychologists serve, and the psychologists who have become impaired, I find it difficult to understand the strong opposition by some members of my association to the establishment of a program.

What seems called for now is an exploration of the reasons for the opposition, along with an indication from those in opposition, of what might enable them to change their views and support the concept. Although focused on the members of a single association who have opposed establishment of such a program, the study could apply more generally to other associations whose members oppose establishing a program for their distressed fellows. The results of this study might enable persons involved in efforts to establish programs elsewhere to present their plans and the data on programs for distressed professionals in a way that would foster support for programs for distressed professionals.

References

American Medical Association Council on Mental Health. (1973). The sick physician: Impairment by psychiatric disorders, including alcoholism and drug dependence. *Journal of the American Medical Association, 2231,* 684–687.

Bissell, L., Fewell, L., & Jones, R. (1980). The alcoholic social worker: A survey. *Social Work in Health Care, 5,* 421–432.

Bissell, L., & Haberman, P. (1984). *Alcoholism in the professions.* New York: Oxford University Press.

Bissell, L., & Jones, R. (1976). The alcoholic physician: A survey. *American Journal of Psychiatry, 733,* 1142–1146.

Bissell, L., & Lambrecht, K. (1973). The alcoholic hospital employee. *Nursing Outlook, 21,* 708–711.

Boyer, C. L. (1984). *The profession's response to distressed psychologists.* Unpublished doctoral dissertation, The University of Arizona.

Dickason, J. (1981). Lawyers assist lawyers. *Illinois Bar Journal, 69,* 546–590.

Garfield, S. L. (1978). Research problems in clinical diagnosis. *Journal of Consulting and Clinical Psychology, 46,* 596–607.

Hoffmann, N. G., Harrison, P. A., & Belille, C. A. (1983). Alcoholics Anonymous after treatment: Attendance and abstinence. *The International Journal of the Addictions, 18,* 311–318.

Isler, C. (1978). The alcoholic nurse. *RN,* 45–49.

Kay, M. G. (1980). The recovered physician: Experiences of the British Doctors' Group. Hazards in recovery, issues, intervention and other roles. *British Journal of Alcohol and Alcoholism, 17,* 155–157.

Kliner, D. J., Spicer, J., & Barnett, P. (1980). Treatment outcome of alcoholic physicians. *Journal of Studies on Alcohol, 41,* 1217–1220.

Laliotis, D., & Grayson, J. H. (1985). Psychologist heal thyself: What's available for the impaired psychologist? *American Psychologist, 40,* 84–96.

Medved, M. (1982). *Hospital: The hidden lives of a medical center staff.* New York: Simon & Schuster.

Nathan, P. E., & Lansky, D. (1978). Common methodological problems in research on the addictions. *Journal of Consulting and Clinical Psychology, 46,* 713–726.

Othmer, E., Penick, E. C., & Powell, B. J. (1981). *Psychiatric Diagnostic Interview* (PDI). Los Angeles: Western Psychological Services.

Robins, L. N., Helzer, J. E., Croughan, J., & Ratcliff, K. S. (1981). National Institute of Mental Health Diagnostic Interview Schedule. *Archives of General Psychiatry, 38,* 381–389.

Skoler, D. L., & Klein, R. M. (1979). Mental disability and lawyer discipline. *The John Marshall Journal of Practice and Procedure, 12,* 227–252.

Srole, L., Langner, T. S., Michael, S. T., Opler, M. K., & Rennie, T. A. C. (1962). *Mental health in the metropolis: The Midtown Manhattan Study* (Vol. 1). New York: McGraw-Hill.

Talbott, G. D. (1982). The impaired physician and intervention: A key to recovery. *Journal of the Florida Medical Association, 69,* 793–797.

Talbott, G. D., Richardson, A. D., & Atkins, E. C. (1977). The Medical Association of Georgia disabled doctors' program: A two-year review. *Journal of the Medical Association of Georgia, 66,* 777–781.

Thoreson, R. W. (1984). The professor at risk: Alcohol abuse in academe. In R. W. Thoreson & E. P. Hosokawa (Eds.), *Employee assistance programs in higher education.* Springfield, IL: Charles C Thomas.

Thoreson, R. W., Budd, F. C., & Krauskopf, C. J. (in press). Perceptions of alcohol misuse and work behavior among professionals: Identification and intervention. *Professional Psychology: Research and Practice.*

Thoreson, R. W., Nathan, P. E., Skorina, J. K., & Kilburg, R. R. (1983). The alcoholic psychologist: Issues, problems and implications for the profession. *Professional Psychology: Research and Practice, 14,* 670–684.

Thoreson, R. W., & Skorina, J. K. (1986). Alcohol abuse among psychologists. In R. R. Kilburg, R. W. Thoreson, & P. E. Nathan (Eds.), *Professionals in distress: Issues, syndromes, and solutions in psychology.* Washington, DC: American Psychological Association.

Vogtsberger, K. N. (1984). Treatment outcomes of substance-abusing physicians. *American Journal of Drug and Alcohol Abuse, 10,* 23–37.

TRAINING ISSUES FOR PROFESSIONALS IN DISTRESS **3**

Richard W. Thoreson

I n the past several decades, there have been major advances in the way psychological procedures are applied in a variety of settings. Psychology is now not only a science, but a fast-growing technology as well (Bevan, 1982; Miller, 1969). Demands for psychological services are at a record level; the increase of educational material, including books, journals, and other media that describe the application of psychological principles to a wide array of human problems is one indication of this increased demand. Parallel to increased interest in and demand for psychological services is the development of programs for employees at all work levels whose job performance is impaired as a result of the destructive impact of distress and a variety of other problems. Industry has discovered that troubled employees can often be restored to adequate levels of work performance through appropriate treatment and intervention. This discovery has led to the development of employee assistance programs within a variety of work environments to identify and treat impaired workers and return them to productive employment (Baxter, 1984; Roman, 1984; Trice & Beyer, 1982).

The growth of employee assistance programs has been rapid and has resulted in the development of programs tailored to the professional employee suffering from distress sufficient to interfere with work performance (Bissell & Haberman, 1984; Skorina, 1982; Thoreson & Hosokawa, 1984; Thoreson, Nathan, Skorina, & Kilburg, 1983). The profession of psychology did not take up this concern until 1980, when a resolution from the APA Council called for the formation of a task force to look at means of providing services to distressed psychologists. Psychologists tend to be perfectionistic, skeptical, self-directed, and reluctant to admit vulnerability and personal distress; and as experts in theory, research, and practice with psychological disorders, psychologists face special difficulties, choices, and concerns in confronting their own distress. Being a psychologist provides no special immunity from those distressing problems that we psychologists diagnose and treat in our clients (see Kilburg, chapter 1). In this chapter I discuss the special issues involved in training psychologists to manage those areas of distress particular to them and to discuss concerns, issues, and considerations in developing such training.

TRAINING THE TRAINERS

Training, according to its dictionary definition, refers to bringing a person to a desired state or standard of efficiency through instruction and practice. This activity constitutes a major growth industry in the United States, for which psychologists serve as experts, the primary managers, developers, and providers of service. Lazarus (personal communication, April 24, 1985) stressed the importance of good self-help materials as an adjunct to therapy. He argued that a good self-help book is worth at least ten therapy sessions, possibly more. For any category of personal distress, one can find an abundance of suggested training strategies in the psychological literature, strategies that consist of the clinical application of basic psychological principles to these areas of human distress.

At this stage in the history of psychology, sophisticated technology for the treatment of a variety of psychological disorders and an impressive supply of reference and self-help materials are available. Furthermore, a focus on the delivery of psychological services exists in our society. The reference materials spell out clearly and concisely how behavioral technology can be applied to mental health, marital, financial, interpersonal, familial, child, parent, and other problems of daily living. Professional psychologists are exposed to a wide array of professionally and personally relevant material on distress. These programs were developed not to reduce personal distress but to increase psychologists' competency in the delivery of services to clients suffering from these various distress syndromes (e.g., Garner & Garfinkel, 1985; Lazarus, 1981; Marlatt & Gordon, 1984; Pattison & Kaufman, 1982; Woolfolk & Lehrer, 1984).

The APA *Monitor* lists numerous conferences, approved for APA continuing education credit, that offer training in the development of technical expertise in the therapy, personality assessment, evaluation, and treatment of every conceivable psychological disorder, and the *American Psychologist* lists more than 200 continuing education opportunities for psychologists (APA, 1985). Thus, psychologists are at the forefront both of the development of training programs for professionals and of technology to use with clients who are suffering from distress.

Although excellent training materials and the technology to implement them exist, there are several factors that impede implementation. First, although there are high-quality materials that cover all areas of distress, the sheer magnitude of the available materials makes selection difficult. How does a professional choose from the array of training resources those that are appropriate to the study of distress among professionals, particularly if the distress is one that he or she is currently experiencing?

Second, and more important, these materials, with the exception of those in the areas of stress and burnout, are directed toward treatment of clients and their problems and not toward treatment of professionals. For specific problem areas, such as alcohol abuse and alcoholism, emotional disorders, drug abuse, clinical stress management, depression, marital distress, and eating disorders, materials are written for psychologists as clinicians to help them to work more effectively with their clients in the specific problem areas.

Third, psychologists are, by inclination and training, resistant to admitting and seeking help for personal vulnerabilities (see Thoreson & Skorina, chapter 5).

Finally, given that resistances and pitfalls can be expected with any planned change, Zaltman and Dunkin (1977) identified principles and guidelines that can enable the social scientist to use the appropriate strategies to implement change. There are several implications of this for training: Implementation of programs for psychologists in distress will be met with resistance, the sources of resistance must be identified, and principles and guidelines must be formulated and included in the training. Only then can the profession of psychology develop the experts needed in the field.

What Defines Distress?

Education is the metier of the psychology profession. Educational services of various kinds are designed, organized, and delivered to a wide variety of constituencies. Gaff (1976) described ongoing training methodologies in higher education to help professors renew themselves and noted that most of these methodologies are being developed by psychologists. Psychologists' livelihood in private practice, higher education, hospital, industrial, and research settings depends, in no small measure, on their capacity to develop programs of education that will enable clients to live more effective, less stressful, and happier lives.

Training has several applications in areas of distress. Training to identify variance in problem definition and solution is needed. Zaltman and Dunkin (1977) noted that once a problem has been defined, a major step has been made in its solution. They suggested that there is likely to be considerable initial variance in definition among the various constituencies concerned with a problem. The larger the number of constituencies, the greater the potential number of problem definitions produced that are at variance with the preferred problem solution, and the greater the difficulty in implementing change. Thus, a major problem in psychology is that the definition of distress depends on who is speaking. The following example illustrates the difficulty.

The Committee Report on Distressed Psychologists

The experience of APA's Committee on Distressed Psychologists, culminating in a final report to the Board of Professional Affairs (BPA), represents an excellent case study of definitional variance in planned change. As described by Kilburg (chapter 1), the Committee was formed in response to a BPA recommendation for action on problems of distress among members of the psychology profession. The committee proceeded to determine the magnitude and scope of the problem, and they developed a survey to gather data on attitudes and experiences of psychologists with respect to distress among their colleagues. The survey, which provided sources of evidence to support the need for the establishment of a program by APA for distressed psychologists, revealed overwhelming positive support (over 90% approved of the idea of the program), insight into the types of service components favored by APA members, strong though indirect evidence of substantial distress among psychologist colleagues, and evidence that efforts to help colleagues in distress were infrequent and far from successful.

A final report was prepared and presented to BPA that proposed a plan of action for dealing with psychologists in distress. BPA initially gave the report high praise for a job well done and then distributed it to the divisions and special interest groups for reactions and recommendations. At that point, a shift occurred from BPA's initial admiring stance to skepticism by certain constituencies and major opposition. Resistance to the proposal centered on three areas: problem definition, problem priority, and methodology. Barriers to change emerged, including a presumed lack of money and resources to do the job and a variety of implementation concerns relating to constituency differences in belief systems and ideology. The principle source of opposition, however, was definitional variance regarding distress, that is, what constituted the distress, what constituted the appropriate treatment, and what constituted acceptable protection of client rights? As a result of this resistance, APA has not yet taken any specific action to deal with distressed psychologists.

What can be learned about program implementation from this case study? Given the special interest groups and constituencies in APA that define distress from different perspectives, variance in the definition of distress seems inevitable. Telfer (1966), Lippitt (1973), and Black (1972) have noted the inevitable resistances to change in organizations. The initial priorities included alcohol abuse and alcoholism, sexual misconduct, major medical and psychiatric problems, and other legal and ethical issues. This organizing scheme, which was based, in large part, on work being done in other professions to deal with their distressed members (Bissell & Haberman, 1984; Thoreson et al., 1983), met with strong resistance. The initial plan called for a "warm line" (24-hour telephone crisis line) with direct service to psychologists (Nathan, Thoreson, & Kilburg, 1983), but this plan was shelved because of the variety and extent of constituency resistance.

Variance in the definition of distress was a strong and legitimate area of resistance. APA members who represented special interests and special constituencies saw the problems of distress and planned change in a manner that reflected the particular focus and needs of their constituencies. This variance led to differences in the way areas of distress were prioritized and in the type of change strategies to be used. To illustrate, components that are developed to help the impaired professional are likely to be reacted to with alarm and skepticism by constituencies whose primary focus is client rights. Such constituencies are likely to perceive these components as having the potential of creating a "safe harbor" for incompetent and unethical psychologists who could continue to harm clients.

The importance of this case study for training is apparent. Areas of definitional variance and resistance are predictable and represent important conceptual differences that are subsumed under the concept of impairment; such resistance can be divided into three categories: (a) variance in problem definition and focus, (b) problem priority, and (c) potential target of the programmatic effort. Special constituencies will redefine distress areas and identify areas to be excluded. The four purposes of such programs—to prevent harm to clients, to protect client rights related to the consequences of the professional distress, to protect distressed psychologists with humane care, and to provide rehabilitative activities directed toward distressed psychologists—will be rank-ordered differently across distress areas by different constituencies. (For a helpful discussion of strategies to cope with resistance to innovative psychosocial interventions, see Backer, Liberman, & Kuehnel, 1986.)

STRATEGIES FOR DEVELOPING TRAINING

Basic Principles

Kutz (1986) confirmed the lack of conceptual clarity in the term *impairment* as contributing to the difficulty in establishing reasonable policies. He argued that the term as it is now used in psychology mixes three separate concepts: impairment, incompetence, and misconduct, and it oversimplifies important issues. Thus, it seems clear that psychology must work on a definition of impairment even as it proceeds to develop programs to address the problem. Given this history and the problem of definitional variance, the following principles and issues must be addressed by the field as it proceeds to cope with its impaired members.

1. Resistance to change will exist as long as the diversity in membership "is given less attention than it deserves" (Zaltman & Dunkin, 1977, p. 59).

2. The focal points of resistance, variance in definition, ranking types of distress in order of priority, and the preferred type and levels of intervention will vary from one constituency to another and must be addressed.

3. The definition and treatment preferences of various APA constituencies are predictable. This variety is healthy and can serve the useful purpose of tempering overenthusiasm and adoption of plans that could inadvertently exclude or harm specific groups. In addition, the differences will provide invaluable data on special needs of constituencies concerned with distress. In the development of training strategies, special attention must be given to types of resistance and types of change strategies that fit particular constituencies.

4. Perception of need for aid and type of services preferred will vary across both constituencies and distress areas. Moderate to high consensus can be expected for areas of dysfunction such as mental illness and alcoholism, where hurt is centered on the individual. Moderate to low consensus is likely to be found in areas such as child abuse and sexual abuse of clients, where distress in the psychologist is linked to harm to clients. Choice of change strategies may vary accordingly across constituencies. Most constituencies can be expected to concur that for psychologists suffering from alcohol abuse and alcoholism, rehabilitative treatment is a first priority. It is unlikely, however, that consensus will exist for direct service as a first priority for a distressed psychologist who presents a sexual abuse problem. Such differences should be given attention in training. In the latter case, some constituencies may favor a multifaceted approach: direct rehabilitative treatment for the psychologist, protection of client rights, and appropriate professional and legal censuring of the psychologist. For other constituencies, safeguarding the client and imposing immediate legal sanctions would be preferred.

5. Level of constituency support will vary according to the type of impairment. Generally speaking, areas involving shame and stigma, such as alcohol

and drug abuse and mental illness, carry moderate to weak public constituency support but stronger private support. Areas of distress involving harm to clients, sexual misconduct, child abuse, or harm to special constituencies such as women, handicapped, and minorities, will tend to have strong public constituencies.

6. Programs for distressed psychologists require diversity in treatment models and in level and type of training strategies. No single treatment or training methodology will suffice.

7. Distress, as defined in this text, refers to at least four distinct syndromes: (a) personally distressing problems related primarily to societal or sociocultural sources of discrimination, for example, problems faced by minorities, gays, women, and handicapped and aging populations; (b) addictive disorders, such as alcoholism, drug abuse, overeating, and smoking; (c) major physical and emotional disorders, which cover the full range of problems from cancer to depression; and (d) violations of legal and ethical standards, which are distressing primarily to others, and include areas of sexual misconduct, sexual abuse, fraudulent advertising, gross professional incompetence, and other such violations. Herbsleb, Sales, and Overcast (1985) urged psychologists to focus their attention on legal and ethical considerations and on the lack of knowledge and the inaccuracy of psychologists' perceptions regarding these critical issues.

Defining the Target and Focus

Training must be broad in scope. The plan will vary with the area of impairment; no single ideology or training model can effectively address all of these concerns. Consequently, both the target of distress and the primary focal point of the training will vary. The focal point for training in areas involving self-inflicted distress, such as the addictive disorders, mental health, or stress and burnout, is the individual psychologist. For areas of distress that are primarily societally or culturally induced, such as problems of discrimination against minority constituencies, the primary focal points are the profession of psychology, APA members, students, clients, training programs, and the public. For areas of distress that involve clear and present danger to the client, the focal points involve training in safeguarding the client and redressing harm through appropriate legal and professional censure and, secondarily, education of the profession and the public.

Developing a Model

It may be concluded that selection of a training strategy in the area of distress depends on an analysis of the special needs of different constituencies. The greater the felt need for change, the greater the commitment to change. Therefore, training directed toward both identifying and increasing consensus on the planned change is needed. The training strategies should start with what must be changed. Once a *definition* of distress is accepted, programs can be designed with acceptable *methodology, targets* of training, *time tables,* and *evalu-*

ation procedures. The model to be described provides a useful example of these components. It concentrates on several of the areas of distress covered in this text: alcohol and drug abuse, stress, and sexual abuse of clients. In each area there is strong consensus on what action should be taken.

Alcoholism, drug abuse, sexual misconduct, and stress are best conceptualized using a tripartite intervention model that involves primary, secondary, and tertiary levels of prevention. For these syndromes, training is needed in diagnosis and treatment and in the services to be provided directly to the distressed psychologist (tertiary prevention); and in early identification, detection of early diagnostic indicators, and consciousness-raising methods and environmental and social support strategies to limit incidence (secondary prevention). Moreover, education is needed on various public issues, the nature of the distress, family involvement, job-related impairment, the importance of posttreatment resources (family, self-, and mutual support systems), characteristics of impaired professionals, and the restructuring of work environments (primary prevention).

For example, training in distress related to sexually exploitative psychologists would be directed toward highlighting the issue; identifying the primary nature, signs, and types of sexual exploitation; specifying appropriate legal and ethical sanctions; and providing treatment options for sexually exploited and abused clients or students. Tertiary prevention would involve training in types of sanctions and direct services necessary to manage sexually exploitative professionals and violators of other ethical and legal norms. Secondary prevention would take the form of early identification of professionals likely to abuse clients or students to reduce the risk and incidence and to increase awareness of the problem. Primary prevention, in the form of education about risk factors and patterns of abuse, would be provided to both the public and the profession.

A TRAINING EXAMPLE: ALCOHOL ABUSE AND ALCOHOLISM

To illustrate how psychologists can be trained in a specific area of distress, a basic model for training in alcohol abuse is provided here. Under each level of prevention, I outline some basic principles.

Primary Prevention

1. The experience of other professions suggests that effective programs can be developed to help professionals who are in distress due to alcohol abuse and alcoholism. This conclusion is supported by our survey (Nathan, Thoreson, & Kilburg, 1983) of the perceptions of alcohol abuse among psychologists, in which over 90 percent of the psychologists polled were in favor of APA developing a program to help psychologists in distress; it is supported also by our survey of alcoholic psychologists, in which they reported severe alcohol problems during active alcoholism, the importance of self-help support systems to their recovery, and exceptionally low relapse rates (see chapter 5).

2. Alcoholism, a major health problem in our society, is a large problem for the profession of psychology and has clearly identifiable and major adverse consequences for afflicted members of the profession.

3. Alcoholism is a complex health problem on which there is no clear agreement in regard to etiology, symptoms, treatment methods, or outcomes. The definition of alcoholism is characterized by ambiguity and diversity in identification and in diagnostic criteria. Definitions vary from conservative definitions based on the clinical population, in which lower estimates of the incidence of the problem are reported, to liberal definitions based on survey research, which tends to overreport the incidence and includes many persons who may not fit into traditional treatment paradigms. Definitions also vary, from those that stress learned and environmental determinants to those that emphasize genetic and constitutional disease components.

Although psychologists tend to favor a behavioral/learning approach over a definition based on the disease model, alcoholism is more appropriately viewed as a twofold illness that includes components of both disease and behavioral disorder. The term *alcoholism* subsumes several subtypes, including three that are found among psychologists. The first subtype uses clinical and behavioral criteria that concentrate on *alcohol dependency;* the second subtype emphasizes *adverse behavioral consequences* of the illness, such as loss of job, driving-while-intoxicated arrests (DWIs), and public intoxication, and *societal and environmental factors;* the third subtype emphasizes *biochemical, constitutional, and genetic determinants.* Each subtype defines and identifies somewhat different populations of alcohol abusers.

4. The debate over controlled drinking versus abstinence has central importance for the profession of psychology. The underlying factors in this debate must be taken into account in the treatment of psychologists who are in distress due to alcoholism. These factors include the following: (a) Behavioral techniques such as careful planning, assessment, and execution of behavioral procedures have been demonstrated to be effective in alcoholism treatment; (b) abstinence is the proper goal for those who have been diagnosed, or have self-diagnosed themselves, as alcoholic; (c) early problem drinkers and other categories of non-alcohol-dependent psychologists can profit from behavioral techniques that lead to the development of healthier drinking habits; (d) the goal of controlled drinking, sometimes used with early problem drinkers, fails to emphasize the importance of the mind-altering function of alcohol for the alcohol-dependent psychologist, and substituting a mild sedative level of alcohol for the mind-altering level will not suffice, because it trivializes the essential mind-altering nature of addiction; and (e) relapse-prevention strategies must be emphasized. These strategies, which rely heavily on behavioral techniques, are critical in enabling the alcoholic psychologist to long-term self-management strategies in relapse prevention.

5. There are special issues and treatment concerns that are unique to alcoholism in women that must be taken into account in working with female psychologists who suffer from alcoholism. The alcohol treatment system has tended to be nonresponsive to alcoholic women. Alcoholic women have lower recovery rates and use treatment programs at a lower rate than alcoholic men. Training is needed in societal–cultural sources of discrimination and in characteristics of treatment that can enhance recovery. Graduate and postgraduate

education programs should emphasize these principles in their preparation of professionals.

Secondary and Tertiary Prevention

1. Alcoholism treatment in the private sector is a major industry in the United States. Such treatment frequently is organized around Alcoholics Anonymous principles, is typically abstinence based, and generally follows an inpatient, medical approach. However, research suggests that alcoholism is a complex, poorly understood illness; that inpatient treatment has no advantage over outpatient treatment; and that effects of treatment have an important but only modest influence on recovery. Therefore, diversity in treatment approaches is needed.

2. Abstinence is the goal best suited for most psychologists who either describe themselves, or who are diagnosed by others, as alcoholic. This is invariably true for psychologists who have developed alcohol dependency.

3. Posttreatment resources such as family, work, self-help support systems, and relapse-prevention strategies are critical and frequently neglected factors in the treatment of alcoholic professionals.

4. Self-help/mutual-help support is an important element in the recovery of alcoholic psychologists.

5. The symptomatology of many psychologists suffering from alcoholism will differ from that usually ascribed to alcoholics. The pattern is likely to be more covert and subtle and more likely to be manifest in alcohol dependence, impaired family relationships, subtle job impairment indicators, and low frequency of job loss.

6. Alcoholism in psychologists is a disorder in its own right, a deeply imbedded, unyielding pattern of behavior that is not amenable to change through individual effort, and, in contrast with other mental health problems, is more difficult to treat; left untreated, it carries greater negative consequences.

7. Psychology should look to other professions for models to use in programs for psychologists who are in distress due to alcoholism. The allied health professions of medicine, dentistry, and nursing, and professions such as law have active programs that vary in voluntary and coercive features, activity level, thoroughness of effort, and reported effectiveness.

8. Psychologists with alcoholism tend to be protected by their peers, clients, and supervisors. Few professional sanctions are applied even to those whose work performance is demonstrably impaired as a result of alcohol abuse. Those who are warned by state boards rarely have licenses revoked and rarely are removed from professional practice.

9. The professional environment of most psychologists encourages alcohol abuse. It involves low visibility and generally low supervision of job performance. Such factors, which are generic to professional practice, constitute significant risks for the development of alcoholism.

Training programs must emphasize these principles in preparing psychologists to enter the field, and treatment programs caring for impaired psychologists need to incorporate these principles into their operations.

OTHER TRAINING ISSUES

Pre- and Postdoctoral Training

Using the foregoing principles, defined by level of prevention, one can easily see the usefulness of providing training programs during the course of education in psychology. Graduate-level courses or advanced undergraduate courses in alcoholism should be part of the educational programs of all predoctoral psychologists. These courses should involve general training in the phenomena of alcoholism and drug abuse, and intervention strategies in the treatment of alcoholism. The courses should provide a careful analysis of the variables in the controlled drinking-versus-abstinence debate. A description of the efforts of the profession and of self- and mutual-help programs should be provided. Experiential components in the form of attendance at open AA and Al-Anon meetings should be included, and evaluation of treatment effectiveness is a must.

At the postdoctoral level workshops and institutes can be developed to enable psychologists to gain knowledge that will help them to work effectively with this population. This could be done through formal APA symposia and presentations, pre-APA-convention workshops, articles in the APA *Monitor,* and information from APA on the ongoing efforts by the profession to meet the needs of distressed psychologists. Similar efforts can be undertaken by state psychological associations.

Defining the Purpose of Training

Should training be tailored to particular syndrome, or, second, given the variance in both definition and consensus on distress, should training be designed to heighten awareness of procedures necessary to implement programs? The former includes standard training procedures in diagnosis and treatment. The latter includes identification of the sources of resistance and the appropriate strategies to use, given variance in problem definition and constituency support. There is merit for selecting training in either one or both of these areas:

Training tailored to a particular syndrome. If the training is directed toward increasing understanding of a particular area of distress, it can be readily implemented. State-of-the-art knowledge on issues and concerns, assessment procedures, intervention strategies, and evaluation procedures in that distress area can be provided immediately in all of the areas identified in this text.

Training in program implementation. If the training is to be directed at increasing the skill and knowledge necessary to develop a program to deal with impaired colleagues, issues in implementation must be taken into account. Wood, Klein, Cross, Lammers, and Elliot (1986) have offered data to support their observation that psychologists would rather take no action to control their impaired colleagues than risk retaliation. They concluded that the public would be better served if psychologists were more willing to regulate rather than treat their own. Such training must be directed toward increasing awareness of factors involved in initiating planned change. Conjoint training in program implementation and specific strategies for work with impaired colleagues should be offered.

Targets of Training

Psychologist as client. Professionals could enter training to gain specific knowledge regarding how they could better manage stress and professional burnout in their lives. Solway (1985) and Suran and Sheridan (1986) have described transition markers, crises, and burnout in the career patterns of psychologists and have recommended training to reduce distress.

Psychologist as mentor. Such training, directed at staff and students, would involve a methodology to train the trainer and would educate the psychologist to be a supervisor and teacher of students, staff, paraprofessionals, and the like. In many ways, this kind of training would be easiest to market, least threatening to psychologists, and most likely to show immediate benefits.

Students and staff. Short courses and conferences, textbooks (such as this volume), and formal courses constitute the kind of training in which most psychologists would participate. Such programs produce little resistance, are easy to market, and are likely to show immediate benefits.

Program implementation. First, all training in the area of distress should involve knowledge of the principles of planned change for the distressed professional, the client, and society. Second, implementation of programs in distress requires high-level administrative support (see Thoreson & Hosokawa, 1984). If such support is available from state association executive councils, university administrations, and the management of organizations, it will facilitate training in the specific procedures and strategies to use in implementation.

Coping With Resistance to Planned Change

Expect resistance to programs for distressed psychologists. It is inevitable and healthy, because there are pros and cons to every issue. Psychologists are predisposed to see alternative explanations or views of a problem. Such variance in perception should be included in the training programs. Because there are identifiable program advocates and critics in every area of distress, heightening awareness of the advocates and critics, the types of resistance, and the strategies for change that follow from these characteristics of the various constituent groups should become an important part of training. Strategies developed for program implementation thus can be contingent upon particular definitions and types of resistance. The timetable for implementation, strong or weak consensus on problem recognition, and consensus and variance on appropriate action will influence the selection of training strategies. When time is not a factor, training in reeducative strategies is in order (Zaltman & Dunkin, 1977). Such strategies would not take a particular position regarding the preferred change strategy but would include an unbiased account of the problem and of the various solutions that have been suggested.

Persuasive strategies constitute the preferred approach when consensus already exists on the need for program implementation by the particular organization (e.g., a state association) but when commitment to change among particular constituencies is low. Training in persuasive strategies could focus on the benefits of adopting a program for distressed psychologists versus the costs of not changing. It could include a plan to present data that would support the plan to be implemented and that, conversely, shows the adverse effects of failure to implement the plan.

SUGGESTIONS FOR IMPLEMENTATION

1. The purpose of the training should be clearly stated. Is the purpose to increase knowledge or skill? To heighten awareness? To change the client? To change attitudes? Is the training directed toward increasing knowledge of individual areas of distress or toward program implementation?

2. The target audience should be identified. There are at least five types of target groups: psychologists, clients, staff, students, program administrators, and the public. The state of the art in each area of impairment needs to be clearly summarized. Particular attention should be given to the issue of how to train the trainer and to the problems related to the characteristics of professional psychologists and their work environments.

3. Training is best received if it has the support of appropriate sanctioning bodies. This is true both for general training in program implementation and for specific training in a given area of distress. Kilburg and Kaslow (personal communication, March 15, 1986) supported using sanctions in doctoral programs to counsel impaired students. They recommended the formulation of training guidelines, explicitly stated in the departmental handbook, that give the university the right and responsibility to remove students found to be impaired in ways that would jeopardize future clients. Knoff and Prout (1985) also described critical procedures and legal issues in terminating students from professional psychology programs. Training is more likely to be effective if accreditation boards, state committees, ethics boards, and so on, give clear sanction to programs that adopt such procedures.

4. Careful attention should be given to the disinclination of psychologists to admit to vulnerability and distress. This characteristic needs to be addressed in the training of psychologists. Prochaska & Norcross (1983) confirmed psychologists' reluctance to admit to vulnerabilities as well as their proclivity to assume that they are healthier than their clients.

5. The process of implementing planned change itself can serve as an excellent case study. Analysis of areas of consensus and diagnosis, of strong and weak constituency support, and of definitional variance can serve to highlight the major issues and concerns in the theory and development of programs that address distress. These analyses can increase the awareness of students and professionals about the problem of impairment.

6. Research support for the effectiveness training and for the validity of concepts in distress is weak and needs to be improved. We know that the long-term effectiveness of training is not clearly supported by research. For example, in reviewing substance abuse training programs, Ewan and Whaite (1983) found short-term but not long-term change. Therefore, we psychologists are challenged to design programs in ways that add to our knowledge base on training in areas of distress. Even the concept of well-being, the other

side of distress, has no generally agreed-upon definition or empirical correlates (Diener, 1984). Conceptualization and measurement problems in life-stress research are noted by Depue and Monroe (1985). Nathan notes (chapter 2) that many of the techniques that have been suggested for use with professionals in areas of distress lack research to support their effectiveness (e.g., tailored treatment, coercion, choice of treater, and prevalence of particular disorders. For recent reviews of advances and directions in research on psychotherapy, one of the major treatment modalities, see Kazdin, 1986, and Vandenbos, 1986.) All of the professions as well as public and private funding organizations have a vested interest in improving the knowledge and training base in the area of distressed professionals.

References

American Psychological Association. (1985). APA-approved sponsors of continuing education in psychology. *American Psychologist, 40,* 695–704.

Backer, T. E., Liberman, R. P., & Kuehnel, T. G. (1986). Dissemination and adoption of innovative psychosocial interventions. *Journal of Consulting and Clinical Psychology, 54,* 111–118.

Baxter, J. (1984). Employee assistance programs in historical perspective. In R. W. Thoreson & E. P. Hosokawa (Eds.), *Employee assistance programs in higher education: Alcohol-related health and professional programming development for faculty and staff* (pp. 7–12). Springfield, IL: Charles C Thomas.

Bevan, W. (1982). A sermon of sorts in three-plus parts. *American Psychologist, 37,* 1303–1322.

Bissell, L., & Haberman, P. W. (1984). *Alcoholism in the professions.* New York: Oxford University Press.

Black, T. R. L. (1972). Ten institutional obstacles to advances in family planning. In M. Potts & C. Woods (Eds.), *New concepts in contraception.* Honolulu: University of Hawaii Press.

Depue, R. A., & Monroe, S. M. (1985). Conceptualization and measurement of human disorder in life stress research: The problem of chronic disturbance. *Psychological Bulletin, 99,* 36–51.

Diener, E. (1984). Subjective well-being. *Psychological Bulletin, 95,* 542–575.

Ewan, C. E., & Whaite, A. (1983). Evaluation of training programs for health professionals in substance abuse: A review. *Journal of Studies on Alcohol, 44,* 885–899.

Gaff, J. G. (1976). *Toward faculty renewal.* San Francisco: Jossey-Bass.

Garner, D. M., & Garfinkel, P. E. (Eds.). (1985). *Handbook of psychotherapy for anorexia nervosa and bulemia.* New York: Guilford Press.

Herbsleb, J. D., Sales, B. D., & Overcast, T. D. (1985). Challenging licensure and certification. *American Psychologist, 40,* 1165–1178.

Kazdin, A. E. (Ed.). (1986). Psychotherapy research [Special issue]. *Journal of Consulting and Clinical Psychology, 54,* 3–118.

Knoff, H. M., & Prout, H. T. (1985). Terminating students from professional psychology programs: Criteria, procedures, and legal issues. *Professional Psychology: Research and Practice, 16,* 789–797.

Kutz, S. L. (1986). Comment: Defining "impaired psychologist." *American Psychologist, 41,* 220.

Lazarus, A. (1981). *The practice of multimodal therapy.* New York: McGraw-Hill.

Lippitt, G. (1973). *Visualizing change: Model building and the change process.* Fairfax, VA: NTL Learning Resources Corp.

Marlatt, G. A., & Gordon, J. R. (1984). *Relapse prevention: Maintenance strategies in addictive behavior change.* New York: Guilford Press.

Miller, G. A. (1969). Psychology as a means of promoting human welfare. *American Psychologist, 24,* 1063–1075.

Nathan, P., Thoreson, R. W., & Kilburg, R. (1983). *Board of Professional Affairs Steering Committee on Distressed Psychologists: Final report.* Washington, DC: American Psychological Association.

Pattison, E. M., & Kaufman, E. (1982). The alcoholism syndrome: Definitions and models. In E. M. Pattison & E. Kaufman (Eds.), *Encyclopedic handbook of alcoholism* (pp. 3–30). New York: Gardner Press.

Prochaska, J. O., & Norcross, J. C. (1983). Psychotherapists' perspectives on treating themselves and their clients for psychic distress. *Professional Psychology: Research and Practice, 14,* 642–655.

Roman, P. M. (1984). The social and organizational precursors of EAPs: Assessing their role in higher education. In R. W. Thoreson & E. P. Hosokawa (Eds.). *Employee assistance programs in higher education: Alcohol-related health and professional programming development for faculty and staff* (pp. 13–44). Springfield, IL: Charles C Thomas.

Skorina, J. (1982). Alcoholic psychologists: The need for humane and effective regulations. *Professional Practice of Psychology, 3,* 33–41.

Solway, K. S. (1985). Transition from graduate school to internship: A potential crisis. *Professional Psychology: Research and Practice, 14,* 50–54.

Suran, B. G., & Sheridan, E. P. (1986). Management burnout: Training psychologists in professional life span perspective. *Professional Psychology: Research and Practice, 16,* 741–753.

Telfer, R. G. (1966). Dynamics of change. *The Clearing House, 41,* 131–135.

Thoreson, R. W., & Hosokawa, E. P. (Eds.). (1984). *Employee assistance programs in higher education: Alcohol-related health and professional programming development for faculty and staff.* Springfield, IL: Charles C Thomas.

Thoreson, R. W., Nathan, P. E., Skorina, J. K., & Kilburg, R. R. (1983). The alcoholic psychologist: Issues, problems, and implications for the profession. *Professional Psychology: Research and Practice, 14,* 670–684.

Trice, H. M., & Beyer, J. M. (1982). Job-based alcoholism programs: Motivating problem drinkers to rehabilitation. In E. M. Pattison & E. Kaufman (Eds.), *Encyclopedic handbook of alcoholism* (pp. 954–978). New York: Gardner Press.

VandenBos, G. R. (Ed.). (1986). Psychotherapy research [Special issue]. *American Psychologist, 41,* 111–214.

Wood, B. S., Klein, S., Cross, H. J., Lammers, C. J., & Elliot, J. K. (1986). Impaired practitioners: Psychologists' opinions about prevalence and proposals for intervention. *Professional Psychology: Research and Practice, 16,* 843–850.

Woolfolk, R. L., & Lehrer, P. M. (Eds.). (1984). *Principles and practice of stress management.* New York: Guilford Press.

Zaltman, G., & Dunkin, R. (1977). *Strategies for planned change.* New York: Wiley.

SECTION II: SYNDROMES

STRESS, BURNOUT, AND WORKAHOLISM 4

Christina Maslach

Work is a central part of our lives. Not only does it occupy a major portion of our waking hours, but it is often the core of our sense of self. "I am what I do" is a key refrain for many people. Not surprisingly, then, how well we handle our work is often more critical for our self-worth and personal health than how well we handle anything else. Work can be a source of satisfaction and success, but it can also be a source of frustration and failure. When such difficulties arise, the personal and social consequences can be very costly. However, these costs can be reduced and the rewards of work increased if we can gain a better understanding of job stress—what it is, why it occurs, and what we can do about it.

STRESS

The concept of *stress* is one that is widely used by both scientists and the general public when discussing the interaction of a person with the environment. The idea that external environmental changes can disrupt the internal stability of the individual found its earliest scientific expression in the work of a French physiologist, Claude Bernard (1867). Later work was done by the American physiologist, Walter Cannon, who used the term *homeostasis* to refer to the internal state of balance and *stress* to refer to those reactions that produced a collapse of the homeostatic mechanisms (Cannon, 1935).

The modern concept of stress, however, was most profoundly shaped by the extensive work of the Canadian endocrinologist, Hans Selye, popularly known as "the father of stress" (Selye, 1936, 1946, 1950, 1974, 1976). Selye discovered that tissue damage could result from diverse stimuli (such as heat, cold, x-rays, and exercise) and was thus a nonspecific response to all noxious stimuli. Subsequently, he proposed that stress is a nonspecific bodily response to any demand made upon the organism. These demands are considered to be stressors. Selye conceptualized the nonspecific stress response as a three-phase General Adaptation Syndrome (GAS). The first, or *alarm* phase, involves major biochemical changes in the body, which occur when a stressor is first encountered. These changes include increases in adrenalin, increases in heart rate and blood pressure, decreases in digestive processes, and a heightening of all senses. The second, or *resistance* phase, occurs when the stressor is being dealt with in some way. The alarm responses disappear, and the physiological changes that then occur are a function of the particular adaptive strategy that is being used. The third, or *exhaustion* phase, occurs when the adaptive energy for resisting the stressor is used up. The alarm phase may be reactivated and the GAS cycle repeated for a new resistance strategy, or, if there is no alternative strategy, the organism may die.

The work of Selye and his predecessors, although enormously influential, was constrained by the focus on physical stressors and physiological stress responses. Current stress research places far greater emphasis on psychological stressors as well as on psychological and social responses to those stimuli. This expansion of the concept of stress has resulted in a proliferation of new definitions of stress, so that now there is considerable disagreement and debate about just what stress is.

Definitions of Stress

Even though *stress* is a popular term that is widely used by both professionals and the general public, its meaning is not always clear. There are many different definitions of stress, most of which fall into one of three categories: stress as stimulus, stress as response, or stress as a stimulus–response interaction.

In the stimulus definition, stress is considered to be a characteristic of the environment that is disturbing or disruptive for a person. Thus, stress is an external force that causes a reaction of strain within the individual. This stimulus definition is analogous to an engineering definition of stress, in which stress is the load, or demand, placed on a physical material (such as a metal beam) and strain is the resultant deformation of that material. If the strain falls within the elastic limits of the material, the material will return to its original condition when the stress is removed. Similarly, if the strain falls within the coping limits of the individual, that person will return to normal and not be permanently affected when the stress is removed. This stimulus definition corresponds most closely to the original conceptions of stress as well as to the most common everyday use of the term. However, this definition has been criticized for its inability to explain individual differences in response to the same level of stress and its assumption that an undemanding (or boring) environment is an ideal one because it is "stress free" (Cox, 1978).

In contrast to the stimulus definition of stress, the response definition considers stress to be a pattern of physiological or psychological reactions exhibited by a person who is under pressure from a disturbing or dysfunctional environment. Thus, stress is an internal response to external stressors. The major proponent of the stress-as-response definition has been Selye who, as mentioned earlier, considered stress to be a nonspecific response to any demand placed on the individual. However, this position has become less popular as evidence has increased that the stress response is variable rather than fixed and unchanging. Also, like the stimulus definition, the response definition of stress does not clearly explain individual differences (Cox, 1978).

A third approach to conceptualizing stress has been to combine the stimulus and the response approaches and define stress as the consequence of the *interaction* between environmental stimuli and individual responses. In addition to focusing on the continuing relationship, or transaction, between the person and the environment, this approach emphasizes intervening psychological processes, such as perception and cognitive appraisal. Stress is considered to occur only when the person perceives an external demand as exceeding his or her capability to deal with it. Thus, the individual's personal evaluation of the nature of the demand, of the available resources and personal skills, and of the presumed outcomes will determine the stress experience. In contrast to the stimulus and the response definitions, this interactional approach both recognizes and deals with individual differences. Its greater complexity, however, can cause more difficulties in deriving clear predictions and applications.

Most discussions of stress emphasize its negative qualities. Stress is considered to be an upsetting or disruptive experience and a problem that needs to be resolved through stress reduction or stress management techniques. However, stress has its positive side as well. External demands can be challenges rather than threats, and challenges can stimulate creativity, improve performance, and yield such personal benefits as satisfaction and self-esteem. The distinction between the negative and positive aspects of stress was recognized by Selye, who used the term *distress* to refer to "bad" or disruptive stress, and *eustress* to refer to "good" stress that has positive outcomes. Throughout this chapter, however, the focus will be on the negative form of stress.

Sources of Stress

What are the major sources of stress? By taking the interactional approach and viewing stress as the result of external demands exceeding the individual's capacity to respond, the question can be addressed in terms of environmental and personal sources. It should be noted, however, that the literature on stress is so vast that a thorough review is not possible within this chapter; thus, the following discussion is necessarily selective.

Environmental sources. At the environmental level, physical stimuli have been identified as sources of stress. For example, stress has been linked to high levels of noise (Cohen & Weinstein, 1981), crowding (Epstein, 1981), heat (Bell, 1981), and air pollution (Evans & Jacobs, 1981). In most cases, attention has focused on excessive levels of these factors, or overstimulation, but there is evidence that too little stimulation is also stressful, as in the case of isolation or sensory deprivation (Suedfeld, 1981). However, it is not the absolute level of the physical stimulus that is most important in producing stress. Rather, it is the person's subjective psychological experience of that stimulus. If the person perceives the stimulus to be predictable and controllable, it will be less likely to induce stress. The social meaning attached to the stimulus will also moderate its stressfulness—compare, for example, the loud noise of a police siren with the loud noise of church bells (Kaminoff & Proshansky, 1982). In general, the more the environment fails to satisfy the person's needs or interferes in the person's pursuit of desired goals, the more stress it will induce (Stokols, 1979).

In addition to physical aspects of the environment, much attention has been given to social events as sources of stress. The initial focus was on stress in extreme situations, such as military combat (Grinker & Spiegel, 1945), traumatic injury (Hamburg, Hamburg, & deGoza, 1953), and bereavement (Lindmann, 1944). The extreme situations receiving more recent attention by researchers include natural disasters, terrorism, war, and migration (see relevant chapters in Goldberger & Breznitz, 1982).

Most stress research, however, has shifted from this focus on extreme situations to a consideration of more normal life events. At first, it was thought that stress would result from any sort of life event involving change or adaptation, and that the greater the change(s), the greater the stress (Holmes & Rahe, 1967). Presumably, both positive life events (e.g., marriage or vacation) and negative life events (e.g., loss of job or death of spouse) involved change and would produce stress. However, this viewpoint has been altered by subsequent research, which shows that the quality of the events is more important than the quantity of changes that are involved. Events that are involuntary, undesirable, or unscheduled and unexpected (e.g., major illness, injury, premature death of a loved one, divorce, or job loss) are the ones most consistently linked to stress outcomes (Pearlin, 1982).

Because of the emphasis on discrete events, there has been a relative lack of attention to chronic, ongoing sources of stress. Such chronic experiences would include daily hassles (Lazarus, 1981), mental strains, parent–child conflict, and job-related problems (Pearlin & Lieberman, 1979). Although less well studied, these chronic experiences appear to be more strongly related to stress than many discrete life events, and researchers would do well to devote more effort to understanding them.

Personal sources. There have been several approaches to elucidating the role of the individual in the stress experience. The first has been to look for personality characteristics that make people more or less susceptible to stress. One such characteristic is trait anxiety, which refers to a dispositional tendency to perceive situations as threatening and to respond to them with greater anxiousness (Spielberger, 1975). Much attention has also been given to the individual with a Type A personality, who typically behaves in an ambitious, aggressive, competitive, and impatient way (Friedman & Rosenman, 1974). This behavior pattern puts the individual at greater risk for heart attacks.

Another approach has focused on individual differences in people's responses to stressful life events. People who have preexisting vulnerabilities may be more likely to respond with some form of psychiatric disorder (Dohrenwend & Dohrenwend, 1981). These vulnerabilities could stem from a genetic predisposition, childhood experiences, or family relationships and could involve deficiencies in interpersonal skills, coping, and access to resources. People with a hardy personality, however, are more likely to remain healthy, even when experiencing stressful life events (Kobasa, 1979). Hardiness is considered to have three general characteristics: control (the belief that one can influence experienced events), commitment (an ability to be deeply involved in life activities), and challenge (the anticipation of change as exciting).

A different approach to personal factors has focused on the cognitive processes that mediate the person–environment interaction. Cognitive appraisal refers to the process by which people evaluate and judge the meaning of a situation. Two types of appraisal have been distinguished (Lazarus, 1966).

PROFESSIONALS IN DISTRESS

In primary appraisal, the person decides whether a situational demand is beneficial or stressful, and if stressful, whether action is called for. In secondary appraisal, the person evaluates what resources are available to cope with the stressful situation. The kind of appraisal that is made can have important consequences for a person's response to stress. For example, the person who appraises a particular situational demand as a challenge may work more persistently or effectively at dealing with it than will the person who appraises the same demand as a threat. Clearly, this cognitive approach can explain individual differences in the stress experience.

Outcomes of Stress

How do people respond to a perceived stressor? As indicated earlier, in the description of the General Adaptation Syndrome (GAS), stress produces a series of changes in bodily functioning. Basically, these changes prepare the organism for any physical actions (such as fight or flight) that are necessary to cope with the external stressor. Muscles get tense, adrenalin starts to flow, and heart rate speeds up—with the result that the body has extra strength and energy to meet any physical demands. However, because many stressors are psychological in nature, rather than physical threats, there is sometimes no need for that sort of physical action. In these instances, the bodily changes of the GAS are inappropriate and even maladaptive, as they may actually interfere with the behaviors necessary for effective coping (such as staying calm and listening carefully).

When the stress response is maladaptive, it can also result in more long-term physiological malfunctioning, or "diseases of adaptation" (Selye, 1976). For example, the increase in adrenalin that occurs in the GAS produces increases in blood pressure, heart rate, and blood clotting. All of these help protect the individual against physical injury, but when the threat of injury is absent, then they serve only to increase the risk of coronary heart disease. Similarly, disorders such as high blood pressure, ulcers, headaches, back pains, and skin problems may be, to some extent, diseases of adaptation. The continual process of adaptation to stressors may also produce a lot of "wear and tear" on the body and eventually exhaust the body's resources to the point where it is overcome by illness.

In addition to physiological outcomes, a number of psychological effects are linked to stress. At the cognitive level, there is a narrowing of attentional focus and a greater reliance on stereotyped and rigid thinking. This process interferes with memory, problem solving, and decision making (Janis, 1982) and can also disrupt complex behaviors. At the emotional level, the major reactions are anxiety, depression, frustration, anger, and irritability. These feelings may get expressed in a number of dysfunctional behaviors, such as excessive use of drugs and alcohol, eating disorders, aggression, and even suicide.

Coping With Stress

A coping activity is any attempt to deal with the demands and problems of a particular situation. There are many different types of coping activities, and they can vary widely in their effectiveness. Two basic categories of coping strategies can be identified: problem-focused coping and emotion-focused coping (Lazarus, 1975). In problem-focused coping, the person deals directly with the stressor and tries to remove or reduce its impact. Examples of problem-focused coping include fight (trying to get rid of the stressor), flight (trying to get away from it), alternative options (e.g., bargaining or compromising), and prevention of future stress. In emotion-focused coping, the goal is not to change the stressor but to reduce its discomfort by changing one's thoughts and feelings about it. Examples of emotion-focused coping are activities to reduce physiological arousal (e.g., relaxation or drugs), cognitive strategies (e.g., distractions and fantasies), and unconscious processes that distort reality.

Various psychological techniques, known as stress management interventions, have been developed to help people cope more effectively with stress. One of the most popular of these is biofeedback, in which people are trained to control specific physiological aspects of their stress response (see Shapiro & Surwit, 1979). For example, biofeedback has been used to teach people to lower their blood pressure and to relax forehead muscles (to reduce tension headaches). Another major approach to stress management has involved cognitive–behavioral therapies (see Meichenbaum & Jeremko, 1982). Here the goal is to change the way people think about stress by altering their cognitive appraisals of stressors or by restructuring their beliefs about themselves and their capabilities. These cognitive changes can alter behaviors that have been maladaptive or self-defeating, and thus they can improve coping effectiveness.

Although people tend to think of coping as an individual response, there is increasing evidence that social ties are an important factor in successful coping. If people have a social network of family and friends to whom they can turn for help, advice, and emotional support, they are better able to cope with various life stressors (Cobb, 1976; Pilisuk, 1982). In contrast, people who are socially isolated and lack such a support system are likely both to experience more stress and to cope with it less adequately.

JOB STRESS

Having completed this quick overview of the stress literature, I will now focus on job-related stress. Like the general concept of stress, job stress has had its share of definitional debates, with proponents arguing for either stimulus or response definitions. The emphasis of more recent conceptualizations, however, has been on the person–environment interaction. For example, job stress has been defined as "a situation wherein job-related factors interact with a worker to change (i.e., disrupt or enhance) his or her psychological or physiological condition such that the person is forced to deviate from normal functioning" (Beehr & Newman, 1978, p. 670) and as "any characteristics of the job environment which pose a threat to the individual" (Caplan, Cobb, French, Van Harrison, & Pinneau, 1975). According to the latter definition, there are two types of threat: environmental demands that the person cannot meet and insufficient environmental supplies to meet the person's needs. In both cases, there is a mismatch, or lack of fit, between the person and the environment (French, Rogers, & Cobb, 1974).

Sources of Job Stress

The experience of job stress has been linked to a variety of causal factors, some of which overlap with those already mentioned as general stressors. Whereas some sources of stress have been defined in objective terms (such as physical hazards or shift work), other stressors are more subjective appraisals by the worker of what is or is not stressful (such as role ambiguity). Moreover, some stressors are found in the physical or social environment, whereas others occur at the individual level.

Environmental sources. Many physical aspects of the work environment have been identified as causes of stress, including noise, extremes of heat or cold, various air pollutants (e.g., asbestos, carbon monoxide, and radiation), vibration and motion (from operating a tool or vehicle), improper lighting or glare, and chronic dangers that expose workers to possible loss of life or limb (Holt, 1982). These physical factors have often been described as blue-collar stressors, because they are more characteristic of those types of occupations (Poulton, 1978).

Another category of environmental stressors involves the structure of the job itself. Nonstandard hours of work, or shift work, is one such stressor that has been tied to disturbances in physiological functioning and social relationships (Tasto & Colligan, 1978). Assembly-line work, which is characterized by machine pacing and often a great deal of monotony, is another structural stressor (Murphy & Hurrell, 1980). Workload is also a relevant structural factor, and particular attention has been paid to overload as an antecedent of stress (French & Caplan, 1973). Quantitative overload refers to having too much work to do in the time available, whereas qualitative overload refers to having work that is too difficult to do because one lacks the necessary skills.

In addition to working conditions, the person's role at work can be a major source of job stress. Two role-related factors have been studied extensively by researchers: role ambiguity and role conflict (Kahn, Wolfe, Quinn, Snoek, & Rosenthal, 1964; Van Sell, Brief, & Schuler, 1981). Role ambiguity exists when there is a lack of clarity about the work role. The worker has insufficient information about the goals and responsibilities of the job and about co-workers' expectations. Role conflict exists when the worker is caught between competing demands or is faced with demands to do things he or she does not want to do. Job roles that are at boundaries (e.g., between departments or between the organization and the public) are often characterized by greater role conflict (Miles, 1980). Another role stressor concerns type of responsibility (Cobb, 1973). Workers who are responsible for people (e.g., subordinates, clients, or patients) experience more stress than workers who are responsible for things (e.g., budget or equipment). Stress is also related to job roles that involve only limited participation in decision making (French & Caplan, 1973; Margolis, Kroes, & Quinn, 1974).

Relationships with other people in the job setting can be sources of stress as well as sources of support. Although less research has been done in this area, there is some evidence to suggest that poor relationships with one's boss, colleagues, or subordinates are linked to negative assessments of the job (Argyris, 1964; Kahn et al., 1964). In addition, poor work relationships with one's clientele or with the general community can be important stressors (Maslach, 1982a).

Other work stressors are related to changes in job status. The most extensively studied job change has been the loss of a job, or unemployment (Cobb & Kasl, 1977), but other stressful changes could include demotion, job transfers, and changes in tasks or responsibilities.

Personal sources. Whatever the nature of environmental job stressors, there are individual variations in people's response to them. Thus, researchers have looked for personal characteristics that increase the worker's risk of experiencing stress and affect how the worker copes with stress. Some attention has been given to demographic variables, such as age or education, but little of major significance has been found. Most of the research has been focused on personality factors, in particular on the Type A personality (Friedman & Rosenman, 1974). As mentioned earlier, the Type A behavior pattern is characterized by a hard-driving competitiveness, aggressiveness, and impatience—and yet it is these characteristics that are encouraged and even rewarded in many occupational settings. Thus, the Type A personality may not be an individual trait so much as it is a learned response style. In either case, its consistent link with coronary heart disease makes it a rather dysfunctional behavior.

Other factors may modify the stress experience. For example, the worker who has a high need for clarity and structure and a low tolerance of ambiguity, should find conditions of role ambiguity more stressful than someone with less of a need and a greater tolerance. Similarly, the worker with high self-esteem should feel less threatened by job demands. Locus of control may be another important personal factor, in that workers who perceive that they have control or mastery in a situation (i.e., internal locus of control) should be less likely to appraise that situation as stressful (Chan, 1977.)

Outcomes of Job Stress

Many researchers have tried to assess the effects of job stress on the worker's health—both physical and mental. In terms of physical health, the major focus has been on coronary heart disease, which is now the principal cause of death in the United States. Job stress has been consistently related to heart disease, as has the Type A behavior pattern. Ulcers have also been linked to job stress, although the findings are not quite as consistent as those for heart disease. Mortality rates have been found to differ by occupation, and varying levels of job stress may be one explanatory factor.

Job stress has also been linked to impairments in psychological well-being, as reflected in reports of depression, dissatisfaction, anxiety, tension, and lowered self-esteem. Job stress bears some relationship to increased use of alcohol and drugs, but much of the evidence is based on self-report rather than on behavioral measures. Surveys of people's use of community mental health centers reveal some striking differences among occupational groups; people in many human service occupations are among the highest users (Colligan, Smith, & Hurrell, 1977). Although this may point to the important role of interpersonal stressors, it may also reflect the fact that human service workers are more informed about mental health facilities and more inclined to take advantage of them.

PROFESSIONALS IN DISTRESS

Although the common-sense assumption is that job stress will lead to impaired job performance, there still has been little research on this issue. There is some evidence, however, to tie job stress to "counterproductive behaviors," such as damaging equipment, stealing from the employer, deliberately doing inferior work, and spreading rumors (Mangione & Quinn, 1975). Job stress may also lead to employee withdrawal from work, as reflected in turnover, absenteeism, or reduced job involvement (e.g., Lyons, 1971).

Burnout Syndrome

Burnout is a type of job stress that has received a great deal of attention in recent years. What is unique about burnout is that it appears to be a response to chronic sources of emotional and interpersonal stress on the job. Thus, burnout is a particular problem for those in people-oriented, caregiving professions, where the provision of care or service often occurs in emotionally charged situations. Helping other people has long been recognized as a noble goal, but only recently has serious attention been given to the emotional costs of achieving that goal.

Burnout is a syndrome of emotional exhaustion, depersonalization, and reduced personal accomplishment that can occur among individuals who work with people in some capacity (Maslach & Jackson, 1981a; Maslach, 1982a). *Emotional exhaustion* refers to feelings of being emotionally overextended and drained by one's contact with other people. As emotional resources are depleted, one feels no longer able to give of oneself to others. As one professional put it, "It's not that I don't want to help, but that I can't—I seem to have 'compassion fatigue'." *Depersonalization* refers to an unfeeling and callous response toward people, often the recipients of one's service or care. This negative attitude may get translated into rude, insensitive, or even inappropriate behavior toward clients as well as to withdrawal from them. The prevalence of this negative attitude toward clients among human service workers has been well documented (Wills, 1978). *Reduced personal accomplishment* refers to a decline in one's sense of competence and of successful achievement in one's work with people. This may develop into more extreme feelings of inadequacy and failure, loss of self-esteem, and even depression.

Although this multidimensional conception of burnout is the predominant one in ongoing research, there are several other definitions as well. Thus, for example, burnout has been defined as a process in which the professional's attitudes and behavior change in negative ways in response to job strain (Cherniss, 1980a); a state of physical, emotional, and mental exhaustion, characterized by physical depletion, by feelings of helplessness and hopelessness, by emotional drain, and by the development of negative self-concept and negative attitudes toward work, life, and other people (Pines, Aronson, & Kafry, 1981); a progressive loss of idealism, energy, and purpose experienced by people in the helping professions as a result of the conditions of their work (Edelwich & Brodsky, 1980); and (as a verb) to deplete oneself, to exhaust one's physical and mental resources, and to wear oneself out by excessively striving to reach some unrealistic expectation imposed by oneself or by the values of society (Freudenberger & Richelson, 1980). Although these (and many other) definitions of burnout may differ in their phrasing and terminology, they actually have much in common. There is general agreement that burnout is a negative internal psychological experience. Furthermore, all of the definitions refer to at least one, if not more, of the three aspects of the burnout syndrome as described at the beginning of this section (Maslach, 1982b). Because this three-dimensional approach represents the overlapping, shared concepts in the other definitions, it can serve as a useful working model of burnout.

Although there may be some shared sense of what burnout is, there is much less consensus on what causes it, what happens as a result of it, and what should be done about it. Research on burnout is still in its infancy, and there is a lot that we simply do not know about the phenomenon. For example, there is little base-rate information (e.g., what percentage of people experience burnout, how often, and for how long), as well as little empirical data on critical outcomes, such as quality of work, turnover, and personal health (Maslach, 1983). Moreover, most of the research to date has consisted of one-shot, correlational studies that can say little about causal relationships or changes over time.

This shortage of facts, however, is not matched by a shortage of ideas. Hundreds of articles and books have been written about burnout, in which numerous proposals are made about causes, effects, and interventions. More integrative models of burnout are beginning to be developed (see, for example, Carroll & White, 1982; Cherniss, 1980b; Golembiewski, Munzenrider, & Carter, 1983), and there are now standardized measures to assess burnout (Maslach & Jackson, 1981a; Jones, 1981a). Clearly, there has been a lot of progress in the burnout field, but there is still a long way to go before complete understanding of the phenomenon is achieved.

Sources of burnout. Many sources of burnout have been proposed, ranging from the personal (expectations, motivations, and personality) to the interpersonal (client contact, relations with co-workers and supervisors, and relations with family and friends) to the organizational (workload, bureaucracy, feedback, and work pressure). No single source has been identified as *the* cause of burnout. Rather, burnout is being viewed as the product of multiple causes, some of which may be more influential than others. To complicate matters even further, different causal factors are related to the three different aspects of the burnout syndrome (Maslach & Jackson, 1984a). For the purposes of this chapter, however, only a summary overview of some major contributors to burnout will be presented.

Given that burnout is a type of job stress, it is not surprising that most of the causal factors identified have been job related. Some of these center around client contact—a key element of the work situation for service and caregiving professionals. As amount of client contact increases, either in terms of a higher caseload or a greater percentage of time spent in direct contact, burnout is more likely to occur (Lewiston, Conley, & Blessing-Moore, 1981; Maslach & Jackson, 1982, 1984b; Maslach & Pines, 1977; Savicki & Cooley, 1983). Moreover, burnout is greater when the nature of the client contact is especially upsetting, frustrating, or difficult (Maslach & Jackson, 1984b; Meadow, 1981; Pines, 1981; Pines & Maslach, 1978).

For professionals working in organizational settings, contact with co-workers and supervisors is another important part of the job. When these

PROFESSIONALS IN DISTRESS

relationships are nonsupportive, unpleasant, or hostile, then the risk of burnout is greater (Cherniss, 1980b; Golembiewski et al., 1983; Leiter & Meechan, 1986; Maslach & Jackson, 1982, 1984b; Pines, 1982; Pines & Maslach, 1978; Savicki & Cooley, 1983).

In addition to interpersonal relations, several other organizational conditions are predictive of burnout. Lack of positive feedback about one's job performance is one such condition (Maslach & Jackson, 1982; Pines, 1982). Another is a lack of autonomy and control in carrying out one's job or a lack of participation in organizational decisions (Golembiewski et al., 1983; Jackson, 1984; Maslach & Jackson, 1982; Maslach & Pines, 1977; Pines, 1982). Conflicting role demands, ambiguity about one's job role, faulty management and supervision, and work pressures have all been linked to greater burnout (Cherniss, 1980b; Jackson, 1984; Maslach & Jackson, 1984b; Pines, 1982; Savicki & Cooley, 1983; Schwab & Iwanicki, 1982a).

Although most attention has been directed toward situational, job-related causes of burnout, there has been some study of personal factors that may make the experience of burnout more likely. Primary among these is one's expectations about the job and personal achievement. When such expectations about the job are unrealistic or unmet, burnout is more likely to occur (Cherniss, 1980b; Edelwich & Brodsky, 1980; Freudenberger & Richelson, 1980; Stevens & O'Neill, 1983; Warnath & Shelton, 1976). Personal values may also be contributing factors; it has been argued that a loss (or lack) of ideological commitment and moral purpose in work can lead to burnout (Cherniss & Krantz, 1983). The risk of burnout seems to be greater for people with certain personality characteristics, including low self-confidence, lack of assertiveness, inability to set limits, a strong need for approval by others, and greater impatience and hostility (Gann, 1979; Heckman, 1980).

In terms of demographic variables, there is some evidence that burnout rates are slightly higher among people who are young (or new to the profession), male (for the depersonalization aspect only), unmarried, and childless (Cherniss, Egnatios, & Wacker, 1976; Maslach & Jackson, 1981b, 1984b, 1985; Schwab & Iwanicki, 1982b). However, these differences are rather small in absolute size, so it is perhaps more accurate to say that demographic factors have little impact on experienced burnout (Golembiewski & Scicchitano, 1983).

Outcomes of burnout. As is the case with contributing factors, different outcomes have been linked to the three different aspects of the burnout syndrome, although only a summary overview will be presented here. Some outcomes involve work-related attitudes and behaviors, and other involve personal well-being and relationships with family and friends.

Among work-related outcomes, job satisfaction has received the most research attention. In general, higher levels of burnout are linked to lower levels of satisfaction (Gann, 1979; Golembiewski et al., 1983; Jones, 1981a; Maslach & Jackson, 1981a, 1984b) and more complaints about the job (Maslach & Jackson, 1981a). Because client contact is a critical contributor to burnout, it is not surprising that burnout leads to a variety of behaviors that involve withdrawal from clients. Thus, people experiencing higher levels of burnout express a desire to spend less time working directly with clients (Maslach & Jackson, 1984b), try to avoid being with people (Maslach & Jackson, 1982), are more likely to be absent from work or to stretch out their work breaks (Jones, 1981b; Maslach & Jackson, 1981a), and have a greater intention of quitting their jobs (Jackson & Maslach, 1982; Jones, 1981a; Maslach & Jackson, 1984b; Pines et al., 1981). Although it is widely believed that burnout leads to a deterioration in the quality of the service or care provided to clients, not much relevant research evidence has been collected beyond anecdotal reports. Jones (1981a, 1981b), however, has found that burnout is associated with more on-the-job mistakes, more "inhumanistic" counseling practices, more aggressive behavior toward clients, and more disciplinary action by supervisors.

Burnout has also been linked to various indices of personal dysfunction. With increased burnout come reports of a decline in physical health and an increase in somatic complaints and illnesses (Belcastro, 1982; Golembiewski, Munzenrider, & Stevenson, 1984; Pines et al., 1981). There may also be a sense of personal inadequacy and failure (Freudenberger, 1982). A greater use of alcohol and drugs is reported by those experiencing greater burnout (Jackson & Maslach, 1982; Jones, 1981b). Finally, although burnout may be due to stresses at work, it can have a negative "spillover" effect on home life in the form of both greater emotional friction and greater withdrawal from family members (Jackson & Maslach, 1982).

Workaholic Syndrome

Much as "burnout" has become a popular term in everyday use, so has "work-aholism." To say that someone is a workaholic is to imply that she or he is addicted to work, obsessed with the job, and, consequently, overloaded and highly stressed. It has even been suggested that workaholism is the root cause of burnout. In spite of the popularity of the term, however, workaholism has received scant attention from researchers. To some extent, this is because workaholism is presumed to be a popular synonym for some other, more scientific construct. In particular, the workaholic is often considered to have a Type A personality, and, as indicated earlier, this personality style and its link to stress have been studied extensively.

The primary research on workaholism has been done by Machlowitz (1980) and will be the source of the information presented here (although, given the lack of corroborative research findings, such information should be viewed with caution). According to Machlowitz, workaholism is an attitude or approach toward work, which has two distinguishing characteristics: an intrinsic desire to work long and hard, and work behavior that often exceeds the requirements of the job and the expectations of the worker's colleagues. In other words, workaholics work hard—and love it. They derive a great deal of happiness and satisfaction from work and would rather spend all of their time working than doing anything else. Thus, contrary to the popular stereotype, workaholics are thriving, not suffering, from working so hard.

Outcomes of workaholism. If this analysis is correct, then workaholics should not exhibit the personal dysfunctions that are commonly associated with job stress. Some supportive evidence comes from Machlowitz (1980), who reports that the workaholics she studied were a remarkably energetic and healthy group.

However, although the workaholic style may not be stressful for the individual, it *is* stressful for the people who work and live with the workaholic. Workaholics expect everyone else to work as long and hard as they do, put heavy demands on others, and are critical of those who do not match their own high standards. They also have difficulties in dealing with their co-workers. They do not like to delegate tasks or responsibilities (because they prefer to do everything themselves), and if they do delegate, they often meddle and interfere. At the same time, they resent any interference by others in their own work and may refuse to cooperate or share essential information. Although workaholics may put in longer hours, they are not necessarily more effective and efficient. Their tendency to do everything means they have difficulties in setting and sticking to priorities. They are more likely to be tied into fixed schedules and rigid approaches to problem solving, rather than being spontaneous and flexible.

The family life of workaholics also suffers. First of all, workaholics are often absent from the family, as a result of their tendency to leave early, work late, and spend their extra free time on the job. Secondly, even when they are home, they are still working or thinking about the job and fail to get involved in family chores and activities. Not only is the quantity of their family contact severely reduced, but often the quality is impaired as well. The family relationships suffer from poor communication and a lack of intimacy and trust. For workaholics, their work clearly comes first, and their spouse and children are a distant second. As one stockbroker put it, "I may be a lousy husband and a lousy father, but when Merrill Lynch needs me, I'm here" (Machlowitz, 1980, p. 65).

Sources of workaholism. What causes workaholism? Because so little research has addressed this question, there are no clear answers yet. Some speculation has centered on factors within the job setting, such as the social pressures to compete, achieve, and be number one. The most emphasis, however, has been placed on personal variables. Parental expectations to exceed and excel, and parental modeling of workaholic behaviors are part of the early socialization experiences linked to later workaholism. Relevant personality traits include the Type A pattern (Friedman & Rosenman, 1974), obsessive-compulsive neurotic style, fear of failure, and a need for control.

EMERGENT THEMES

Several important themes emerge from this review of the literature on stress, job stress, burnout, and workaholism. The first of these is ambiguity. For none of these phenomena is there clear agreement as to what they are or are not. The list of varying, and sometimes inconsistent, definitions is long for all of them (with the exception of workaholism, where ambiguity arises from the *lack* of research attention). This conceptual fuzziness is not simply a minor matter of academic quibbling but has some major consequences for any attempts to deal with these issues. To put it bluntly, if we do not know what the problem is, we are in no position to figure out solutions for it. Any treatment or intervention is based on some assumptions about what is causing the problem and with what effects, but a clear understanding of those causes and effects is impossible without a clear conception of the phenomenon itself. We cannot always consolidate the information gleaned from various research studies because the phenomenon under investigation may actually be different in each case, even though the conceptual label is the same. Until there is greater definitional clarity, any interpretations of research findings or recommendations for intervention have to be made with a great deal of caution.

A second emergent theme in the literature is that of complexity. However these stress phenomena are defined, the conceptualizations are not simple. Rather, these phenomena are seen as multifaceted and as occurring at many different levels—cognitive, emotional, physiological, behavioral, and interpersonal. There are multiple causes—not single ones—and multiple effects, both immediate and long-term. Furthermore, these multiple factors are being viewed less often as functioning additively (e.g., the more causal factors, the more stress). Instead, the trend is toward assuming that more complex interactions exist between personal and environmental factors. Although it may be that these more complex conceptualizations are better models of stress phenomena, there are some drawbacks. First, it is much more difficult to test and validate these models empirically. Second, they do not always lend themselves to practical applications—it is hard to take a complicated model, with so many parts of it still unknown, and extract some clear guidelines regarding what factor can be changed in what way to have what effect. If these models are correct in their complexity, however, then that may help to explain why some interventions fail to work or even backfire. Thus, these complex conceptualizations have the potential for producing more clearcut answers about stress.

A third theme that has received increasing attention in recent years is the importance of subjective response to objective stimuli. Although there is a lot of intuitive appeal to the idea that stress is simply a function of the quantity and quality of external stressors (and that, therefore, the appropriate treatment strategy is to modify those stressors), that concept has been found to be far too simple and limited. Instead, greater weight is being given to how the person perceives and interprets the stressor. The notion of cognitive appraisal is a key concept in this area, as well as psychological variables such as personal expectations, a sense of personal autonomy, and commitment. Changing these subjective responses is the goal of various treatment strategies, which include self-help books, workshops, inservice programs, job training programs, and counseling or therapy. It is important to keep in mind, however, that it is just as erroneous to assume that stress is "all in the person's head" as it is to assume that it is "all out there." As mentioned earlier, there are complex interactions between personal and environmental factors.

A fourth theme in the literature, the effectiveness of various interventions, is distinguished more by its absence than by its presence. Although there are numerous ideas, proposals, and recommendations for dealing with job stress, there are very few instances of systematic implementation and evaluation (Newman & Beehr, 1979). Consequently, there is a real shortage of facts on what works—we simply do not know what treatments are effective, under what circumstances, for which people, for how long, at what cost, and so forth. Because job stress is such a critical problem and there is such a strong demand for solutions to it, studies that evaluate treatment strategies should be a top priority.

TREATMENT APPROACHES

Given the lack of clear evidence about effective interventions for job stress, the following discussion is, of necessity, highly speculative. What will be presented are ideas, suggestions, hunches, and best guesses about what should be helpful for dealing with either workaholism or burnout. There is a certain face validity to these approaches, but only that—at least at this point in time.

Treating Workaholism

A special issue for the treatment of the workaholic is that the workaholic often does not want to be treated. He or she is working hard and enjoying it and thus does not perceive a personal problem that needs to be solved. Rather, workaholism is a problem for those who have to live or work with a workaholic. The impetus for change is more likely to come from family, friends, or co-workers than from the "busy but happy" worker. Therefore, treatment of a workaholic style may be most likely to occur in the context of treatment for some other problem, such as marital discord, children's difficulties in school, clashes over office policy, and so forth.

Assuming that the workaholic can be motivated to modify his or her style, what should be targeted for change? Interactions with co-workers are one key area. Workaholics need to learn how to share their workload with others rather than trying to handle it all by themselves (a strategy that is often less efficient than they might think and that conveys a negative message of distrust). For example, workaholics could profit from learning how to delegate responsibilities to others, which would allow them to reduce their workload and concentrate on the tasks they enjoy most. Even more importantly, through delegation they would express a respect and trust in the competency of their colleagues. In addition, relations with co-workers could improve if the workaholic learned how to work cooperatively with them and how to both give and receive constructive feedback. Furthermore, being more sensitive to others, whether colleagues or family members, could be crucial in improving relationships with them. This sensitivity involves an understanding of other people's needs and feelings, a recognition of their strengths and weaknesses, and a willingness to look at things from their perspective. Learning how to enjoy leisure activities and how to develop interests outside of the workplace might be other goals of treatment strategies for the workaholic.

Treatment strategies for the family and colleagues of workaholics might be an alternative way of dealing with the problem. For families, the focus might be on how best to adapt to the workaholic's style—how to reduce sources of friction, how to take advantage of the style's positive aspects, and how to initiate changes. For co-workers, the focus might be on such issues as how to get clarity and commitment from a workaholic peer, how to set limits with him or her, and how to get deserved rewards. Interventions for workaholism could also occur at an organizational level in terms of such issues as job redesign and retirement policies.

Treating Burnout

Compared to workaholism, burnout has been the target of far more speculation about effective solutions—yet the evidence of actual effectiveness is still rather sparse. Consequently, although there is more to say about treating burnout, little is really known about it.

A wide range of coping strategies have been proposed for combating burnout. Some strategies focus on alleviating the sources of emotional exhaustion or by providing better resources for dealing with it. Some strategies attempt to counteract a depersonalized view of clients by modifying the structure of the client contact or by changing the worker's expectations. Other strategies try to forestall a negative evaluation of one's accomplishments by emphasizing positive experiences and developing rewarding activities and relationships outside of the work setting. These coping strategies can occur at several different levels—personal, social, and organizational. Personal strategies refer to things that the individual can do on his or her own to cope with burnout. Social strategies require the collaborative efforts of a group of people (such as one's co-workers). Organizational strategies involve administrative decisions with respect to institutional policy, organization, resources, and staff services.

Personal strategies. Strategies that can be implemented by a single individual are especially important to offset the pervasive tendency to feel that "this problem is just too big for any one person to handle; I'm helpless—there's nothing I can do about it." Although situational factors may be the major causes of burnout, it would be erroneous to conclude that therefore only situational solutions can be effective. There are many ways in which an individual can modify the impact of a stressful situation and, in so doing, exert some personal control over it. One set of coping techniques focuses on the work process; a second set focuses on the individual.

A common response to job demands is to work harder—to do the same things as before but do more of them more quickly. The "work harder" response may increase the risk of overload and burnout, so recommendations are often made to "work smarter" instead. "Working smarter" can be done by changing the things one does or the style in which one works with people. For example, a person can alter the opening remarks of an interview, adopt a new teaching technique, try a different strategy for giving medication, and so forth. Such changes in personal work patterns, even if they seem trivial, can give people a sense of control, can get them out of a rut, and can break the pervasive tendency to stick with what is safe and familiar (but not necessarily effective).

In addition to changing work behaviors, people can change their work expectations from abstract, overly high ideals to more concrete, achievable goals. If people can develop a series of meaningful goals that are steps toward the realization of a cherished ideal, then they will have a clearer sense of their accomplishments and evidence of their own self-worth.

The effective use of work breaks is another aspect of working smarter and beating burnout. All too often, breaks are used to catch up on assignments, squeeze in a few more people, and work even harder. However, breaks can serve as emotional breathers, allowing a person to unwind, relax, and recharge before dealing with more people and problems. Breaks can also function as safety valves, by allowing the individual to blow off steam before saying or doing something that might be regretted later. Furthermore, "downshift" breaks (in which one makes a special arrangement to do less stressful, non-people work as a substitute for the regular contact with others) provide a legitimate basis for a temporary withdrawal from stressful situations while at the same time making a useful contribution to the organization.

In addition to working smarter, people can deal with burnout by taking better care of themselves. People who are strong in both physical health and psychological well-being may be in a better position to handle sources of stress and to be of maximum help to others. What sorts of strategies could boost self-esteem, prevent the development of negative feelings about others, and promote resistance to the emotional exhaustion of burnout? Seeking out and developing positive interactions with people is one way of countering the negative focus on problems that so many helping professions have. Such enjoyable activities can serve to emphasize how rewarding human interaction is and offset the work experience of how difficult it can be. In addition to positive contact with people, it is important to develop sources of positive feedback as well. Because good work is all too often taken for granted, people may have to actively seek out the praise and compliments they deserve (e.g., "Let me know if things go wrong, but I'd also like to hear when they go right"). Positive feedback can come from a number of others—the recipients of one's services, co-workers or supervisors, and family or friends—as well as from oneself.

Another aspect of self-care is to know oneself—one's strengths, weaknesses, attitudes, feelings, and so forth. If people can make a realistic appraisal of their abilities and know their own limits, they may be able to recognize the times when they should say "no," take a break, get help from others, or even change jobs. If they are sensitive to shifts in their feelings about other people and about the job, they may be better able to discover the sources of those shifts and take some appropriate action.

Because so many people-oriented jobs are so personally demanding, it is important to have times for rest, relaxation, and recharging. These rest periods can be incorporated within regular breaks, utilized as emotional breathers between contact sessions, or developed as part of a "decompression" period between leaving work and arriving home. Decompression activities allow one to unwind, get away from the pressures and problems of working with people (both physically and psychologically), and shift into a different style of dealing with others such as family and friends. These activities often involve a mode of behavior different from the highly cognitive and emotional approach required by the job; most typical are physical exercise and sports, as well as music, "fun" reading, meditation, hot baths, and so forth.

One's home life represents a highly significant break from work and has the potential to be an important resource in the battle against burnout. This is best accomplished when one's home life has a certain degree of separation from job demands and includes a variety of rewarding interests, activities, and personal relationships. To the extent that one's home life is impinged upon by one's job (as when one is "on call," puts in overtime, takes work home, or thinks or talks about the job while at home), one is far more at risk for emotional exhaustion as well as for a collapse in self-esteem if the work does not go well. Having another life outside of one's job means that there is less dependence on the work alone as a source of self-validating information and that there are important accomplishments and positive experiences to offset the negative biases inherent in people work. These resources include good relationships with a spouse, family, and friends; interesting hobbies; enjoyable leisure activities; a meaningful religious faith; and so on.

Social and organizational strategies. As suggested by the previous section, many of the proposed treatments for burnout have been directed toward individual action. However, the individual can also be helped by the efforts of other people, both at home and on the job. Social support is the key element here. Social support refers to relationships among people in which they provide each other with various types of help and comfort. If there are people who care about you and who are able and willing to assist you, then you can cope more effectively with stress. Other people provide many things that you cannot always provide for yourself—new information and insights, training in new skills, recognition and feedback, advice, emotional support, social comparison, and material aid.

Family and friends can be important sources of social support, as can work colleagues. For this reason, treatment strategies are often aimed at people who are socially isolated or whose social relationships have been disrupted (because of death, divorce, loss of job, etc.), with the goal of developing new social ties. In terms of treating burnout, the predominant approach has been to develop supportive relationships on the job rather than at home. To some extent, this reflects the privacy accorded home life and the reluctance to intervene there unless specifically requested to do so. However, it also reflects the belief that a problem caused by the job is best solved on the job. If burnout is a response to chronic sources of emotional and interpersonal stress on the job, then the people who are best qualified to provide job-related help and support are work colleagues.

Co-workers can provide social support through informal get-togethers, such as chatting over lunch or socializing after work. There are also more formal, official mechanisms, such as staff meetings, conferences, and retreats. In some cases, a formal support group is organized for the express purpose of helping staff cope with job stress. Such groups are often run by a trained leader who can keep the group on a constructive track, avoiding the hazards of a confrontation or bitch session. Establishing supportive relationships on the job is not always easily done, especially if feelings of competition, rivalry, and dislike already exist among the staff. It may take time and extensive organizational commitment to develop supportive ties.

Improving co-worker relations is only one of several organizational strategies that have been proposed as antidotes to burnout. To the extent that burnout is linked to work overload, any actions that would reduce the overload (e.g., more resources or changes in staffing) should reduce burnout. Similarly, burnout may be ameliorated by organizational policies that limit the amount of job spillover into people's home life (e.g., policies regarding overtime, on-call duty, or relations with clients outside of the organization). Time off from the job can also be a constructive way of coping with burnout, particularly if the time can be used for job enrichment and professional growth, as is the case for sabbaticals and various staff development programs. Burnout may also be lessened by policies that promote greater variety in job tasks, encourage new

PROFESSIONALS IN DISTRESS

approaches to old problems, and give staff a greater sense of personal autonomy and involvement in the organization (e.g., participative decision making).

In some cases, people may try to deal with burnout by seeking professional help, and this treatment strategy can be affected by organizational policies. Organizations can encourage it by providing psychological services for the staff (either in-house or contracted to an outside agency) or by offering health insurance coverage for employees' psychological treatment. However, it is critical that an employee's decision to seek the counseling or therapy be completely confidential. If a person's use of psychological treatment is made known to the personnel office (as when insurance claims are filed) or can be seen by other staff (as when the therapist's office has a very central and visible location), it is almost certain that available services will not be utilized.

Prevention strategies. Most treatment approaches are designed to deal with an already established problem. It may be better, however, to prevent the problem from occurring in the first place. Remedial efforts may be more difficult and less effective overall than preventive actions. For example, trying to change burned-out helpers' cynical views of recipients may be a far more futile effort than trying to maintain the humanized view of recipients that most helpers start with.

Several suggestions have been made regarding the prevention of burnout. Early detection of the first signs of burnout, when the problems are minor and the person is still open to change, may be a critical aspect of prevention. Regular reviews or checkups of a person's progress may be quite helpful in this regard. Better preparation for the emotional hazards of people-work occupations is also crucial. If new professionals were already aware of the emotional demands of the job, had more accurate expectations about the work they would be doing, and knew about the risk of burnout and how to cope with it, they might handle the job more successfully. Better training in interpersonal skills, such as how to discuss sensitive issues with clients or how to deliver bad news, is something that many practitioners cite as a critical need.

CONCLUSION

Burnout, workaholism, and other types of job stress constitute an issue of major concern to psychologists and other professional caregivers. The primary question has been "What do I do about it?", and the push has been toward discovering practical and effective solutions. Yet, as this chapter has shown, the problems themselves are not very well understood, and thus the proposal of treatment strategies may be premature. Nevertheless, the outlook for future knowledge and understanding is optimistic. It may not be very long before we have some solid solutions to job stress—solutions that may indeed validate our current speculations.

References

Argyris, C. (1964). *Integrating the individual and the organization.* New York: Wiley.
Beehr, T. A., & Newman, J. E. (1978). Job stress, employee health, and organizational effectiveness: A facet analysis, model, and literature review. *Personnel Psychology, 31,* 665–699.
Belcastro, P. A. (1982). Burnout and its relationship to teachers' somatic complaints and illnesses. *Psychological Reports, 50,* 1045–1046.

Bell, P. A. (1981). Physiological comfort, performance, and social effects of heat stress. *Journal of Social Issues, 37,* 71–94.

Bernard, C. L. (1867). *Rapport sur les progrès et la marche de la physiologie générale.* Paris: Baillière.

Cannon, W. B. (1935). Stresses and strains of homeostasis. *American Journal of Medical Science, 189,* 1–14.

Caplan, R. D., Cobb, S., French, J. R. P., Jr., Van Harrison, R., & Pinneau, S. R. (1975). *Job demands and worker health: Main effects and occupational differences.* Washington, DC: U.S. Government Printing Office.

Carroll, J. F. X., & White, W. L. (1982). Theory building: Integrating individual and environmental factors within an ecological framework. In W. S. Paine (Ed.), *Job stress and burnout* (pp. 41–60). Beverly Hills, CA: Sage.

Chan, K. B. (1977). Individual differences in reactions to stress and their personality and situational determinants. *Social Science and Medicine, 11,* 89–103.

Cherniss, C. (1980a). *Professional burnout in human service organizations.* New York: Praeger.

Cherniss, C. (1980b). *Staff burnout: Job stress in human services.* Beverly Hills, CA: Sage.

Cherniss, C., Egnatios, E., & Wacker, S. (1976). Job stress and career development in new public professionals. *Professional Psychology, 7,* 428–436.

Cherniss, C., & Krantz, D. L. (1983). The ideological community as an antidote to burnout in the human services. In B. A. Farber (Ed.), *Stress and burnout in the human service professions* (pp. 198–212). New York: Pergamon Press.

Cobb, S. (1973). Role responsibility: The differentiation of a concept. *Occupational Mental Health, 3,* 10–14.

Cobb, S. (1976). Social support as a moderator of life stress. *Journal of Psychosomatic Medicine, 38,* 300–314.

Cobb, S., & Kasl, S. V. (1977). *Termination: The consequences of job loss.* Cincinnati, OH: National Institute for Occupational Safety and Health.

Cohen, S., & Weinstein, N. (1981). Nonauditory effects of noise on behavior and health. *Journal of Social Issues, 37,* 36–70.

Colligan, M. J., Smith, M. J., & Hurrell, J. J. (1977). Occupational incidence rates of mental health disorders. *Journal of Human Stress, 3,* 34–39.

Cox, T. (1978). *Stress.* Baltimore, MD: University Park Press.

Dohrenwend, B. S., & Dohrenwend, B. P. (1981). Life stress and illness: Formulation of the issues. In B. S. Dohrenwend & B. P. Dohrenwend (Eds.), *Stressful life events and their contexts.* New York: Watson.

Edelwich, J., with Brodsky, A. (1980). *Burn-out: Stages of disillusionment in the helping professions.* New York: Human Sciences Press.

Epstein, Y. M. (1981). Crowding stress and human behavior. *Journal of Social Issues, 37,* 126–144.

Evans, G. W., & Jacobs, S. V. (1981). Air pollution and human behavior. *Journal of Social Issues, 37,* 95–125.

French, J. R. P., Jr., & Caplan, R. D. (1973). Organizational stress and individual strain. In A. J. Marrow (Ed.), *The failure of success.* New York: AMACOM.

French, J. R. P., Jr., Rogers, W., & Cobb, S. (1974). Adjustment as a person–environment fit. In G. U. Coelho, D. A. Hamburg, & J. E. Adams (Eds.), *Coping and adaptation.* New York: Basic Books.

Freudenberger, H. J. (1982). Counseling and dynamics: Treating the end-stage person. In W. S. Paine (Ed.), *Job stress and burnout* (pp. 173–185). Beverly Hills, CA: Sage.

Freudenberger, H. J., with Richelson, G. (1980). *Burn-out: The high cost of high achievement.* Garden City, NY: Doubleday.

Friedman, M., & Rosenman, R. (1974). *Type A behavior and your heart.* New York: Knopf.

Gann, M. L. (1979). *The role of personality factors and job characteristics in burnout: A study of social workers.* Unpublished doctoral dissertation, University of California, Berkeley.

Goldberger, L., & Breznitz, S. (Eds.). (1982). *Handbook of stress.* New York: Free Press.

Golembiewski, R. T., Munzenrider, R., & Carter, D. (1983). Phases of progressive burn-out and their worksite covariants. *Journal of Applied Behavioral Science, 19,* 461–482.

Golembiewski, R. T., Munzenrider, R., & Stevenson, J. (1984, April). *Physical symptoms and burnout phases.* Paper presented at the Second Annual Conference on Organizational Policy and Development, Louisville, KY.

Golembiewski, R. T., & Scicchitano, M. (1983). Testing for demographic covariants: Three sources of data rejecting robust and regular association. *International Journal of Public Administration, 5,* 435–447.

Grinker, R. R., & Spiegel, J. P. (1945). *Men under stress.* New York: McGraw-Hill.

Hamburg, D. A., Hamburg, B., & deGoza, S. (1953). Adaptive problems and mechanisms in severely burned patients. *Psychiatry, 16,* 1–20.

Heckman, S. J. (1980). *Effects of work setting, theoretical orientation, and personality on psychotherapist burnout.* Unpublished doctoral dissertation, California School of Professional Psychology, Berkeley.

Holmes, T. H., & Rahe, R. H. (1967). The Social Readjustment Rating Scale. *Journal of Psychosomatic Research, 11,* 213–218.

Holt, R. R. (1982). Occupational stress. In L. Goldberger & S. Breznitz (Eds.), *Handbook of stress* (pp. 419–444). New York: Free Press.

Jackson, S. E. (1984). [Burnout and the nursing work environment]. Unpublished raw data.

Jackson, S. E., & Maslach, C. (1982). After-effects of job-related stress: Families as victims. *Journal of Occupational Behaviour, 3,* 63–77.

Janis, I. L. (1982). Decisionmaking under stress. In L. Goldberger & S. Breznitz (Eds.), *Handbook of stress* (pp. 69–87). New York: Free Press.

Jones, J. W. (1981a). Diagnosing and treating staff burnout among health professionals. In J. W. Jones (Ed.), *The burnout syndrome* (pp. 107–126). Park Ridge, IL: London House Press.

Jones, J. W. (1981b). Dishonesty, burnout, and unauthorized work break extensions. *Personality and Social Psychology Bulletin, 7,* 406–409.

Kahn, R. L., Wolfe, D. M., Quinn, R. P., Snoek, J. D., & Rosenthal, R. A. (1964). *Organizational stress.* New York: Wiley.

Kaminoff, R. D., & Proshansky, H. M. (1982). Stress as a consequence of the urban physical environment. In L. Goldberger & S. Breznitz (Eds.), *Handbook of stress* (pp. 380–409). New York: Free Press.

Kobasa, S. C. (1979). Stressful life events, personality, and health: An inquiry into hardiness. *Journal of Personality and Social Psychology, 37,* 1–11.

Lazarus, R. S. (1966). *Psychological stress and the coping process.* New York: McGraw-Hill.

Lazarus, R. S. (1975). A cognitively oriented psychologist looks at biofeedback. *American Psychologist, 30,* 553–561.

Lazarus, R. S. (1981, July). Little hassles can be hazardous to your health. *Psychology Today,* pp. 58–62.

Leiter, M. P., & Meechan, K. A. (1986). Role structure and burnout in human services. *Journal of Applied Behavioral Science, 22,* 47–52.

Lewiston, N. J., Conley, J., & Blessing-Moore, J. (1981). Measurement of hypothetical burnout in cystic fibrosis caregivers. *Acta Pediatrica Scandinavica, 70,* 935–939.

Lindemann, E. (1944). Symptomatology and management of acute grief. *American Journal of Psychiatry, 101,* 141–148.

Lyons, T. F. (1971). Role clarity, need for clarity, satisfaction, tension, and withdrawal. *Organizational Behavior and Human Performance, 6,* 99–110.

Machlowitz, M. (1980). *Workaholics.* Reading, MA: Addison-Wesley.

Mangione, T. W., & Quinn, R. P. (1975). Job satisfaction, counterproductive behavior, and drug use at work. *Journal of Applied Psychology, 60,* 114–116.

Margolis, B. L., Kroes, W. H., & Quinn, R. P. (1974). Job stress: An unlisted occupational hazard. *Journal of Occupational Medicine, 16,* 659–661.

Maslach, C. (1982a). *Burnout: The cost of caring.* Englewood Cliffs, NJ: Prentice-Hall.

Maslach, C. (1982b). Understanding burnout: Definitional issues in analyzing a complex phenomenon. In W. S. Paine (Ed.), *Job stress and burnout* (pp. 29–40). Beverly Hills, CA: Sage.

Maslach, C. (1983, April). *New directions in burnout research.* Invited address at the meeting of the Western Psychological Association, San Francisco.

Maslach, C., & Jackson, S. E. (1981a). *The Maslach Burnout Inventory.* Palo Alto, CA: Consulting Psychologists Press. Second edition published 1986.

Maslach, C., & Jackson, S. E. (1981b). The measurement of experienced burnout. *Journal of Occupational Behaviour, 2,* 99–113.

Maslach, C., & Jackson, S. E. (1982). Burnout in the health professions: A social psychological analysis. In G. Sanders & J. Suls (Eds.), *Social psychology of health and illness* (pp. 227–251). Hillsdale, NJ: Erlbaum.

Maslach, C., & Jackson, S. E. (1984a). Burnout in organizational settings. *Applied Social Psychology Annual, 5,* 133–153.

Maslach, C., & Jackson, S. E. (1984b). Patterns of burnout among a national sample of public contact workers. *Journal of Health and Human Resources Administration, 7,* 189–212.

Maslach, C., & Jackson, S. E. (1985). The role of sex and family variables in burnout. *Sex Roles, 12,* 837–851.

Maslach, C., & Pines, A. (1977). The burn-out syndrome in the day care setting. *Child Care Quarterly, 6,* 100–113.

Meadow, K. P. (1981). Burnout in professionals working with deaf children. *American Annals of the Deaf, 126,* 13–22.

Meichenbaum, D., & Jeremko, M. (Eds.). (1982). *Stress prevention and management: A cognitive behavioral approach.* New York: Plenum Press.

Miles, R. H. (1980). Organization boundary roles. In C. L. Cooper & R. Payne (Eds.), *Current concerns in occupational stress* (pp. 61–96). New York: Wiley.

Murphy, L. R., & Hurrell, J. J., Jr. (1980). Machine pacing and occupational stress. In R. M. Schwartz (Ed.), *New developments in occupational stress.* Cincinnati, OH: National Institute for Occupational Safety and Health.

Newman, J. E., & Beehr, T. A. (1979). Personal and organizational strategies for handling job stress: A review of research and opinion. *Personnel Psychology, 32,* 1–43.

Pearlin, L. I. (1982). The social contexts of stress. In L. Goldberger & S. Breznitz (Eds.), *Handbook of stress* (pp. 367–379). New York: Free Press.

Pearlin, L. I., & Lieberman, M. A. (1979). Social sources of emotional distress. In R. Simmons (Ed.), *Research in community and mental health: Vol. 1.* Greenwich, CT: JAI.

Pilisuk, M. (1982). Delivery of social support: The social inoculation. *American Journal of Orthopsychiatry, 52,* 20–31.

Pines, A. (1981). Burnout: A current problem in pediatrics. *Current Problems in Pediatrics, 11*(7), 3–31.

Pines, A. M. (1982). Changing organizations: Is a work environment without burnout an impossible goal? In W. S. Paine (Ed.), *Job stress and burnout* (pp. 189–211). Beverly Hills, CA: Sage.

Pines, A. M., Aronson, E., & Kafry, D. (1981). *Burnout: From tedium to personal growth.* New York: Free Press.

Pines, A., & Maslach, C. (1978). Characteristics of staff burn-out in mental health settings. *Hospital & Community Psychiatry, 29,* 233–237.

Poulton, E. C. (1978). Blue collar stressors. In C. L. Cooper & R. Payne (Eds.), *Stress at work* (pp. 51–79). New York: Wiley.

Savicki, V., & Cooley, E. (1983, April). *The relationship of work environment and client contact to burnout in mental health professionals.* Paper presented at the meeting of the Western Psychological Association, San Francisco.

Schwab, R. L., & Iwanicki, E. F. (1982a). Perceived role conflict, role ambiguity, and teacher burnout. *Educational Administration Quarterly, 18,* 60–74.

Schwab, R. L., & Iwanicki, E. F. (1982b). Who are our burned out teachers? *Educational Research Quarterly, 7*(2), 5–16.

Selye, H. (1936). A syndrome produced by diverse nocuous agents. *Nature, 138,* 32.

Selye, H. (1946). The general adaptation syndrome and the diseases of adaptation. *Clinical Endocrinology, 6,* 117–230.

Selye, H. (1950). *Stress.* Montreal: Acta.

Selye, H. (1974). *Stress without distress.* New York: Lippincott.

Selye, H. (1976). *The stress of life* (2nd ed.). New York: McGraw-Hill.

Shapiro, D., & Surwit, R. S. (1979). Biofeedback. In O. F. Pomerleau & J. P. Brady (Eds.), *Behavioral medicine: Theory and practice.* Baltimore MD: Williams & Wilkins.

Spielberger, C. D. (1975). Anxiety: State-trait process. In C. D. Spielberger & I. G. Sarason (Eds.), *Stress and anxiety: Vol. 1.* New York: Wiley.

Stevens, G. B., & O'Neill, P. (1983). Expectation and burnout in the developmental disabilities field. *American Journal of Community Psychology, 11,* 615–627.

Stokols, D. (1979). A congruence analysis of human stress. In I. G. Sarason & C. D. Spielberger (Eds.), *Stress and anxiety: Vol. 6.* Washington, DC: Hemisphere.

Suedfeld, P. (1981). *Restricted environmental stimulation.* New York: Wiley.

Tasto, D., & Colligan, M. (1978). *Health consequences of shiftwork* (DHEW-NIOSH Publication No. 78–154). Washington, DC: U.S. Government Printing Office.

Van Sell, M., Brief, A. P., & Schuler, R. S. (1981). Role conflict and role ambiguity: Integration of the literature and directions for future research. *Human Relations, 34,* 43–71.

Warnath, C. F., & Shelton, J. L. (1976). The ultimate disappointment: The burned out counselor. *Personnel and Guidance Journal, 55,* 172–175.

Wills, T. A. (1978). Perceptions of clients by professional helpers. *Psychological Bulletin, 85,* 968–1000.

ALCOHOL ABUSE AMONG PSYCHOLOGISTS 5

Richard W. Thoreson
Jane K. Skorina

DEFINING, DIAGNOSING, AND IDENTIFYING ALCOHOLISM

Models of Alcoholism

The term *alcoholism* has idiosyncratic connotations and usually means what the user chooses it to mean. Much disagreement and controversy abound regarding what constitutes alcoholism. On the one hand, no one quarrels with the fact that alcohol abuse, be it a disease, a bad habit, or a culturally induced behavior pattern, carries with it a multitude of medical, familial, social, and work problems that dwarf those of any other so-called disease in our society (Vaillant, 1983). On the other hand, alcohol misuse comes in so many guises with so many variations in form and symptoms that fitting all of these manifestations into a well-delineated disease model seems impossible (Jacobson, 1976; Pattison & Kaufman, 1982; Peele, 1984).

Throughout the ages, using alcohol as a means of altering consciousness has had an extraordinary appeal to humankind. This simultaneous fascination with and dread of alcohol was depicted by Oliver Wendell Holmes, Jr. (1918), who suggested that there is in all of us "a demand for the superlative, so much so that the poor devil who has no other way of reaching it attains it by getting drunk" (p. 40). Weil (1972), in studying the universal use of chemical agents to induce alterations in consciousness, concluded that the desire to alter consciousness is an innate, normal drive analogous to hunger or the sexual drive. He emphasized that drugs are but one way of satisfying this drive; many others exist. Glasser (1976) coined the term "positive addiction" to define the attempt to refocus negative addictive behaviors into positive, mind-altering addictions, for example, running and meditating. The classification of alcohol misuse as a moral failing, a bad habit, or a disease has been the subject of major attention over the past 20 years. Fortunately, the view that alcoholism is a moral problem has, in part, been rejected. Yet the skepticism that is attached to self-inflicted diseases remains.

The scientific/treatment community has tended to take either of two major positions on this issue. Those on the social science side tend to prefer the term *alcohol misuse* to *alcoholism* and to view the syndrome as a deeply imbedded habit or behavioral excess that carries with it a variety of problems. The use and misuse of alcohol from this perspective is viewed primarily as being a behavior disorder. It is a learned habit. It has familial and cultural correlates and is considered amenable to change through the use of methods known to the social sciences for altering behavioral patterns. On the other hand, the medical/treatment community tends to prefer the term *alcoholism* and to place it within the framework of the disease model.

Consistent with their behavioral base in science, psychologists tend to be sensitive to the current trend in our society toward medicalization of self-induced problems (see Conrad & Schneider, 1980). Conversely, much of the medically based alcohol treatment community points to the reluctance of the behavioral scientists to accept fully the grim reality that alcohol misuse, although characterized by a highly variable symptom pattern, is an illness that, left untreated, has severe and life-threatening consequences (Madsen, 1974). Vaillant (1983), arguing for the disease position, reported results of an 8-year follow-up sample of 100 alcoholics posttreatment. Roughly one third of the sample maintained abstinence, one third continued to drink, and one third were dead, primarily as a result of medical complications of sustained alcohol misuse. Vaillant offered this biting caveat to the behavioral scientists: Although alcohol misuse is in part a behavioral disorder that is similar to nail biting, it differs radically from nail biting in mortality rate.

The model one chooses has profound significance, with respect to both type and numbers of persons who are classified as having alcohol problems. Seixas (1976) noted that limiting alcoholism to mean only those who have developed cell tolerance, withdrawal states on stopping, and the diseases associated with alcoholism excludes alcohol-dependent people who may have suffered few or none of these consequences. It is known, for example, that drinking reaches its peak for people in their early 20s, and that for 20-year-olds who abuse alcohol and suffer adverse consequences, the criteria just mentioned do not apply. It seems clear that family, interpersonal, school, and work problems associated with alcohol misuse occur for many people who are not physiologically dependent on alcohol.

Cahalan (1970) argued for substituting the term *problem drinking* for alcoholism to avoid permanent labeling and stigmatization. This change places the focus on behavior rather than on the person and promotes inquiry into different patterns and types of drinking problems and problem drinking. Jones (1979) questioned "whether alcoholism is or should be the dominant force of alcohol research" (p. 105). He based his conclusion on two factors: first, the inadequacy of the definition, and second, the major negative effects of alcohol misuse by people who are not classified as alcoholic. Any conceptualization of alcoholism must include consideration of how much loss of control there is, how much physical dependence there is, and how problematic the drinking is and to whom. The complexity of the issue has led some observers to suggest that there are as many alcoholisms as there are alcoholics. Alcoholics Anonymous takes a phenomenological stance, that is, that alcoholism is defined by individual perceptions of powerlessness and unmanageability regarding alcohol use (Alcoholics Anonymous, 1975–1983; Thoreson & Budd, in press). On the other hand, there are a variety of diagnostic schemes that have validity in delineating symptoms and problems related to alcohol abuse. They provide a means of classifying alcohol problems in ways that lead to some consistency in definitions and diagnosis.

Existing Definitions of Alcoholism

Definitions of alcoholism are diverse. The definition used by the investigator influences prevalence rates, the resulting magnitude of the problem, and subsequent treatment strategies. Criteria for diagnosing alcoholism are generally divided into one of three categories or "tracks," as exemplified in the criteria stipulated by the National Council on Alcoholism (NCA, 1972). These are (a) physical dependency, (b) clinical medical symptoms, and (c) behavioral, psychological, and social aspects. Particular definitions stress one or the other of these criteria and may, in turn, add a special emphasis on the interrelationship of alcohol abuse or alcoholism with work and socially related problems. In general, the more stringent the criteria, the more confident the diagnosis, and the more limited the number of alcohol misusers who fit these criteria. Conversely, the more liberal the criteria, the less confident the diagnosis, and the greater number of alcohol misusers so classified.

Mendelson and Mello (1979, 1985) noted that the diagnosis of alcoholism has always been complicated by the criterion problem. They pointed to the resulting lack of precision in standards for what really constitutes alcohol misuse and noted that the stigma associated with alcoholism is an important and often unrecognized factor in the decision regarding which criteria to include in the definition of alcoholism. To illustrate, the NCA's previously mentioned criteria—serious problems associated with drinking, physiological dependency, and medical complications—are diagnostic indicators that are used in several definitions of alcoholism. Because of the stigma and the well-documented denial of alcoholism in our society, people with symptoms in any or all of these categories will be excluded from diagnosis of alcoholism and included only if serious health or job-related problems ensue.

An example of more liberal definitions that include behavioral and cultural criteria of alcoholism is that of the World Health Organization (World Health Organization [WHO], 1952), which replaces the term *alcoholism* as follows: "Drug dependence of the alcohol type may be said to exist when the consumption of alcohol by an individual exceeds the limits that are accepted by his [or her] culture. If he [or she] consumes alcohol at times that are deemed inappropriate within that culture or his [or her] intake of alcohol becomes so great as to injure his [or her] health or impair his [or her] social relationships" (Mendelson & Mello, 1979, p. 3). The WHO definition stresses acceptable limits of alcohol consumption and appropriateness of time and place of that consumption. It takes into account the marked variation across cultures as to what constitutes acceptable drinking practices, both within and between countries, and focuses on the behavioral and social indicators and signal violations of normal standards and social deviance. By their breadth, such definitions tend to provide higher prevalence rates, with implications for a primary and secondary prevention approach to treatment programs (Edwards, 1985; Edwards, Gross, Keller, Moser, & Room, 1977).

A more limited definition of alcoholism is proposed in the *Diagnostic and Statistical Manual* (DSM-III) (American Psychiatric Association, 1980; Robins, 1982). The DSM-III contains two sections related to the abuse of alcohol: (1) Alcohol organic disorders and (2) substance abuse disorders. Under substance abuse disorders, the DSM-III distinguishes between the alcohol abuser and the alcohol-dependent person. In a sense, the DSM-III may be said to offer a definition of alcohol abuse as well as alcoholism (Mayer, 1983). The classification *alcohol dependence* and the classification *alcohol organic mental disorders* depict serious and grave conditions associated with excessive alcohol consumption over a prolonged period. These conditions include diagnoses such as dementia associated with alcoholism, alcohol hallucinosis (visual and auditory hallucinations), withdrawal delirium, and amnesic disorders (short- and long-term memory disturbances).

The classification *alcohol abuse* does not, however, necessitate inclusion of alcohol dependence or clinical and medical problems. Mayer (1983) asserted that in order to be effective in treating alcoholism, health professionals should focus on helping alcohol abusers. Most alcohol abusers, he noted, hold jobs, live with families, and are reasonably healthy or at least have a good treatment prognosis. This point has significance for the treatment of psychologists and other professionals with alcohol problems. Psychologists and other professionals are more likely to be characterized by alcohol abuse than by patterns that are typical of alcoholism, because alcoholism includes the public indicators or more severe alcohol problems that, owing to a variety of psychological and social factors, tend to be uncommon among professionals until the later stages of alcoholism.

The search for diagnostic indicators is strongly influenced by Jellinek (1960). The scientific study of alcoholism can be traced to the work of Jellinek, who studied a group of alcoholics in abstinence-based recovery through the self-help organization, Alcoholics Anonymous. Through retrospective accounts of these alcoholics in recovery, Jellinek identified the following five types of alcoholism: (a) Alpha, in which there are symptoms of psychological but not physical dependence; (b) Beta, in which there are medical symptoms but no physical dependence; (c) Gamma, in which there are both symptoms and physical dependence; (d) Delta, in which there is physical dependence but few or no symptoms; (e) Epsilon, in which there is binge drinking. Vaillant (1983) pointed to the major problem in this classification scheme. It represents a good cross-sectional, but not longitudinal, classification. In long-term studies, a person may move from one category to another. For example, the Epsilon disappointed fiancé may return to social drinking, or the Alpha housewife may progress to become a Gamma alcoholic. Thus, the cardinal principle of alcoholism, a progressive disease with clearly distinguishable symptoms by stages, is not supported by longitudinal studies.

For the purposes of this chapter, alcohol misuse is termed alcoholism; it exists on two continua: a time continuum from early to late and a severity continuum ranging from mild to severe virulence. Although we favor the disease model, we concur with Vaillant (1983) that alcoholism comes in so many guises and contains so many stages, particularly when viewed from a cross-sectional perspective, that it is not clear whether it should be conceptualized as a unitary medical problem, as a disease with wide variation in symptom patterns, as many diseases, or even as many behavioral patterns. We view alcoholism both as a primary disease and as a behavior disorder, defined by a redundancy of symptoms, whose etiology is not entirely known and which, if not treated, may become a life-threatening illness.

Diagnostic Criteria for Defining Alcoholism

Definitions of alcoholism are contingent upon the diagnostic criteria used. Consequently, we examine the common diagnostic schemas, their strengths, and their limitations and describe how they fit with our definition.

1. National Council on Alcoholism (NCA) Criteria (1972). The NCA has proposed a three-track criterion for the diagnosis of alcoholism. The criterion distinguishes among three kinds of data: behavioral (psychological and attitudinal), physiological, and clinical. Signs and symptoms designated under *diagnostic level 1* contain classic signs of alcoholism. Physiologically, there may be dependence, increased tolerance, and heavy daily consumption. Clinically, the illnesses of alcoholic hepatitis and alcoholic cerebellar degeneration are diagnostic criteria. Behavioral criteria includes drinking despite strong medical and social contraindications of known consequences. *Diagnostic level 2* represents probable alcoholism. The physiologic criterion is alcoholic blackouts. Clinically, there are a variety of illnesses such as Laennec's cirrhosis, Wernicke-Korsakoff syndrome, and alcoholic myopathy or cardiomyopathy that may be evident. The behavioral criterion is the subjective complaint of loss of control of alcohol consumption. *Diagnostic level 3* is characterized as potential or incidental for the diagnosis of alcoholism. No physiological or behavioral criteria are designated at this level. Clinical manifestations such as anemia, pellagra, and gastritis may be evident but are insufficient diagnostic criteria.

2. American Psychiatric Association Criteria. The DSM-III emphasizes similarity between alcoholism and other forms of drug abuse. Alcoholism and alcohol abuse are included in the category "Substance Abuse Disorders," which is further subdivided into "substance abuse" and "substance dependence." Substance abuse, including alcohol abuse, involves three criteria: a pattern of pathological use, impairment in social or occupational functioning caused by the pattern of pathological use, and duration of at least one month. Substance dependence requires evidence of tolerance or withdrawal. The diagnosis of alcohol dependence requires, in addition to tolerance or withdrawal, evidence of social or occupational impairment from the use of the substance or a pattern of pathological use. *Tolerance* is defined in the DSM-III as follows: "increased amounts of the substance are required to achieve desired effect or there is a . . . diminished effect with regular use of the same dose" (p. 165). *Withdrawal* is indicated by "morning shakes" and "malaise" that are relieved by drinking, as well as by the occurrence of this syndrome "after cessation or reduction of drinking" (p. 165). The diagnostic criteria for alcohol dependence or alcoholism in the DSM-III are relatively specific, because the pharmacological criteria of tolerance and physical dependence are clearly defined and unambiguous.

The diagnostic criteria for alcohol abuse are more ambiguous than those for alcohol dependence. The category alcohol abuse includes impaired social relations with family and friends and a pattern of pathological use but may or may not include substance dependence. Our clinical experience, supported by research data (Thoreson, 1982), is that professionals can fall in either or both the abuse or dependence categories without the usual public indicators of job loss, fights, absenteeism, or hospitalization for alcohol treatment that are present in other alcoholic populations. Edwards and his colleagues (Edwards, 1982, 1985; Edwards et al., 1977) have offered the concept of addiction with alcohol dependence. This framework assumes a difference between alcohol dependence and related problems. The distinction recognizes that a person can exhibit clear symptoms of alcohol dependence without manifesting obvious public alcohol-related problems.

A variety of diagnostic instruments have been used for identifying alcoholics and problem drinkers, in the form of questionnaires and inventories of psychological and behavioral variables. Mayer (1983) concluded that such inventories are the most sensitive instruments for identifying alcoholism. They vary in form from those that are long and time consuming to administer to those that are brief and can be used in quick screening to assess pathological drinking practices. Jacobson (1976) has provided an excellent review of the tests that have been used to diagnose alcoholism. He argued the point that is operationalized in the DSM-III criteria that not all "so-called alcoholics experience blackouts, lost control of the drinking, change jobs frequently, undergo delirium tremors, drink in the morning, get into trouble with the law, or have in common any other symptoms besides drinking too much or too often" (p. 16). (A description of the most commonly used of these instruments is found in Jacobson, 1976; Knox, 1982; Miller, 1976.)

Problems in Diagnosing Alcoholism

From the analysis of the variation in symptom pattern and type, some observers have concluded that there are a variety of alcoholisms rather than a unitary disease with wide variation in symptoms. Others, in answering the question "What is alcoholism?" have concluded that it is both disease and behavior disorder. Vaillant (1983) has asserted that the proper assessment of alcoholism should include four basic criteria: The diagnosis should (a) imply causative factors that are independent of the presence or absence of social deviance; (b) convey shorthand information about symptoms and course; (c) be valid cross-culturally and not dependent on mores or fashion; and (d) suggest appropriate medical response to treatment. Vaillant further concluded from his longitudinal study of a sample of alcoholics that a number of alcohol-related problems, not a particular cluster, best predicts alcoholism.

Wanburg and Horn (1983), in summarizing their research on the assessment of alcohol use, concluded that because phenomena referred to under the heading of alcoholism are diverse, assessment of alcoholism should begin with multiple measures. They pointed out that this approach would enable one to discover whether the phenomena are in fact unitary in response to some feature of etiology or treatment or outcome. They believed that, if the phenomena are unitary, the results of the multiple measures will coalesce. They noted that, on the other hand, if the phenomena are diverse in reference to the external criteria, this diversity can be discerned through unambiguous definitions of alcoholism that will emerge in the results of the multiple assessments.

We have described factors that complicate the definition and diagnosis of alcoholism among professionals and have argued that despite increased enlightenment, substantial stigma still surrounds alcoholism. As a result of this stigma, psychologists strongly resist accepting their own alcohol abuse or alcoholism as a serious, life-threatening illness. As a result in part of the stigma and in part of inclination, psychologists prefer to see their problem from an intrapsychic or a learning perspective that is subject to the control of the intellect. Another important deterrent to diagnosing alcohol abuse or alcoholism is the failure to distinguish dependency that develops from sustained heavy alcohol use and its consequent medical sequelae from problem drinking with or without physiological dependency but with behavioral sequelae including absenteeism, tardiness, job loss, arrests, job accidents, and fights (Edwards et al., 1977; Thoreson, 1976, 1984; Thoreson, Nathan, Skorina, & Kilburg, 1983).

We are persuaded by clinical experience and by our literature review that alcoholism cannot be defined solely as a disease; rather, it should be viewed as both an illness and a form of social deviance (Shaw, 1979; Thoreson, 1976). The stigma that alcoholism carries has a direct bearing on how alcoholics are identified and treated. When alcoholism is viewed as an illness that brings harm to the alcoholic, society tends to react with sympathy and acceptance. When it is perceived as a potential threat to others, alcoholism is met with fear and revulsion. According to Blum and Blum (1974), most societies have this ambivalent, "harm–hurt orientation." The effect that these attitudes can have on treatment is obvious. The greater society's tendency to consider the alcoholic's behavior to be dangerous to others, the greater the focus will be on punishment. The greater society's tendency to consider the behavior as a threat to the individual, the greater the focus will be on humanitarian treatment.

The general public tends to define alcoholism as deviant behavior. People whose behavior is openly deviant—people who exhibit public drunkenness, family disputes, violations of laws, and destructive behavior to self or others—are easily identified as alcoholics. These alcoholics can be categorized in one of two groups: those considered by society to be morally inferior or delinquent and those whose drinking habits are shared by only a minority of others in the community (see also Roman, 1982; Room, 1979, 1983). Thus, for the small percentage of alcoholics whose behavior is markedly deviant from societal norms, or for those who exhibit demonstrable physical symptoms, the diagnosis and treatment of alcoholism is straightforward.

For the remainder of alcoholics and alcohol abusers, however—such as professionals who are often plateau drinkers instead of binge drinkers, hold regular jobs, and have intact families—diagnosis is not so simple. Because society is ambivalent toward alcoholism and because many of the behaviors are not dangerous to society, many alcoholics are not easy to identify. In order to identify and treat humanely the professional suffering from alcohol abuse and alcoholism, it is necessary to delineate these cornerstones of ambivalence: hurt to the individual and harm to society. The diagnosis of alcoholism among professionals such as psychologists mandates the development of symptomatology that is appropriate to professionals. Symptoms of alcohol abuse within professional groups are far less likely to be harmful to society than they are to be harmful to the individual.

ALCOHOLISM AMONG PROFESSIONALS: A SPECIAL CASE

Dimensions of the Problem

In the past decade there has been a significant increase in public and professional attention to the topic of alcohol abuse and alcoholism as well as in research on treatment and evaluation. Despite this overall increase, most of the treatment efforts and research on the effects of alcohol abuse and alcoholism on job performance have concentrated on the blue-collar worker and not on the professional. Bissell and Haberman (1984) stated: "Specific information about alcoholism in the professions is still relatively scarce" (p. 3). Information on the alcoholic psychologist in particular is similarly judged to be sparse (Laliotis & Grayson, 1985; Larson, 1981; Skorina, 1982; Thoreson et al., 1983).

Although little is known about the specifics of alcohol abuse and alcoholism among professionals and executives, this topic is now receiving attention in the literature (e.g., Bissell, 1980; Bissell, Fewell, & Jones, 1980; Bissell & Haberman, 1984; Bissell & Jones, 1976, 1981; Bissell, Lambrecht, & Von Wiegand, 1973; Cosentino, 1981; Exo, 1981; Laliotis & Grayson, 1985; Thoreson, 1981a, 1981b, 1981c, 1982, 1984; Thoreson & Hosokawa, 1984; Thoreson, Hosokawa, & Talcott, 1982; Thoreson et al., 1983). Two concomitant professional and humanitarian concerns of the profession emerge from these studies: First, the need to set standards for professional practice and ethical conduct; second, the need to care for those members of the profession who are themselves suffering from a disease that is frequently both life- and career-threatening.

Alcohol dependency seems more characteristic than problem drinking among psychologists, who, like other professionals and executives, operate within a set of social norms that eschew deviant behavior and encourage control. Thus, psychologists are more likely to engage in daily drinking by spacing drinks. The spacing serves the dual function of maintaining a moderately elevated blood-alcohol level to create a sustained high while masking the more obvious public indicators of drunkenness. Socially deviant behavior such as open intoxication, arrests, belligerence, and job loss are rarely found in professionals with problems of alcohol abuse and alcoholism. These cardinal symptoms of alcoholism are more acceptable in the norms for male blue-collar employees, among whom there is greater tolerance for such presumed alcoholic misbehavior. (For female employees at all social and work levels, open drunkenness still appears to be censured; hidden drinking and denial of heavy drinking constitute the norm. Professional women are at risk for developing alcoholism as a result of denial (Hore & Plant, 1981; Robe, 1977; Rubington, 1972; Shore, 1985; Follman, 1976; Wilsnack, 1976, 1982; Wilsnack, Wilsnack, & Klassen, 1984–1985).

Generally speaking, studies of professionals and executives suggest that the higher the status of the worker, the more there is to lose if alcoholism is detected. Sanctions against professionals, executives, and other high-status workers who show an alcohol-related decline in job performance tend to be less frequently and more privately applied. When sanctions are applied, however, they are more severe than for workers in occupations that are considered to be lower in status. Thus, professionals in high-status jobs tend to be confronted less frequently for their alcoholism and, because of the stigma and the severity of sanctions, tend to keep their alcoholism hidden. A study of psychologists' perceptions of the nature and incidence of alcoholism among their colleagues revealed a general reluctance to confront colleagues who have alcohol problems (Thoreson, Budd, & Krauskopf, 1986). Furthermore, outcomes of confrontations were judged to be less desirable than for comparable confrontations with colleagues who presented mental health problems (see also Rubington, 1972; Skorina, 1982; Thoreson et al., 1983).

The increased attention to the adverse effects of alcohol abuse on performance in the health professions and in other high-status, high-visibility groups has led to increased public awareness of the deleterious effects of alcoholism and to the need for programs to help professionals who have alcohol problems. Such programs include efforts by the professions and by recovered alcoholics within the professions to extend help to colleagues. Dual-track formal treatment and self-help programs have been developed in law, dentistry, nursing, social work, and other professional–executive groups (Bissell & Haberman, 1984; Larson, 1981; Nathan, 1982; Skorina, 1982; Thoreson et al., 1983).

The Prevalence of Alcoholism Among Professionals

Survey research suggests that approximately 70 percent of Americans drink and that more than 90 percent of college-educated people drink. The Department of Health, Education, and Welfare (DHEW) estimated that between 9.3 and 10 million people, or 7 percent of the population, could be considered problem drinkers (De Luca, 1981). Of these, approximately 6 percent to 10 percent develop alcoholism (Cahalan, Cisin, & Crossley, 1969). A review of the literature on incidence (Nathan, Thoreson, & Kilburg, 1983), however, revealed a lack of reliable data on the numbers of people in the professions affected by alcoholism or drug dependency: Most figures were estimates based either on data from treatment groups or on hunches from clinical experience.

Steindler (1975) estimated that 3 percent to 5 percent of practicing physicians suffer in varying degrees from alcoholism or drug dependency. Laliotis and Grayson (1985) reviewed estimates of impairment of physicians due to alcoholism, drug dependency, or major psychiatric illness and found that prevalence rates reported in various studies ranged from 5 percent to 15 percent. Steindler (1975) argued that, because of their status and the stigma, many professionals who suffer from alcoholism are not in the alcoholic treatment system. He concluded that the clinical treatment estimates that 1 percent to 2 percent of professionals suffer from alcohol abuse and alcoholism were underestimates. He offered 5 percent to 6 percent as a more valid estimate.

In the study of alcohol consumption rates of male and female managers and professionals, Shore (1985) found that 88.3 percent of the men and 94.6 percent of the women responded affirmatively when asked if they drank. Heavy drinking (in terms of quantity or frequency) was reported as 10.9 percent for women and 19.1 percent for men, but only 1.4 percent of the women and 3.1 percent of the men labeled their own drinking as either "heavy" or "too heavy." Shore speculated that this discrepancy relates to the professionals' refusal to acknowledge, or denial of, heavy drinking and that such denial prevents them from attempting to limit intake or develop means of protecting themselves from the negative consequences of their behavior. Consequently, denial constitutes a major risk factor for professionals.

Prevalence rates are typically determined from several diverse methodologies. The most common are (a) the Jellinek revised estimation formula, in which estimates of the number of alcoholics are based on number of deaths each year due to cirrhosis of the liver (Argerioui, 1974); (b) the Schmidt and DeLindt formula, which is similar to the Jellinek formula and is also based on deaths due to cirrhosis of the liver (Ford & Luckey, 1976); (c) the Schmidt and DeLindt suicide formula, which estimates the number of alcoholics alive in a given year from the number of suicides; (d) the Marden age/sex matrix, which estimates the number of problem drinkers on the basis of prevalence in various population subgroups (Ford & Luckey, 1976). (See Keller, 1975, for a discussion of the inclusion of problem drinkers in estimating prevalence rates.)

If we extrapolated from the high consumption rates for professionals, we would predict a relatively high prevalence rate. Indications from survey research findings, however, caution against such direct extrapolation. Rates of alcoholism are influenced by cultural and demographic variables and tend to occur on a lower per capita basis for professionals and executives (Marden, 1975). Bissell and Haberman (1984), in their report of alcoholism in the professional, concluded that there are as yet no accurate estimates of prevalence rates of alcoholism among specific professional groups. They contended, however, that professionals have at least the same level of risk of becoming alcoholic as other American adults who drink, that is, roughly 1 in 10 for males and 1 in 20 for females. They considered 5 percent to 6 percent a reasonable estimate for the profession of medicine. (For a discussion of the issues of reliability and validity in self-report measures of alcohol consumption, a further problem in establishing prevalence rates, see Polich, 1982; Sobell, Maisto, Sobell, & Cooper, 1979; Sobell & Sobell, 1975; Sobell, Sobell, & Vanderspek, 1979; Williams, Aitken, & Malin, 1985.)

Thoreson et al. (1983) selected 6 percent as a reasonable estimate of the rate of alcoholism within the profession of psychology. Bissell and Haberman (1984), Boyer (1984), Laliotis and Grayson (1985), Nathan et al. (1983), and Thoreson et al. (1983) all agree that at present no reliable studies exist on the prevalence of alcoholism among members of professional groups. Current prevalence rates for the professionals are based on data provided by disciplinary bodies, impaired-physicians committees, impaired-attorney committees, and so on. Such groups report on numbers that are brought to their attention; however, because the sampling that is reported is selective, there is no valid way to extrapolate to a general incidence for the professions. Bissell and Haberman (1984) were convinced, notwithstanding, that the alcoholism rate among physicians is probably higher, not lower, than reported. They based their conclusions on medical data that has shown that physicians have a high mortality rate from cirrhosis of the liver (3.5 times that of the general population). Nonetheless, on the basis of an "exhaustive literature review," Bissell and Haberman concluded that they cannot say "with any degree of certainty how many members of any profession already are or will become an alcoholic" (p.

27). We agree that despite the plethora of statements on the incidence of alcoholism and alcohol abuse among professionals, the true incidence of alcohol abuse and alcoholism remains a mystery that may never be solved. Determination of exact rates appears infeasible, because estimates are a function of both particular methods and the definition of alcoholism.

As a result of the arbitrary lumping of respondents into various levels of consumption that may or may not constitute alcohol misuse for a given person, survey research methods tend to overreport incidence rate. Conversely, given the strong probability that much alcohol abuse and alcoholism remains untreated, clinical studies from hospitalized patients probably underreport the true incidence of alcohol abuse and alcoholism. The following conclusions seem to be warranted. First, given the present state of knowledge, there is no way of determining the exact prevalence rates for alcohol abuse and alcoholism among psychologists. Second, however, it is also known from perceptions of psychologists regarding alcohol problems among their colleagues and from data from the survey of actual problems during active drinking provided by alcoholic psychologists in abstinence-based recovery, that (a) alcohol abuse and alcoholism are present among psychologists, and (b) when present, these syndromes produce a clearly identified set of adverse family, health, and job-related consequences. Third, surveys by Thoreson et al. (1986) and by Thoreson, Budd, and Krauskopf (in press) confirm, that the term *alcoholism* denotes a problem that is intractable, of long duration, resistant to treatment, and which, when present in a colleague, constitutes a problem in which psychologists are reluctant to intervene.

Although it is not feasible to determine an exact prevalence rate for psychologists who suffer from alcohol abuse and alcoholism, we consider that 6 percent constitutes a reasonably accurate estimate of psychologists who suffer adverse consequences from alcohol misuse; and it is likely that the incidence is higher for male than for female psychologists. We propose establishing an incidence band rather than a rate for alcoholism among psychologists. The lower portion of the band would show incidence rates of approximately 6 percent for men and 3 percent for women. The higher portion of the band would show rates of 9 percent for men and 4 percent for women. On the basis of 100,000 PhD-level psychologists in the United States and a male–female ratio of 2 to 1, we could extrapolate these totals: 7,000 psychologists (5,800 males, 1,400 females) at the high prevalence level, and 4,950 psychologists (3,900 males, 1,050 females) at the lower prevalence level.

The critical factor is not to estimate the exact number but that a substantial number of psychologists are suffering adverse consequences due to alcohol abuse, including work-related impairment. Both rates suggest sufficient numbers to establish a need for psychology professionals to attend to this problem. This need is confirmed by the Thoreson et al. (1986) study of a random sample of APA members regarding their perceptions of prevalence and type of alcohol and mental health problems. Over 90 percent of the respondents favored APA developing a program for the profession to help psychologists in distress. Moreover, approximately one third of those surveyed indicated that they knew of a colleague who had a serious problem with alcoholism or alcohol abuse. Those who knew of such a problem among their colleagues rated it as severe and debilitating and as more damaging and more permanent, and with greater negative impact on job, health, and family components than was true for mental health problems.

As noted earlier, Thoreson et al. (in press) confirmed these perceptions in their survey of psychologists in abstinence-based recovery. These psychologists reported major work, family, and health consequences during their prior active alcoholism. We concur with the analysis of Laliotis and Grayson (1985) that we can ill afford to ignore the need of our impaired colleagues, however small their numbers. This admission of impairment does not reflect poorly on psychology; no profession is immune. The failure to detect and treat impairment, however, is a serious omission that would ultimately create a negative image of the profession of psychology.

The Covert Nature of Alcohol Abuse Among Professionals

Alcohol abuse is relatively well hidden among professionals, a fact that constitutes a problem in the detection and determination of the nature and extent of alcohol abuse and alcoholism in the professions. Several factors confound easy identification. One of these is the societal–cultural variation in alcohol use patterns and beliefs regarding what constitutes alcohol misuse among different social classes and occupational groups (Newlove, 1981; Robe, 1977; Thoreson, 1976). Moreover, alcohol abuse and alcoholism among professionals present a special dilemma in that the tangible indicators of alcoholism, such as public drunkenness, violence, legal problems, drunken driving, and job loss, which are typical of blue-collar alcoholism, are usually not seen until relatively late in the addiction process. The drinking practices of most professionals are characterized by control, and the symptoms of alcoholism among professionals are more internal than external. The more obvious external indices and deterioration in social relations, work behavior, and appearance generally are not characteristic symptoms. This is true despite the likelihood that the alcoholic professional shares during his or her active alcoholism the keen suffering and pain found in other groups (Thoreson et al., 1983).

A second set of factors that complicate identification are norms in the professional's work environment that sanction use and permit abuse of alcohol. These risk factors, identified by Roman and Trice (1970), include minimal supervision, low visibility of job performance, freedom from time demands, and standards for performance that are vaguely defined or unenforced. Cosper (1979) summarized the research on occupational differences in drinking patterns and concluded that empirical evidence confirmed differential risk factors in occupations, and he urged efforts to study drinking practices of various occupational groups. Thoreson (1984a, 1984b) identified risk factors in the work environment and risk factors in characteristics of professionals that coalesce to sanction alcohol abuse. These factors appear to have direct relevance to psychologists:

1. *Role bifurcation.* In role bifurcation, the individual has both a professional and an institutional identification. This dual identity, which requires a major investment of time and energy by the professional in extracurricular and off-job-site meetings, leads to much hidden time away from the work setting in socially sanctioned, high-drinking environments (e.g., conventions, vacations).

2. *Tenure and academic freedom.* These safeguards for the academic, which have their counterpart in nonprobationary status in most state and civil service professional positions, also provide the opportunity to drink abusively. The nature of professional work involves autonomy and minimal accountability for performance to peers or supervisors. Thus, autonomy and freedom from interference, which are vital and indigenous to both professional and academic practice, enable alcohol abuse to flourish.

3. *The high esteem bestowed upon professionals.* Professionals are given "idiosyncrasy credits" for behavior that can be symptomatic of alcohol abuse. Attitudes such as arrogance, aloofness, impatience, agitation, and irritability, and behaviors such as missed appointments, missed classes, and time away from the office, tend to be accepted and sanctioned as evidence of eccentricity and as essential attributes of the lonely scientist/scholar.

4. *Subordinate-status dependency and isolation.* Centra (1978) indicated that the independent position of the academic professional is paradoxically characterized by a subordinate status and sense of dependence, separateness, and alienation from society. Psychologists often spend a good deal of time in solitary work performance. It is typical of those in private practice to function with minimal or no supervision and limited contact with other professionals. For many professionals, a substantial part of their job is inevitably an unchallenging, lonely one that places frustrating limits on creativity and accomplishment. Thus, boredom, frustration, and isolation exist that are conducive to alcohol abuse.

5. *The commitment to discovery and expanded awareness.* Psychologists as scientists are committed to discovery and altering awareness to achieve new perspectives. Consequently, the use of mind-altering drugs and alcohol in the pursuit of such perspectives is common among professionals, artists, and poets (Newlove, 1981; Root-Bernstein, 1981; Thoreson, 1976; Weil, 1972). This tendency is confirmed in a study by Thoreson et al. (in press), who found that alcoholic psychologists in abstinence-based recovery reported substantial use of mind-altering substances in addition to alcohol during their active drinking days. Slightly over 40 percent of the sample reported having using stimulants, such as amphetamines, and psychodelics, such as LSD, mescaline, or marijuana.

6. *Denial.* Denial is one of the diagnostic canons of alcoholism. Alcoholism is the only disease that does everything to inform the patient who has it that she or he does not have it (Gitlow & Peyser, 1980). Skorina (1982) argued that the alcoholic psychologist tends to replace the external reality of her or his alcoholism with a wish-fulfillment fantasy of control and nonimpairment or potency. The myth of invulnerability, the professional's raison d'être, serves to increase the magnitude of resistance and of the denial of alcohol problems. Skorina noted that psychologists with serious alcohol problems sincerely believe in their ability to control and solve problems. Their intellectual pride and feeling of omnipotence constitute powerful obstacles to admitting failure. Psychologists tend to look upon their inability to control alcohol misuse as a major failure, a form of narcissistic injury. One of the morbid fears of psychologists in a clinical practice is that they may become impaired in the same way that their clients or patients are impaired. The counterpart for the academic psychologist

resides in the panic that goes with the thought of becoming unknowledgeable and thus comparable to students. Pride, as it relates to this narcissistic injury, has its origin in the shame surrounding lack of control over alcohol. When we fail to live up to what we believe a professional should be (positive ego ideal) and become failures, or what a professional should not be (negative ego ideal), we develop an overwhelming sense of worthlessness. Denial is used by the alcoholic professional as a means of escaping these intense feelings. Denial, then, for many alcohol abusers or active alcoholics, becomes the means of controlling an uncontrollable situation. The use of selective attention and inattention serves as a defense against shame and reinforces the belief system that nothing is wrong.

7. *The myth of power and invulnerability.* This myth, which is characteristic of most scientists and academics and is critical to the scientific enterprise, has the adverse effect of reinforcing the irrational belief that professionals can, solely through the use of their intellectual resources, solve all personal problems. This denial of essential limitations is a major problem for individuals who are trapped in alcohol addiction (Kurtz, 1979, 1982). Kurtz argued that refocusing on vulnerability and accepting human limitations is essential to recovery and to comfortable living without the use of chemicals. Many professionals are firmly committed to the belief that achievement denotes power and control and that competency prevents alcoholism. Such professionals who are caught in the web of alcohol abuse have particular difficulty focusing on "essential limitations of being." Yet according to Kurtz, it is precisely in this acceptance of essential limitations that professionals can come to terms with their problems of alcohol abuse.

8. *Difficulty in accepting the intractable nature of alcoholism.* Alcoholism is a deeply imbedded, intractable, long-term pattern of behavior that cannot be overcome by conscious, deliberate effort. This fact seems especially frustrating and antithetical to the predisposition and training of psychologists as scientists. The training of psychologists predisposes them to a commitment to behavioral change and learning. The professional–scientist is also characterized by high internal controls. These traits complicate the acceptance of a deeply imbedded, intractable habit or disease. The beliefs in the possibility of behavioral change and in the capacity to solve problems for self and other are strongly reinforced and indigenous to the scientific community. Therefore, it is not surprising that psychologists generally prefer intrapsychic or learning–behavioral concepts of alcoholism to the disease model (Bissell & Haberman, 1984; Marlatt, 1983; Moos & Finney, 1983; Peele, 1984; Thoreson et al., 1983).

9. *The proclivity to self-treat.* The professional psychologist with a serious alcohol problem is likely to attempt by his or her own resolve to change behavior and cognitions in order to solve the alcohol problem. This effort is likely to fail. The deeply imbedded alcohol abuse resists definition, data collection, and data analysis and makes it unlikely that the psychologist can come to conclusions about the problems. The perceived need for change is convoluted and the power of denial and rationalizations so imbedded in the habit of alcohol misuse that grossly inaccurate conclusions about behavior are reached that do not lead to a commitment to change. The result is that the denial system becomes even more firmly established, such that the psychologist may ignore or be completely unaware that his judgment is impaired. Johnson

(1973) suggested that impaired judgment, by definition, excludes self-perception of impairment.

Despite objective evidence of lack of success, psychologists are likely to engage in self-treatment to solve their alcohol problems. Seeking out treatment from another professional is difficult, for this necessitates relinquishing control and accepting the likelihood that change without help from others is not possible. One vehicle that is often used for self-treatment is medication. Psychologists may self-medicate with drugs or alcohol. The retrospective study by Thoreson et al. (in press) of alcoholic psychologists in abstinence-based recovery provided clear evidence that during active drinking, psychologists used a wide variety of prescription and nonprescription drugs. On the other hand, professionals may also use behavioral change strategies to change belief systems regarding their pathology ("it is not so bad") or may use other behavioral approaches to change actual behaviors (when, where, or how they ingest alcohol) in an attempt to gain control over their drinking. Because obsession with control, rather than loss of control, tends to be the key characteristic of professionals with severe alcohol problems, the latter is a likely alternative (Wallace, 1985).

10. *The confounding of high achievement and alcoholism.* Many alcoholic psychologists tend to be high achievers in their fields (Skorina & Bissell, 1986), but because a modest performance level is often set for job performance, those impaired by alcohol abuse can drop off considerably in productivity and still be viewed as performing satisfactorily, albeit marginally, in their work. On the basis of clinical observation and research, Bissell and Jones (1976) reported high performance for professionals. Thoreson (1984a) described it as the "20-widgets-an-hour" problem; that is, satisfactory levels for most jobs are set at a mediocre "20-widgets" level that any high-performing professional can accomplish with ease. In addition, assessing the decline in performance is further complicated by the difficulty in separating out the alcohol-impaired performance from the natural tailing off of performance due to aging (Gross, 1977).

11. *Overcompensation.* The tendency to overcompensate as a means of hiding an alcohol problem is particularly prevalent during the middle stages of alcoholism. Appropriate and timely intervention may be hampered if the professional continues to perform at a high level, possibly in a more limited and narrow area of the job. Frequently this area of performance is quite visible to colleagues and superiors and diverts their attention from signs of alcohol misuse in the professional's job performance (Thoreson et al., 1983).

The distinction made by Edwards et al. (1977) and Edwards (1980) between the alcohol-dependent person and the person whose drinking leads to adverse social consequences can be applied with caution to psychologists. Edwards argued that the alcohol-dependent person can become psychologically addicted to alcohol without any tangible social or economic consequences. As noted earlier, except in the late stages, alcoholism among psychologists and other professionals is not manifested in obvious deviations from accepted work norms, and it impinges only subtly on job performance (Rubington, 1972; Thoreson, 1981a, 1981b; Roman & Trice, 1970; Thoreson et al., 1983). In the late stages of alcoholism, obvious decrement in job performance is likely to be apparent (Thoreson, 1984a), whereas impairment in interpersonal and, particularly, family relationships is obvious at earlier stages.

12. *Infrequent sanctions.* Bissell and Haberman (1984) reported that although approximately 60 percent of their sample of physicians with alcohol problems were admonished about their drinking by colleagues and approximately 25 percent of those physicians were warned by their employers or the professional medical society and lost hospital privileges, alcoholic physicians were rarely fired during their drinking days. Skorina and Bissell (1985) are finding the same general patterns of sanctions in their study of psychologists. Although internal indicators of despair are likely and a variety of external indicators of job decline are noticeable to both the alcoholic professional and to his or her colleagues, threats of sanctions and actual job loss are infrequent, and when they do occur, the alcohol misuse has progressed to the latter stages of alcoholism, where serious irreparable damage may have occurred (Thoreson, 1984b).

The twelve points have illustrated risks in the professional work environment and characteristics of professionals that complicate the identification of alcohol abuse and alcoholism. Although these factors have interfered with the development of treatment programs for alcoholic professionals, professionals have been aware of serious problems of alcohol abuse in their colleagues. This awareness has resulted in a few carefully designed treatment programs; however, the problem of what to do with the alcohol-abusing professional is now becoming a major concern and focus for most organizations that represent and are responsible for the professional. A historical perspective on such efforts follows.

ALCOHOLISM TREATMENT FOR PROFESSIONALS

Historical Perspective

Issues concerning the provision of alcoholism treatment to professionals are currently receiving major attention in the literature (Bissell, 1980; Bissell et al., 1980; Bissell & Haberman, 1984; Bissell & Jones, 1976; Bissell et al., 1973; Cosentino, 1980; Exo, 1981; Kliner, Spicer, & Barnett, 1980; Thoreson, 1981a, 1981c, 1982; Thoreson & Hosokawa, 1984; Thoreson et al., 1982; Thoreson et al., 1983). This literature reflects two related professional–humanitarian responsibilities: the responsibility of the professions (a) to set standards for professional practice and conduct and (b) to care for their members who suffer from a life- or career-threatening problem. Alcoholism is one of the major health problems of our society (Efron, Keller, & Gurioli, 1974), and chemical dependency has been noted as the major cause of decline in performance among professionals (Steindler, 1975; Talbott, Richardson, Mashburn, & Benson, 1981).

Several implications can be drawn from these findings. First, maintaining work-role respectability, which in this instance involves hiding alcohol problems, is of vital importance to high-status employees, including psychologists (Layne & Lowe, 1979). Second, despite the increase in public attention to alcoholism as a disease, at a covert level alcoholism still tends to be viewed as a weakness of character rather than as a disease. Hence, the stigma of alcoholism, alluded to earlier, continues to constitute a major deterrent to the treatment of psychologists and other professionals who have alcohol problems. Third, given these conditions and dilemmas, professionals tend to develop a complex array of strategies related to their alcoholism that serve to divert attention, rationalize, and maintain problem drinking.

Thus, in recent years, increased attention has been given to the adverse effects of alcoholism in the professions and other high-status, high-visibility groups. This attention has led to increased public awareness of the damaging effects of alcoholism both on the professional and on his or her clients and to the development of successful efforts to help professionals who have alcohol problems. In this portion of the chapter, we look at the efforts that a variety of other professions have made to deal with problems of alcohol. We conclude the section with a discussion of efforts of the American Psychological Association that have focused on problems of alcohol abuse.

Bissell and Haberman (1984) have provided an extensive review of efforts currently underway in the professions to help colleagues with alcohol problems. They noted an increased interest in impaired professionals, mainly those with alcohol problems. They suggested that at the same time, concealment to protect a colleague's reputation is common even though the stigma of alcoholism seems to have diminished somewhat in recent years. Laliotis and Grayson (1985) provided a historical perspective on the efforts in various professions, particularly in medicine, to establish programs for impaired professionals. Dickason (1981) reviewed similar efforts in law and described efforts in the legal profession to establish programs and procedures that contain both disciplinary and therapeutic components.

Efforts in medicine began with the development of the "sick doctor" statute and subsequently led to the current "disabled physician" act as drafted by the American Medical Association in 1974. This act recommends to the state medical societies that they be given authority to examine physicians who are alleged to be impaired and in this way to serve as agent or advisor to the medical licensing boards (Raskin, 1977). The state statutes were observed to vary somewhat, but all had in common the goal of early recognition and treatment of impaired physicians. Laliotis and Grayson (1985) have noted that all 50 state medical societies have established impaired-physicians' committees to deal exclusively with the problem of impairment. The committees vary in how they handle the problem of impairment, the extent to which they are involved in treatment facilities, and their relationship to the state examining board.

Generally speaking, these programs vary on the continuum of voluntary to coercive features. The programs at one end of the spectrum are strictly voluntary and keep no records, whereas programs at the other end use a more assertive outreach approach whereby uncooperative physicians are offered a choice of treatment or a loss of licensure (Robertson, 1980). The majority of programs fall somewhere between these two extremes. Bissell and Haberman (1984) concurred with Laliotis and Grayson (1985) that state efforts vary considerably in level of activity and in degree, and in voluntary and coercive features. They also noted considerable variation in quality. The Bissell and Haberman text contains an excellent summary of efforts in other health professions in our society, including osteopathic medicine, dentistry, nursing, the legal profession, social work, and psychology.

Laliotis and Grayson (1985) confirmed a reluctance on the part of professions, particularly psychology, to become involved in programs for their distressed members. In their survey of the activities of state psychological associations regarding efforts to help distressed psychologists, they concluded that state associations have done little to assist colleagues. Indeed, a number of responses to their request indicated complete ignorance of the problem. Similar findings have been noted in the responses of six other professions regarding services for impaired professionals. Laliotis and Grayson suggested several alternative explanations, a number of which have been noted in this chapter: (a) denial (it is easier to see impairment elsewhere than in oneself); (b) the existence of more pressing issues; (c) the relatively recent attention to consumer rights; (d) possible low incidence of reported alcohol problems.

Pearson (1982) noted that the physician has been accustomed to being the one who does the treatment, not to being treated by others. Nathan et al. (1983), reporting on psychologists, and Steindler (1975), reporting on physicians, noted a similar need for infallibility and omnipotence among the members of these professions, a need that is reinforced by expectations of their patients or clients. This reluctance to admit to difficulties, which constitutes a deterrent to treatment, is a basic part of the role and function of high-status executives and professionals. Thoreson et al. (1986), reporting on a survey of perceptions of alcohol problems among psychologists, found that few psychologists are confronted for alcohol problems, and of the few who are confronted, even fewer seek help or treatment. This finding stands in stark contrast to the view of alcoholism held by the same respondent-psychologists, that alcoholism is a relatively permanent and severe affliction with discernable adverse consequences for work, interpersonal relationships, and family relationships.

Although psychologists are unlikely to be confronted for alcohol problems or to seek help for it, they are, however, likely to seek help from psychologists or psychiatrists for mental health or personal development (Thoreson et al., 1982; Thoreson et al., 1986; Vaillant, 1983). As suggested by Thoreson (1984b), Thoreson et al. (1986), and Boyer (1984), stigma remains a major deterrent to help-seeking behavior by professionals for alcohol problems, because their reputation and earning capacity could suffer.

The pattern of response by the professions has been remarkably similar. Initially little attention is paid to individuals in trouble even though one may know about it (Thoreson et al., 1986). The erroneous assumption that such cases are rare is also common. Furthermore, there is, at first, considerable debate over who will control and who will take credit for the programs that are established. Issues of advocacy versus coercive methods are dealt with, and some professional organizations such as Lawyers Concerned for Lawyers and Dentists Concerned for Dentists take a noncoercive advocacy position. More detailed descriptions of several of these programs, representing both coercive and noncoercive features, are found in Dickason (1981) and in Gitlow and Peyser (1980).

Support advocacy groups consisting of recovered alcoholics have recently come to the fore to help colleagues in distress. Such support groups, as earlier suggested, are found in the professions of law, medicine, dentistry, nursing, social work, and psychology (e.g., Bissell & Haberman, 1984; Larson, 1981; Nathan, 1982; Skorina, 1982; Thoreson et al., 1983). Many of these self-help groups are modeled on the principles of Alcoholics Anonymous (AA), which has been suggested as an important resource for executive-professionals with problems of alcohol abuse and alcoholism (Layne & Lowe, 1979; Roman & Trice, 1970). AA support groups constitute for many alcoholics an important component of long-term recovery (Hoffman, Harrison, & Belille, 1983; Robinson, 1979). AA appears to be a significant posttreatment support system for many alcoholics, including professionals, and can help prevent relapse.

Self-help has been a trend of the 1980s. van der Avort and Van Harberden (1985), describing the process of mutual identification that encourages each member to relate to his or her own experience, referred to the major element in self-help groups as mutual identification or "identification resonance." The authors further identified four values that play a major role in self-help groups: self-determination, authenticity, hope, and solidarity, in addition to the central characteristic, the gaining of experiential knowledge.

Members of self-help groups frequently develop attitudes that clash with professional training. These include an emphasis on affection, appreciation of personal experience, common sense and intuition, direct responsibility and self-assistance, emphasis on spontaneity, and practical problem solving. These elements, considered to be critical to the maintenance of sobriety via the Alcoholics Anonymous programs, are of importance to the alcoholic professional. Mutual self-help promotes the discovery of support, hope, vulnerability, and openness to the possibility of receiving help for an alcohol problem from powers beyond the self. Perhaps of more fundamental significance is the discovery that people can help and forgive each other while at the same time reacting with competence and compassion (Bolan, 1985). These actions are fundamental to the recovery of professionals suffering from alcoholism.

Support-Advocacy in Psychology: Psychologists Helping Psychologists

Bissell and Haberman (1984) have described four stages in the development of efforts in the professions to help their alcoholic members: (a) Professionals deny the problem and extrusion of noticeably impaired persons, (b) alcoholic individuals in the profession struggle, enter into recovery, and finally seek affiliation with Alcoholics Anonymous as a posttreatment support system, (c) professionals in AA establish self-help advocacy within the profession, and (d) these professionals advocate increased problem awareness and outreach programs for members of the profession who are distressed by alcohol and other major health problems; this advocacy results in programs to assist distressed professionals. A similar sequence was seen in psychology.

In addition to APA's formal efforts to address the general problem of distressed professionals, a group of psychologists has developed an organization, Psychologists Helping Psychologists (PHP), to provide support for alcohol-impaired colleagues. The initial planning efforts for PHP began in the fall of 1980. The efforts were patterned after research on impaired physicians, social workers, and nurses (Bissell et al., 1980; Bissell & Jones, 1976; Bissell et al., 1973).

An initial committee focused on their common needs and interests in creating an advocacy–support group for psychologists. The planning group believed that PHP could provide an opportunity for recovered psychologists to share, in the language of AA, their "experience, strength and hope." Planning-committee members, all in recovery from alcoholism, found that their initial denial, in the face of incontrovertible evidence to the contrary, seemed to have been a cardinal sign of their alcoholism. The committee recognized that psychologists, committed to a belief in their capacity to control behavior, affect behavioral change, and solve human problems, were reluctant to ask for help for alcohol problems. The combination of scientific skepticism, intellectual pride, and feelings of invincibility constitute a powerful obstacle to identification and treatment of alcoholism among psychologists. The members found a consensual need for mutual support that led to the planning and formation of PHP (see Skorina, 1982; Thoreson et al., 1983).

Membership in PHP is open to alcoholic or drug-dependent doctoral-level psychologists (including doctoral candidates) who are interested in sharing their "experience, strength, and hope with one another to improve the quality of their sobriety." Members are interested in helping colleagues, doing research, and educating peers about experiences with alcohol and drugs, because PHP members believe that the psychology profession has failed to provide adequate training regarding this impairment. Psychologists Helping Psychologists is an international organization with membership from all over the United States, Canada, and Australia. Membership as of 1985 consisted of 150 psychologists and was growing at a rapid rate. Because abstinence is the treatment goal of PHP and its members who are in excellent recovery, members constitute a significant resource for other psychologists who are in abstinence-based recovery from alcoholism and substance abuse.[1]

Bissell and Haberman (1984) have summarized the special issues, promise, and difficulties that have been encountered in developing and implementing programs that protect clients' rights as well as members of the profession in cases of alcohol abuse. They observed that members of the professions are reluctant to tattle on one another. Thus, most professionals tend to put off confronting colleagues with difficult alcohol problems until such problems are in an advanced state. At the same time, disciplinary boards and committees can be ineffective, slow, and destructive rather than helpful. It may be concluded that more than one approach is needed by the professions in getting a colleague into treatment. At any point, a noncoercive self-help advocacy group such as PHP may be asked to assist. Employee assistance programs and committees at the workplace can sometimes help, the state society may succeed, and if all else fails, a state disciplinary board can intervene. The one action that is certain to be wrong is to do nothing, ignoring the problem until it becomes a major deterrent to practice and is dangerous to both the professional and to users of professional services.

In the next section, we discuss treatment of psychologists with alcohol problems, including paradoxes, dilemmas, and barriers to treatment, as well as specific treatment recommendations for alcoholic psychologists.

[1]Further information on PHP can be obtained from Jane K. Skorina, PHP, 23439 Michigan, Dearborn, MI 48124.

The Effectiveness of Intervention

Bissell and Haberman (1984) chronicled the efforts of the professions to cope with the problem of alcoholism among their members and concluded that the status of the subject has moved from the unmentionable to becoming almost stylish, complete with "experts," schemes for intervention, and even prevention. However, despite the marked increase in attention being shown to the problem and the increase in research and consequent new knowledge, the understanding of alcoholism remains strikingly incomplete, and controversy abounds in the search for understanding. The population of alcoholics is not at all homogeneous, and the effectiveness of conventional treatment methods is in serious question (Emrick, 1975, 1983; Emrick & Hansen, 1983). Thoreson et al. (in press) noted that alcoholism is often presented in bipolar fashion, either as a behavioral excess akin to the "mythical beast" or as the "inexorable, progressive disease" (e.g., Edwards, 1982; Edwards & Grant, 1980; Miller, 1983; Peele, 1983a; Thoreson et al., in press; Vaillant, 1983).

While the controversy continues, many people with severe alcohol problems die. Death may result from accidents, particularly auto accidents, from illnesses such as cirrhosis or pancreatitis, from malignancies related to the toxic effects of alcohol, as well as from the same physical illnesses that kill everyone else but are exacerbated by alcohol abuse. Clinical evidence suggests that alcoholics die younger and at a higher rate—two to four times that of nonalcoholics (Nichols, Edwards, & Kyle, 1974; Peterson, Kristenson, Sternby, Trell, Fex, & Hood, 1980; Thorarinsson, 1979; Vaillant, 1983). In his 8-year follow-up study of a sample of 100 clinic treatment alcoholics, Vaillant found significantly higher rates of mortality. As noted earlier, one third were abstaining, 26 percent continued to drink, and 29 percent were dead (5 percent drank asymptomatically). These findings provide support for an abstinence model, that is, people with severe alcohol problems appear to move toward abstinence or toward a premature death but only rarely to successful controlled drinking. This model is supported both by the AA self-help position and by the conventional wisdom regarding the need for abstinence.

Those who represent the alcohol treatment community concede that some people do manage to stop drinking on their own. Some problem drinkers, typically those in the early stages without physiological dependency and with environmental resources, are able to return to social or controlled drinking. For the most part, however, conventional wisdom dictates that those with severe alcohol problems require abstinence and outside assistance in order to cope effectively with their alcohol problems. (See also Miller, 1983, and Miller & Caddy, 1977, for a critique of the disease concept and a description of drinkers who are likely to profit from a nonabstinence goal.)

This issue leads to an important question: Given the stigma and the theory preference of psychologists, what are the types of assistance that are sought by psychologists with alcohol problems? Bissell and Haberman (1984), in reporting on a longitudinal study of physicians, dentists, nurses, and social workers, concluded that the alcoholic will seek help only when "home remedies" have failed and when they are forced either by circumstances or by other people. In a study reported by Bailey and Leach (1965), AA members were asked where they had gone for help. About one third had sought help from the medical professions; slightly less than 20 percent had sought the clergy in their first attempt to get help for their alcohol problem. Professionals who seek help for alcohol problems seem to go in large numbers to other professionals, particularly therapists. Vaillant (1983) reported that more than 60 percent of his Harvard college sample of alcohol abusers, as compared to only 8 percent of a disadvantaged core city sample, received psychotherapy. Similar findings were reported by Bissell and Haberman in their study of physicians with alcohol problems. They found that approximately 50 percent of the physicians had sought help from psychiatrists for their alcohol problems.

Vaillant (1983) presented a convincing case that psychotherapy is remarkably ineffective as the treatment for active alcoholism. In his Harvard sample, 26 subjects with severe alcohol problems had received a combined total of 5,000 hours of psychotherapy. Of these 26, only 2 ever attained sobriety, and one of these 2 relapsed and became a member of AA. The implications of the negative psychotherapy outcomes were clear. Those with severe alcohol problems will do anything to solve their problem except not drink; therefore, psychotherapy, be it dynamic or behavioral, with persons who have severe alcohol problems and who continue to drink abusively is likely to be at best ineffective and at worst harmful to the alcohol-abusing professional. We concur with Vaillant but offer this important exception: Psychotherapy conducted with individuals in abstinence-based recovery, as opposed to those in active alcoholism, is very useful as an aftercare support. It permits the client to work toward uncovering persistent and unproductive patterns of behavior, to develop problem-solving behaviors, to gain a new understanding of internal dynamics, and to acquire a set of strategies to prevent relapse.

The increase in treatment resources available to those with alcohol problems has led to increased referrals to AA from counseling or treatment centers. Approximately one third of those who entered the AA program since 1977 indicated that they were referred by counseling and treatment centers (Alcoholics Anonymous, 1981). AA has also been identified as a significant aftercare support for the recovering alcoholic (Armor, Polich, & Stambul, 1978; Desoto, 1983; Hoffman et al., 1983; Norris, 1976; Robinson, 1979; Skorina, 1982; Thoreson, 1984a, 1984b; Vaillant, 1983).

Thoreson et al. (1986) reported on a study of perceptions of alcohol misuse and work behavior among a random sample of 507 APA members. In this study, respondents were asked for knowledge of psychologists with alcohol problems, efforts made to confront such persons, and referral resources used in dealing with these problems. Results showed that approximately one third of the sample were aware of alcohol misuse among their colleagues. Symptoms included intoxication at inappropriate times, hangover symptoms, and significant impairment in a variety of work behaviors. These work behaviors included late or incomplete job assignments and a decrease in the quality of work. Only a minority of those who confronted their colleagues indicated that the psychologist's work performance remained good in spite of the problems.

These results were consistent with those reported by Bissell and Haberman (1984) for other health professionals: Confronting colleagues about alcohol problems was uncommon. Despite the adverse effects of alcohol problems on psychologists' personal and professional lives, roughly one half of the respondents who reported observing that their colleagues had severe alcohol problems also reported that the colleagues had done nothing about their alcohol problem except become more cautious about their drinking. Although one third of the psychologists reported being aware of alcohol problems among their colleagues, only one third of these, or 10 percent of the total sample, actually confronted a colleague regarding his or her alcohol problem. The typical method of confrontation was to talk with their colleagues about the problem, and one half of those who confronted a colleague referred the colleague to treatment resources. The majority of referrals were to AA; the next most frequent referrals were to private psychologists and inpatient alcoholism treatment facilities. Thoreson et al. (in press) found that about one half of their sample of psychologists in abstinence-based recovery sought treatment without ever having been confronted about work performance.

Thoreson et al. (in press) suggested that two findings from their study merit special attention. First, despite the extent of alcohol misuse, the decrement in work performance, and the impairment in reputation and health that have been identified, intervention is infrequent, a situation that constitutes a serious dilemma for the profession. In the study, reported confrontation was rare, and when it did occur, it led to results that were less encouraging than results of confrontation of colleagues who had mental health problems. Fewer of those confronted for alcohol problems sought treatment, and fewer were thankful; most denied that they had a problem, and in most cases, nothing at all happened. Nevertheless, alcoholism was seen by respondents both as being more permanent and as having more deleterious consequences on health, reputation, and work than are mental health problems.

In the Thoreson et al. study (in press), 74 percent of psychologists who had sought abstinence-based treatment reported decreased quality in their work, 68 percent reported a narrowed scope of work activity, and 56 percent reported late or incomplete job performance. The respondents also identified work factors in the setting that complicated identification and provided an opportunity for continued drinking: 62 percent reported that criteria for their work performance evaluation were nonspecific; 30 percent reported that they did their work independent of observation; 27 percent reported that they had no supervision; and 69 percent reported that their job performance was rarely or never reviewed. These results provide confirmation for the conclusions that characteristics of the work environment tend to be instrumental in delaying identification of professionals who have alcohol problems and also that severe alcohol problems carry with them major job-related decrements. It is important to consider characteristics of both the work environment and the professional in establishing treatment strategies (Moos & Finney, 1983).

It is also important to note that in the Thoreson et al. study (in press), alcohol-abstinent psychologists showed a remarkably stable pattern of recovery. The average length of sobriety was slightly less than 4 years; only 3 percent of the sample were not currently sober, and only 10 percent had been sober for less than one year. High satisfaction with current life areas was reported, with excellent or good relationships noted with significant others, children, and peers, and high ratings on job performance, physical health, and self-image. The majority enjoyed life and felt able to cope with anxiety, depression, and difficult situations. Recovery from alcohol problems had led to avoidance of legal difficulties and greater success in managing financial affairs. In only two areas were some difficulties reported: ability to seek and to accept help, and ability to accept limitations in oneself or in others. However, the majority of the respondents rated their abilities in these areas as excellent or good. The excellent recovery for this sample of alcoholic psychologists, despite a substantial number of job-related problems, severe symptomatology, and abuse of drugs other than alcohol during the stage of active alcoholism, offers a note of optimism to the profession in regard to positive outcomes from intervention programs.

Treatment Goals and Methods in the United States

Jaffe (1980) reported that the vast majority of treatment programs in the United States, Canada, and a number of other Western countries are built primarily around affiliations with the AA groups in the surrounding communities. Abstinence as a treatment goal and traditional treatment methodology undergird most alcoholism treatment programs in the United States. Although applicable to clinical populations of alcoholics, this view is unduly restrictive for alcohol treatment in general. On the basis of a review of treatment strategies for alcohol misuse, Jaffe (1980) arrived at six conclusions that have relevance to treatment of professionals:

1. Within the broad category of alcoholism there are a number of distinct subgroups.

2. To be understood, alcoholism must be viewed in multidimensional and quantitative terms, that is, on several dimensions, each of which may vary in severity.

3. Much remains unknown about the dimensions of the disorder of alcoholism.

4. Apart from any biological vulnerability, the major determinants of alcohol-related problems in any given society are the cultural arrangements that encourage or discourage alcohol use.

5. Although the natural history of some subgroups involves a steady and inevitable deterioration, there are subgroups of alcoholics in which this is not the case.

6. Once the alcohol syndrome is firmly established in an individual, it is relatively insensitive to changes in the intensity of psychological treatment.

The increase in interest shown in alcoholism has led to a concomitant increase in treatment capacity. This, in turn, has led to a sharp increase in case-finding methods and in the attention given to people with alcohol problems. Many more people are now being identified as alcoholics and are getting care and assistance who in past times would have received none. Competition for funding, whether through direct appropriations or through grants and contracts, is strong. This competition has led to a major emphasis on the selling of alcoholism services, on public relations, fancy brochures, and optimistic reports and evaluations rather than on hard facts regarding treatment successes. The entrepreneurial character of the treatment system tends to be antithetical to the scientific mind and deters alcoholic psychologists from admitting to alcohol problems.

The increase of services for alcohol problems in our society has led to a rapid increase in treatment services available in the private treatment sector, which are funded primarily by employment-based group health insurance plans. The result is at least four kinds of responses by the providers of alcoholism treatment:

- Making the treatment more attractive to clients, such as having an attractive seaside resort atmosphere for alcohol clients.
- Seeking out client populations for provision of special alcohol services, noteworthy examples being the specific alcoholism treatment services for various ethnic groups, women, and youth.
- Diversifying treatment for specific problem areas and redefining alcoholism. Special groups (such as those in treatment for drunken driving) may be closer to the general population of problem drinkers than to clinically defined alcoholics (Room, 1980).
- Making treatment compulsory. For example, in industry-based employee assistance programs, treatment professionals may diagnose an individual with job impairment as being alcoholic, and industry officials threaten to fire the individual unless he or she receives treatment immediately.

Room (1980) was troubled by the mixing of direct economic benefits with sound treatment procedures. He believed that often too little attention is paid to the potential conflict between the ethical responsibilities of the treatment team to their client and the practical and ethical dilemmas inherent in a coercive case-finding approach. What is troubling in this approach to alcoholism treatment is that although private sector treatment programs market alcoholism services, issues such as where clients come from, under what conditions, with whom treatment works, and what the treatment misses have not been carefully studied. (For a provocative discussion of the issues and trends in alcoholism and alcoholism research from an interdisciplinary perspective, see Keller, 1976, 1979; Moos, Cronkite, & Finney, 1982; Moos & Finney, 1983).

We are convinced that it is critically important to give careful attention to the ethical and moral dilemmas intrinsic to the current approach to treating alcoholism. This attention includes maintaining an openness to the limited state of knowledge and examining both clinical and research findings in developing a coherent and defensible treatment strategy for psychologists with severe alcohol problems. Edwards (1982) offered several recommendations that are consistent with this aim.

1. Because alcoholic populations are not homogeneous, patients require different types of help. This suggestion seems applicable to dealing with the problem of alcoholism within the profession of psychology, wherein heterogeneity exists in both job function and membership characteristics.

2. The particular moment at which help is sought by the person with an alcohol problem has its own significance. Mulford (1982) stated that abstinence-based recovery from alcoholism comes as a culmination of a series of treatment, work, and familial experiences. Those who treat professionals must be sensitive to this issue of timing. Everything possible, as Edwards (1982) noted, needs to be done to confirm the potential of this particular moment.

3. Goals should be agreed upon rather than imposed. This recommendation is especially important for working with psychologists, because joint decision making is a critical factor in motivation for treatment and recovery. Furthermore, the type of therapist is important. Erez and Kanfer (1983) found that a supportive therapeutic style increases the client's ability to set goals. We

concur with this point. Miller (1985) stated that the therapist factor is a major but infrequently considered factor in both motivation for treatment and recovery for a person suffering from severe alcohol problems. He emphasized that a high level of therapist empathy is a significant factor in maintaining gains in posttreatment and in reducing the incidence of relapse in persons with alcohol problems.

4. Participants in treatment who relapse should be identified and plans should be made for treatment and prevention of relapses. This recommendation fits particularly well with an emphasis on posttreatment aftercare planning for the professional that focuses on self-monitoring and other relapse-prevention strategies.

5. The family should be included as an integral part of the recovery process. The spouse or family should be involved in initial assessment, in treatment, and in posttreatment planning. This suggestion is consistent with the research that has identified the critical role of a maximally supportive, consistent environment in treatment outcomes (Finney, Moos, & Chan, 1981; Moos, 1974).

Edwards believed that treatment should occur in an outpatient setting except for detoxification or treatment for underlying or accompanying medical conditions. This treatment recommendation is a radical departure from current practice. It is consistent, however, with the outcome studies that show limited effects of alcoholism treatment and with recommendations for more emphasis on posthospital treatment and relapse prevention or sobriety maintenance experiences (e.g., Emrick, 1974, 1975, 1982; Emrick & Hansen, 1983; Marlatt & George, 1984; Marlatt & Gordon, 1984).

Emrick and Hansen (1983) argued that the high level of abstinence reported in the literature for posttreatment alcoholics is likely to be based on biased subgroups. They point to the 7 percent long-term abstinence rate reported by Polich (1980) as being more "internally valid and generalizable to the treatment populations similar to those seen at NIAAA funded agencies" (p. 1086). Considering the likelihood that alcoholism is a chronic, long-term medical condition and that continuous sobriety is more often the exception than the rule, it is of critical importance to develop posthospital support systems and to establish methods to reduce relapse in working with alcoholic psychologists. A comprehensive review of the literature on social support in health maintenance is provided by Caplin (1974), Cohen and Syme (1985), Cohen and Wills (1985), and Gottlieb (1983).

Thoreson and Budd (in press) emphasized the importance of AA as a posttreatment aftercare resource that helps maintain a drug-free, positive posthospital adjustment. The Thoreson et al. study (in press) revealed that a subsample of alcoholic psychologists in abstinence-based recovery had relied heavily on AA as an aftercare resource and reported a minimal amount of relapse and a considerable amount of sustained sobriety. The average length of sobriety of this subgroup was approximately 4 years, and more than 60 percent of the sample reported no relapse since they first sought AA for help. A careful analysis of the coping strategies used by this group to maintain their drug-free, problem-free status would be helpful, because this group reported satisfaction in virtually all areas of life. The importance of AA was supported by Edwards (1980), who recommended that AA be routinely offered when an abstinence goal has been selected. The importance of using AA as a posthospital support and of actively pursuing a healthy, nonchemical life-style seems to have been established (see Desoto, 1983; Hoffman, Harrison, & Belille, 1983; Thoreson & Budd, in press).

Counterbalancing AA's undeniable success in treating alcoholics, Tournier (1979) has pointed out the potentially negative consequences of the dominance of Alcoholics Anonymous in the alcoholism field. Tournier argued that lumping all drinking problems under the rubric of alcoholism does an injustice to the complexity of alcohol problems and to the persons included and limits innovations in approaches. For a critique of the Tournier position, see Madsen (1979), Rosenberg (1979), and Schulman (1979).

Abstinence Versus Controlled Drinking and Implications for Treatment

The evidence we have presented leads us to conclude that, with the exception of a relatively small category of "early problem drinkers" and persons who misuse alcohol but have not yet become physiologically dependent, abstinence—not controlled drinking—represents the optimal solution. The controversy that surrounds the use of controlled-drinking strategies has been heated, often has been divisive at both extremes, and has served to obscure what is obviously true: Alcoholism is both a learned behavior and a chronic diseaselike, medical condition.

What seems clear is this: Learning to drink moderately on a daily basis, or controlled drinking, no problem for most people, can be accomplished by some. But for most professionals suffering from alcoholism, it is not the appropriate treatment goal. Those who rely on controlled-drinking strategies fail to consider sufficiently the likelihood of alcohol dependency, the primary nature of alcohol addiction, and the need for substituting healthy alternative nonchemical means of gaining new perspectives and insights into a new life without the use of alcohol (e.g., Glasser, 1976). The problem of dealing with life's stresses in a healthy way is not limited to alcoholics. It is the challenge of the human condition to find a healthy means for dealing with the inevitable pain, obstacles, and ambiguities of life.

The controversy over abstinence versus controlled drinking has had the positive effect of establishing the primacy of an abstinence goal for persons with severe alcohol-misuse problems. The fact that most alcoholics have difficulty in maintaining uninterrupted abstinence supports the vital need both for relapse-prevention strategies and for attention to the posttreatment phase of recovery for alcoholic psychologists. Data show that certain subgroups—for example, the sample of alcoholic psychologists in abstinence-based recovery—show good psychological health, excellent rates of continued abstinence, and low relapse rates (Thoreson et al., in press). It is important to evaluate carefully the experiences of groups such as this to determine the appropriate array of aftercare and relapse-prevention strategies for enhancing resistance to relapse.

The controversy has had the unfortunate effect of calling into question the use of valid behavioral techniques and has inhibited free inquiry into the study of alcoholism. This failure to appreciate the value of conducting careful behavioral assessments of, and using behavioral strategies with, persons who have severe alcohol problems has led to a cleavage between the psychological scientific community and the ongoing alcoholism treatment enterprise. Because alcoholism is a complex and poorly understood problem, it is unrealistic to expect that the present form of alcoholism treatment constitutes the best possible form and is effective for all people with alcohol problems. That alcohol abuse is in large part learned and is based on operant and classical conditioning procedures seems well established, and the use of behavioral strategies in treatment logically follows. The involvement of other factors seems equally well established. In addition to alcoholism being a learned behavior, at least four other factors need to be considered in developing an optimal plan of relapse prevention for alcoholic psychologists: (a) genetic predisposition, such that some people can ingest large amounts of alcohol without noticeable ill effects; (b) psychological predisposition, such that some persons become more socialized toward drinking; (c) physiological, cell-adaption factors, such that some individuals become more dependent on alcohol; and (d) absence of a stable social environment, such that alcohol is used to increase stability (Tarter, Alterman, & Edwards, 1985; Vaillant, 1983).

An excellent summary of the literature on controlled drinking can be found in Heather and Robertson (1981). (For further detail on the controlled-drinking-versus-abstinence controversy, refer to Conrad & Schneider, 1980; Delint & Schmidt, 1971; Finney, Moos, & Chan, 1981; Fisher, 1982; Keller, 1972; Marlatt, 1983, 1985; McCrady, 1985; Peele, 1983a, 1984; Pendery, Maltzman, & West, 1982; Royce, 1985; Sobell & Sobell, 1976, 1984; Thoreson, 1976; Wallace, 1985. For review of the relapse-prevention literature, refer to Annis, 1984; Chaney, O'Leary, & Marlatt, 1978; Litman, 1980; Marlatt & George, 1984; Marlatt & Gordon, 1984.)

Alcoholic Psychologists: A Psychological Profile

A look at characteristics of psychologists will help clarify sources of their attraction to alcohol use and resistance to treatment. First, psychologists tend to be involved in matters of the mind and have a particular interest in gaining insight into the meaning of life. Drugs and alcohol are often used in the endeavor to enhance such meaning (Weil, 1972). Psychologists are also trained and involved in science. They are trained to objectively analyze research, their clients or patients, and themselves. They are disinclined to seek help from others or to perceive a need to seek help. Thoreson et al. (in press) reported that difficulty in receiving help was one of the few problem areas listed by psychologists who were in good abstinence-based recovery. In almost all other areas of their life, these psychologists reported excellent psychological adjustment and major satisfaction. This intrinsic difficulty in accepting help is manifest in the psychologists' reluctance to view their own severe, deeply imbedded alcohol problems as requiring outside help. Instead, they tend to revert to their analytical, scientific training and greatly increase the time and attention given to careful analysis and control of the alcohol problem. This contention was supported by Gitlow (personal communication, 1985) who stated that alcoholics attempt to control "everything" in order to control alcohol and alcoholism. The problem of professionals, however, is less with control than it is with obsession with control. Most alcoholics, particularly professionals, are successful most of the time in controlling most of the adverse embarrassing effects of their drinking (Chalmers, 1984). It is more the obsession with controlling alcohol intake that counts professionals among the alcohol population. This obsession leads to the "overcompensating" behavior of alcoholic psychologists who continue to drink and to struggle, often at great personal sacrifice, to make their lives manageable within the constraints of continued drinking and physiological dependence on alcohol.

A second relevant characteristic of psychologists is their commitment to behavior change, with its emphasis on the power and control to solve problems in self and others. This tendency complicates the admission of an alcohol problem. Many people enter the profession of psychology because defining and solving others' problems is a safe means of working out their own problems. Ironically, however, the profession's characteristic of analyzing human behavior offers alcoholic psychologists an excellent opportunity to avoid dealing with their own alcohol problem, in that they can hide behind one of their worst fears: of becoming impaired (helpless) like a client, or helpless and unknowing like a student.

Paredes, Gregory, and Jones (1974) identified the inability to overcome problems by volitional control as one of the major deterrents to treatment for those suffering from alcohol abuse problems. The lack of control and autonomy inherent in the admission of an alcohol problem promotes regression and denial and, in our opinion, is common among psychologists, who typically use obsessive-compulsive emotional controls.

Psychologists have a tendency toward perfectionism that promotes denial and heightens resistance to change. The admission of helplessness and problems represents the antithesis of the professionalism and perfection that psychologists tend to seek. The need to deny the fallibility involved in a severe, intractable alcohol problem creates an imperviousness to change. If by chance the alcohol problem is so severe that the need for change breaks through this layer of imperviousness, a defense of denial is quickly asserted, and an attempt is made to change without seeking outside help. Self-treatment, or "home remedies," then ensue. Self-treatment efforts generally include (a) treatment within one's own modality, that is, application of behavioral procedures to one's own alcohol problems; (b) self-medication with strict controls on the use of alcohol or drugs; (c) seeking a colleague who rejects the disease model of alcoholism and will likely permit continued drinking while one looks for underlying causes of one's own alcohol problems; (d) continued struggling with the particular modality of treatment one has selected even when it is not working; and (e) using "euphoric recall" (conveniently forgetting the negatives), thus leading one to be oblivious to any alcohol-related impairment in judgment or performance.

Isolation and limited supervision constitute strong enabling factors in the continued misuse of alcohol by psychologists. The second most frequent place of employment for psychologists is in private clinical practice (American Psychological Association, 1981). The study by Thoreson et al. (1986) of psychologists in abstinence-based recovery from alcoholism confirmed that isolation is a factor in the work setting and work role of alcoholic psychologists. Twenty-seven percent of the sample said they had no supervision whatsoever, and 69 percent of the sample said that their job performance was seldom or never reviewed. As noted earlier, Thoreson et al. (1986) reported that confrontation by colleagues is rare, and when done, tended to lead to outcomes that were less positive than for colleagues with mental health problems. Skorina and Bissell (1985) found that confrontation by colleagues and by society is virtually unknown by psychologists; only one third of psychologists had been admonished by colleagues.

Protection is another powerful enabling factor. Professionals tend to protect their colleagues. There is also the "celebrity syndrome," a power position that helps to protect them. Patients, clients, and students rarely confront their alcohol-abusing therapists or teachers. Hosokawa (1986) found that peers and elected chairs in a state university were generally reluctant to confront their academic colleagues who presented alcohol-related job problems. Only appointed chairs, with presumed legitimate power, showed a willingness to do so. Skorina (1982) found that a majority of psychologists in abstinence-based recovery were confronted by family, not employers, for their alcohol problems. Furthermore, Bissell and Haberman (1984) reported that only 7 physicians and 3 nurses in their sample of over 150 lost their licenses to practice their professions. Skorina and Bissell (1985) concluded that although their research sample was composed of professionals, many of whom were psychologists who were in the late stages of alcoholism, virtually none were confronted by legal, peer, or societal sanctions. Implicit in this conclusion is collegial protection by the "conspiracy of silence" that works to solidify the already existing denial system of the psychologist, the profession, and all of the psychologist's significant others.

RECOMMENDATIONS FOR TREATMENT

1. *Deal with the presenting problem, but listen for alcoholism.* Psychologists with alcohol problems are resistant to recognizing and accepting the problems. At the same time, psychologists' curiosity about new learning coupled with the presence of a variety of alcohol-related problems makes them receptive to services. It is important to listen to marital, family, financial, legal, stress, burnout, and midcareer change problems with a "third ear" for the likely role of alcohol in these problems. We believe that this model can identify underlying alcohol problems. Thoreson et al. (1982) reported that 40 percent of clients with alcohol problems initially presented family or marital problems as their primary focus of concern. Talbott et al. (1981) found that physicians in an alcoholism treatment program reported that families are the first to be affected by alcoholism and the profession the last. In helping the psychologist gain insight into his or her alcoholism, it is more effective to provide services that include an educative/developmental component rather than to focus exclusively on alcohol problems.

Psychologists' high inner- and self-directedness as well as keenness of intellect contraindicate the use of the abrasive confrontation techniques that are typically advocated in alcoholism treatment for breaking down the denial system. It is necessary to break through the denial that covers the shame and to turn that shame into guilt, by helping the psychologist to look at his or her behavior and the guilt over the behavior rather than at the shame of being an alcoholic. A program that involves respect for the psychologist's need for self-direction and that takes into account individual needs and uses finesse would be workable. If the therapist can for a brief time focus on a variety of "socially acceptable" problems and provide services such as stress reduction, marital enrichment, and financial planning, the alcoholic psychologist can be helped to draw appropriate inferences regarding the role of alcohol in creating these problems. However, we offer this caution: If this process is carried on for an extended period, the treater may find that it plays into the sophisticated alcoholic denial system to the point that neither the treater nor the patient will look at the underpinning of alcohol in the many problems that ensue.

2. *Disengage from the learned-behavior-versus-disease controversy.* Becoming locked in conflict over whether the psychologist is suffering from the disease of alcoholism is both gratuitous and potentially harmful. It is gratuitous because the real issues are powerlessness over alcohol, severity of alcohol problems, and willingness to deal with these problems. Forcing the psychologist to admit that he or she has a disease when there is a lack of consensus in the scientific community about the disease concept seems both cruel and unnecessary. The important point is to help psychologists who are suffering from alcohol misuse to gain as much clarity about their problem as is possible— about the extent to which alcohol misuse is interfering with their lives—and to develop appropriate strategies for coping with the problem. The potential harm done by a direct attack on the alcoholic's denial system is supported by Miller (1985), who reported that a direct attack that focuses on the negative aspects of denial and rationalization is akin to forcing the alcoholic client to fit into your particular view of therapy, is destructive, and leads to higher relapse rates.

3. *Use finesse in your confrontation.* In lamenting the difficulty in confronting academics who have alcohol problems, Madsen (1983) suggested the use of finesse. This confirms our experience that finesse rather than direct, abrasive confrontation over decline in job performance, is the key. Madsen observed that it is difficult, if not impossible, to invoke professional university sanctions on senior-level academics. Furthermore, he argued that the academic with serious problems of alcohol misuse is frequently so ego driven and feeling so guilty that he or she will far outstrip colleagues in teaching and writing. Thus, despite the likelihood of some subtle indicators of decline, there is frequently no clear basis for confrontation based upon demonstrable decline in job performance. We believe that the same dictum holds true for psychologists.There is likely to be a relationship, but only a subtle one, between decline in job performance and alcoholism, and this can be determined only by reference to an individual's performance over time. Using finesse will enable the psychologist with an alcohol misuse problem to look at her or his own picture of decline. To illustrate the use of finesse, any psychologist in the active phase of alcoholism is likely to experience a decline in cognitive functioning and memory. Such a decline leads to feelings of panic and deep shame. For the therapist to refer gently but openly to such likely decline ("Is your work as good today as it was a year ago?") is likely to serve as a great source of relief, slowly opening the psychologist to face the unbearable inner despair and shame felt over this problem of alcoholism.

4. *Make use of the psychologist's scientific proclivities.* It is important to exercise patience coupled with consideration, awareness, and respect for the

skeptical scientific minds of psychologists who suffer from alcohol misuse. Inviting them to observe a variety of issues, alternative hypotheses, relationships among the various problems in their lives and the particular influence of alcoholism as a moderator variable for these problems will be less threatening and will promote self-esteem. Encourage the psychologists to use their training in the scientific method, their interest, and careful assessment in working with their alcohol problems. This approach is particularly helpful in establishing the relationship between excessive alcohol use and life problems.

5. *Empower psychologists to be consultants on their own alcohol problem.* Encourage them to bring all of their resources to bear in attaining a full understanding of their problem. Providing a variety of carefully selected written materials for review, including homework assignments, sometimes helps the treatment process enormously (Alcoholics Anonymous, 1975; Marlatt & Gordon, 1984; McCrady, 1985).

6. *Stress the complexity of alcohol problems and the "life-of-its-own" aspects.* Alcohol problems are very complex. The "life of its own" refers to the concept that the alcoholic lives only to drink and drinks to live. He or she is at the mercy of this "other life" and has no means of controlling it while currently imbibing; however, it is controlling him or her. Moreover, maintaining a facade of normalcy while enmeshed in alcoholism requires enormous effort as well as a set of strategies to enable the psychologist's alcoholic drinking to continue.

7. *Give permission not to use the disease label.* Emphasize behavior, not labels. Focus directly on the behavior that results from using alcohol.

8. *Provide models of sobriety.* Provide the psychologist with an opportunity to gain exposure to psychologist peers who have similar alcohol problems and occupational characteristics and are likely to share their personal experiences with alcohol, their solutions, and their experiences in living life nonchemically. This exposure can help the psychologist to cope with the omniscience and omnipotence so common among scientists.

9. *Acknowledge the presence of guilt and shame.* It is important to help the psychologists to deal with the inevitable guilt and shame that comes from their inability to manage a problem that they believe should be amenable to self-control. Be prepared to discuss the paradox involved in gaining power over the addiction through admission of powerlessness over alcohol (Thoreson & Budd, in press). We would like to point out that there is nothing in the self- or mutual-help program that requires invoking the disease concept or that requires not drinking. (The AA preamble [AA, 1984] states that the only AA requirement for membership "is a desire to stop drinking.") What is important is a "willingness" to consider powerlessness over alcohol as the critical issue. An analogy to the smoking habit would seem apt. One does not need to feel guilt or shame over smoking, nor is a program of controlled smoking likely to be successful for the person with a chronic smoking habit. Psychologists can be encouraged to view their alcoholism as a debilitating habit that can be changed, just as cigarette smoking can be changed, through both a sobriety-maintenance program that includes developing a healthy pattern of living and a cognitive–behavioral program that includes daily attention to the means of implementing a new life-style.

10. *Develop a relapse-prevention protocol.* Encourage the psychologists to develop a set of self-management strategies that can be used to prevent re-

lapse, increase their sense of empowerment and self-control, and take advantage of their problem-solving orientation. Brown (1985) found that posttreatment stressors, limited social support, and drinking expectancies predicted relapse. She recommended that treatment include relapse-prevention strategies to deal with the drinking expectancies and limitations in environmental support. The combination of professional treatment that emphasizes relapse-prevention strategies and mutual self-help support from psychologist peers via AA is consistent with this recommendation. For the private practitioner, this could also include peer-consultation groups as a support system to prevent stress (Greenburg, Lewis, & Johnson, 1985).

11. *Reframe alcoholism as a positive force.* Help psychologists to reframe their alcohol problem and resulting abstinence as an opportunity to establish and maintain a healthy life-style. Encourage them to use as much energy in developing appropriate nonchemical patterns of living and relapse-prevention strategies as they used in maintaining their debilitating alcohol problem. Help them to enjoy the freedom that they now experience in not being trapped in alcoholism.

12. *Insist on an alcohol- and drug-free status.* Our position is that the psychologist be willing to be drug and alcohol free as a prerequisite to psychotherapy. The road to recovery for those with severe alcohol problems begins when the individual becomes free of the toxic effects of alcohol. A valid separation of alcohol-induced behavior from drug-free patterns is not possible until the individual becomes detoxified.

Psychotherapy for those who are drug free constitutes a positive treatment. Such therapy permits the individual to undertake the careful analysis of patterns, strategies, daily hassles, and means of establishing a new life-style. Psychotherapy for those who are actively drinking, as a means of eliminating problems other than alcohol, is likely to fail, to be personally unsatisfying to the psychotherapist, and to be potentially damaging to the psychologist-client.

13. *Be cautious regarding other drug use.* The use of drugs other than alcohol should be considered a positive factor only under these circumstances: (a) if needed for medical problems such as diabetes, epilepsy, arthritis, or heart disease; (b) in the instance of demonstrable psychopathology such as diagnosed schizophrenic or manic depressive conditions; and (c) when needed for the short term as a means of abating a crisis, for example, the use of antidepressants such as tricyclics. The latter use should be considered positive, but only on a temporary basis. Minor tranquilizers except when used in detoxification, are contraindicated. Many alcoholic professionals also have been addicted to minor tranquilizers. The psychologist who is using minor tranquilizers should be encouraged to eliminate their usage as quickly as is feasible. The use of illegal recreational drugs is considered hazardous to sobriety and is also contraindicated.

Our data on male and female psychologists in abstinence-based recovery show the use of a variety of prescription and nonprescription drugs during active alcoholism. Generalizing from this sample, it seems likely that psychologists with alcohol problems will have experimented with and have used a variety of drugs including the minor tranquilizers, the stimulants—including nicotine, amphetamines, and cocaine—the psychedelics, and barbiturates. Some (10 percent or more) will have used opiates and narcotics. In addition, a very large percentage will have used marijuana either regularly or occasionally. All of these prescription and nonprescription drugs are considered to be hazardous for the psychologist to continue to use in an abstinence-based, nonchemical program of recovery. It is our experience that a number of professionals in recovery continue to take certain drugs such as marijuana or minor tranquilizers during their initial abstinence from alcohol. Over the long term, persons who stay in good recovery internalize the abstinence norm and come to realize that their program of recovery is being compromised by the continuous use of other drugs. Thus, most professionals in abstinence-based recovery eliminate other drug use. The use of minor tranquilizers in the early stages of recovery may be necessary for some professionals who need to gain sufficient confidence in their abstinence from alcohol through a program of recovery before they are able to give up the remaining external mood-altering support systems. It is important to caution, however, that the use of such drugs often serves as a precursor to relapse into active alcoholism.

CONCLUSION

Psychology as a profession has been a latecomer in the development of strategies and programs to help its members who are distressed by problems such as alcoholism. By training and inclination, psychologists are predisposed to favor a learning model and frequently discount the deleterious health effects and the disease concept of alcoholism; this situation tends to permit and sanction alcohol abuse. The tendency among psychologists toward a high degree of inner control and problem solving makes the problem of alcoholism an elusive, baffling, intractable illness that is difficult to comprehend and accept. Although there is a significant amount of job-related impairment among alcoholic psychologists as well as major impairment of the family during active alcoholism, few sanctions are applied to professionals, including psychologists. Based upon our retrospective data on psychologists in abstinence-based recovery there is evidence that considerable use of both alcohol and of drugs other than alcohol is typical. However, despite this substantial misuse these psychologists report long-term stable sobriety, excellent recovery and health status, and professional success. Thus, self-help advocacy programs, such as Psychologists Helping Psychologists, of major importance as a peer-support system for alcoholic psychologists, seem clearly beneficial to long-term recovery. We have described a variety of treatment strategies tailored to characteristics of psychologists, their work environments, and societal attitudes, which may be helpful for working with psychologists suffering from alcohol abuse.

References

Alcoholics Anonymous. (1975–1983). *Living sober*. New York: AA World Services, Inc.
Alcoholics Anonymous. (1981). *Alcoholics Anonymous membership survey*. New York: AA World Services, Inc.
Alcoholics Anonymous. (1984). *AA Grapevine, Inc., 41*(6), 1.
American Psychiatric Association. (1980). *Diagnostic and statistical manual of mental disorders* (3rd ed.). Washington, DC: Author.

American Psychological Association. (1981). Human resources in psychology [Special Issue]. *American Psychologist, 36*(11).

Annis, H. M. (1984). A relapse prevention model for treatment of alcoholics. In D. Carson & H. Rankin (Eds.), *Alcoholism relapse*. London: Alpha.

Argerioui, M. (1974). The Jellinek estimation formula revisited. *Quarterly Journal of Studies on Alcohol, 35*, 1053–1057.

Armor, D. J., Polich, J. M., & Stambul, H. B. (1978). *Alcoholism and treatment*. New York: Wiley.

Bailey, M. B., & Leach, B. (1965). *Alcoholics Anonymous: Pathway to recovery: A study of 1058 members of the AA fellowship in New York City*. New York: National Council on Alcoholism.

Bissell, L. (1980). Reaching the autonomous self-sufficient alcoholic professional. In E. A. Pascoe & R. W. Thoreson (Eds.), *Employee assistance programs in higher education—1979 Conference Proceedings*. Columbia, MO: University of Missouri, Office of the Provost.

Bissell, L., Fewell, C. H., & Jones, R. W. (1980). The alcoholic social worker: A survey. *Social Work in Health Care, 5*, 421–432.

Bissell, L., & Haberman, P. W. (1984). *Alcoholism in the professions*. New York: Oxford University Press.

Bissell, L., & Jones, R. W. (1976). The alcoholic physician: A survey. *American Journal of Psychiatry, 133*, 1142–1146.

Bissell, L., & Jones, R. W. (1981). The alcoholic nurse. *Nursing Outlook, 29*, 96–101.

Bissell, L., Lambrecht, K., & Von Wiegand, R. A. (1973). The alcoholic hospital employee. *Nursing Outlook, 21*, 708–711.

Blum, E. M., & Blum, R. H. (1974). *Alcoholism: Modern psychological approaches to treatment*. San Francisco: Jossey-Bass.

Bolan, J. S. (1985). *Godesses in every woman: A new psychology of women*. New York: Harper Colophon.

Boyer, C. A. (1984). *The profession's response to distressed psychologists*. Unpublished doctoral dissertation, University of Arizona, Tucson.

Brown, S. A. (1985). Reinforcement expectancies and alcoholism treatment outcomes after a one-year follow up. *Journal of Studies on Alcohol, 46*, 304–308.

Cahalan, D. (1970). *Problem drinkers*. San Francisco: Jossey-Bass.

Cahalan, D., Cisin, I. H., & Crossley, H. M. (1969). Measuring massed versus spaced drinking. In *American drinking practices*. New Brunswick, NJ: Rutgers Center of Alcohol Studies.

Caplin, G. (1974). *Support systems and community mental health*. New York: Behavioral Publications.

Centra, J. A. (1978). Types of faculty development programs. *Journal of Higher Education, 49*, 151–162.

Chalmers, D. G. (1984). Evaluation research. In R. W. Thoreson & E. P. Hosokawa (Eds.), *Employee assistance programs in higher education: Alcohol, mental and professional development: Programming for faculty and staff* (pp. 285–310). Springfield, IL: Charles C Thomas.

Chaney, E. F., O'Leary, M. R., & Marlatt, G. A. (1978). Skill training with alcoholics. *Journal of Consulting and Clinical Psychology, 46*, 1092–1104.

Cohen, S., & Syme, S. L. (Eds.). (1985). *Social support and health*. New York: Academic Press.

Cohen, S., & Wills, A. W. (1985). Stress, social support and the buffering hypothesis. *Psychological Bulletin, 98*, 310–357.

Conrad, P., & Schneider, J. W. (1980). *Deviance and medicalization: From badness to sickness*. St. Louis, MO: C. V. Mosby.

Cosentino, J. P. (1981). A diversion program for impaired physicians. In J. Johnston & E. P. Hosokawa (Eds.), *Employee assistance programs in higher education (Conference Proceedings)*. Columbia, MO: University of Missouri, Office of the Provost.

Cosper, R. (1979). Drinking as conformity. *Journal of Studies on Alcohol, 40*, 868–891.

Delint, J., & Schmidt, W. (1971). The epidemiology of alcoholism. In Y. Y. Israel & J. Mardones (Eds.), *The biological basis of alcoholism*. New York: Wiley.

De Luca, J. R. (Ed.). (1981). U.S. Department of Health, Education and Welfare. *Fourth Special*

Report to the U.S. Congress on Alcohol and Health (DHHS Publication No. ADM 81-1080). Washington, DC: U.S. Government Printing Office.

Desoto, C. B. (1983, August). Long-term changes in abstinent alcoholic professionals and nonprofessionals. In J. Skorina (Chair), *Alcoholism: Issues in treatment and recovery of professionals*. Symposium conducted at the meeting of the American Psychological Association, Anaheim, CA.

Dickason, J. S. (1981). Lawyers assist lawyers. *Illinois Bar Journal, 546*, 590.

Edwards, G. (1980). Alcoholism treatment: Between guesswork and certainty. In G. Edwards & M. Grant (Eds.), *Alcoholism treatment in transition* (pp. 307–320). Baltimore, MD: University Park Press.

Edwards, G. (1982). *The treatment of drinking problems*. New York: McGraw-Hill.

Edwards, G. (1985). A later follow-up of a classic case study series: D. L. Davie's 1962 report and its significance for the present. *Journal of Studies on Alcohol, 46*, 181–195.

Edwards, G., & Grant, M. (Eds.). (1980). *Alcoholism treatment in transition*. Baltimore, MD: University Park Press.

Edwards, G., Gross, M. M., Keller, J., Moser, J., & Room, R. (Eds.). (1977). *Alcoholic-related disabilities* (Offset Publications No. 32). Geneva, Switzerland: World Health Organization.

Efron, V., Keller, M., & Gurioli, C. (1974). *Statistics on consumption of alcohol and on alcoholism*. New Brunswick, NJ: Rutgers Center of Alcohol Studies.

Emrick, C. D. (1974). A review of psychologically oriented treatment of alcoholism: I. The use and interrelationships of outcome criteria and drinking behavior following treatment. *Quarterly Journal of Studies on Alcohol, 35*, 523–549.

Emrick, C. D. (1975). A review of psychologically oriented treatment of alcoholism: II. The relative effectiveness of different treatment approaches and relative effectiveness of treatment versus no treatment. *Quarterly Journal of Studies on Alcohol, 36*, 88–108.

Emrick, C. D. (1982). Evaluation of alcoholism psychotherapy methods. In E. M. Pattison & E. Kaufman (Eds.), *Encyclopedic handbook of alcoholism* (pp. 1152–1169). New York: Gordon Press.

Emrick, C. D., Hansen, J. (1983). Assertions regarding effectiveness of treatment for alcoholism: Fact or fantasy? *American Psychologist, 38*, 1078–1088.

Erez, M., & Kanfer, F. H. (1983). The role of goal acceptance in goal setting and task performance. *Academy of Management Review, 8*, 454–463.

Exo, K. J. (1981). *Substance abuse among professionals: Weaving the fabric of partnership* (CSEP Occasional Papers No. 5). Chicago: Illinois Institute of Technology, Center for the Study of Ethics in the Professions.

Finney, J., Moos, R., & Chan, B. (1981). Length of stay and program component effects in the treatment of alcoholism: A comparison of the techniques for process analysis. *Journal of Consulting and Clinical Psychology, 49*, 120–131.

Fisher, K. (1982, November). Debate rages on 1973 Sobell study. *APA Monitor*, pp. 8–9.

Follman, J. F. (1976). *Alcoholics and business: Problems, costs, solutions*. New York: Avacom.

Ford, W. E., & Luckey, J. (1976). *An alcoholism needs assessment technique*. Lincoln, NE: Nebraska Department of Public Institutions.

Gitlow, S. E., & Peyser, H. S. (1980). *Alcoholism: A practical treatment guide*. New York: Grune & Stratton.

Glasser, W. (1976). *Positive addiction*. New York: Harper & Row.

Gottlieb, B. H. (1983). *Social support strategies*. Beverly Hills, CA: Sage.

Greenburg, S. L., Lewis, G. L., & Johnson, M. (1985). Peer consultation groups for private practitioners. *Professional Psychology: Research and Practice, 16*, 437–447.

Gross, A. (1977). Twilight in academia: The problem of the aging professoriate. *Phi Delta Kappan, 58*, 752–755.

Heather, N., & Robertson, I. (1981). *Controlled drinking*. New York: Methuen.

Hoffman, N. G., Harrison, P. A., & Belille, C. A. (1983). Alcoholics Anonymous after treatment: Attendance and abstinence. *The International Journal of Addictions, 18*, 311–318.

Holmes, O. W. (1918). Natural law. *Harvard Law Review, 32,* 40–44.

Hore, B. D., & Plant, M. A. (Eds.). (1981). *Alcohol problems in employment.* London: Groom Helm Ltd.

Hosokawa, E. P. (1986). *An analysis of the ecology of the academic work setting and its influence on helping behavior among faculty.* Unpublished doctoral dissertation, University of Missouri, Columbia.

Jacobson, G. R. (1976). *The alcoholisms: Detection, diagnosis and assessment.* New York: Human Sciences Press.

Jaffe, J. H. (1980). What alcoholism isn't borrowing. In G. Edwards & M. Grant (Eds.), *Alcoholism treatment in transition* (pp. 32–48). Baltimore, MD: University Park Press.

Jellinek, E. M. (1960). *The disease concept of alcoholism.* Highland Park, NJ: Hill House.

Johnson, V. (1973). *I'll quit tomorrow.* New York: Harper & Row.

Jones, B. M. (1979). Research priorities in alcohol studies: The role of psychology. *Journal of Studies on Alcohol, 40*(Suppl. 8), 104–111.

Keller, M. (1972). On the loss of control phenomenon in alcoholism. *British Journal of Addiction, 67,* 153–166.

Keller, M. (1975). Problems of epidemiology in alcohol problems. *Journal of Studies on Alcohol, 36,* 1442–1451.

Keller, M. (1976). The disease concept revisited. *Journal of Studies on Alcohol, 37,* 1694–1717.

Keller, M. (1979). Afterwards. *Journal of Studies on Alcohol, 40*(Suppl. 8), 7–10.

Kliner, D. J., Spicer, J., & Barnett, B. S. (1980). Treatment outcome of alcoholic physicians. *Journal of Studies on Alcohol, 41,* 1217–1220.

Knox, W. J. (1982). Diagnostic psychological testing. In E. M. Pattison & E. Kaufman (Eds.), *Encyclopedic handbook of alcoholism* (pp. 55–63). New York: Goodman Press.

Kurtz, E. (1979). *Not-God—A history of Alcoholics Anonymous.* Center City, MN: Hazelden.

Kurtz, E. (1982). Why AA works: The intellectual significance of Alcoholics Anonymous. *Journal of Studies on Alcohol, 43,* 38–80.

Laliotis, D. A., & Grayson, J. H. (1985). Psychologist heal thyself: What is available for the impaired psychologist? *American Psychologist, 40,* 84–96.

Larson, C. (1981). Psychologists ponder ways to help troubled colleagues. *APA Monitor,* pp. 16, 50.

Layne, N. R., & Lowe, G. D. (1979). The impact of loss of career continuity on the later occupational adjustment of problem drinkers. *Journal of Health and Social Behavior, 20,* 187–193.

Litman, A. L. (1980). Relapse in alcoholism: Traditional and current approaches. In G. Edwards & M. Grant (Eds.), *Alcoholism treatment in transition.* Baltimore, MD: University Park Press.

Madsen, W. (1974). *The American alcoholic: The nature–nurture controversy in alcoholic research and therapy* (2nd printing). Springfield, IL: Charles C Thomas.

Madsen, W. (1979). Alcoholics Anonymous as treatment and as ideology: Comments on the article by R. E. Tournier. *Journal of Studies on Alcohol, 40,* 323–327.

Madsen, W. (1983). Reaching the alcoholic academic: An anthropological perspective. In R. W. Thoreson & E. P. Hosokawa (Eds.), *Employee assistance programs in higher education: Alcohol, mental health and professional development programming for faculty and staff* (pp. 145–158). Springfield, IL: Charles C Thomas.

Marden, P. (1975). *A procedure for estimating the potential clientele of alcoholism service programs.* Rockville, MD: National Institute on Alcohol Abuse and Alcoholism.

Marlatt, G. A. (1983). The controlled drinking controversy: A commentary. *American Psychologist, 38,* 1097–1110.

Marlatt, G. A. (1985). Controlled drinking: The controversy rages on. *American Psychologist, 40,* 374–375.

Marlatt, G. A., & George, W. H. (1984). Relapse prevention: Introduction and overview of the model. *British Journal of Addictions, 79,* 261–273.

Marlatt, G. A., & Gordon, J. R. (1984). *Relapse prevention: Maintenance strategies in addictive behavior change.* New York: Guilford Press.

Mayer, W. (1983). Alcohol abuse and alcoholism: The psychologist's role in prevention, research, and treatment. *American Psychologist, 38,* 1116–1121.

McCrady, B. J. (1985). Comments on the controlled drinking controversy. *American Psychologist, 40,* 370–371.

Mendelson, J. H., & Mello, N. K. (1979). Diagnostic criteria for alcoholism and alcohol abuse. In J. H. Mendelson & N. K. Mello (Eds.), *The diagnosis and treatment of alcoholism* (pp. 1–19). New York: McGraw-Hill.

Mendelson, J. H., & Mello, N. K. (1985). Diagnostic criteria for alcoholism and alcohol abuse. In J. H. Mendelson & N. K. Mello (Eds.), *The diagnosis and treatment of alcoholism* (2nd ed. pp. 1–20). New York: McGraw-Hill.

Miller, W. R. (1976). Alcoholism scales and objective assessment methods: A review. *Psychological Bulletin, 83,* 649–674.

Miller, W. R. (1983). Controlled drinking: A history and critical review. *Journal of Studies on Alcohol, 44,* 68–83.

Miller, W. R. (1985). Motivation for treatment: A review with special emphasis on alcoholism. *Psychological Bulletin, 98,* 84–107.

Miller, W. R., & Caddy, G. R. (1977). Abstinence and controlled drinking in the treatment of problem drinkers. *Journal of Studies on Alcohol, 38,* 986–1003.

Moos, R. H. (1974). *Evaluating treatment environments.* New York: Wiley.

Moos, R. H., Cronkite, R. C., & Finney, J. W. (1982). A conceptual framework for alcoholism treatment evaluation. In E. M. Pattison & E. Kaufman (Eds.), *Encyclopedic handbook of alcoholism,* (pp. 1120–1134). New York: Gardner Press.

Moos, R. H., & Finney, J. W. (1983). The expanding scope of alcoholism treatment evaluation. *American Psychologist, 38,* 1036–1044.

Mulford, H. A. (1982). The epidemiology of alcoholism and its implications. In E. M. Pattison & E. Kaufman (Eds.), *Encyclopedic handbook of alcoholism* (pp. 441–457). New York: Gardner Press.

Nathan, P. E. (1982, December). Psychologists need psychologists too. *APA Monitor,* p. 5.

Nathan, P. E., Thoreson, R. W., & Kilburg, R. R. (1983). *Board of professional affairs steering committee on distressed psychologists: Final report.* Washington, DC: American Psychological Association.

National Council on Alcoholism. (1972). Criteria for diagnosis of alcoholism. *Annals of Internal Medicine, 77,* 249–258.

Newlove, D. (1981). *Those drinking days: Myself and other writers.* New York: Horizon.

Nicholls, P., Edwards, G., & Kyle, E. (1974). Alcoholics admitted to four hospitals in England: II. General and cause-specific mortality. *Quarterly Journal of Studies on Alcohol, 35,* 841–855.

Norris, A. J. (1976). Alcoholics Anonymous and other self help groups. In R. E. Tarter & A. A. Sugerman (Eds.), *Alcoholism: Interdisciplinary approaches to an enduring problem.* Reading, MA: Addison-Wesley.

Paredes, A., Gregory, D., & Jones, B. M. (1974). Induced drinking and social adjustment in alcoholics: Development of a therapeutic model. *Quarterly Journal of Studies on Alcohol, 35,* 1279–1293.

Pattison, E. M., & Kaufman, E. (1982). The alcoholism syndrome: Definitions and models. In E. M. Pattison & E. Kaufman (Eds.), *Encyclopedic handbook of alcoholism,* (pp. 3–30). New York: Gardner Press.

Pearson, M. M. (1982). Psychiatric treatment of 250 physicians. *Psychiatric Annuals, 2,* 194–206.

Peele, S. (1983a). Is alcoholism different from other substance abuse? *American Psychologist, 38,* 963–964.

Peele, S. (1983b, April). Through a glass darkly: Can some alcoholics learn to drink in moderation? *Psychology Today,* 38–42.

Peele, S. (1984). The cultural context of psychological approaches to alcoholism: Can we control the effects of alcohol? *American Psychologist, 39,* 1337–1351.

Pendery, M. L., Maltzman, I. M., & West, L. J. (1982). Controlled drinking by alcoholics? New findings and a re-evaluation of a major affirmative study. *Science, 217,* 169–175.

Peterson, B., Kristenson, H., Sternby, N. H., Trell, E., Fex, G., & Hood, B. (1980). Alcohol consumption and premature death in middle-aged men. *British Medical Journal, 280,* 1403–1406.

Polich, J. M. (1980). Patterns of remission in alcoholism. In G. Edwards & M. Grant (Eds.), *Alcoholism treatment in transition* (pp. 95–112). Baltimore, MD: University Park Press.

Polich, J. M. (1982). The validity of self-reports in alcoholism research. *Addictive behaviors, 7,* 81–90.

Raskin, H. A. (1977). The impaired physician: An overview. In M. B. Hugunin (Ed.), *Helping the impaired physician. Proceedings of the AMA conference on the impaired physician: Answering the challenge* (pp. 7–12). Chicago: American Medical Association.

Robe, L. B. (1977). Rich alcoholics: How dollars buy denial. *Addictions, 24,* 42–57.

Robertson, J. J. (Ed.). (1980). *Legal aspects of impairment. Proceedings of the fourth AMA conference on the impaired physician: Building well-being.* (pp. 45–48). Chicago: American Medical Association.

Robins, L. N. (1982). The diagnosis of alcoholism after DSM-III. In E. M. Pattison & E. Kaufman (Eds.), *Encyclopedic handbook of alcoholism,* (pp. 40–54). New York: Gardner Press.

Robinson, D. (1979). *Talking out alcoholism: The self-help process of alcoholics anonymous.* Baltimore, MD: University Park Press.

Roman, P. (1982). Sociological models for deviant drinking behavior. In E. M. Pattison & E. Kaufman (Eds.), *Encyclopedic handbook of alcoholism* (pp. 367–382). New York: Gardner Press.

Roman, P. M., & Trice, H. A. (1970). The development of deviant drinking behavior. Occupational risk factors. *Archives of Environmental Health, 20,* 424–435.

Room, R. (1979). Priorities in social science research on alcohol. *Journal of Studies on Alcohol, 40* (Suppl. 8), 248–268.

Room, R. (1980). Treatment seeking populations and larger realities. In G. Edwards & M. Grant (Eds.), *Alcoholism treatment in transition* (pp. 205–224). Baltimore, MD: University Park Press.

Room, R. (1983). Sociological aspects of the disease concept of alcoholism. In R. L. Smart, F. B. Glaser, Y. Israel, Y. Kalant, R. E. Popham, & W. Schmidt (Eds.), *Research advances in alcohol and drug problems* (Vol. 7, pp. 47–91). New York: Plenum Press.

Root-Bernstein, N. (1981). Science and skepticism [Letter to the editor]. *Science, 212,* 1446.

Rosenberg, C. M. (1979). Alcoholics Anonymous as treatment and as ideology. Comments on the article by R. E. Tournier. *Journal of Studies on Alcohol, 40,* 330–333.

Royce, J. E. (1985). Alcoholism: A disease? *American Psychologist, 40,* 371–372.

Rubington, E. (1972). The hidden alcoholic. *Quarterly Journal of Studies on Alcohol, 33,* 667–683.

Schulman, G. D. (1979). Alcoholics Anonymous as treatment and as ideology: Comments on the article by R. E. Tournier. *Journal of Studies on Alcohol, 40,* 335–338.

Seixas, R. (1976). Afterword. In G. R. Jacobson. *The alcoholisms: Detection, diagnosis and assessment.* New York: Human Sciences Press.

Shaw, S. (1979). A critique of the concept of the alcohol dependence syndrome. *British Journal of Addiction, 74,* 339–348.

Shore, E. R. (1985). Alcohol consumption rates among managers and professionals. *Journal of Studies on Alcohol, 46,* 153–156.

Skorina, J. (1982). Alcoholic psychologists: The need for humane and effective regulations. *Professional Practice of Psychology, 3,* 33–41.

Skorina, J., & Bissell, L. (1986). The alcoholic psychologist. Manuscript in preparation.

Sobell, L. C., Maisto, S. A., Sobell, M. B., Cooper, A. M. (1979). Reliability of alcohol abusers. Self-reports of drinking behavior. *Behavioral Research and Therapy, 17,* 157–160.

Sobell, L. C., & Sobell, M. B. (1975). Out-patient alcoholics give valid self reports. *Journal of Nervous and Mental Disorders, 161,* 32–42.

Sobell, M. B., & Sobell, L. C. (1976). Second year treatment outcome of alcoholics treated by individualized behavior therapy: Results. *Behavior Research and Therapy, 14,* 195–215.

Sobell, M. B., & Sobell, L. C. (1984). The aftermath of heresy: A response to Pendery et al.'s critique of "Individualized behavior therapy for alcoholics." *Behavior Research and Therapy, 22,* 413–440.

Sobell, M. B., Sobell, L. C., & Vanderspek, R. (1979). Relationship among clinical judgments, self-report, and breath analysis measures of intoxication in alcoholics. *Journal of Consulting and Clinical Psychology, 47,* 204–206.

Steindler, E. M. (1975). *The impaired physician: An interpretive summary of the AMA conference on the disadvantaged challenge of the profession.* Chicago: American Medical Association.

Talbott, D. G., Richardson, C. H., Mashburn, J. S., & Benson, E. B. (1981). The medical association of Georgia's disabled doctors program—A 5-year review. *Journal of the Medical Association of Georgia, 70,* 545–549.

Tarter, R. E., Alterman, A. I., & Edwards, K. L. (1985). Vulnerability to alcoholism in men: A behavioral–genetic perspective. *Journal of Studies on Alcohol, 46,* 329–357.

Thorarinsson, A. A. (1979). Mortality among men alcoholics in Iceland, 1951–1974. *Journal of Studies on Alcohol, 40,* 704–718.

Thoreson, R. W. (1976). Current views on alcoholism: Their implication for treatment. *Addictions, 23,* 58–69.

Thoreson, R. W. (1981a). Alcohol problems in academe: The renaissance man, the inscrutable scholar and other myths. In J. Johnston & E. P. Hosokawa (Eds.), *Employee assistance programs in higher education. Conference Proceedings.* Columbia, MO: University of Missouri, Office of the Provost.

Thoreson, R. W. (1981b). Alcoholism in the profession: The dilemma of reaching the chemically dependent or alcoholic psychologist. In P. Nathan (Chair), *Psychologists in distress.* Symposium conducted at the meeting of the American Psychological Association, Los Angeles, CA.

Thoreson, R. W. (1981c). The professional–executive alcoholic: A sabbatical perspective. *ALMACAN, 12,* 5.

Thoreson, R. W. (1982). Their cup runneth over: Achievements, accolades and alcohol abuse. In J. Johnston, E. P. Hosokawa, & R. W. Thoreson (Eds.), *Employee assistance programs in higher education—1981.* Conference Proceedings, Columbia, MO: University of Missouri, Office of the Provost.

Thoreson, R. W. (1984a). The professor at risk: Alcohol abuse in academe. *Journal of Higher Education, 55,* 56–72.

Thoreson, R. W. (1984b). The professor at risk: Alcohol problems in academe. In R. W. Thoreson & E. P. Hosokawa (Eds.), *Employee assistance programs in higher education* (pp. 123–143), Springfield, IL: Charles C Thomas.

Thoreson, R. W., & Budd, F. C. (in press). Self help groups and other group procedures for treating alcohol problems. In W. M. Cox (Ed.), *Treatment and prevention of alcohol problems.* New York: Academic Press.

Thoreson, R. W., Budd, F. C., & Krauskopf, C. J. (1986). Perception of alcohol misuse and work behavior among professionals: Identification and intervention. *Professional Psychology: Research and Practice, 17,* 210–216.

Thoreson, R. W., Budd, F., & Krauskopf, C. (in press). Alcoholism among psychologists: Work related behavior and patterns in recovery. *Professional Psychology: Research and Practice.*

Thoreson, R. W., & Hosokawa, E. P. (1984). *Employee assistance programs in higher education: Alcohol related health and professional programming development for faculty and staff.* Springfield, IL: Charles C Thomas.

Thoreson, R. W., Nathan, P., Skorina, J., & Kilburg, R. (1983). The alcoholic psychologist: Issues, problems and implications for the profession. *Professional Psychology: Research and Practice, 14,* 670–684.

Thoreson, R. W., Hosokawa, E., & Talcott, W. (1982). Reaching distressed faculty and staff: The employee assistance program in higher education. *EAP Digest, 2,* 30–35.

Tournier, R. E. (1979). Alcoholics Anonymous as treatment and as ideology. *Journal of Studies on Alcohol, 40,* 230–239.

Vaillant, G. E. (1983). *The natural history of alcoholism, causes, patterns and paths to recovery.*

Boston: Harvard University Press.

van der Avort, A., & Van Harberden, P. (1985). Helping self-help groups: A developing theory. *Psychotherapy: Theory, Research, & Practice, 22,* 269–272.

Wallace, J. (1985). The alcoholism controversy. *American Psychologist, 40,* 372–373.

Wanberg, K. W., & Horn, J. C. (1983). Assessment of alcohol use with multi-dimensional concepts and measures. *American Psychologist, 38,* 1055–1069.

Weil, A. (1972). *The natural mind: A new way of looking at drugs and the higher consciousness.* Boston: Houghton-Mifflin.

Williams, G. D., Aitken, S. S., & Malin, H. (1985). Reliability of self-reported consumption. *Journal of Studies on Alcohol, 46,* 223–227.

Wilsnack, S. C. (1976). The impact of sex roles on women's alcohol use and abuse. In Greenblatt, M., & Schuckit, M. A. (Eds.), *Alcoholism problems in women and children.* New York: Grune & Stratton.

Wilsnack, S. C. (1982). Alcohol abuse and alcoholism in women. In E. M. Pattison & E. Kaufman (Eds.), *Encyclopedic handbook of alcoholism* (pp. 718–733). New York: Gardner Press.

Wilsnack, S. C., Wilsnack, R. W., & Klassen, A. D. (1984–1985). Drinking and drinking problems among women in a U.S. national survey. *Alcohol Health & Research World, 9*(2), 3–25.

World Health Organization (1952). *Expert Committee Report No. 48.* Geneva, Switzerland: Author.

SOURCES OF EMOTIONAL AND MENTAL DISORDERS AMONG PSYCHOLOGISTS: A CAREER DEVELOPMENT PERSPECTIVE

6

Theodore Millon
Carrie Millon
Michael Antoni

Our original intent in writing this chapter was to review what is known concerning the emotional and mental disorders prevalent among psychologists. Unfortunately, but not surprisingly, the empirical literature in this area is sparse; what little is to be found is methodologically weak or biased and, hence, for the most part impressionistic (Farber & Heifetz, 1981). At best we can ascertain that psychologists suffer from the same variety of psychic ailments, in similar proportions, as do others of their socioeconomic and education levels, with depression, anxiety, and alcoholism at the top of the list.

The two major systematic studies of recent decades that relate to the prevalence of mental disorders, one carried out in a major metropolitan city, the other in a rural area, concluded alike that at any given time approximately one-fifth of the general population is sufficiently disturbed to justify the therapeutic services of a psychologist or psychiatrist (Leighton, Harding, Macklin, MacMillan, & Leighton, 1963; Srole et al., 1978). This figure contrasts with the fact that less than 2 percent of the general population is involved in mental health treatment at any point, the majority of whom (approximately 65 percent) are seen either in federally funded community health centers or in private outpatient settings (Rosenstein & Milazzo-Sayre, 1981). Of relevance to this chapter is the recent increase reported in the number of suicides, especially among adolescent children of upper-middle-class families, and among adult health professionals, including psychiatrists and psychologists (Murphy 1977; Murphy & Wetzel, 1980). Although there are no systematic data specifying which variants of psychopathology are most prevalent among psychologists and other mental health professionals—a fact suggesting that we may be no different in this regard than comparable professional groups—those who wish to update their acquaintance with the nature of mental disorders in general may wish to review any number of good abnormal psychology or clinical psychiatry texts (e.g., Cameron & Rychlak, 1985; Coleman, Butcher, & Carson, 1984; Davison & Neale, 1982; Millon, 1981).

Although empirical data with regard to the etiology of disorders among psychologists are no more available than are those relating to prevalence and distribution, it appeared to us to be substantially more useful to the reader were we to focus on the sources (e.g., failed expectations, role conflicts) that may be somewhat unique to the profession of psychology and to those who follow careers within it. Given these sources of stress and disappointment, psychologists are likely to react no differently from others, that is, to cope with them in a manner consonant with their premorbid personality dispositions (Millon, 1981). For some, these adaptations are constructive and healthful; for others, they are disordered emotionally or mentally.

We intend to follow a career-development sequence in this review, beginning with graduate school training and progressing through the mid-life period, stopping on the way to offer impressionistic assessments of those sources that initiate and aggravate the stressors of psychological work.

THE HARDSHIPS OF GRADUATE SCHOOL

Anointed as one of the chosen to gain entrance to graduate school, each new student brings with him or her past vulnerabilities and the proclivities of a distinctive type of personality. Somewhere between graduate school matriculation and the dissertation defense, a shaping process occurs. Carving a professional status to fit within the framework of established personality dispositions involves adaptations and changes in one's psychic self. For many, achieving either academic or clinical competence—the hallmarks of a burnished professional—is gained only after considerable expenditure and emotional sacrifice. The outlay can be a most taxing one, ranging from the tangible and concrete to the more ethereal and abstract.

Students must contend with many ambivalent messages on the way through the academic maze. Trained to think of themselves as "la crème de la crème," they are carefully selected to participate in a distinguished profession on the basis of their competencies and past accomplishments; ultimately, this career choice should lead them to financial security, social status, and a life of useful work and comfort. Despite the recognition they gain for their promising potentials, the experience of graduate school proves to be a curious paradox in that it is in large measure an infantilizing experience. Students are implicitly required to subjugate their own views to those of their faculty and supervisors. Despite protestations to the contrary, rare is the doctoral program that encourages independent thought. As a consequence, an unhealthy conformity is fostered that is at variance with the growth of self-esteem and the autonomy of a future professional. Students have moved up the academic ladder only to be treated as novices again.

The fledgling student stands at the edge of a burgeoning field and is often intimidated by the enormous task that lies ahead (Chessick, 1971). Many and varied demands must be met, and the feverish pace required often results not only in a lack of academic synthesis, but also in a lack of self-confidence

(Wallerstein, 1981). This doubting of one's competence is enhanced by the "soft" nature of the science. In contrast to other professions, the empirical facts of psychology are fuzzy at best, and there are few clear indices of the efficacy of clinical work.

It is not only the day-to-day coordinating of diverse courses, such as psychotherapy, statistics, assessment, and research design, that tests the limits of intellectual coherence but also the ever-present evaluation of professional adequacy that tinges the graduate school experience with unrelenting anxiety. All too often the only reinforcement for successfully crossing one academic hurdle is the "privilege" of moving on to face another (Kubie, 1971). It is not only the quantity and diversity of the workload that create stress, but also the repetitive and endless steps that compose the academic ladder.

Not to be overlooked as a stressor is the financial struggle so common to graduate school life. Pressure to hold down outside jobs invariably takes its toll on academic effort and energy via late hours and lost sleep. For some, it instills the habit of being a jack-of-all-trades as a prerequisite for becoming a professional—one of many conflicting signposts marking the way through graduate school. No less contradictory is the fact that the acquisition of knowledge on matters such as family systems, interpersonal development, and self-actualization contrasts with a daily existence characterized by delayed family life, frequent social isolation, and a hyperconformity to the values of academic supervisors.

Self-doubt often peaks for the clinical graduate student with the introduction of therapeutic responsibilities. Confidence as a developing professional usually lags far behind actual competence in clinical work (Ungerleider, 1965). Interaction with patients is often processed as a "performance" of a regimented technique or as a "flying by the seat of one's pants" activity. Little may get internalized, and an early sense that one has successfully pulled it off may quickly fade, to be replaced by a gnawing awareness that clinical work is not an academic game but a matter deserving deep human concern. This worrisome realization adds to the student clinician's feeling of self-doubt and mortification. To ensure a measure of security in the therapeutic role, the student is likely to acquire a collection of pat techniques and strategies (Schlict, 1968). The student's attempt to dilute his or her vulnerabilities as a therapist may lead him or her to distance further from the personal qualities and affective content of clinical work.

To many people, the prospect of uncovering one's own psychic dynamics, fallibilities, and idiosyncracies is a frightening process. Introspection and self-disclosure can be particularly troublesome because of the quandaries they set up (Greenson, 1966). Psychology graduate students receive contradictory messages that present seemingly unresolvable dilemmas. On one hand, the young clinician is asked to expose his or her frailties as a step toward greater self-understanding and patient sensitivity (Wheelis, 1966). On the other hand, "deviant" ideas and open emotional displays rarely fare well in academic settings. The best course for many is to flatten one's individuality, especially emotionality. Others become cynical and learn to "play the system":

> The survival techniques the therapist often acquires, with a kind of
> cynicism, in the institutional scene, are many. Not the least of these are
> the "tricks of the trade" he learns. . . . He carefully avoids risking such

labels as "acting out" or "impulse ridden" being tacked on to him. He notices that it is wiser and more prudent to appear perhaps even a little dull, to appear compulsive, conformist, controlled and safe. (Freudenberger & Robbins, 1979, pp. 278–279)

There are other graduate school experiences that promote anxiety and conflict. Psychology students are more likely to be sensitive to human relations than are their natural science, law, or medical school peers (Book, 1973). Competition and schisms among students and faculty disturb illusions of an idyllic life-style, especially when relationships are temporary and good performance criteria are as nebulous as they are in psychology. Furthermore, whatever impulse toward individuality may exist is often stopped cold, because good standing within a department is gauged by obedience and intellectual conformity. Should one express more than one's share of unconventional thought or challenge a cherished faculty viewpoint, one may be the object of rebuttals, not only by faculty but also by fellow students who adopt the prevailing academic fashion.

Deviating too far from the dominant belief system often results in both professional and personal abandonment while inviting troublesome obstacles that may place one's career in jeopardy. Rarely are such threats expressed directly, but their subtle signs and inexorable consequences are well known. Although faculty ostensibly favor open and unreserved expression, students fare best when they follow the mainstream. It is indeed ironic that a science oriented largely to the study of individual differences has so little tolerance of them. Moreover, although doctoral pursuits are supposed to encourage a quest for new knowledge, creative explorations are often restricted to the seeds of well-sown crops.

Furthermore, few students escape unscathed the ever-present threat and the fear of dismissal. Such fears can adversely affect a student's intellectual courage and innovative thinking, and they can foster a defensive and protective posture whereby a student may close off affect, interpersonal intimacy, and therapeutic sensitivity. Emerging from the bewildering graduate school boot camp, the fledgling professional can receive a hard-earned reward: entry into an internship, postdoctoral training, or the job market. Unfortunately these places are noted for their propensity to perpetuate the stressors of the preceding four or five years.

THE TRAVAILS OF AN ACADEMIC PROFESSION

Being a professor of psychology places one in an ambiguous position in academia, a position best illustrated by the perennial difficulties that many university faculties face when seeking an answer to the question of whether psychology is a social science, a life science, a behavioral science, or something else (Clagett, 1980; Pankin, 1973). Broad in scope, diverse in its relations with other disciplines, and located on the shifting sands between the highly regarded, fully legitimized, and technologically secure physical sciences, on the one hand, and the equally respected, traditional, and scholarly erudition of the humanities, on the other, the field of psychology and its professors must contend not only with an uncertain self-image but also with deep and intrinsic ambivalences (Abram, 1970; Bess, 1973). Whatever direction they turn, be it toward the scientism and precision of the physicist and chemist or the artistry and analyses of the historian and philosopher, psychology faculty come face to face with an invidious comparison.

Recognizing the firmer grounds upon which other disciplines rest can lead, at some level, to a sense of inferiority and self-contempt on the part of academic psychologists—be they experimentally oriented colleagues who look to the rigorous technology of the natural sciences as their reference point, or the more subjectively oriented clinicians who look to the reflective probings of those in the humanities as their standard. Whether or not this self-denigration is admitted publicly, there is often an inexorable decline in self-esteem attributable, in part at least, to the impact of being a member of an irresolute and enigmatic discipline that seems incapable of fulfilling the ambivalent standards of a "true" branch of science (Light, 1974).

Adding to these vexations are the perceived aspersions of colleagues from other academic disciplines. Because psychologists are sensitive to their own subjectively judged shortcomings, they may assume that their nonpsychologist colleagues derogate them for their shortcomings. This appraisal may be correct, but for other reasons as well (Hartnett & Centra, 1974). Although much faculty lunchroom banter may be characterized as jocular attacks on psychology's deficits, such attacks are likely to spring defensively from the ever-present suspicion experienced by "outsiders" that psychologists are intruders into people's private lives—that they invade spheres of thought and emotion that are best guarded and kept unexposed. It matters little whether one is a psychophysiologist, comparative animal researcher, or clinician; all are yoked together as potential encroachers and transgressors, unwelcome meddlers in the personal world of others. Such derogation from those outside the discipline probably comes from their feeling threatened by the psychologist's explicitly stated intent to know the sources of human behavior and thought, as well as from their mistrust of the inaccessible and arcane methods that psychologists employ to uncover these sources.

Psychology lays claim to specialized and esoteric procedures by which it ascertains matters of which others have no direct knowledge. Would this not incur the discomfort and ultimate disfavor, even ridicule, of colleagues outside the discipline? Moreover, psychologists are assigned voyeuristic motives and revelatory powers far beyond their due. It is no wonder, then, that psychology and psychologists are admired and envied but also feared and condemned in academia. Thus, in addition to coping with their own ambivalences about who they are and where they belong, psychologists must deal also with the ambivalences that nonpsychology colleagues experience toward them. Are they the all-powerful and all-knowing seers, as feared by others, or are they fraudulent quasi-scientists who deserve disdain and condemnation?

To cope with feelings of diminished self-esteem or status, many psychologists engage in internecine struggles. One classic example is that of experimental psychologists versus clinical psychologists. Typically, one of the factions identifies with the aggressor (nonpsychologist academics) and attacks the other faction. In some instances, each faction harms the other; in other instances, there is a clear victor, who smugly claims to be the sole purveyor of the department's philosophy. Regardless of who wins, invidious intradepartmental rivalries injure the department as a whole, in no small part because they provide further justification for outsiders' distrust of the psychological enterprise.

Whether or not one agrees with the aims and methods of one's discipline, it is difficult if not impossible for most established academics to give up their university careers; there is too much at stake, there are few alternatives from which to choose, and, frankly, there is not much to lose by staying. Despite intense disillusionment, many professors, having achieved tenure and having allowed the youthful striving for excellence and recognition to wane, simply retire to a sinecure, increasingly indifferent to academic matters and apathetic toward formerly valued goals (Sawyer, 1981). Once bright and promising PhDs may permit ordinariness to take hold, finding refuge in the routines of uninspired teaching and research, activities that once were challenging but are now devoid not only of enthusiasm and creativity but also of simple attention and responsibility (Furniss, 1981). As a result of the ambiguous standards by which teaching and research are gauged, it becomes possible for the demoralized, tenured professor to plod along performing services with few negative consequences (Volgyes, 1982). The murky modus operandi of academic life tolerates diversity and enables the disheartened academic to function within acceptable boundaries. The shoddiness with which he or she discharges responsibilities reflects a deep sense of personal failure and disillusionment.

As noted previously, professors were once the most promising of the young, upwardly mobile PhDs. Academic deficits are not necessarily the cause of failure to maintain one's promise, nor are disillusionment and internecine problems. Early successes may have set up unrealistic aspirations, such as a desire to be omnipotent or omniscient. Moreover, whatever one's potential or yearnings may have been, circumstances may not have produced a setting or a timing in which the aspirant's talents could find a niche. Inability to measure up to potential may lead not only to disappointment and shame but also a rejection of that which was once yearned for, particularly for many of the most able. Failure to meet unrealistic expectations can cause one to be cynical about formerly cherished ideals and to be specifically critical toward one's more fortunate peers. Seeking to deviate as far as possible from conventional professorial norms, demoralized academics not only renounce past values and standards but may seek to undo them. Hence, rather than live with only partial successes, they press matters toward the end of total failure. Unable to succeed well, they aim not only to fail badly but to draw others down with them as well.

THE VICISSITUDES OF A CLINICAL/COUNSELING CAREER

Two occupational routes are open to those with clinical/counseling PhDs: affiliation with a public institution and independent or shared private practice. The former route is most common in the early years, gradually overlaps with the latter over time, and is increasingly replaced by private work. During the transitional years, fledgling clinicians acquire the methods and skills of developing and maintaining reliable referral sources. In addition, although serendipity plays a large role in a psychologist's success, it is also necessary for a psychologist to engage in a broad range of professional activities—for example, to join county and state psychological associations, to display a willingness to serve on relevant professional boards and committees, to regularly attend local workshops, to develop one or two areas of special expertise, to present a few papers or workshops, and to provide supervision (usually gratis) to clinical practicum students at nearby universities. In effect, it is necessary for a psychologist to build a reputation as a mature, responsible, and competent professional who deserves a respected and growing practice.

Success and recognition breed more of the same, and with them come materialistic gains. In time the practitioner achieves what he or she has set out to achieve: a respected position in a useful profession and an enviable standard of living. Soon the boundaries of practice begin to stretch and encroach on other activities. It is the unusual clinician who can put the brakes on opportunities for successful expansion—more patients, a few additional evenings a week, a prestigious consultantship or two, just this additional course to teach, and so on (Wallerstein, 1981). Before long the business of building a successful practice has taken over, consuming leisure time and activities (Wheelis, 1966). Gratifying and lucrative as these developments may be to one's self-esteem and pocketbook, they constitute the basis for an "ironic paradox," as Freudenberger and Robbins (1979) have put it:

> Many of the patients seem to live more fully than the therapist . . . as their therapy moves along they seem to be more a part of life than the therapist. The therapist's controlled, objective, professional stance seems to mold all his relationships. . . . the therapist becomes trapped into the position of listening to the sounds of others. Ironically, he may be listening too intensely to be able to hear or follow his own personal drumbeat. Somewhere along this busy path of professionalism, a personal self tends to become lost. (p. 281)

As time proceeds, the fabric that intertwined the drive for personal and material success with humanistic and caring impulses begins to unravel. Slowly but inexorably, the prerequisites of financial comfort and professional recognition eclipse the caring impulses, changing both the hue and texture that had characterized the early fabric (Chessick, 1971). Drawing upon rationalizations heard from more established clinicians, the now mature clinician begins to advise patients of lesser interest or economic means to join affordable therapeutic groups or to seek treatment at publicly supported agencies.

This drift from more humane sensibilities is not limited to clinicians in the private sector. It occurs for quite different reasons among those in the public domain. Institutional rules and restrictions, excessive workloads, and organizational politics add to the despair of treating recalcitrant or otherwise unsatisfying patients (Pines & Maslach, 1978). Such settings transform formerly creative and socially committed clinicians into petty and robotic bureaucrats (Rogow, 1970). With empathy drained and treatment success low, clinicians treat patients in an increasingly routine or detached way and refer to them with diagnostic labels rather than with care and understanding.

Although this variant of dehumanization evolves in distinctive ways in private and public settings, it is a form of demoralization in both. A common negative experience shared among clinicians is the low frequency of significant improvement among patients. Many clinicians have a strong need to rescue, which is not readily fulfilled, if for no reason other than the length of time it takes before real results are seen (Maslach, 1978; Menninger, 1984). In addition, the signs of therapeutic progress are varied and difficult to discern. Tolerating the ambiguities of progress and the sporadic successes of one's patients is one of the most problematic and disheartening aspects of long-term clinical work. As Maslach (1978) has noted:

> This is especially true when the same client keeps coming back with the same (or similar) problems. Staff people often feel that their successes go away but their failures keep coming back to haunt them and provide constant visible proof that they are incompetent or make mistakes. To ward off these feelings of failure and ineffectiveness, staff may shift the blame for lack of positive change from themselves to the clients and view them as inherently defective, unmotivated, bad, or weak. (p. 116)

The recognition that often patients cannot reshape the course of their lives, even with expert therapy, becomes increasingly painful. Perhaps even more distressing is the recognition that despite extensive knowledge, experience, and commitment, therapists themselves are largely powerless to effect change. As a consequence, clinicians may face the possibility that their life's work is for naught, that their methods are weak, and that other factors in their patients' lives are more powerful and relevant to treatment outcome.

Worthy of note is a source of stress experienced especially by independent practitioners as a result of the autonomy and social isolation characteristic of their practice. Without secretary or receptionist for the most part, the solo practitioner's day is devoted to an intense world of symbols and tangential meanings shared in a secluded setting. This contrasts considerably with the activities of academic psychologists, whose responsibilities place them in a goldfish bowl. Not only are their successes and failures visible to all, but reality-based correctives are often explicit and direct. The private and hermetic transactions of solo clinicians not only deprive them of opportunities for obtaining affirmation, but they also fail to provide safeguards against personal, if not idiosyncratic and autistic, reveries. Daily and repetitive immersion in an isolated world of metacommunications engenders more than a sense of loneliness (Forney, Wallace-Schutzman, & Wiggers, 1982). Standing in a symbolic "as-if" relationship to patients, dealing with the allusions and metaphors of transference and countertransference, the autonomous clinician spends his or her time in an experience that is unreal and may seem increasingly inauthentic. Beyond its seeming insubstantiality, the therapist–patient relationship may assume a ritualized quality.

ADVERSITIES ON THE INDUSTRIAL/ORGANIZATIONAL PATH

Few graduate students initiate their educational careers with the industrial/ organizational (I/O) route in mind; nor do graduate schools, with mentors who are predominantly clinical and academic, offer a setting or role models to legitimize the status of a consulting or business career. Psychologists who venture beyond the pale of an academic or clinical locale for their work usually stay within the wide boundaries of either education or medicine-related activities. Only those whose business career goals were clearly in mind beforehand or who fortuitously attended departments with strong I/O mentors were likely to view the commercial world as a possible, no less acceptable or prestigious, career line.

These less than welcome origins presage a comparably troublesome future for many. The business route is one that often leaves the psychologist with a sense of being an outsider, not only among fellow psychologists, but among business peers as well; it is a dislocating reality and tenuous status that continues for many throughout their careers. Being accepted neither by one's psychology nor business colleagues, being defined as neither fish nor fowl, struggling to integrate opposing values and goals, all challenge one's coherence and identity, as well as setting in motion a persistent undercurrent of doubting one's self and career (House & Rizzo, 1971).

Regardless of his or her specialization, the young psychologist has been imbued with a sense of ethics, personal integrity, humanistic goals, and an appreciation for scientific evidence—values that are reinforced regularly by professional licensing boards and continuing education requirements. Although they are not necessarily in contrast, the roles of the I/O psychologist must fit within the framework and goals of a business enterprise, and hence, require one to employ the methods and to support the objectives of the commercial world. The upshot is a dual identity and dual loyalties, which need not lead inevitably to internal conflicts, but which are stressful in that they require integrative solutions that are not readily achieved. It is the persistence of this bifurcation of self that may cumulate to the point of psychic disorder (Gardner & Hall, 1981). The following few paragraphs briefly describe the struggle to maintain one's psychic coherence while functioning as a psychologist in the business and industrial world.

Psychologists are taught to approach human problems from the perspective of the individual, that is, to value and foster the aims of personal growth and self-realization (French & Caplan, 1973). In commerce and industry, however, it is the organization that counts. To those in business what matters is how the individual contributes to the welfare and productivity of the organization, not whether the individuals within the organization are fulfilling their personal goals. How comfortably can the psychologist deal with dual loyalties when a mismatch occurs between the needs of individuals and those of the organization? Employed by a company and being responsible for adhering to its methods and aims, the I/O psychologist must give primacy to the organization. The price one pays with each decision of this nature is to deny a part of self, to become less sensitive to the values of individuality. If one presses the needs of individuals, especially those in psychological distress, one can go just so far before sacrificing one's overall credibility within the organization. An inner dissonance may be inescapable, regardless of one's choice.

Confidentiality is another two-way street composed of conflicting roles and loyalties. Staff or consulting psychologists often possess more information of a private, if not secretive, nature than anyone else in the organization. By virtue of the willingness of both managers and employees to confide in them, psychologists must not only be scrupulous about confidentiality, but must also maintain a perspective on a number of ethical, personal, and organizational considerations (Schein, 1969). Here, again, in this major consulting role, the psychologist faces the stress of divided loyalties.

No less troublesome are misgivings about the explicit nature with which the profit motive guides business activities. It is not that money is a dirty word, but when one's work arena ostensibly values money over people, it becomes difficult to see one's self as not having "sold out." Harboring ambivalent feelings about the juxtaposition of profit and humanistic motives simply will not do in the business world. To survive one must put aside such ambivalences and act wholeheartedly to foster profitability. The assumption that business and humanistic goals are antagonistic may be all too simplistic, if not erroneous, but it does remain a sticking point owing to its occasional validity. And for those troubled by this view, it can only undermine what sense of high purpose many gain by virtue of their professional activities.

Other business activities also undermine one's identity. For example, in the case of the psychologist-scientist, careful methodologies, research designs, and statistical analyses are central to the training of doctoral-level psychologists, whatever their speciality may be. They have learned to draw conclusions only after a thorough evaluation of systematically obtained data. Those in the business world employ different standards. Here, evidence can be limited or ambiguous; decisions are often made quickly; subjective feelings of what seems likely to work determine action as much, if not more than objectively obtained or quantitative data. Recognizing the changing and probabilistic nature of unfolding events, the business person will take risks to seize opportunities rather than await the gathering of precise evidence favoring one course or another. Hence, here again the I/O psychologist will ride the horns of another dilemma of divided loyalty. Does one join in making "crystal ball" decisions, or does one insist on the tenets of scientific objectivity and quantitative precision?

The schisms of dual loyalties and bifurcated identities are problematic enough, but there are stressors that go beyond those which undermine one's psychic coherence (Adams, 1980; Cooper & Payne, 1978). For example, no matter how committed one may be to the goals of the business enterprise, psychologists qua psychologists inevitably remain outsiders—peripheral, if not suspect figures within the environs of commercial life. It is rare that psychologists are part of an inner circle of decision makers; they are sought for expert opinions or for different perspectives. Finding that one's talents and advice on how best to achieve a particular goal takes second place to considerations of money, space, and human resources is a troubling reality. And to complicate this feeling of being peripheral, it is rare, except in very large corporations, to find even one other professional psychologist in the organization with whom one can join forces or commisserate. And adding to the discomforts of being peripheral and isolated as a spokesperson for humanistic matters, there is often little faith that psychology has a legitimate or worthwhile contribution to make. Many in business doubt that psychological know-how "pays off," that is, enhances the organization's profit margin (Hall, 1976). Questioned repeatedly as to one's worth to the company's goals, hearing one's best contributions given secondary consideration, and lacking the colleagueship of like-minded peers can only add to an increasing sense of personal doubt, job insecurity, and problematic behaviors.

Indifference and devaluation in the business world are troublesome enough, but to these must be added the belief of many that psychologists are foreign intruders in the commercial domain, voyeuristic investigators who question its values and expose their "baser" motives (O'Toole, 1980). Even more than academic psychologists, who feel unsure of their acceptance in the larger university context, I/O psychologists and consultants find themselves even further afield, evoking among their peers a mixture of fear and suspicion. Feeling isolated and demoralized is not an unlikely consequence of conditions such as these.

THE DISILLUSIONMENT OF MID-CAREER

Whether choosing a clinical, industrial, or academic career, psychologists reach a point when their early idealism and aspirations wane. This period is often a continuation of earlier developmental trends rather than a change of life-style or a reward for having made it. Difficulties in one's early career may have been written off as having paid one's dues to gain passage to the good life, but mid-life disappointments are not so easily dismissed. The topic of mid-life crises has become popular, but, interestingly, psychologists have been inclined to see themselves as immune to this "disease." Despite this assumption, psychologists, especially therapists, appear to be among the professionals who suffer from this ailment most frequently and feel its manifestations strongly (Peters, 1980; Pines, Aronson, & Kafrey, 1981).

Psychologists cultivate, as their distinctive professional skill, an ability to gain insight into human behavior. This heightened understanding of mental processes, the prize that motivates many to seek a psychological career, may be the very ingredient that accounts for the depth of psychologists' mid-life problems. Insight is accompanied by attention focused on interior processes, and this internal focus invites the risk of narcissistic preoccupations as well as reduced empathy and a pervasive difficulty in tuning into social matters. To complicate life further, this growing self-examination is likely to focus on short-comings, and these, in turn, are likely to lead to an anxious egocentricity that, in turn, may further constrict one's problem-solving skills.

Many psychologists abandon all creative or high-risk activities, seeking in their stead to find simple and routine solutions that may have worked to resolve similar preoccupations in the past. Although they may maintain job efficiency, both academics and clinicians may begin to feel incapable of breaking this vicious circle, withdrawing more into themselves and losing touch increasingly with external events (Potter, 1980). As noted previously, some may acquire a self-protective dehumanizing attitude toward patients and students. In this objectivizing process, other people are viewed as if they were devoid of their distinctive human qualities. Sustained for extended periods, these attitudes may lead the individual to withdraw from all personally demanding interactions and to turn further inward to obsessive internal explorations (Ables & Brandsma, 1977).

Among clinicians, this detachment may manifest itself through avoiding patients, experiencing a variety of ill-defined ailments, using drugs or alcohol, and growing indifferent to social and work-related responsibilities. Psychologists who are disillusioned or detached may eventually be judged to be incompetent and may feel that they no longer fit in socially (Milburn, 1981). Depending on personality style, demoralized psychologists may express feelings of hopelessness, vent anger in a caustic manner, or adopt a robot-like demeanor.

This demoralization may leave the person ill equipped to cope with the routines of everyday life (Hodgkinson, 1974). The psychic overload may be aggravated by feelings of powerlessness and frustration. The individual may experience job-related anxieties associated with decreased performance adequacy and the dismay of losing control of and a sense of purpose in life (Ripley & Dorpat, 1981). This existential crisis is often moderated by defensive apathy accompanied by significant and erratic changes in activity—a robotic compulsivity one time, physical lethargy another, peculiar sleep–wake cycles, and so on.

Detached from students, patients, or colleagues, the psychologist in the mid-life period may become absorbed by pervasive egocentric preoccupations. Colleagues, once seen as a reliable source of reinforcement, are avoided lest they become reminders of the psychologist's failures and self-disdain. Self-preoccupations are no doubt carried home, and the individual may shun family and friends (Ables & Brandsma, 1977; Peters, 1980; Wallerstein, 1981). It is at this point of increasing demoralization and alienation that more severe levels of psychopathology may become evident. Depression, guilt, sexual acting out, substance abuse, psychosis, and suicide may be end-point manifestations of this downward trend.

Watkins (1983) grouped the consequences of mid-life traumas into four categories: cognitive, affective, behavioral, and physical. Cognitive symptomatology is expressed in rigid thought, detachment, defensiveness, and pessimism. Affectively, the individual experiences conflicting and disturbing emotions such as guilt, helplessness, hopelessness, and depression. Behavioral symptoms range from compulsivity to lethargy and may include alcohol and drug abuse. Finally, physical manifestations, although highly variable, tend to be the outcome of prolonged anxiety, arousal, and, ultimately, exhaustion. These physical signs often lead to an increased susceptibility to viral and bacterial maladies, accident proneness, and symptoms secondary to substance abuse. As these consequences wax and wane, they may pave the way for more severe outcomes. Perhaps one of the most well-known statistics in our time is the finding that psychologists and psychiatrists commit suicide at a rate five to six times greater than the general population (Farber, 1983). Suicide and other serious end-point outcomes (i.e., severe mental disorders) seem to be especially prevalent among mental health professionals.

Demoralized psychologists in mid life have little faith in their own profession, a life raft to which they could cling that might rescue them from the turbulent seas around them. Alienated psychologists are truly in despair, for many believe they know better than to invest their faith in psychotherapy as a healing art. Indeed, it is the very understanding of the complexities of human behavior that leads them to judge the situation as hopeless. Devoid of hope, many may sink into either a psychosis or suicidal action. Although many aging academics and clinicians sidestep all of these dilemmas, other psychologists—

more than we know—settle for a life of apathy, constriction, and quiet frustration. This "suicide of the spirit" is in most cases the most painful end that can befall the professional.

SOME REFLECTIONS ON THERAPY

Therapeutic work relates to the amelioration of emotional discomfort. Regardless of one's theoretical orientation, diagnostic methodology, or therapeutic technique, the treatment process seeks to neutralize psychic pain. Despite decades of thought and research, however, there is a surprising dearth of knowledge regarding effective solutions to unhappiness and discontent among professionals. A review of the literature unearths little pertinent information regarding practices that can be used to help the discontented practitioner. There is a great quantity of speculative literature, most of which derives from a humanistic orientation and is almost entirely addressed to the burnout phenomenon. Burnout, or whatever label one wishes to use, is not a new syndrome—only the formal designation of the experience is new. This fact leads to a dismaying and curious awareness—that those in the psychological profession require a "disease" label prior to admitting personal and professional fallibility.

With few exceptions, most recommendations for treating distressed professionals are oriented toward organizational issues first and toward the individual only secondarily. The terminology of most articles addresses the "agency" or "clinic" and the "worker's" inherent difficulties within these settings. The problems of organizations are recognized via indices such as job turnover, and difficulties are seen as amenable to administrative policy and structural changes. In contrast, difficulties encountered by the individual practitioner appear to be known only to that individual, and changes necessary to enhance her or his life result solely from the practitioner's own efforts. Once the disturbed professional has recognized that help is needed, locating a source of help is difficult. Unfortunately, channels for help-oriented consultation with colleagues rarely are open, and those in need are not disposed to expose their vulnerabilities.

Reticence is the biggest roadblock to the professional's pursuit of therapy. Psychologists may hold to an even greater extent than do lay people negative attitudes toward therapy. Although mental health professionals stress the importance of providing services to all persons in need, psychologists and psychiatrists alike tend to exclude one group—their own colleagues. Because of the great emphasis on self-reliance and professional autonomy, there exists an unspoken expectation that healers should need no healing. This tacit standard is reinforced by a parallel and equally unrealistic expectation on the part of patients. Viewing themselves and being viewed by others as paragons of mental health prevent needy psychologists from admitting weakness and seeking help.

Practitioners in psychology are generally ill prepared to offer help to one another. Boice (1982) noted the "inherent awkwardness in a situation where peers admit to weakness" (p. 240). The hesitancy to treat another therapist may also stem from an unwillingness to test one's competence before a fellow professional as well as from a more general skepticism concerning the efficacy of therapy.

Another stumbling block to treating the treater has been the lack of guidelines. Fortunately, progress is being made in identifying problems and in establishing procedures and rationales. Formal therapeutic groups appear to be a promising beginning, but they typically have been implemented casually or have been geared primarily to organizational problems rather than to personal difficulties (Pines, Aronson, & Kafry, 1981; Pines & Maslach, 1979). Groups serve many functions, from discussions of work-related ideals and objectives to the ventilation of personal difficulties and fears. Freudenberger and Robbins (1979) spoke of the roles and values the peer relationship can serve, such as (a) examining the areas an individual practitioner may take for granted or feel overly confident about, (b) providing an emotional checkpoint that can have a stabilizing effect, and (c) providing a "safe" setting in which to validate and gauge countertransference issues.

Research indicates that effective support systems at work settings reduce the incidence of burnout (Pines & Maslach, 1978). However, these studies relate to the alleviation of problems within organizations, not to difficulties incurred by individual practitioners. Nevertheless, Pines, Aronson, and Kafry (1981) suggest that such groups often achieve several useful functions, notably (a) offering receptive listening, (b) affirming competencies, (c) providing technical information, (d) giving emotional support, (e) achieving psychological insight, and (f) sharing a "social reality."

CONCLUSION

It seems ironic that the profession of psychology has documented the mental health problems of others at length but has only recently begun to examine their prevalence and character among its own practitioners and academics. These emotional and mental difficulties should be approached both preventively and therapeutically. Early professional training should include a realistic assessment of professional expectations, and safety valves should be provided for the unsuspecting novice. Freudenberger and Robbins (1979) have noted the importance of private time and nonprofessional activities, as well as "the unstinted sharing of professional ideas and goals with colleagues." Nonprofessional vacations and sabbaticals are also thought to promote health. The formation of therapy groups for therapists seems a natural way to help the troubled professional. Indeed, most psychologists find that many of their everyday confidants are in mental health fields, because mental health professionals speak the same language—affectively and intellectually. Furthermore, those professionals encounter similar life difficulties because they have similar careers—and perhaps because they have in common predisposing characteristics that drew them initially to their fields. As has been learned from the study of psychotherapeutic processes, few gains are made in emotional life without taking risks, and professionals must use that knowledge to help themselves and colleagues who are in distress.

References

Ables, B. S., & Brandsma, J. M. (1977). *Therapy for couples.* San Francisco: Jossey-Bass.

Abram, M. B. (1970). Reflections on the university in the new revolution. *Daedalus, 99,* 122–140.

Adams, J. (1980). *Understanding and managing stress: A book of readings.* San Diego: University Associates.

Bess, J. L. (1973). Patterns of satisfaction of organizational prerequisites and personal needs in university academic departments. *Sociology of Education, 46,* 99–144.

Boice, R. (1982). Counseling colleagues. *Personnel and Guidance Journal, 60,* 240–242.

Book, H. (1973). On maybe becoming a psychotherapist, perhaps. *Canadian Psychiatric Association Journal, 18,* 487–493.

Cameron, N., & Rychlak, J. F. (1985). *Personality development and psychopathology* (2nd ed.). Boston: Houghton Mifflin.

Chessick, R. D. (1971). How the residents and the supervisor disappoint each other. *American Journal of Psychotherapy, 25,* 272–283.

Clagett, C. A. (1980). *Teacher stress at a community college: Professional burnout in a bureaucratic setting.* Largo, MD: Prince Georges Community College, Office of Institutional Research.

Coleman, J. C., Butcher, J. N., & Carson, R. C. (1984). *Abnormal psychology and modern life* (7th ed.). Glenview, IL: Scott, Foresman.

Cooper, C. L., & Payne, R. (Eds.) (1978). *Stress at work.* New York: Wiley.

Davison, G. C., & Neale, J. M. (1982). *Abnormal psychology* (3rd ed.). New York: Wiley.

Farber, B. A. (Ed.). (1983). *Stress and burnout in the human service profession.* New York: Pergamon Press.

Farber, B. A., & Heifetz, L. J. (1981). The satisfactions and stresses of psychotherapeutic work: A factor analytic study. *Professional Psychology, 12,* 721–730.

Forney, D. S., Wallace-Schutzman, F., & Wiggers, T. T. (1982). Burnout among career development professionals: Preliminary findings and implications. *Personnel and Guidance Journal, 60,* 435–439.

French, J. R. P., & Caplan, R. (1973). Organizational stress and individual strain. In A. J. Morrow (Ed.), *The failure of success.* New York: AMACOM.

Freudenberger, H. J., & Robbins, A. (1979). The hazards of being a psychoanalyst. *Psychoanalytic Review, 66,* 275–296.

Furniss, W. T. (1981). Reshaping faculty careers. *Change, 13,* 38–57.

Gardner, E., & Hall, R. (1981). The professional stress syndrome. *Psychosomatics, 22,* 672–680.

Greenson, R. (1966). That "impossible" profession. *Journal of American Psychoanalytic Association, 14,* 9–27.

Hall, D. (1976). *Careers in organizations.* Pacific Palisades, CA: Goodyear.

Hartnett, R. T., & Centra, J. A. (1974). Faculty views of the academic environment: Situational vs. institutional perspectives. *Sociology of Education, 47,* 159–168.

Hodgkinson, H. L. (1974). Adult development: Implications for faculty and administrators. *Educational Record, 55,* 263–274.

House, R., & Rizzo, J. (1971). Role conflict and role ambiguity as critical variables in a model of organizational behavior. *Organizational Behavior and Human Performance, 7,* 467–505.

Kubie, L. B. (1971). The retreat from patients. *Archives of General Psychiatry, 24,* 98–106.

Leighton, D. C., Harding, J. S., Macklin, D. B., MacMillan, A. M., & Leighton, A. H. (1963). *The character of danger.* New York: Basic Books.

Light, D. W., Jr. (1974). The structure of the academic professions. *Sociology of Education, 47,* 2–28.

Maslach, C. (1978). The client role in staff burnout. *Journal of Social Issues, 34,* 111–124.

Menninger, W. W. (1984). Dealing with staff reactions to perceived lack of progress by chronic mental patients. *Hospital and Community Psychiatry, 35,* 805–808.

Milburn, B. M. (1981). Burnout. *Personnel and Guidance Journal, 59,* 484.

Millon, T. (1981). *Disorders of personality: DSM-III, Axis II.* New York: Wiley.

Murphy, G. E. (1977). Suicide and attempted suicide. *Hospital Practice, 18,* 73–81.

Murphy, G. E., & Wetzel, R. D. (1980). Suicide risk by birth cohort in the United States, 1949 to 1974. *Archives of General Psychiatry, 37,* 519–523.

O'Toole, P. (1980). The menace of the corporate shrink. *Savvy.*

Pankin, R. (1973). Structural factors in academic mobility. *Journal of Higher Education, 44,* 95–101.

Peters, D. S. (1980). Why professors leave: Stress in the organization. *Professional Educator, 3,* 6–7.

Pines, A., Aronson, E., & Kafry, D. (1981). *Burnout: From tedium to personal growth.* New York: The Free Press.

Pines, A. M., & Maslach, C. (1978). Characteristics of staff burnout in mental health settings. *Hospital and Community Psychiatry, 29,* 233–237.

Potter, B. A. (1980). *Beating job burnout.* San Francisco: Harbor Publishing.

Ripley, H. S., & Dorpat, T. L. (1981). Life change and suicidal behavior. *Psychiatric Annals, 11,* 32–47.

Rogow, A. (1970). *The psychiatrists.* New York: Putnam.

Rosenstein, M. J., & Milazzo-Sayre, L. J. (1981). *Characteristics of admissions to selected mental-health facilities: 1975.* Rockville, MD: U.S. Dept. of Health and Human Services.

Sawyer, D. O. (1981). Institutional stratification and career mobility in academic markets. *Sociology of Education, 54,* 85–97.

Schein, E. J. (1969). *Process consultation: Its role in organization development.* Reading, MA: Addison-Wesley.

Schlict, W. J. (1968). The anxieties of the psychotherapist. *Mental Hygiene, 52,* 439–444.

Srole, L., Langner, T. S., Michael, S. T., Kirkpatrick, P., Opler, M. K., & Rennie, T. A. (1978). *Mental health in the metropolis: The midtown Manhattan study* (rev. ed.). New York: New York University Press.

Ungerleider, J. T. (1965). The most difficult year. *American Journal of Psychiatry, 122,* 542–545.

Volgyes, I. (1982). Is there life after teaching? Reflections of a middle-aged professor. *Change, 14,* 9–11.

Wallerstein, R. S. (1981). The psychoanalyst's life: Expectations, vicissitudes and reflections. *International Review of Psychoanalysis, 8,* 285–298.

Watkins, C. E. (1983). Burnout in counseling practice: Some potential professional and personal hazards of becoming a counselor. *Personnel and Guidance Journal, 61,* 304–308.

Wheelis, A. (1966). *The illusionless man.* New York: Norton.

CHEMICAL ABUSE AMONG PSYCHOLOGISTS: SYMPTOMS, CAUSES, & TREATMENT ISSUES

7

Herbert J. Freudenberger

During the past 10 years mental health professionals have become increasingly concerned about their colleagues who are impaired. These impairments manifest themselves in "physical and mental disability, alcoholism, substance abuse, debilitation through aging, loss of motor skills, and sexual involvement with patients" (Freudenberger, 1984b, p. 175). Mental health professionals might in fact be in a higher risk category than is the general population for having these impairments.

Most of the data that have been gathered in the last 10 years are on physicians and nurses. Medved (1982), for example, evaluated the personal lives of American physicians and arrived at some very startling conclusions. The rate of drug addiction among physicians is approximately 30 to 100 times that of the general population; 47 percent of responding physicians indicated that they were in unhappy marriages and 13 percent reported having sex with their patients. Skoler and Klein (1979) indicated that approximately 100 physicians commit suicide every year and that the alcoholism rate among physicians and attorneys exceeds 10 percent of that population as opposed to 7 percent of the general population.

Pfifferling, Blum, and Wood (1981) suggested "that the incidence of mental illness is higher among practicing physicians than among members of similarly educated groups." Isler (1978) conjectured that there were 40,000 alcoholic nurses in the United States, a figure that has probably increased in the past 7 years. Although most studies of physicians and nurses have not differentiated between chemical dependence and alcoholism, all indicators point to a significant increase in abuse.

Although there is very little in the literature regarding the impairment of psychologists, material does exist regarding the profession's concern with psychotherapists, psychiatrists, and psychoanalysts. In the field of psychology it was not until 1982 that the Board of Professional Affairs of APA voted for the following: "That the Steering Committee on Distressed Psychologists prepare a detailed plan for an action research design for a model of service delivery to distressed psychologists for presentation to BPA by the Fall of 1983" (Nathan, Thoreson, & Kilburg, 1983). This was the first time that psychologists addressed the issue of impaired colleagues in a serious way, and this volume is one of the first outgrowths of that commitment.

SIGNS OF IMPAIRMENT

Signs of impairment among professionals who are potential chemical abusers or alcoholics manifest themselves in many ways. Physical symptoms include headaches, spasms, backaches, gastrointestinal difficulties, constipation, lingering colds, false cardiac problems, hives, unexplained itching, and frequent tiredness or insomnia.

Mental and behavioral signs may manifest themselves in an inability to concentrate or make decisions, mood swings, and feelings of resentment at having to work. An impaired professional may also become easily irritated, argumentative, or angry and make cynical, arrogant, and noncaring remarks to family members, loved ones, or friends that ultimately are translated to patients, students, or clients. Impaired professionals often forget or are late for meetings, are unable to organize their schedules, and seem generally unprepared. Often there is a noticeable deterioration in the impaired person's grooming and attire. They may also exhibit unprofessional behavior such as discussing personal problems or their social life with students or clients, or they may demonstrate difficulties with colleagues or corporate management clients.

An impaired professional's work tends to become more ritualistic and rigid and is guided by the feeling that "my approach, theory, or technique is *the* one that will help people or provide the answers that everyone is looking for." The approaches of other colleagues are perceived as being inferior, and their research is downgraded or perceived as not worthy of reflection or scrutiny. Further indications that chemical or alcohol abuse may be taking place are excessive borrowing from financial institutions, going into debt, and lying.

Having sexual relations with clients or abusing chemicals or drugs is often a sign that an impaired professional is manifesting a feeling of omnipotence. The breeding ground for the shift to chemical abuse is littered with individuals who believed that they would never "get hooked," and certainly could handle the use of drugs without any problems. For a professional, to enter into serious chemical abuse requires a significant break with reality, a distortion of the self-system, a sense of arrogance and omnipotence, as well as poor reality perception.

One of the current definitions of addiction is provided by Jaffe (1984): "A behavioral pattern of compulsive drug use, characterized by an overwhelming involvement with the use of a drug, the securing of its supply and a high tendency to relapse after withdrawal" (p. 8). According to Blum (1984), dependency is "The chronic abuse of drugs. This condition which is common to all types of long-term drug and alcohol abuse, reflects the user's attitude and the intensity of the habit that is the need to seek a particular substance over and over again." The degree of psychological dependence tends to dictate the use or abuse of a substance at a level necessary to maintain an optimal state of well-being.

To ascertain whether a professional is chemically impaired, one needs to determine his or her tolerance to the drug, the degree of physical dependence, and whether the individual is cross-dependent on other drugs. Tolerance suggests that repeated doses of the identical drug have had, over a period of time, a diminishing effect on the individual. Therefore, an individual who has acquired a tolerance requires more of a drug in order to attain those feelings that previously were gained with lesser amounts. Physical dependence is, according to Blum, "a condition in which the body has adjusted to the presence of a drug and when forced to function without the drug reacts with characteristic illness or withdrawal signs" (p. 6).

Cross-dependence refers to the person's physical dependence on other drugs of a particular or related class. For example, an alcoholic who is unable to obtain alcohol may resort to barbiturates or other depressants to gain some degree of a high feeling. Drugs act as behavior reinforcers in that the initial use of a particular drug enables the person to "feel good," "make it through the day or night," "get a high," or "get out of bad feelings."

Although all of the underlying factors that make a particular individual prone or predisposed to abusing a specific chemical are not known, there are some common patterns that can be watched for. For example, many professionals who become chemical abusers initially abused tobacco. Some, over a period of time, may have shifted to marijuana. Those who seek assistance for chemical abuse, are, for the most part, barbiturate, cocaine, and alcohol abusers. Their predilections for the abuse may stem from a combination of psychological, constitutional, biological, genetic, and chemical factors.

I have worked with at least 60 impaired professionals, psychologists, social workers, dentists, physicians, and attorneys during the past ten years and have found certain personality characteristics to be common. For the most part, impaired professionals are between 30 and 55 years of age. This is in essential agreement with Farber and Heifetz (1981) who suggested that "suicides of physicians, when they happen, are most likely to occur in the 35–54 age group" (p. 296). Early childhood impoverishment is another common characteristic. This is in agreement with Vaillant, Brighton, and McArthur (1970), who pointed to the "lack of consistent support and concern from their parents" in his study of drug-using physicians.

Most, if not all, of the patients I worked with led consistently unhealthy lifestyles. They tended to be masochistic, to have low self-images, and to be self-destructive in their personal and professional lives. Eighteen of the 60 had been married more than one time, 10 were bachelors, and the remainder were separated or divorced. Those who were married had frequent extramarital affairs. They all worked excessively long hours and, as Pearson and Strecker (1960) suggested, "had poor organizational habits . . . seldom took vacations, lunch hours and had few outside interests" (p. 916).

Their masochism made them prone to give to their patients beyond their own personal limits. All tended to be perfectionists and were usually never pleased with their work. "I know I can be better, I'm not good enough, I could have done more" are frequently heard refrains. They tended to conduct their lives, both at home and in the office, in such a way that they found little, if any, relief from their chores. They had a desperate need to be needed and rationalized taking drugs as doing something for themselves. As one psychologist said, "I had a right, I worked hard enough." He was a cocaine abuser.

Others used narcotics because they needed something to get them out of their state of exhaustion. They rationalized, denied, and overcompensated to an excessive degree. While expressing a sense of dedication and commitment, they denied that abusing drugs or alcohol or sexually abusing clients might eventually lead to their destruction. As a group they were risk takers with their own as well as their patients' lives.

CAUSES OF IMPAIRMENT IN THE MENTAL HEALTH PROFESSIONS

Individuals are motivated to enter professions for a variety of reasons. Some of these reasons may ultimately contribute to problems. Motivations for working in the helping professions may include the need for achievement, the desire for personal growth, financial rewards, prestige, intellectual stimulation, self-awareness, and, of course, a desire to help those in need.

It is important for professionals to differentiate between healthy and unhealthy motives. Healthy motives are those given conscious, thoughtful, realistic appraisals by an individual; these motives are inherent in the value system of that person. Unhealthy motives are usually expressions of unconscious needs such as an excessive need to compete, be perfect, or not feel inferior; to resolve early childhood conflicts; to fulfill childhood fantasies of omnipotence and grandiosity; to earn a lot of money; or to attain a personal identity. Professionals who are motivated by needs such as these are likely to experience difficulties as they function within the profession.

In seeking to answer why is there such a proportionately high rate of suicide among psychiatrists, Chessick (1978) suggested that many of the following pressures and expectations might be causes: a need to seek truth; the need to feel useful to the community; a need to receive and dispense relationships to others with justice, the need for a complete or whole sense of self based primarily on a sense of personal integrity; the need to have some feeling of relatedness to God, to nature, or to the world; the need for tradition and rootedness; and, above all, a need to feel that one has transcended oneself and belongs to something more long lasting and of greater value than one's individual life.

In studying the causes of burnout among psychoanalysts, Robbins and I have identified several sources of pressure: high expectations placed on psychoanalysts during training, the loneliness and aloneness that are characteristic of this practice, and the "continued psychic draining, the wear and tear of daily practice, wherein much anger, hate, dislike, and hurt are verbalized toward the therapists" (Freudenberger & Robbins, 1979, p. 285).

Farber and Heifetz (1982) stated that when difficulties are exceeded by "intolerable working conditions or by unusually stressful therapeutic work . . . personal pressures may intensify drastically, and stressors may appear disproportionate to satisfaction, and burnout may occur" (p. 298). Farber (1979) further suggested that suicidal ideation, aggression, hostility, premature termination, agitated anxiety, and apathy are significant stressors for therapists. According to Wallerstein (1981), as a member of a healing profession a psychoanalyst develops the attitude of the healer. Wallerstein stated that "the frustration of the limited cures, and even the non-cures, the disillusionment with the analyst's awareness of the limited efficacy of insight, and the potential flooding with the effect of unmitigated psychic turmoil, make for very special exposures and may serve as precursors for future stress" (p. 292).

Searles (1981) referred to his experience as a supervisor and consultant and discussed "with what toughness, tenacity and sadistic virtuosity [his or her] colleague's patients tend to coerce these therapists into the ever-alluring role of the dedicated physician treating the supposedly weaker patient" (p. 840). Recently Deutsch (1984), in a study on self-reported sources of stress among psychotherapists, found that a "client's suicidal statements are the most stressful work-related occurrence, as well as a perceived inability to help an acutely distressed client."

A review of this literature reveals several possible reasons for impairments among psychotherapists, psychoanalysts, and psychiatrists, which may lead to alcohol and chemical abuse: training, or lack of it, personal value systems, attitudes with which one approaches one's work, and realistic or unrealistic self-expectations. Impairment appears to be furthered by loneliness, the seriousness of making decisions alone, the wear and tear sustained over the years, the aging process, as well as the influence of serious disturbances that the majority of patients have. But what of the impairments of psychologists?

OCCUPATIONAL STRESSES IN THE PROFESSION OF PSYCHOLOGY

Training for Psychology

The training facilities from which professionals graduate can be a potential source of impairment. Institutes, hospitals, agencies, and universities often either overtly or covertly encourage competition. "The survival techniques that the therapist often acquires, with a subtle cynicism, may be many" (Freudenberger & Robbins, 1979, p. 287). In learning the tricks of the trade, students learn techniques to help them maneuver through training. They may observe that the values of those who will graduate are determined more by colleagues, faculty, and supervising mentors than by themselves. Within this pressured graduate school environment, certain attitudes evolve. Psychologists may believe that, in view of the fact that they have expended so much time, energy, and money, they are now deserving of a certain life-style and income. This is reinforced by colleagues and friends in other professions who speak of their high earning power. As time wears on, a tinge of callousness may creep into some lives, with accompanying varied degrees of rationalization and cynicism. As Pfifferling (1980) suggested, "I wouldn't say physicians are greedy. They use money to make up for things missing from their lives" (p. 210).

Institutional Settings

Bureaucratic intrusion. A major impact that is felt by psychologists who work in institutional, school, university, or research settings is the bureaucratic intrusion on their professional autonomy. According to Farber (1985), "Psychologists working in institutional settings, e.g., hospitals or clinics, are often faced with a whole new set of professional issues that must be negotiated" (p. 12). He found that "nearly half (48.1%) of those working in institutional settings feel that they have been frustrated by administrative redtape. 59.7% feel that they have been frustrated by budgeting considerations, and 59.7% feel disheartened by their working conditions" (p. 13). Cherniss (1980) suggested that "bureaucracy is perhaps the greatest enemy of professionalism. In general respects, 'the professional ideal' and 'bureaucratic ideal' are completely incompatible" (p. 430).

Psychologists often find themselves in subordinate positions, having to wait for instructions from an administrator or supervisor. They may view themselves, therefore, as not being in charge of their professional autonomy and view their status or role to be seriously interfered with, in time perceiving their functions as being relatively unimportant. Professionals who work in institutional settings learn early that they may have virtually no control over the political process that may have impact on their lives and work. This precariousness is most profoundly felt by consultants, researchers, and academics, and it tends to promote a sense of helplessness and powerlessness. A feeling that one's job is not permanent may additionally lead to anxiety, stress, and burnout.

Administrators. According to Veninga (1979), the psychologist-administrator experiences one of the most stressful of all occupations. Burnout among managers and administrators may be caused in part by a manager's philosophy of work. Many managers believe in functioning in an autocratic manner and believe that reliance upon authority and obedience are paramount. This philosophy may also manifest itself in a belief that subordinates do not need to be in on planning decisions. By not enlisting the cooperation of subordinates in making decisions, managers may engender resentment to the centralized planning process; as a result, subordinates may take out their frustrations and resentments on the administrator. The administrator then may counter with the attitude "I will succeed even if it kills me." Burned-out administrators tend to further promote their agony by taking fewer and fewer risks, and as Veninga indicates, "structure their administrative actions to promote their own security and to minimize hassles. They obstruct with bureaucratic gibberish employees who have creative suggestions for improving the organization" (p. 48). These maneuvers serve only to isolate an administrator even further, and the accompanying minimal contact with, or feedback from, anyone further promotes the burnout process or the loss of the job.

Educators. Quite a bit of attention has been given recently to another group that experiences a good bit of stress—psychologist-teachers. As tends to be the case with psychologist-therapists, psychologist-teachers enter their field with a sense of dedication and sincerity. In time, a number of problems tend to emerge for those in the teaching profession. Lack of salary, respect, and status;

a feeling of isolation; and red tape seem to be major issues that confound the academic. Like institutional psychologists, academic psychologists may feel a sense of powerlessness over their teaching assignments, their expected participation in sometimes meaningless university committees, and the pressure to publish or perish. They also must confront the attitude that some students have that if the teacher could have made it, then he or she would not be teaching. Consequently, academics may view themselves as being stepchildren to the practitioners who are sometimes thought of as being in the more financially rewarding part of the field.

Problems of Practitioners

Patients' demands. I suggest that psychologists examine their value systems, life-styles, and motivations for seeking out the profession of psychologist as a way to prepare them for the kinds of stress they may encounter. Psychologists ought to also consider the kinds of patients that they may be called upon to help: drug-addicted, paranoid, alcoholic, narcissistic, and affect-impoverished people who feel empty and are unable to be intimate. These patients have deep needs; therefore they may demand an inordinate amount of energy and dedication from a psychologist. Patients' expressions of anger, lack of observable progress in treatment, and lack of motivation may also be continued sources of stress to psychologists (Freudenberger, 1983).

Psychologists may also experience conflict between their own and patients' needs. In their desire to be caring and serving individuals, psychologists may become overcommitted to patients and make themselves available 24 hours a day. Although it is rewarding to be a caring person who can influence and have impact, a psychologist's overinvolvement can become a source of self-gratification that is eventually narcissistic and not growth promoting. Conversely, years of caring and giving too much to patients, students, and colleagues can result in not giving enough to oneself.

Achievement demands and competition. High achievers are especially prone to eventual impairment and burnout (Freudenberger & Richelson, 1980). Their happiness is intimately tied to their success at work. All other gratifications, such as those provided by family or friends, pale in comparison. As they work increasingly hard, they may eventually deplete the resources and energies they once had. The aging process as well as years in the field take their eventual toll: These individuals may fail to maintain earlier levels of performance and to derive the same level of gratification from their efforts. The toll tends to manifest itself not only in their work but also in their home lives. Omnipotence gradually turns to exhaustion, feelings of emptiness, experienced failures, and the desire to be more than other colleagues. In part, the desire to be more creates some of the problems. High achievers are seldom satisfied with their accomplishments and do not respond well to failure; they are likely to feel self-loathing and self-derisiveness.

Achievement demands can also lead to feelings of envy and jealousy. Psychologists who are dissatisfied with themselves may feel threatened when a colleague is promoted, completes significant research, is published, makes a significant theoretical contribution to the field, or achieves national professional status and prominence. The pressure of needing to be contemporary and keep "up to date" may also bring one's competence into doubt. A psychologist's self-doubt can be further heightened when he or she perceives that high-achieving colleagues are younger or appear to be engaged in more exciting or varied work.

Along with this feeling of incompetence or inferiority comes an awareness that one cannot cure all who seek treatment, reach all students, or control every aspect of one's corporate organization. Frustration with the limitations of technology may lead to a disillusionment with oneself and with the field of psychology. This disillusionment may prompt some to leave the field or to respond by removing themselves emotionally from any activity that might threaten their "I'm OK" stance. They may, as Wallerstein (1981) suggested, "not go to the movies, the threatre, the other performing arts, even to read, except narrowly professionally" (p. 296). In this way, threatened or self-doubting professionals protect themselves from further energy drain while trying to keep up and to continue to build a rigid and inflexible system of functioning and survival as a form of self-defense.

Self-image. According to Jacobsen (1954), "'a normal self-feeling' derives from the individual's awareness of an integrated self." Self-esteem and self-regard reflect a combination of affective and cognitive components functioning reasonably well. As Kernberg (1970) suggested, "A lack of an integrated self is also characterized by a chronic feeling of unreality, puzzlement, emptiness or general disturbances in the 'self feeling,' as well as in a marked incapacity to perceive oneself realistically as a total human being" (p. 110). Professionals can develop low self-esteem in response to a variety of pressure and demands, which ultimately can affect their interactions with their patients. For example, an impaired therapist may cease to analyze a patient's positive or negative transference feelings, because to do so would call into question the therapist's own self-esteem and self-system, about which he or she is having increasing doubts.

Alienation and aloneness. Impairment can also result from the essential isolation and aloneness within which a psychologist-therapist functions. This is particularly true of therapists who work mostly in one-to-one relationships with clients. Clients may transfer their feelings or ascribe their good or bad feelings to the therapist. Furthermore, without the support of a group or peer supervisory group, therapists have little opportunity for feedback. Working alone with clients, without feedback from peers, can lead therapists ultimately to distort reality and to have difficulty distinguishing the patients' feelings from their own, and their effectiveness as therapists may be hampered, as well as their own well-being.

Furthermore, feelings of aloneness, which can be engendered by working without peer support or feedback or can result from other circumstances previously discussed (e.g., an increased sense of emptiness, lack of fulfillment, frustration, or depletion of energies that may in part be a function of the daily work of doing therapy, teaching, or conducting research, etc.), can promote a risk-seeking attitude. It is my belief that some therapists become sexually involved with their clients as a direct result of these feelings of aloneness. It is interesting that, as more women enter the field, an increasing number of lawsuits are being brought against women psychologists for sexual involvement with both male and female clients, or for alienating the affections of spouses. It appears that this expression of impairment is no longer exclusively confined to the male professional.

Special Problems of Women Psychologists

Women psychologists face even more monumental and complex issues than do men. Women are pulled in many directions by the enormity of the expectations placed on them, both personally and professionally, including demands that they simultaneously achieve, be aware that their biological clock may be running out, and continue to keep pace with a hectic personal and professional work week (Freudenberger & North, 1985). As Solomon (1984) suggested, many women "continue to experience the burden of the dual career with the associated time demands and responsibilities. If the professional woman chooses to pursue her career goals without simultaneously pursuing more domestic interests, she risks facing the pressures imposed by a family oriented society" (p. 136). Women with children have additional responsibilities to juggle, and women psychologists who are single parents have even greater responsibilities. Not only do they have less support with domestic chores and child care, but they must also cope with the pressures of seeking companionship and love relationships.

Imes and Clance (1984) raised a significant issue in their perception of the high-achieving woman. They postulated that women believe that they are imposters, that "they are not bright, capable, or creative, despite ample evidence to the contrary" (p. 72). They suggested that women professionals are secretly convinced that they have fooled all those who compliment and think highly of them and that high-achieving women live with an anxiety and fear that they will eventually be found out. These women have difficulty sustaining a sense of personal pride in their accomplishments and seem to negate their abilities by feeling that luck or other factors beyond their control are responsible for their success.

Thus, women psychologists, in order to diminish or prevent impairment, need continually to ask: "How will I function professionally?" "What areas do I wish to excell in?" "How may I maintain my integrity and self-systems?" And last, but by no means least, "What sort of a human being and professional will I be, and at what cost to myself, if I continue at this pace?" The inability of women psychologists to resolve these questions may lie at the root of future role confusion, minimal professional identification, functioning on the edge of professional involvement, and an eventual impact on physical or emotional well-being.

The ever-increasing number of women who suffer from alcoholism, heart disease, breast cancer, and chemical abuse suggests the immense stress and burnout that confront the woman professional today. The rising female death rate reflects an unfortunate trend for more and more women; their lifestyles include various life-endangering habits that formerly were the exclusive domain of men.

TREATMENT ISSUES FOR IMPAIRED PROFESSIONALS

Reasons for Seeking Treatment

The reasons for seeking treatment are varied, but some of the more common reasons for self-referral are the ending of relationships or marriages; feelings of depression, aloneness, or loneliness; the attempt or the actual suicide of a patient; and feelings of failure or rejection in working with patients. An administrator may be in danger of losing his or her job; a teacher may have come face to face with poor faculty and student evaluations. All of these circumstances are made even more difficult to face if the psychologist has served in a particular position for a number of years.

Some seek treatment because they are involved in malpractice suits and are troubled by either false or real accusations of the complainants for sexual or financial offenses; alienation of affection; child, patient, or student abuse; as well as for alcohol or chemical abuse. There are other instances wherein the psychologist experiences an excessive number of depressive episodes, sometimes accompanied by suicidal panic or psychosis. Still others, because of poor judgment, may lose a great amount of money in risky financial ventures or through gambling. Taking such risks may be an individual's way of denying his or her depression or lack of purpose and of bringing excitement once again into his or her existence.

Aging can also be stressful and may promote impairment. As psychologists age, their own life-threatening illnesses or the illness of a spouse or a child may call into question their own sense of mortality and make them feel vulnerable. They often experience difficulty in dealing with or recognizing the need to slow down and cut back on their work as they grow older and may confront the situation with a denial coping mechanism. Traumatic experiences, such as the death of a loved one, can also impair a psychologist's functioning; the psychologist may be unable to cope with tragedy, thus impairing his or her ability to concentrate or to work with patients, students, clients, or staff members. Therapists, in particular, begin to feel burned out or depleted simply as a result of the continued demands made on them by patients. "I have nothing further to give, I am a void, vacuumed out" is a typical comment that one hears from such therapists. Some of these individuals eventually contemplate leaving the profession. Some do. Unfortunately, the decision to leave can be yet another form of denial—a denial that stress and burnout have taken their toll.

Because of articles, lectures, and symposia at conventions, an ever-increasing number of professionals are seeking therapy and admitting to their struggles with alcohol and chemical abuse. A large percentage of these professionals, however, enter therapy with strong resistances. They begin therapy usually upon the urgings of attorneys or members of their family. An attorney, for example, may suggest that being in treatment might assist a colleague in plea-bargaining. Initially, therefore, the motivation for change for some of these men and women is minimal. They are in treatment under duress and tend to voice these thoughts to the therapists either subtly or overtly. This coercion into treatment certainly places the treating therapist in a difficult position. He or she needs to convey to the patient-colleague that he or she is there to assist in whatever way is needed but will not be used as a cover for the client. The client, in time, will need to see that the reasons for his or her being in therapy are serious, both personally and professionally, and that the treating therapist can and will not be used as a means of avoiding future legal issues.

Obstacles to Seeking Treatment: Denial

To admit illness, professionals must admit to themselves that their image as health providers, teachers, and administrators and their continued functioning as professionals are in question. In their frame of reference, they exist to assist others. Thus, a major coping mechanism used by impaired psychologists is denial. Denial, according to Lazarus (1983), "is the negation of something in a word or act. The negation can be . . . an impulse, feeling . . . thought, or of an external demand or reality" (p. 349). Along with denial there may be guilt, avoidance, unreasonableness, or illogical thinking. One's concepts of realities of self, work, and family are distorted or dismissed. A person using denial becomes increasingly rigid, unresponsive, and closed to constructive criticism, information, or knowledge from others. Declining health and ability to function are also subject to denial—a denial that life is finite and that people are capable of becoming ill and are thus unable to go on at the pace that they have set for themselves.

The use of denial as a coping mechanism may also manifest itself in counterphobic and counterdependent responses. The physical and psychological signs that suggest difficulty, such as exhaustion, increased irritability, poor judgment, and physical illness, are denied and dismissed. The counterphobic mechanism is expressed by the professional's working harder and longer. Denial can also be manifested by an unwillingness to seek help for experienced symptoms. To admit need would be to admit dependency on another for aid. This is an especially difficult admission for people who are themselves helpers, and it often serves as a significant deterrent to seeking therapeutic assistance.

Chemical and alcohol abusers are especially prone to denial. Bean and Zinberg (1981) suggested that alcoholics not only deny the problem, but they obstruct any interference with their drinking. Chemical abusers have a reputation for being able to manipulate their families, friends, colleagues, and therapists. They may not be able to see what is going on in themselves, but their ability to bully, wheedle, charm, or promote misplaced compassion and understanding is truly profound. They also have special skills they gained through graduate or specialized education and through their own experience in working with clients or patients. As a result, a special forthrightness is required of the treating therapist in order to confront and break through to the truth in a disturbed colleague who abuses alcohol or drugs.

The denial mechanism prevents impaired professionals from seeking treatment; it is also employed by the impaired professional's colleagues to the same effect. Psychologists tend not to recognize or acknowledge that a colleague is impaired for a number of reasons. Either the psychologist does not perceive that a colleague is in difficulty, or because the colleague is a friend, co-worker, or acquaintance, the psychologist is unwilling to become involved. Psychologists tend to take the attitude that their colleagues' problems are none of their business. They are also hesitant to stigmatize a member of their own profession and unwilling to bring an individual to the attention of appropriate boards or committees for fear that this person's livelihood will be jeopardized. It is also possible that a psychologist might be sued for slandering the character of a colleague or for making false accusations.

It is unfortunate that, although many psychologists know colleagues who are depressed, sadistic with clients, sexually abusive with patients and students, alcoholic, chemical abusers, or suicidal, they do not confront these colleagues and use coping mechanisms such as denial, avoidance, and rationalization. As one colleague said recently, "to become involved is just not worth the risk and the hassles." In her work with alcoholic therapists, Skorina (1982) pointed out that "denial is one of the diagnostic canons of alcoholism. External reality regarding one's alcoholism is replaced by a wish fulfillment of control or potency" (p. 38). Sadly, psychologists too often take the same route in denying the observed difficulties of fellow psychologists.

It is important to recognize that psychologists may seek to deny the truth about colleagues because they themselves may be in a process of burning out (Freudenberger, 1976, 1977). It is also possible that a psychologist tends to overidentify with the impaired colleague and, in seeking to deny his or her own process of impairment, denies the colleague's impairment. As Schreiber (1977) suggested, "the lack of recognition of a physician's distress is related to the colleague's conscious or unconscious denial that a physician can be emotionally disturbed and is likely related to the personal threat to oneself of "there but for the grace of God go I" (p. 323).

STEPS TOWARD BEGINNING TREATMENT FOR ALCOHOL- AND CHEMICAL-ABUSING PSYCHOLOGISTS

Accepting the Role of Patient

Regardless of the patient's history and the type of treatment indicated, recovery for alcohol and chemical abusers includes three distinct steps: admission, acceptance, and surrender. That is, the patient must admit to abusing substances, accept the role of patient, and be willing to follow the steps of the treatment indicated.

Healers find it particularly difficult to move into the role of patient. They verbalize fears of losing dignity; they experience injury to their sense of self, pride, and power; they believe themselves to be foolish; and they are disturbed about their loss of self-esteem. Their actions may be accompanied and complicated further by feelings of guilt or a sense of shame. A most difficult task for them is to let go of their "therapeutic power" and, in the process, they need to puncture their narcissism or grandiosity. Since many are resistant to treatment, they also are hesitant to accept interpretations. They have been accustomed to enlightening others, rather than being enlightened. Some view the process of entering therapy as a sign of being weak and vulnerable and suggest that to seek to help must mean that they have become "very sick, and possibly close to a mental breakdown." Some indeed may have initially experienced signs of breakdown, such as subtle delusions, severe sleep disturbances, or an inability to concentrate. The majority, however, are not in a process of a mental breakdown. Rather, these feelings cover anxiety about a felt powerlessness over their lives and work.

Initial Assessment

As indicated, treating therapists need to be cognizant that clinicians are often reluctant to seek therapy and to see themselves as patients—they are slow to shift their self-image from that of helper to helpee. Understanding that, treating therapists need to begin treatment with an evaluation of the patient's history, including the following information:
1. Was there previous therapy? If so,
   a. When did it occur?
   b. How long did it last?
   c. What kind of therapy was it?
   d. What issues were resolved or left unresolved?
2. When did the process of impairment begin?

Next, the therapist needs to ascertain the nature of the patient's impairment, what the symptoms are, and what led him or her to seek treatment. The following two examples illustrate many of the signs and causes of impairment discussed in this chapter. This kind of information, gathered from the treating therapist at the outset of treatment, can provide the therapist with insight into an individual's sources of impairment, thereby helping the therapist to design the appropriate treatment.

A 38-year-old, self-referred, woman psychologist had been abusing chemicals since she was an adolescent. This woman came from a lower socioeconomic background. Her father, a laborer, and her mother, an alcoholic, had essentially abandoned her. After she graduated from high school, she had drifted into a peer drug culture and had used LSD and marijuana excessively. Through extensive therapy, which she sought out herself, she was able to eliminate drugs from her life and graduate from college with a PhD in psychology. She had practiced for approximately 7 years when a long-standing love affair broke up. She experienced quite a bit of loneliness, and, unfortunately, at about the same time one of her patients committed suicide. This made her question her worth as a psychologist, and she found herself drifting into first occasional, then addictive, cocaine abuse. She began to experience anxiety, depression, frequent headaches, paranoia, dizziness, nausea, vomiting, dry throat, and twitching of her small muscles—all symptoms of serious cocaine abuse.

A 40-year-old psychiatrist, who had been abusing marijuana for 20 years, sought treatment under pressure from his wife. Within the past year he had been experiencing profoundly disorganizing psychological changes, particularly in the presence of excessive stress or fatigue. He would tend to forget what he, someone else, or a patient had said; his anxiety had measurably increased, he felt he was losing control of himself; and he was suffering from severe sleep disturbances. He had always seen himself as a hard-working man and a person who had enjoyed the responsibilities of adulthood and being a professional. He admitted, after a number of probing sessions, that he was finding his work increasingly meaningless. He was tired of the many patients, of the routine of his work along with having to face the pressures of a recently born retarded son. He commented that in order to take "the pressure off," and to feel less burned out, he smoked marijuana more and more.

The treating therapist needs to continually explore a patient's history and ascertain from them what signs and symptoms have been observed over a period of time. Have they noticed becoming careless, callous, cynical, blunted, or less compassionate with their patients? Over what length of time have they noticed these changes in their behavior—3 months, 6 months, or longer? Have family members or friends commented on behavioral changes?

It is also important to inquire about shifts in their intellectual, physical, and emotional lives. Have they become less creative or sharp or found their mind wandering while treating others? Have they experienced excessive fatigue or insomnia? Have their attitudes toward themselves, their work, and life changed? Are they essentially optimistic or pessimistic, positive, negative, or disillusioned? If they are pessimistic, what are they disillusioned about? Is it that their hoped-for expectations have not been met in their work? Do they feel disappointed in themselves or their contributions? Some patients talk of being so excessively involved with their work for years that all else had ceased to exist.

Have they become increasingly isolated or less involved with people? Is this a change or have they always been loners? Do they have a familial or social support system? It is sometimes helpful to know whether the patient has had a spiritual or religious support system and whether their beliefs had undergone a change.

Medical assessments. With chemical and alcohol abusers, it is essential to obtain a thorough medical history. This history needs to include the following information: the type of drug and amount being abused, how recently the drug was last ingested, and whether the patient abuses more than one drug. With barbiturates, a tolerance may have built up, and the user may be prone to going into a coma. The degree of damage to the body from alcohol or chemical abuse needs to be clearly understood. The patient may need to be referred to a physician for a thorough medical evaluation, to a dentist because of teeth and gum deterioration, or to a physician-pharmacologist for combined psychotherapy and drug treatment. Medication is often prescribed to help patients through the initial periods of withdrawal or to more readily deal with the underlying depression, anxiety, and sleeplessness. Some patients may need to be hospitalized for 28 to 35 days for detoxification.

It is essential that therapists who are working with drug-abusing patients have good access to physicians who understand the problems of substance abuse. As Beitman and Klerman (1984) suggested: "The research literature supports combined treatment in a variety of disorders, e.g. alcoholism, polydrug abuser and depression" (p. 80). When more than one professional is involved in treatment, the patient needs to understand the roles of each professional, and there are several issues that all parties must understand clearly before treatment begins: the issue of confidentiality, the necessity for the professionals involved to share information, the need for developing explicit and clear goals for the combined treatment, and the need for working through the resistances and transference distortions of each person.

Setting goals. Initially a cognitive, dynamic approach appears to be most suitable for treating therapists who abuse chemicals and alcohol (Freudenberger, 1982). As Greenberg and Kaslow (1984) indicated, therapists have certain advantages over other patients when seeking assistance: "They know which therapists are available in the community and so can make a better choice. Another advantage is that they know what the therapy process is likely to be and are better prepared for its vicissitudes. Additionally, almost always therapists are verbal and intelligent."

In using a cognitive approach, it is initially important to establish short-range goals. An immediate goal is to work out procedures to stop abusing the chemicals, or to work on a significant diminution of intake. This will take time and lapses will occur; therefore the therapist needs to structure the treatment and set firm guidelines. Chemical abusers tend to overgeneralize, be erratic, lie, and think or act impulsively. Thus it is essential to work as rapidly as possible toward the achievement of abstinence. They must be confronted with their lying and manipulative character. As Ehrlich and McGeehan (1985) suggested: "There can be little, if any, treatment of worth if the patient continues to take one drink or a "bit" of cocaine every once in a while, and the therapist is conned into believing that progress is taking place" (p. 60).

Once treatment has begun, initial work addresses itself to clarifying patients' personal value systems. Are they idealists, perfectionists, or high achievers? Were they unable to continue this self-imposed pace? How much dedication and commitment have they experienced as therapists, teachers, researchers, consultants, and administrators, and how successful have they been? It may be necessary to help them redefine the meaning of dedication and commitment during these discussions. Seek to determine whether they are hung up on unconscious childhood parent models, or professional persons that they have modeled themselves after. Do they believe they have let them down? Seek to determine their manner, technique, and philosophy of work in order to ascertain the stressors inherent in their daily activities and how diligently they have followed their training in their practice. It is interesting to note that Prochaska and Norcross (1983) found that when therapists are "faced with their own psychic distress, they tend to be more pragmatic, cost-efficient and 'middle-of-the-road,' rather than relying on classical theories of psychotherapy" (p. 648). This implies that they tend to abandon how they work in their office once they are faced with their own limitations.

This further implies that, in the treatment of psychologists, the change processes that therapists value may significantly differ from those they offer their clients, or from those they consider to be within their therapeutic competence. Therefore treatment of psychologists may need to be thought of more in the direction of the practical, the cost effective and the "realistic." Drawn-out treatment, without significant intervention except in severely disturbed colleagues, tends not to be appropriate, and the client may leave treatment prematurely.

Support Networks

Chemical and alcohol abusers are intense and compulsive about their abuse and have come to view it as a salvation from daily stressors. Furthermore, their pattern of abuse usually has behavioral effects that can make treatment difficult. Abusers often find it difficult to maintain a schedule, they break promises, they telephone at all hours, and wreak havoc with others' schedules. Therefore it is extremely important for the therapist to assist the client in developing other techniques for coping with ineffectuality and impairment. A network support system made up of the therapist, a therapy group, and the family must be put into place as rapidly as possible.

I find that it is essential, for example, when working with an alcoholic to enlist the support of both Alcoholics Anonymous and the family. Drinking is the alcoholic's major concern; therefore he or she needs assistance in order to recognize and admit to addiction and to acknowledge that he or she is unable to handle the problem alone. It may happen that they will undergo treatment several times before they finally acknowledge that they cannot do it by themselves. As long as the impaired person does not acknowledge that he or she is in imminent danger, the therapist can do only a minimum amount of intervention.

Transference

Therapists need to know when they are treating a client who is a fellow professional. The helper now in the position of needing help cannot subtly be turned into a "friend." The clear demarcation of the client-therapist relationship is critical for treatment. The therapist who treats a colleague needs to be cognizant of the possibility that such a client will demand more of a therapist's time than the usual patient. The colleague-patient may be in the midst of a custody battle; fighting for the retention of his or her license; need to appear before local, state, or national ethics committees and boards; or be the subject of publicity. Court appearances by the treating therapist may be necessary. All these considerations need to be taken into account before deciding to treat a colleague as client. Therapists who treat impaired colleagues also run the risk of experiencing counter-transference: they may begin to feel frustrated or angry when they feel that they are not making any progress. Often progress is made by taking one step forward and one-half step backwards.

SUMMARY

The overall process for treatment is one that requires one to concentrate on the personal and professional reasons for abuse and impairment. It needs to be used to assist colleagues in reevaluating their life-styles, their goals, and their manner of functioning in their profession. They need to be made aware that treatment may take a long time and that in the process some may lose their licenses to practice, while others may leave the field or shift their treatment populations. They all need to acknowledge that they cannot use alcohol or chemicals in moderation.

A colleague under stress who abuses chemicals or alcohol can be helped, but it demands dedication, experience, knowledge of pharmacology, awareness of resistances to treatment, and objectivity on the part of the treating therapist, as well as the involvement of the patient's family. The helper population is a group difficult to treat. If the treating therapist is not aware of the limitations of his or her treatment with this group and the importance of ascertaining the motivations of the client, then the therapist is him- or herself vulnerable to becoming burned out and impaired in the process of helping.

References

Bean, M. H., & Zinberg, N. E. (1981). *Dynamic approaches to the understanding and treatment of alcoholism.* New York: The Free Press.

Beitman, B. D., & Klerman, G. L. (1984). *Combined psychotherapy and drug therapy in clinical practice.* New York: Spectrum Publications, Inc.

Blum, K. (1984). The background for abuse. In K. Blum (Ed.), *Handbook of abusable drugs* (p. 8). New York: Gardner Press.

Cherniss, C. (1980). *Professional burnout in human service organizations.* New York: Praeger.

Chessick, R. D. (1978). The sad soul of the psychiatrist. *Bulletin of the Menninger Clinic, 42*(1), 1–9.

Deutsch, C. J. (1984). Self-reported sources of stress among psychotherapists. *Professional Psychology: Research and Practice, 15*(6), 833–845.

Ehrlich, P., & McGeehan, M. (1985). Cocaine recovery support groups and the language of recovery. *Journal of Psychoactive Drugs, 17*(1), 11–17.

Farber, B. A. (1979). The effects of psychotherapeutic practice upon the psychotherapist: A phenomenological investigation. *Dissertation Abstracts International, 40,* 447B. (University Microfilms No. 7916611)

Farber, B. A. (1985). Clinical psychologists' perceptions of Psychotherapeutic Work. *The Clinical Psychologist, 38*(1), 10–13.

Farber, B. A., & Heifetz, L. H. (1982). The satisfactions and stresses of psychotherapeutic work: A factor analytic study. *Professional Psychology: Research and Practice, 12*(5), 621–630.

Freudenberger, H. J. (1976). The professional and the human services worker: Some solutions to the problems they face in working together. *Journal of Drug Issues, 6*(3), 273–282.

Freudenberger, H. J. (1977). Burnout: Occupational hazard of the child care worker. *Child Care Quarterly, 6*(2), 90–100.

Freudenberger, H. J. (1982). Counseling and dynamics: Treating the end-stage burnout person. In W. S. Paine (Ed.), *Job stress and burnout: Research, theory and intervention perspective* (pp. 173–186). Beverly Hills, CA: Sage.

Freudenberger, H. J. (1983). Hazards of psychotherapeutic practice. *Psychotherapy in Private Practice, 1*(1), 83–89.

Freudenberger, H. J. (1984a). Burnout and job dissatisfaction: Impact on the family. In J. C. Hansen & S. A. Cramer (Eds.), *Perspectives on work and the family.* Rockville, MD: Aspen Publications.

Freudenberger, H. J. (1984b). Impaired clinicians: Coping with "burnout". In P. A. Keller & L. G. Ritt (Eds.), *Innovations in clinical practice: A source book* (vol. 3, pp. 223–229). Sarasota, FL: Professional Resource Exchange.

Freudenberger, H. J., & North, G. (1985). *Women's burnout: How to spot it, how to intervene and how to prevent it.* New York: Doubleday.

Freudenberger, H. J., & Richelson, G. (1980). *Burnout: How to beat high cost of success.* New York: Bantam Books.

Freudenberger, H. J., & Robbins, A. (1979). The hazards of being a psychoanalyst. *The Psychoanalytic Review, 66*(2), 275–297.

Greenberg, S., & Kaslow, F. W. (1984). Psychoanalytic treatment for therapists, residents and other trainees. In F. W. Kaslow (Ed.), *Psychotherapy with psychotherapists* (pp. 19–32). New York: Haworth Press.

Imes, S., & Clance, P. R. (1984). Treatment of the imposter phenomenon. In C. M. Brody (Ed.), *Women therapists working with women* (pp. 78–82). New York: Springer.

Isler, C. (1978, July). The alcoholic nurse. *RN,* 45–49.

Jacobsen, E. (1954). Contributions to the metapsychology of psychotic identifications. *Journal of American Psychoanalytic Association, 2*(239), 239–262.

Jaffe, J. (1984). Pharmacology and clinical applications of narcotic antagonists. In K. Blum (Ed.), *Handbook of abusable drugs* (p. 94). New York: Gardner Press.

Kernberg, O. F. (1970). A psychoanalytic classification of character pathology. *Journal of American Psychoanalytic Association, 18*(270), 800–822.

Lazarus, R. S. (1983). The cost and benefits of denial. In S. Breznitz (Ed.), *The denial of stress* (pp. 1–10). New York: International University Press.

Medved, M. (1982). *Hospital: The hidden lives of a medical center staff.* New York: Simon & Schuster.

Nathan, P., Thoreson, R., & Kilburg, R. (1983). *Board of Professional Affairs Steering Committee on Distressed Psychologists: Draft report.* Washington, DC: American Psychological Association.

Pearson, M. M., & Strecker, E. A. (1960). Physician as psychiatric patients: Private practice experience. *American Journal of Psychiatry, 116*(10), 915–919.

Pfifferling, J. H. (1980). Wounded healers. *Medical Self Care, 10,* 8–14.

Pfifferling, J. H., Blum, J., & Wood, W. (1981). The prevention of physician impairment. *Journal of Florida Medical Association, 68,* 268–272.

Prochaska, J. L., & Norcross, J. C. (1983). Psychotherapists' perspective on treating themselves and their clients for psychic distress. *Professional Psychology: Research and Practice, 4*(5), 642–655.

Schreiber, S. C. (1977). Emotional problems of physicians: The nature and extent of problems. *Arizona Medicine, 34*(4), 323–324.

Searles, H. J. (1981). The "dedicated physician" in the field of psychotherapy and psychoanalysis. In H. F. Searles (Ed.), *Counter transference and related subjects* (pp. 71–89). New York: International University Press.

Skoler, D. L., & Klein, R. M. (1979). Mental disability and lawyer discipline. *The John Marshal Journal of Practice and Procedure. 12,* 227–252.

Skorina, J. K. (1982). Alcoholic psychologists: The need for humane and effective regulation. *Professional Practice of Psychology, 3*(2), 33–41.

Solomon, L. J. (1984). Working women and stress. In C. M. Brody (Ed.), *Women therapists working with women* (pp. 135–144). New York: Springer.

Vaillant, G. E., Brighton, J. R., & McArthur, C. (1970). Physicians' use of mood altering drugs. *New England Journal of Medicine, 282,* 365–370.

Veninga, R. (1979). Administrator burnout: Causes and cures. *Hospital Progress, 60*(2), 45–52.

Wallerstein, R. S. (1981). The psychoanalyst's life: Expectations, vicissitudes and reflections. *International Review of Psychoanalysis, 8*(3), 285–298.

THE DISTRESSED PSYCHOLOGIST: SEXUAL INTIMACIES AND EXPLOITATION

8

Annette M. Brodsky

When one imagines a distressed psychologist, there is usually an empathic feeling for the subjective anguish of the professional in distress. There is a desire to help the individual cope with the distress so that he or she can be more comfortable and more functional in personal and professional situations. In the case of the psychologist who is sexually intimate with patients or students, an important factor is that the psychologist involved is never the only party in distress. Sexual intimacy with patients and students implies exploitation, which in turn implies distress or damage to the recipient of the psychologist's behavior. This chapter concerns issues for both the psychologist and the patient or student involved in a sexually intimate situation. What are the boundaries of sexual intimacies? What kinds of psychologists and patients are vulnerable? What kind of remediation makes sense and for whom? Finally, what can be done to prevent the behaviors that lead to exploitation?

DEFINING SEXUAL INTIMACY

The American Psychological Association (APA) states under Principle 6A of its ethical principles of psychologists (APA, 1981) that sexual intimacies between patient and therapist are unethical. However, sexual intimacies are not defined. Almost anyone with a cursory knowledge of the issues involved might understand that it is unethical to have sexual intercourse with one's patients, or even with one's students. But, it should be asked, what other behavior can be considered to constitute intimacy or sexual exploitation? This question presents the first difficulty in defining sexual intimacy. People's varying perceptions of intimacy poses another difficulty. Surveys of professionals indicate a persistent minority belief that there may be a positive aspect to sexual intimacy between patients and therapists (Bouhoutsos, Holroyd, Lerman, Forer, & Greenberg, 1983; Gartrell, Herman, Olarte, Feldstein, & Localio, 1986; Holroyd

& Brodsky, 1977; Kardener, Fuller, & Mensh, 1973). There are several other issues that influence how intimacy is defined; they involve the intent and the judgment of the therapist. Part of the difficulty in delineating what is exploitive about a sexual relationship has to do with the intent of the activity. It may seem clear that the intention to sexually arouse one's patient or student to satisfy one's own needs would be a violation of an ethical code; however, the word *intent* itself has a variety of parameters. The first question concerns whose intent. With regard to the intent of the therapist (or professor), is it acceptable for the patient to become sexually aroused by something the therapist does, as long as the therapist disclaims the intention to sexually arouse? Courts have skirmished around this issue in cases in which the patient has maintained that the actions of the therapist came through loud and clear as sexual intention, whereas according to the therapist, the patient may have been aroused without cause or intention. One can imagine that the therapist who engages in physical touching of patients for the purpose of affectionate support or acknowledgment of caring might be inadvertently behaving in ways that a patient might misinterpret as erotic or sexual. Thus kissing, hugging, affectionate touching, or stroking could easily have more than one meaning to either of the parties involved (Holroyd & Brodsky, 1980).

There is a distinct difference, however, between the kind of touching that occurs when a therapist is himself or herself aroused and has an intention to elicit a reciprocal reaction from the patient, and the kind of nonerotic touching and holding given by a therapist with benign, caring intentions. A patient is frequently aware of the subtle difference, even when the therapist does not consciously intend for the patient to recognize the erotic feelings of his or her countertransference. Thus, a female patient can distinguish the intent of eroticism when a male therapist rubs his hand up and down on her arm from the intent to console when the therapist puts his arm around her shoulder when she is distraught and crying. Therapists who are accused of sexual intimacies, however, often deny such refinements of intent (Brodsky, 1984).

Those of us working with patients who have complained about therapists being sexually intimate are inclined to extend the definition of sexual intimacy from *intention* to arouse to the *effect* of arousing the patient. That is, if a therapist is so naive that he or she is not aware that the physical touching or seductive statements being made in therapy are sexually arousing the patient, then the therapist is dangerously in need of further sensitivity training. If the behaviors have the effect of sexually arousing the patient, one might conclude that sexual intimacy has occurred (Brodsky, 1984). I know of at least one legal case in which this issue was brought to the fore because the patient produced evidence, corroborated by the therapist's own notes, that she had told the therapist explicitly that his physical touching—stroking her arms, hugging her, and rocking her back and forth—were sexually arousing to her and that she had sexual feelings toward him. Thus, when he continued these behaviors, she could only assume that he was encouraging her sexual arousal, which extended her own belief that he was interested in having a sexual alliance with her. His defense that he was mothering her, rather than being sexual, was hard to accept, given that he had acknowledged her direct feedback that those particular behaviors were sexually arousing to her.

A second factor in defining a sexual intimacy in therapy involves the judgment of the therapist. Is the therapist truly competent if he or she is not aware of the major emotional states of a client or a patient? Is it truly possible that a competent therapist can miss the signs of sexual arousal in a patient with whom he or she has engaged in physical touching or in the intimate discussion of sexual details? This is not to suggest that a therapist and patient should not discuss the patient's sexual feelings and sexual fantasies; it is rather to say that the therapist needs to know where discussion leaves off and arousal and action may begin. A confounding factor in this issue is that some therapists believe that although the unusual, innovative approaches they use may violate the more traditional boundaries of touching in therapy, these innovations are beneficial to the patient and therefore justify violation of traditional personal boundaries (Holroyd & Brodsky, 1977). Thus, the therapist who engages in intense physical touching, such as rocking a patient back and forth, holding or hugging for several seconds, or more than momentary stroking, may consider himself or herself a brave pioneer into uncharted territory. Such techniques, however, are not really innovative; if they were, they would have been adopted more widely decades ago when previous therapists experimented with them.

In the 1960s, Masters and Johnson became aware of the need to eliminate any actual sexual behavior by the therapist or a surrogate during the treatment of sexual dysfunctions. Masters and Johnson no longer provide sexual surrogates in therapy, let alone permit the therapist to engage in any sexual acts with the patient (Masters & Johnson, 1975). Other so-called innovators promoting physical touch that might intimate sexual behavior, such as McCartney (1966) with his overt transference, or Shepard (1971) with his love treatment, found to their dismay that the initial interest in their proposals was temporary at best and resulted in their dismissal from their respective professional organizations. Modern day reinventors of erotic psychotherapeutic techniques are even less likely to be considered surveyors of a brave, new cure (Keith-Spiegel, 1979).

Dual relationships are another aspect of the definition of sexual intimacies. A sexual intimacy between patient and therapist is one example of a dual relationship. Dual relationships involve more than one purpose of relating. A therapy relationship is meant to be exclusive and unidimensional. The therapist is the expert, the patient the consumer of that expertise. Once a patient accepts an individual as a therapist, that individual cannot, without undue influence, relate to that patient in any other role. Relating to the patient as an employer, business partner, lover, spouse, relative, professor, or student would contaminate the therapeutic goal. This contamination is much more intense in a psychotherapy relationship than it would be in the relationship between a client and a professional in any other field—for example, between a client and an internist, a dentist, a lawyer, or an accountant.

Acting upon a sexual feeling or the development of a personal relationship beyond the professional one would not have consequences nearly as serious for nonpsychotherapeutic dyads, because in the psychotherapy relationship, the relationship is part of the service being contracted for by the patient, whereas in other professional dyads, it is not. Almost all psychotherapies, except perhaps a few technical behavioral programs, involve the development of a relationship between the therapist and the patient. This relationship is not egalitarian; the therapist comes into the relationship with all the power and authority of the expert who has something to sell. In the case of therapy, what is being sold is a promise that the relationship will help the patient improve his or her personal life. Indeed, it is the mismanagement of love relationships in a patient's life that is so frequently at least one major presenting complaint. For the therapist to contaminate and deobjectify his or her role in helping to resolve the patient's problems is unforgivable. Therapy is not the selling of friendship, the selling of one's body, a mating game, or a place for lovers to meet. In fact, such misuses of therapy clearly would be ethical and moral violations (APA, 1981).

Nonsexual dual relationships between therapists and patients are also unethical but are probably less damaging. For example, bartering goods for therapy is a practice that was more common and more acceptable in the past but that is now being recognized for its potential problems, and individual situations have resulted in negative sanctions by ethics committees. (Hare-Mustin & Hall, 1983). The therapist who hires a patient to mow a lawn, to paint a portrait, to babysit for his or her children, or to buy a house is creating a dangerous situation that may be as damaging to the therapist as to the patient. Business deals that fail, investments that lose money, and contracts, services, or products that do not meet expectations all can affect the transference and countertransference in the therapeutic relationship. But none of these matches the humiliation and the devastation to one's self-esteem that results from the discovery that the promise of a sexual or romantic relationship that had been awakened in therapy was only exploitation (Freeman & Roy, 1976). It is an interesting finding that patients who have sexual relationships with their therapists also tend to have intimate knowledge about their therapists' personal lives and to have other types of dual relationships with their therapists. The therapist who crosses the boundary from the professional relationship to any other tends to cross in more ways than one and to be at high risk for being involved with a patient sexually (Belote, 1977; Bouhoutsos et al., 1983; D'Addario, 1978).

Another aspect to be considered in defining sexual intimacy also involves the therapist's judgment: selectivity. Those therapists most likely to be involved with their patients treat patients differentially on the basis of age, sex, and attractiveness. Thus, the male therapist who touches, holds, kisses, or hugs female patients but not male patients is at higher risk for sexually exploiting his patients (Holroyd & Brodsky, 1980).

CHARACTERISTICS OF PSYCHOLOGISTS AT RISK

When I get a call from a lawyer somewhere across the country who has a patient wanting to sue a therapist for sexual intimacy involvement, I can often describe the involved therapist before the lawyer says a single word. The following characteristics constitute a prototype of the therapist being sued: The therapist is male, middle aged, involved in unsatisfactory love relationships in his own life, perhaps in the process of going through a divorce. His patient caseload is primarily female. He becomes involved with more than one patient sexually, those selected being on the average 16 years younger than he is. He confides his personal life to the patient, implying to her that he needs her, and he spends therapy sessions soliciting her help with his personal problems. The therapist is a lonely man, and even if he works in group practice, he is somewhat isolated professionally, not sharing in close consultation with his peers. He may have a good reputation in the psychological or psychiatric community, having been in practice for many years. He tends to take cases through referrals only. He is not necessarily physically attractive, but there is an aura of power or charisma about him. His lovemaking often leaves much to be desired, but he is quite convincing to the patient that it is he above all others with whom she needs to be making love (Butler & Zelen, 1977; Chesler, 1972; Freeman & Roy, 1976; Smith, 1982; Taylor & Wagner, 1976).

There are several variations of the prototype of sexually abusive therapist, some of which I will describe now. First are therapists in love. These therapists are more likely to be younger, to be inexperienced in therapy, and to be genuinely, emotionally involved with only one patient. They have difficulties with professional boundaries, particularly with the sanction against dual relationships. They do not recognize, or have not been adequately trained to realize, that a therapy patient is not free enough of the influence of the therapeutic relationship to make an informed, voluntary, consenting decision about an extratherapeutic relationship with the therapist. Should these therapists realize that their feelings toward a patient are more than that of a caring parent figure, or of a professional treating a vulnerable needy patient, they may recognize their previous poor judgment in the situation and genuinely wish to remedy the situation—or at the very least clarify what has happened. Being inexperienced, however, these therapists may think that the solution is giving up the therapeutic sessions and moving into a full-fledged affair, which they believe to have long-term potential, including marriage. In those cases in which the therapist and patient end therapy and move into a lover or marriage relationship, the ending is what counts. That is, when they live happily ever after, the fact that the therapist originally courted his or her love in the therapy hour does not seem to be a problem. It may be only when the current love relationship sours that the former patient is able to appreciate that the relationship developed as a result of the therapist's taking advantage of the patient's transference in the therapeutic situation.

Another type of vulnerable therapist consists of those with a personality disorder, usually classified as antisocial personality. These therapists truly abuse their power through playing the role of expert. Their byline is "trust me." Unfortunately, these therapists are the last people in the world whom patients should trust. They have only their own needs uppermost in mind and can sometimes be recognized by the fact that they engage in sexual intimacies with many patients no matter what their presenting complaints are. They may be unable to form meaningful relationships themselves, and their alliances with patients rely heavily on persuasive power, dishonesty, and charm. These therapists are often likely to do the greatest damage. They may encourage patients to act in ways that are diametrically opposed to behavior that would be therapeutic. For example, a male therapist may encourage an inhibited female patient to become sexually promiscuous, or he may tell her that incest is all right and that she should look to him as her father. Therapists may also engage patients in other dual relationships, bilking them out of their money, using them as cheap labor, and otherwise exploiting them. They will not be interested in resolving any issue a patient might bring up related to the poor treatment, and they will deny intent to arouse or seduce. Such therapists can be very dangerous and may lie when confronted, but they may be supported by colleagues who, not being aware of the extent of the behavior, overidentify with their claims of being "victimized."

Another variation of the prototype is the charismatic professor (who is usually male and with whom female students are more at risk). Whereas the personality-disordered therapist misuses the power of the relationship by assuming the role of the expert helping a dependent patient in need, the charismatic professor misuses his or her role as the expert in an academic specialty area to impress and entice vulnerable students. The relationships become more complicated if he or she sees students as therapy patients as well. The student-patient is in a particularly vulnerable position to be exploited, because she or he feels honored to have been chosen from among peers to be selected as a therapy patient of this powerful, brilliant, respected professor, and the addition of a personal/sexual relationship becomes an easy step to take. Such professors may be involved in relationships with students or therapy patients for many years before anyone brings a case against them. Although their behavior may be well known throughout the institution, the power of their positions is such that colleagues and students of both sexes are often too intimidated to make a complaint. They may go as far as to convince students that not only are sexual intimacies between professors and students proper, but intimacies between therapists and patients are proper, and that those who disagree are naive (Marmor, 1953). Their line is likely to be, "everyone does it, it's no big deal."

The last type is the falsely accused professional. False accusations are rarer than valid ones, but they do happen, and it may be useful to identify some characteristics of the therapist at risk. The false accusation may occur because of a perceptual problem between therapist and patient. For example, a therapist's behavior may encourage or permit a patient to misinterpret; a therapist may not be aware that a patient is sexually aroused; or a therapist may misinterpret a patient's romantic comments, hoping that they are just affectionate, caring comments rather than sexually related comments.

Thus, the therapist who feels complimented when a patient says "you are special to me," "I am in love with you," or "I dreamt I went to bed with you last night," must recognize that such pronouncements may well be direct sexual confrontations. A therapist who interprets these comments from a patient as merely being evidence of a need for a nurturing relationship or of a normally developing therapeutic alliance may be surprised later. The therapist who physically pats or strokes a patient who has just verbalized very positive feelings toward the therapist may stimulate the patient's sexual desires rather than reassure the patient of the mutuality of the caring. Although the therapist's intent may be innocent, the patient's interpretation may not be. It is the therapist's responsibility in such situations to evaluate the situation and to keep the boundaries of the relationship and the limits of the behavior in that relationship clear (Brodsky, 1985).

Cases in which women are the perpetrators and men the victims of sexual intimacies in therapy are rare (Cummings & Sobel, 1985). In the few known cases, the situation appears to fall in the categories of therapist in love or therapist with boundary problems. A less rare occurrence is the homosexual alliance. In the case of women, an older lesbian therapist is most likely to be involved with a younger patient, and the situation may follow any of the subtypes just described. In the case of gay therapists, the age spread between therapist and patient may be the widest of any combination; frequently minors are involved. Increasing numbers of therapists are being brought to the attention of licensing boards and increasing numbers are being delicensed for having sexual intimacies with patients. An interesting aspect of the cases is that complaints from patients who have had sex with their therapists only after officially terminating therapy do not seem to be taken any less seriously by ethics committees and licensing boards than are those cases in which sex more clearly occurred during ongoing therapy (Gottlieb, Sell, & Schoenfeld, 1985).

CHARACTERISTICS OF PATIENTS OR STUDENTS AT RISK

If psychologists can be identified as being at risk by virtue of their demographic characteristics, then patients at risk can also be so identified. Patients at risk for becoming sexually intimate with their therapists are most likely to be female or to be homosexual patients of either sex with a homosexual therapist. The patient is frequently reasonably attractive, young, naive, dependent, and needing to work on relationships, particularly love relationships. Most patients who become sexually involved with their therapists do not enter therapy with presenting complaints about their sexuality. Sexual difficulties are often interpreted first by the therapist. A major characteristic across most types of patients who become involved with their therapists is their trust of the therapist. Patients do not question that "the doctor knows best." Though they may feel at the time that the sexual innuendos or overtures during therapy are improper, they repress or submerge these feelings and try to live up to the therapist's expectations of them. They may or may not be sexually attracted to the therapist, and if they are sexually attracted, it may be because they already confuse their respect and awe of the therapist with sexual desire and love. By the time a sexual relationship is imminent, these patients are so invested in the therapeutic relationship that whether or not they participate sexually is far less important to them than that the doctor approve of them and not abandon them.

These patients do not question the therapist's judgment; they question their own when it conflicts with the therapist's judgment. If they are not sexually aroused, they may hide this "deficit." When the therapist's behavior is identified to them later as being unethical and as having exploited them, these patients feel devastated at their own inability to have recognized this earlier (Brodsky, 1984). Patients with genius-level IQs, patients in extremely responsible positions, patients in happy marriages, and patients normally suspicious to the point of paranoia in other situations may all be unwittingly sexually exploited in a therapeutic situation.

A common type of patient who becomes sexually involved with his or her therapist is the patient who has been physically or sexually abused as a child by his or her own parents. These patients tend to play out the role of abused child with the therapist and to become extremely vulnerable to the therapist's demands, however subtle. Thus, these patients do not question statements by the therapist such as "what we are going to do is secret; don't tell anyone," or "this is what you need to do because I know best." In effect, these statements translate to them as "your role is not to question me but to please me, and if you do not please me, I might leave."

For example, a woman incest victim is usually not that surprised if a father figure such as the therapist is interested in a sexual relationship. In fact, she may have already given cues that she expects to give something of her body or self to the therapist in exchange for his attention. She has learned to relate to men in authority in ways that become readily sexualized. It may be the discussion of her confusion about previous sexual relationships with an incestuous father that encourages a therapist to begin to fantasize a sexual relationship with her (Bouhoutsos & Brodsky, 1985). In the case of the physically abused patient, the sexuality may not necessarily be there, but the same dynamics appear to play a part in her looking to the therapist as someone who must be obeyed in order to receive caring and love. Such patients frequently report that during the sexual episodes they have out-of-body experiences or other related disassociative coping mechanisms. They attempt to isolate the sexual experience, disown it, and move on to take the rest of the therapy hour for what it is (Brodsky, 1984).

Patients who have not been abused, either by family or authority, and may be extremely naive about abuse by anyone, can also be vulnerable to sexual intimacies with the therapist. For example, women patients who have led sheltered, protected lives in which their ministers, uncles, fathers, and brothers have been honest and caring, may be ill prepared for entrance into relationships with men outside the family. Thus, one patient whose caring father died when she was 15 years old later started dating men who did not treat her in the trusted, protective way that the men in her life previously had. She entered therapy to work on her difficulties with a boyfriend. The therapist exploited her trusting nature by encouraging her to become intimate with him. She was convinced that she had been overprotected in the past and would therefore be naive now in not going along with the solutions the doctor offered. If the trusted doctor said that having a sexual relationship with him would help her learn to deal with men in her life, then doctor knew best and as a good patient she should comply even if it felt wrong.

This particular type of patient is most likely to be misunderstood by others and to be faulted for having gone along with the therapist's suggestions. In fact, this patient may be fairly well integrated otherwise, very intelligent, and easy prey only in this particular type of situation. For patients of this type, the experience may be devastating when they realize later that again they have been wrongly naive and trusting and cannot differentiate between when someone is going to hurt them or is genuine. Such patients may develop posttraumatic stress disorders complete with nightmares, somatic complaints, and confusion long after the episodic relationship with the sexually abusing therapist has ended (Brodsky, 1984).

Another type of personality who may be vulnerable to sexual intimacies with the therapist is the woman with a personality disorder, who is demanding and acting out. This type of patient becomes involved sexually with her therapist by confronting him with the full force of her personality, daring the therapist to follow through. The therapist falls into her trap and complies with the demanding, flirtatious, seductive pattern she has developed to interact with others to get her way. What she needs from the therapist is limits on, not collusion with, the behavior. How can such a patient learn the limits and reality related to her demands when she finds that even the exalted therapist is putty in her hands? Therapists who fall for the demands of such a patient, whether the patient is diagnosed as antisocial, borderline, or as having other personality disorders, are essentially incompetent. Therapists are trained to be sensitive to the needs, dynamics, and diagnostic categories of the patients with whom they are working. It may be very ego-inflating to a therapist for the patient to make a sexual overture, but to give in to this overture, even tentatively, only reinforces the patient's belief that such techniques will always work and—especially in the case of women—that sex is all that men want.

Another variant is the hero-worshiping student, students who (again, usually female) find a professor in whom they see a shortcut for gaining stature. Such students are very vulnerable to professors who also have prominent positions in the community or in their departments or universities. The relationship may begin honestly enough but then may progress to a level at which these students begin to have doubts about maintaining the relationship adequately on an academic level or need to cut out the competition with other students. They are likely to justify the alliance by stating that having sex with the professor is no different from having sex with a fellow student. Frequently students such as these have self-doubts about their competency, and being chosen by a charismatic leader bolsters their egos and allows them to identify with the hero. Some student–professor relationships have indeed led to long-term alliances, even marriage. The gray area here is the student's willingness and freedom from coercion. Setting aside the academic ethical issue of having sex with someone who is in a position to evaluate you, there is the issue of the professor's power over the student, of which the student may not be fully aware. Nevertheless, as in the case of the therapist who marries a patient, such relationships can result in long-term marriages as long as nothing goes wrong between the two parties.

Problems arise when one party wants to end the relationship. If the professor ends the relationship prematurely, the student may interpret this as evidence that he or she is not good enough. This perception may affect the student's academic career and make the student feel humiliated. A student who becomes sexually involved because of sexual harassment may have already felt the loss of power in his or her inability to initially reject the professor's advances, but may also be seen by peers as the cheat who trades sex for grades or status.

The fact that such alliances exist in so many graduate programs of psychology (Pope, Levenson, & Schover, 1979) leads one to be concerned that sex between students and professors has not been clearly delineated as being either unethical or illegal. The ethics of such a situation seem to arise only if the student feels a sense of harassment when he or she wishes not to become involved. There is little that prohibits professors and students from freely choosing to have sexual alliances.

Certainly, intimacies with students are not identical to intimacies with clients. Students are supposed to be well integrated, aware, and certainly able to differentiate having sex with the professor from doing academic work. These alliances, however, tend to be between male professors and those female students who are either very naive, desperate, or themselves lacking in boundaries between different aspects of their lives. Such students often feel that this behavior is never wrong and that the professor can never be wrong. I have heard students testify on behalf of such professors with blanket statements of the professor's competence and therapeutic skills, even in ignorance of what the professor does in the classroom or therapy setting. The statement runs, "If Professor X did it, it must be wonderful, because he would never do anything that wasn't wonderful."

SITUATIONS AND CIRCUMSTANCES CONDUCIVE TO SEXUAL INTIMACY

Patients at risk and psychologists at risk may often get together in situations at risk. Just as there are boundaries in relationships between professional and patient or student, so there are boundaries in professional settings. The environment in which a patient is seen communicates the degree to which the relationship can be expected to be strictly professional. Most patients expect to be seen in an office with typical office furniture, such as desks and chairs. They expect the therapist to be fully clothed and in business attire. They expect a waiting room or secretary and consistency in office hours, length of therapy sessions, and payment schedules. Patients who become intimate with their therapists are more likely to see the therapists during evening or weekend hours. There may be no other personnel in the building, or therapy may be conducted in a house, coffee shop, or other casual place. There may be unusual furnishings, like pillows on the floor, soft or unusual lighting, or closed drapes. To the extent that the setting in which the patient is seen varies from the traditional office, the risk for sexual intimacies is higher (Brodsky, 1985).

Therapists' verbalizations can also be conducive to sexual intimacy. Therapists are trained in verbal techniques to make patients comfortable, emotional, open, truthful, and talkative. The therapeutic jargon that therapists learn can also be handy for the sexual seduction of patients. Therapeutic language includes statements that give messages such as telling a women "you need to trust men and this is a safe place for you to learn that"; "I hear what you're saying, only I understand"; "others may be awful, but I really care for you"; "you can do anything you want here—it's safe"; or "it's okay to talk about anything; you can trust me." All such "psychologese" can be aimed at relaxing and opening up patients therapeutically but can be misused to encourage patients to agree to sexual intimacies. Some therapists are not even aware that the techniques they use can be misapplied in this way. They delude themselves into believing that patients are really head over heels in love with them because of their own personal magic rather than because of the fluent verbalizations in which they have been trained and the power of the setting in which they are used.

Seduction may involve the gradual relaxation of a patient, whether this be a formalized relaxation therapy session, a hypnosis session, or something quite informal. Some of the Gestalt techniques of referring to body language and other nonverbal cues can be extremely seductive, and certainly any physical touching can be construed as an invitation to be intimate.

Frequently, women who have been involved with their therapists report that prior to the sexual intimacy, there was a personal intimacy in which the therapist began to disclose more and more about his own life. It is very seductive, particularly to women who want to feel needed, to hear the therapist's problems with his wife, children, officemates, academic rivals, and bosses. Although self-disclosure by the therapist may indeed be therapeutic when used judiciously to help a patient realize that she is not alone in having problems, in being humiliated, or in feeling like a failure, it is not helpful to a patient when the disclosure reveals the therapist's personal relationships, particularly with other women in his life.

When intimacies have occurred, termination of the relationship becomes fraught with difficulty. Some therapists, instead of getting help when such a situation has obviously gotten out of hand, want to hide the implications of what has happened from their own as well as their patients' awareness. Thus, after one or two intimate situations, the therapist may recognize the danger and try to terminate hastily or inform the patient that therapy is not going to work anymore. In such a case, the therapist is avoiding the resolution of a situation iatrogenically induced. In other cases, when patients find out that others are also involved with the therapist, they may become very jealous and precipitously terminate the relationship. In a third scenario, a therapist wants to continue a sexual relationship with a patient but recognizes that he or she is no longer functioning as therapist; the therapist has rationalized, therefore, that if therapy is terminated formally, the patient is free to respond independent of the therapeutic relationship. Unfortunately, the impact of past experiences is not so easily nullified. Finally, there is the type of termination whereby the patient recognizes that something has gone awry and wants to discuss it with the therapist. If the patient becomes angry or accuses the therapist of inappropriate behavior, the therapist may fear litigation. In this situation, the therapist may become angry and refuse to speak to the patient again, leaving in doubt the patient's questions, perceptions, feelings, and continuing need for therapy.

Grievances and litigation may be the final result of sexually intimate relationships between therapists and patients. Obviously, while the relationship is ongoing, patients are in no position to complain. Either they have not yet recognized that there is a problem, or they are in collusion with the therapist, or worst of all, they are so needy that the greater fear is abandonment. The grievances and litigation come only when the patient has recognized that something is wrong, has enough anger toward the therapist to be able to seek a grievance, and has enough ego strength to be able to handle what may be a very trying conflict of words and wills. In fact, one of the biggest problems in litigation in such cases is the "he says, she says" dilemma. Everything has occurred behind closed doors, without witnesses.

The therapist may be the more credible person in situations like this and can usually find a couple of colleagues to attest to his or her character. It is the rare therapist who is so isolated and so alienated from fellow professionals that not even a few colleagues will come to the defense. On the other hand, a patient is likely to have all kinds of enemies and problems with relationships in the outside world. He or she may not be a reliably truthful person in other situations, may not be very well integrated, may even be psychotic. And, as with rape, when a woman accuses a man of sexual abuse, it is often true that the accuser is examined more closely than the accused. Furthermore, therapists may also have much at stake: their reputation, practice, license, and money are all endangered during such a grievance (Keith-Speigel, 1979).

Rehabilitation

When an ethics committee, licensing board, or civil court has convicted a therapist of sexual intimacy with a patient, the question of rehabilitation arises. Obviously, rehabilitation will vary with the parameters of the intimacy. One can easily consider rehabilitation for a therapist who had fallen in love with a patient and had problems with the boundaries of therapy but who was genuinely remorseful and had attempted to get consultation about the mismanagement of the situation. The naive therapist who makes a one-time error and the therapist in a midlife crisis who loses perspective on his or her impact on a patient can be helped. Even some therapists who are guilty of incompetence can be rehabilitated through education. They can take remedial courses in ethics or therapeutic techniques, be supervised by a designated, objective supervisor on a regular basis, or read the research and clinical literature in their areas of weakness.

On the other hand, the therapist whose motives were less than honorable, who had intimacies with several patients, and who, in the case of men, is chronically problematic in relationships with women outside of therapy is probably not easily rehabilitated. In some cases of personality disorder, it is questionable whether or not retraining of the therapist is possible. Rehabilitation as it is sometimes now practiced serves more as a minor form of punishment, perhaps to expiate the guilt of the offending therapist and, maybe even more, of the sanctioning committee or court. Alternatively, the revocation of a license and practice is a very severe punishment. To give a therapist who has made a gross error a method to regain that license would appear honorable, but this gesture needs to be balanced against the profession's duty to protect the public. As mental health workers, psychologists need to come to terms with their weak ability to predict future behavior on the basis of past unethical, immoral, or illegal behavior. In one case, a state board debated at length the merits of renewing the revoked license of a therapist who had committed multiple infractions and had already undergone a "supervised" period during which a new patient brought a complaint of a sexual intimacy. This case raises the question: At what point should a therapist be refused further chances to reform?

A thorny issue in rehabilitation is the development of criteria. What should be known about a sexually abusive therapist before he or she is allowed to do therapy again with a vulnerable population? Should there simply be a time period in which to expiate everyone's guilt? Is such a time period tantamount to being on probation? Does one expect merely remorse and contrition from an abusive therapist or a certain level of achievement? Should the therapist learn through reading and coursework, should there be supervision and guidance, and, if so, how should progress be monitored? Questions about supervision include the following: Who is a good supervisor? Should a male therapist's supervisor be a woman? Should the supervisor be someone familiar with sexual intimacy issues? Should the supervisor be someone with whom the therapist has had no previous contact? What should be the content of supervision? Should the supervisor do co-therapy with the supervised therapist? Should there be audiotapes of sessions with patients? How frequently should the supervisor meet with the therapist?

In some of the initial attempts by state boards to rehabilitate sexually abusing therapists, the therapist was given a choice of supervisors, and of course the supervisor chosen was often the most lenient. In a case previously mentioned, the supervisor is being sued by a patient abused during the rehabilitation period (Brodsky, 1984). These questions frequently raise heated debates in ethics committees, licensing board hearings, and among the lawyers and patients involved in specific incidents. The answers are not simple. Guidelines would be useful, but, ultimately, sensitivity to the case at hand should dictate procedures to be followed.

ALTERNATIVES TO REHABILITATION

When rehabilitation is not the answer, other alternatives need to be considered. If the therapist is not willing to mediate with the client, does not appear to be a candidate for supervision, or cannot be trusted to work with patients in the future, several alternatives may be pursued. First, ethical sanctions may be administered. Often, the therapist takes a sexual intimacy situation seriously only when a patient files a complaint with an ethics committee. The investigation itself may bring the therapist to the realization that a serious infraction has been committed. If ethical sanctions are issued, they may vary according to degree of severity. In a situation in which a therapist has damaged the patient only minimally and, upon investigation, becomes remorseful and contrite, the issue may be resolved by a reprimand or a censure rather than by more severe punishment. Often the patient involved is delighted to have the situation resolved in a manner in which everyone is treated confidentially, no one is brought up to public censure, and yet a judgment goes against the therapist, thereby satisfying the need of the patient to have the therapist admit error.

Second, when the damage to the patient is considerable, such that she or he may have attempted suicide, needed hospitalization, or suffered a complete disruption in a love relationship, then the sanctions probably should be more severe. In some cases, state law provides for delicensure to protect the public when there has been sexual intimacy with a patient. In such states, steps toward delicensure may be the first recourse, because state associations and licensing boards are more likely to have personnel who will proceed with an investigation than are national organizations. Punishment in terms of suspension or revocation of licensure is indeed a sanction that the therapist is likely to take extremely seriously. But in some states, the professional and penal codes are not explicit about sexual intimacies and may not protect the public adequately from such practices. Thus, ethical sanctions by the profession may represent the only deterrent to this behavior.

A third alternative to rehabilitation is litigation in civil or criminal court, depending on state law and the nature of the sexual intimacy. If assault or rape has occurred, criminal court may be the more appropriate avenue. On the other hand, civil litigation may provide for evaluation of psychological and physical damage to the patient and result in monetary compensation. Again, patients seem more concerned with a judgment against the therapist than with a large amount of compensation. However, large amounts are being awarded partly as a punitive measure when the behavior of the therapist has been particularly out of line or the damage has been severe. The majority of cases of sexual intimacy between patients and therapists are settled out of court (Lerman, 1982; Wright, 1981). The prospects of reliving the embarrassment and humiliation of the experience and of a cross-examination are fraught with anxiety for both patient and therapist. Lawyers of patients in such situations often become quasi-therapists to their clients.

In the cases of professors who become involved with students, academic hearings may be held with faculty as judges. At stake is the reputation of an institution whose professors are known to engage in sexual intimacies or harassment of students and patients. Such behaviors are no longer humorously endured by the academic community (Pope et al., 1979). Although such proceedings may deal with censure or dismissal of the faculty member, another issue prominent in academic institutions is the effect of the behavior on students in training. There is some clinical evidence that professors who have sexual intimacies with their patients and students serve as role models in producing future generations of offending therapists and professors. The value of punishment over rehabilitation in these situations is that it emphasizes the seriousness of a situation that has been the subject of private and professional jokes for decades. Fortunately, the professor or therapist who has sex with a patient is no longer seen as a rascal who has the chutzpah to get away with it.

Reports of sexual intimacies and sexual harassment have been increasing. In the last few years, the greatest single category of complaints to the APA ethics committee has been sexual intimacy (APA, 1986). Judgments against therapists, dismissal of professors, revocation of licenses, and large civil court damage awards are no longer unusual.

Prevention

Preliminary to prevention is the acknowledgment that sexual intimacies in therapy are unethical, illegal, damaging—and prevalent. There has been professional outrage over victimization through child abuse, rape, and spouse battering. That there may be abuse within the professional therapy relationship is more difficult for psychologists to own. We psychologists must recognize not only that some of our colleagues are hurting themselves (and indirectly affecting their patients) through distressed behavior such as alcoholism or burnout but also that they can be directly and devastatingly abusive to their patients. This acknowledgment needs to be not only a professional one but a public one as well. We need to educate potential victims as well as potential perpetrators. There is a beginning effort in this direction by planned publication of documents such as the pamphlet being prepared by the Committee on Women of the American Psychological Association to enlighten consumers of psychotherapy in the identification of inappropriate sexual behavior between therapists and patients and sources of information regarding grievances and emotional support. These documents may be useful for therapists in training as well.

Training is the locus for primary prevention of sexual intimacies between patients and therapists and between students and their professors. Students currently being trained in a few enlightened programs are addressing issues such as personal involvement in managing potentially erotic transference and countertransference with patients (Brodsky, 1977). In these programs, students gain valuable insights about their own vulnerability and about techniques to avoid becoming involved without being rejecting.

Although several kinds of training resources are available now in the form of videotapes, workshops, and readings (Lerman, 1984), they are rarely sought out by traditional academic programs or by mainstream therapists in continuing education. It is more likely that feminists already aware of the problems will attend voluntary workshops on sexual intimacy between patients and therapists. Judging from the attendance at national and regional workshops given by the American Psychological Association and its divisions on sexual intimacies and sex roles in therapy, the most vulnerable demographic group, the middle-aged male private practitioner, is probably the least likely to choose such continuing education training, although ethics committee and state board members are increasingly prominent in workshops and conferences in recent years (Brodsky, 1986). Perhaps one day documentation of training in this area will be required for all licensed psychologists, as California has mandated for the areas of human sexuality and child abuse. Training with videotapes of situations with potential for sexual intimacy is one technique I have used frequently and beneficially (Brodsky, 1979), and which has become a recommended tool for trainers by the Women's Committee of the American Psychiatric Association, which has just completed a training tape for use by psychiatrists. It is not possible, however, to say at this point that any training has been particularly effective, because there are no outcome studies. Although it is known who is vulnerable under what conditions, it is not known if any particular training really reduces vulnerability. Nevertheless, knowledge of high risk, the awareness of the impact on the patient and on the therapist, and the deterrent of litigation and ethical sanctions all play a part in the primary prevention of this behavior.

At the secondary prevention level are the confrontation of a suspected therapist by colleagues and the use of consultation by more aware therapists who recognize their own involvement before damage has become inevitable. Some therapists are able to recognize when a patient is difficult to handle or when the patient may be misconstruing statements and actions or becoming personally involved with the therapist beyond the therapy hour. The feelings of omnipotence and pan expertise of the older, experienced therapist do not seem to be as great in the younger generation of therapists, who have been trained to be more egalitarian and more respectful of their patients. Moreover, most male therapists are becoming aware of the need to consult with female therapist colleagues about female patients who are difficult because of the intensity, persistence, or erotic overtones of the transference.

In fact, documentating of such consultations will be most helpful to the therapist if an unjustified complaint is made. Taking comprehensive notes on sessions in which transferences become eroticized can also be very valuable. One should note professions of love by the patient, the therapist's response, and any consultation with a therapist of the same sex as the patient. Documenting this progress in the chart or the notes minimizes the possibility of gross misperceptions and misunderstandings on the part of either the patient or the therapist.

Another level of secondary prevention is mediation, which can helpful when a patient has already confronted the therapist or when therapy has terminated precipitously. Schoener, Milgrom, and Gonsiorek (1983) have been doing mediation with patients who have been sexually abused or intimately involved with their therapists. They have developed a formal technique whereby a mediator confronts both the therapist and the patient about the situation, in order to help them resolve it. Such mediation can be successful. In one case, I was a mediator for a session that included a patient, the confronted therapist with whom she had terminated therapy, the current therapist as the patient's support, and a support person for the confronted therapist (Bouhoutsos & Brodsky, 1985). The resolution was a happy one. The patient had sought further therapy because she had reacted strongly to having had a sexual relationship with her previous therapist and was dealing very poorly with her own questions of how she got involved and what it meant to her therapist-lover. She needed to get back in touch with the previous therapist but not without support. The therapist was frightened of the prospect of being sued and was concerned over his negative impact on the patient. The mediation session served to clear the air for everyone involved and left everyone feeling safe from fear of further action and comforted that the previous therapist did indeed care for the patient enough to acknowledge his misjudgment in the situation. He reassured the patient that he had learned from his mistakes and would not become involved with other patients.

Unfortunately, at this time mediation is a mechanism only for those who agree to it. The California State Ethics Committee is now experimenting with incorporating mediation sessions into their procedure for handling sexual intimacy complaints. Perhaps like divorce mediation, an institutionalized procedure can handle many situations at the secondary prevention level.

At the tertiary prevention level, most important is making rehabilitation realistic. On the one hand, some therapists should simply not see patients anymore and perhaps should not have been licensed in the first place. It is unfortunate that bringing a therapist to a committee, a judge, or a licensing board because of a sexual infraction may be the first opportunity for preventing an incompetent or psychopathic therapist from continuing to see patients. On the other hand, rehabilitation makes sense in cases of erroneous judgment, such as a single-episode mistake or a one-patient involvement by a therapist who falls in love. Most licensing boards and other sanctioning bodies have experienced problems with developing rehabilitation models for professionals who have been sexually intimate with patients.

Part of the problem may be that the sanctioning institutions are composed mainly of high-risk individuals—middle-aged men in private practice. It may be that some of them tend to overidentify with the problem, recalling in their own practice having had a sexual feeling for a particular female patient with whom they may have fantasized or actually considered a romantic relationship (Pope, Keith-Spiegel, & Tabachnick, 1986). Such individuals might find it difficult to punish transgressors in this area if they believe that they themselves have narrowly escaped. There is a considerable difference, however, between having a fantasy or one weak moment and engaging in a continuing sexual relationship.

It is important to have on any sanctioning committee someone with knowledge of the sexism involved in the choice of victims and an appreciation of the differential impact of the behaviors that are motivated by personal gain versus those that represent unintended involvement. Thus, educating sanctioning committee members might be the best tertiary prevention. Rehabilitation is realistic as tertiary prevention only when it deals with the problematic dilemmas of supervision, such as finding appropriate supervisors, developing tight criteria for time limits, defining achievement levels, evaluating therapists' motivations, developing a program of retraining, and removing the causative factors that would make a particular therapist more vulnerable than the average therapist.

CONCLUSION

Although it would be foolish to expect therapists who have had sexual intimacies with their patients to turn themselves in upon discovering that this behavior is unethical, it is not foolish to anticipate that at the moment of crisis, a confidential source of legal, ethical, and professional guidelines on this issue would be welcome. Even if the situation had already occurred, a hotline type of consultation could indeed save the situation by helping the therapist to go back to the patient to work things out, to acknowledge rather than deny the patient's perceptions, to try to resolve the issue with the patient by offering to bring in a consultant to the session, or to offer to transfer the patient to someone else. All of these responses are superior by far to the more common responses: The therapist denies that anything sexual happened, denies that he or she may have contributed to the patient's sexual perceptions, denies that the intimacy had any negative effect on the patient, or denies that it might be helpful to ever see the patient again to resolve the situation.

Sexual intimacies between patients and therapists or between professors and students are not frivolous matters. Although discussions of them may elicit nervous laughter from the naive, those of us who have worked with these populations know far too well the damage and distress the situation can mean for both patients and therapists (Bouhoutsos et al., 1983; Feldman-Summers, 1984). Whether the distress of a psychologist is based on a psychosis, a character disorder with loss of boundaries, a character disorder built on lack of remorse or compassion for others, lack of judgment, or lack of training, the therapist who engages in such behavior can indeed be dangerous. Prevention is the best solution.

References

American Psychological Association. (1981). Ethical principles of psychologists. *American Psychologist, 36*(6), 633–638.

American Psychological Association, Ethics Committee. (1986). Report of the Ethics Committee: 1985. *American Psychologist, 41,* 694–697.

Belote, B. J. (1977). Sexual intimacy between female clients and male psychotherapists: Masochistic sabotage. *Dissertation Abstracts International, 38*(2–B), 887.

Bouhoutsos, J. C., & Brodsky, A. M. (1985). Mediation in therapist–client sex: A model. *Psychotherapy: Theory, Research, & Practice, 22*(2), 189–193.

Bouhoutsos, J., Holroyd, J., Lerman, H., Forer, B. R., & Greenberg, M. (1983). Sexual intimacy between psychotherapists and patients. *Professional Psychology, 14*(2), 185–196.

Brodsky, A. M. (Producer). (1979). *Sex fair psychotherapy stimulus films. Series 1–Relationships between clients and therapists.* A 30-minute videotape available from Educational Media, University of Alabama.

Brodsky, A. M. (1984). *Issues in the litigation of a sexually abusive therapist.* A symposium presented at the meeting of the American Psychological Association, Toronto, Canada.

Brodsky, A. M. (1985). Sex between therapists and patients: Ethical gray areas. *Psychotherapy in Private Practice, 3*(1), 57–62.

Brodsky, A. M. (1986, May). Sex between patient and therapist: Psychology's data and response. Paper presented at the meeting of the American Psychiatric Association, Washington, DC.

Butler, S. E., & Zelen, S. L. (1977). Sexual intimacies between therapists and patients. *Psychotherapy: Theory, Research and Practice, 14*(2), 139–145.

Chesler, P. (1972). *Women and madness.* New York: Doubleday.

Cummings, N. A., & Sobel, S. B. (1985). Malpractice insurance: Update on sex claims. *Psychotherapy, 22,* 186–188.

D'Addario, L. J. (1978). Sexual relations between female clients and male therapists. *Dissertation Abstracts International, 38*(10–B), 5007.

Feldman-Summers, S., & Jones G. (1984). Psychological impacts of sexual contact between therapists or other health care practitioners and their clients. *Journal of Consulting and Clinical Psychology, 52*(6), 1054–1061.

Freeman, L., & Roy, J. (1976). *Betrayal.* New York: Stein & Day.

Gartrell, N., Herman, J. Olarte, S. Feldstein, M., & Localio, R. (in press). Psychiatrist-patient sexual contact: Results of a national survey. *American Journal of Psychiatry.*

Gottlieb, M. C., Sell, J. M., & Schoenfeld, L. (1985, August). *Ethical considerations of social/romantic relationships with present and former clients.* Paper presented at the meeting of the American Psychological Association, Los Angeles, CA.

Hare-Mustin, R. T., & Hall, J. E. (1983). Sanctions and the diversity of ethical complaints against psychologists. *American Psychologist, 38*(6), 714–728.

Holroyd, J., & Brodsky, A. M. (1977). Psychologists' attitudes and practices regarding erotic and nonerotic physical contact with patients. *American Psychologist, 32*(10), 843–849.

Holroyd, J. C., & Brodsky, A. M. (1980). Does touching patients lead to sexual intercourse? *Professional Psychology, 11*(5), 807–811.

Kardener, S. H., Fuller, M., & Mensh, I. V. (1973). A survey of physicians' attitudes and practices regarding erotic and nonerotic contact with patients. *American Journal of Psychiatry, 130*(10), 1077–1081.

Keith-Spiegel, P. (1979, August). *Sex with clients: Ten reasons why it is a very stupid thing to do.* Presented at the meeting of the American Psychological Association, New York, NY.

Lerman, H. (1982). Misconduct by therapists. *American Psychologist, 37*(11), 1289–1290.

Lerman, H. (1984). *Sexual intimacies between psychotherapists and patients: A bibliography.* Unpublished manuscript. Available from Patricia Hannigan, California State University at Fullerton.

Marmor, J. (1953). The feeling of superiority: An occupational hazard in the practice of psychotherapy. *American Journal of Psychiatry, 110*(5), 370–373.

Masters, W. H., & Johnson, V. E. (1975, May). *Principles of the new sex therapy.* Paper presented at the meeting of the American Psychiatric Association, Washington, DC.

McCartney, J. L. (1966). Overt transference. *Journal of Sex Research, 2,* 227–237.

Pope, K. S., Keith-Spiegel, P., & Tabachnick, B. G. (1986). Sexual attraction to clients: The human therapist and the (sometimes) inhuman training system. *American Psychologist, 41,* 147–158.

Pope, K. S., Levenson, H., & Schover, L. R. (1979). Sexual intimacy in psychology training: Results and implications of national survey. *American Psychologist, 34*(8), 682–689.

Schoener, G., Milgrom, J., & Gonsiorek, J. (1983). *Responding therapeutically to clients who have been sexually involved with their psychotherapists.* Unpublished manuscript. Available from Walk-In Counseling Center, 2421 Chicago Ave. S., Minneapolis, MN.

Shepard, M. (1971). *The love treatment: Sexual intimacy between patients and psychotherapists.* New York: Peter Wyden.

Smith, S. (1982). *The sexually abused patient and the abusing therapist: A study in sadomasochistic relationships.* Paper presented at the meeting of the American Psychological Association, Washington, DC.

Taylor, B. J., & Wagner, N. N. (1976). Sex between therapists and clients: A review and analysis. *Professional Psychology, 7*(4), 593–601.

Wright, R. H. (1981). Psychologists and professional liability (malpractice) insurance: A retrospective review. *American Psychologist, 36*(12) 1485–1493.

LEGAL LIABILITY 9
AND PSYCHOLOGISTS

Randolph P. Reaves

Aside from lawyers, the professionals who spend the most time in courtrooms these days are psychologists. They appear in a number of different roles, often simply as expert witnesses. In this chapter I focus on those legal entanglements that involve potential liability for psychologists. Principally there are three areas to consider: civil liability, criminal liability, and license-related liability.

In the section on civil liability I explore most of the causes of action that have been brought against psychologists for compensatory and punitive damages. In the section on criminal liability I explore certain activities that can lead to criminal prosecution. Finally, in the section on licensure liability I review an often overlooked area that should concern psychologists—administrative action against a professional's license. It is difficult for practicing psychologists to avoid legal liability while functioning at full capacity. Therefore, I assume that the impaired professional will experience even greater difficulty in this highly litigious society. I acknowledge the lack of data to support this assumption, except in professional disciplinary cases, but proffer the assumption nevertheless.

CIVIL LIABILITY

A civil lawsuit is, of course, different in many respects from a criminal trial. In a civil lawsuit, a defendant is not charged with having violated a criminal statute, although violations of certain statutes sometimes play a role. In a civil action, a defendant is charged with having committed a tort upon the person of another individual or entity. Simply defined, a tort is a civil wrong for which the law provides a remedy if another person has been damaged.

Civil trials differ markedly from criminal trials. The actors involved are different. A plaintiff in a civil suit is represented not by a state prosecutor but by a trial lawyer of his or her choosing. The defendant or defendants are, of course, represented by another lawyer of their choosing or chosen by their insurance carrier. The case is tried most often before a jury, although the number of jurors may vary according to the jurisdiction and the tribunal in which the case is tried. Most states still require unanimous verdicts by 12-

person juries, although many states now have laws that allow for civil verdicts with less than unanimity. Federal court civil juries are limited to six individuals.

Other differences include the burden of proof and damages. It is well known that in a criminal trial, the state must prove the defendant guilty beyond a reasonable doubt. That is not the case in civil law. In civil law, the burden of proof is normally a preponderance of the evidence; however, the burden of going forward with the evidence rests on the plaintiff.

Malpractice

The term *malpractice* is frightening to most practitioners, but few realize that it results in a legal advantage. In order for a plaintiff to prove that a lay person involved in ordinary everyday pursuits negligently caused him or her harm, he or she must prove the following:

1. that the defendant owed the plaintiff a duty recognized by law requiring the defendant to exercise reasonable care not to harm the plaintiff;
2. that the defendant breached the duty of care;
3. that the defendant's actions were the cause of the harm done to the plaintiff; and
4. that indeed the plaintiff suffered an injury.

In a malpractice case, the plaintiff's burden is much the same with respect to 3 and 4 in the preceding paragraph. However, in proving 1 and 2, the plaintiff is no longer dealing with an average "reasonable-person" standard. The plaintiff in malpractice actions must establish a duty recognized by law requiring a professional to exercise the degree of care, skill, and diligence that is ordinarily possessed and exercised by those in the same general line of practice under similar circumstances. Furthermore, the plaintiff must prove breach of that particular duty.

Although that certainly can be done, it is much simpler to prove that John Doe drove his car in a negligent manner when he ran a red light and struck another vehicle. Most jurors drive cars and can determine easily enough whether someone else has driven a car in a negligent manner. Most jurors are not mental health professionals, and consequently, the difficulty in proving the duty of a mental health professional and the breach of that duty is much more difficult.

As a matter of fact, in order to carry the plaintiff's burden of proof in a malpractice case, the plaintiff must establish the standard of care and its breach through an expert witness, a task far more difficult than my example of proof of simple negligence. In states where a "locality" rule still exists, the expert must be knowledgeable or must practice in the same locality with the defendant. That type of cooperation is almost impossible for the plaintiff to obtain, but in most professions, it is quite easy to find willing experts to testify for the defendant.

There are many forms of malpractice. A catalog of all of them would be of little use to the reader. Consequently, only the most important are discussed: sexual relations with clients, negligent supervision of hospitalized patients, negligent release of suicidal or dangerous patients, failure to warn, inadequate or inappropriate prescribing, and negligent release of confidential information. Also, it is important to note that although I refer to these forms as "malpractice", they are in fact manifestations of malpractice. In any of its forms, malpractice is professional negligence.

Sexual Relations With Clients

The lawsuit brought against a practitioner alleging sexual activity with a client or clients is devastating from the day it is filed. The press always prints these allegations, and the effects can be destructive and even dangerous. From the legal point of view, these cases are difficult to defend. First, there is some authority in the law that says such a claim sounds not only in professional negligence but also in assault and battery, a cause of action that needs no expert testimony. If a trial judge so rules, the case can easily become nothing more than a swearing match. Many lawyers say that there is nothing harder than trying to prove that a client did not do something. Second, Principle 7 of the American Psychological Association's "Ethical Principles of Psychologists" (APA, 1981) specifically prohibits sex with clients. It is hard to put a defendant on the stand who has engaged in sex with a client or former client and not have him or her make damaging admissions regarding his or her ethical behavior. These cases are usually inflammatory, and the potential for significantly large jury verdicts exists. Moreover, many insurers are trying to deny liability in this area, further endangering the defendant's livelihood.

The case of *Evelyn Walker v. Zane D. Parzen* was tried in or around San Diego, California, in 1981. The plaintiff apparently suffered from depressive anxiety and low esteem, among other things, and sought psychiatric treatment from Dr. Parzen. Dr. Parzen had been recommended by other physicians, and the plaintiff was told that he was the top psychiatrist in La Jolla, California.

A sexual relationship ensued between Parzen and Walker. Parzen freely admitted to having had sex with Walker during a two-and-a-half-year period, during which time he charged her $55.00 per session. The plaintiff ultimately divorced her husband, lost her rights under California Community Property Law, and lost custody of her two children. Parzen had also prescribed excessive medication for the plaintiff, who alleged that she tried to commit suicide more than a dozen times using pills obtained from Parzen or his office. Parzen ultimately referred the plaintiff to another doctor; his notes indicated that at the time he referred her she was a "borderline psychotic."

She sued Parzen for ethical and professional misconduct, including his abuse of the transference and countertransference phenomenon by seducing and sexually abusing her. According to her theory, the therapy she had received not only had not helped her but had actually harmed her psychologically. The plaintiff sought compensatory damages exclusively and did not seek punitive damages. The jury awarded significant compensatory damages in the amount of $4,631,666.

This is certainly not the only significant jury verdict or settlement involving a case of sexual misconduct. These cases are proliferating around the country. For example, *Rosenstein v. Barnes* involved a woman who had a sexual relationship with a California psychologist over a 10-year period. The psychologist sued her for failing to pay her bill, and her counter-claims for sexual misconduct resulted in a jury verdict of $250,000. A Massachusetts case, *Kulick v. Gates,* concerned a 40-year-old woman who alleged a sexual relationship with her psychologist. Damages in the case included distrust of people, mental health professionals in particular; severe depression; and two suicide attempts. The jury, although finding the woman partially at fault, returned a verdict for the plaintiff of $180,000 and $80,000 for her husband. In New York County, New York, the case of *Breitbard v. Leonard* was not settled and went to trial, and a jury returned a $230,000 verdict for a 43-year-old woman who suffered a breakdown after being sexually assaulted by her psychiatrist.

Negligent Supervision Of Hospitalized Patients

Remember that when lawsuits are initially filed, the plaintiff's attorney may not know who the negligent parties are. In order to protect the client, not to mention themselves, most will sue all those who could possibly be guilty of some act of commission or omission leading to injury to that client. Thus, in negligent supervision cases, anybody who could have been responsible is sued.

Negligent supervision is another cause of action that sounds in negligence. Due to the special relationship that exists between a therapist and a patient, a recognizable duty often arises to protect the patient from him- or herself. Breach of the duty occurs when the therapist does or more often fails to do something, which allows the patient to harm him- or herself.

A good example of such a case is *Smith v. Rush Presbyterian St. Luke's Medical Center,* a Chicago, Illinois, case, in which a jury brought back a $75,000 verdict in 1980. The verdict came on behalf of the survivors of a 24-year-old male who killed himself while he was an inpatient in the hospital psychiatric unit. Upon his admission to the unit, he was diagnosed as having a paranoid personality. He cut his wrists on the first night with a soft drink pop-top tab, after which he was placed on a suicide risk list. He was supposed to be observed every 15 minutes. He became more difficult to handle, barricaded himself in his room, and was unresponsive to hospital staff.

Eventually the patient raised his electrically operated bed, placed his head within the frame and lowered the bed onto his neck and head. He managed to crush his neck, was in a coma for nine days, and then died. Not only did the plaintiffs allege that the hospital failed to maintain the appropriate surveillance, but it also alleged, and rightfully so, that the hospital was negligent in placing a suicidal patient in a room where an electrically operated bed was available.

This is a small verdict compared with some of the other incidents of failure to supervise properly. For example, in *Pisel v. The Stamford Hospital,* a Stamford, Connecticut, case, a jury rendered a verdict for $3.6 million in 1978. The plaintiff was then a 26-year-old patient who was semicomatose as a result of brain damage sustained when she wedged her neck between the rails of a hospital bed while she was unattended. She was in a seclusion room in the security wing at the time of her injury; however, the defendant hospital had no policy of constant observation. The plaintiff's experts testified that a proper seclusion room for a patient in the state that the obviously disoriented individual was in should not contain such a hospital bed, unless the patient was under constant observation. Other experts, including psychiatrists and psychiatric nurses, also testified that the hospital's procedure of "frequent checks" was inadequate. In fact, in this case, the nursing procedures of all of the general hospitals in Connecticut were introduced to demonstrate the standard of care that that community required for such patients. In addition, the semicomatose state of the plaintiff affected the size of the verdict.

Another large verdict came in the case of *Radzikowski v. Metcalfe.* In this Indiana case, a jury returned a $1.6 million verdict for the survivors of a psychiatric patient. The defendant psychiatrist had placed the patient in the psychiatric ward at a local hospital, and the patient soon escaped and committed suicide by shooting himself with a pistol.

In *Roesler v. Menorah Medical Center,* a psychiatric patient strangled herself to death, apparently with a pillow case, while unobserved at the defendant hospital. The jury returned a verdict of $200,000 for the survivors.

Even the federal government has been found liable in such cases. In *Smith v. U.S.,* a court awarded damages for a mental patient who escaped from a Veterans Administration hospital and killed himself by throwing himself in front of a train. The patient apparently suffered from paranoid schizophrenia and had led an unproductive life. He had made at least three previous suicide attempts and on occasion exhibited violent tendencies. The court held that the individual should not have been transferred from a locked ward to the open facilities from which he escaped.

In *Campbell v. U.S.,* a Navy hospital was the principal defendant when a 19-year-old woman was brain damaged in a suicide attempt at the hospital. Admitted with a diagnosis of paranoid schizophrenia with an active psychosis, she had a history of past suicide attempts and indicated her present intention to commit suicide. Six days into her hospital stay, she shot herself with her husband's revolver. Apparently, the hospital had failed to search the plaintiff upon admission. The structured settlement came to $1.6 million.

In another difficult case, *Dunn v. Washington Hospital Center,* a jury returned a $750,000 verdict for the death of a woman who had set herself on fire in the defendant hospital. She was a chronic alcoholic who was admitted for treatment of in-stage liver disease and other problems. After wandering in the halls and attempting to leave the hospital, as well as smoking in bed, she was placed in restraints. She then suffered second- and third-degree burns while attempting to burn the restraints with matches that the defendants had failed to find on her person. She died a few weeks later. Among the allegations that the plaintiffs made were the failure to properly supervise a sedated and confused patient, as well as the failure to search a patient who had broken smoking rules.

Negligent Release Of Suicidal Or Dangerous Patients

Failing to properly supervise a hospitalized patient can lead to liability, but failing to admit or releasing a suicidal or dangerous patient can also result in liability. For example, in *Martin v. Washington Hospital Center,* a jury returned a verdict of over $200,000 for the wrongful death of a 26-year-old male who was prematurely discharged from the hospital emergency room. In the emergency room, a physician diagnosed the patient's condition as "anxiety reaction with drug abuse." No psychiatric consultation was requested, nor was the patient hospitalized. He was simply discharged with instructions not to drink or take drugs for at least a week.

Later that day, the decedent drove his car into a parked vehicle at a high rate of speed and was killed. The jury returned this verdict against the attending physician and the hospital, despite the fact that no alcohol or drugs were found in the decedent's system during the autopsy following his death. Although the trial court overturned the jury's decision, the district court of appeals reversed, holding that expert testimony regarding the probable duration of decedent's condition was unnecessary, because the plaintiff had shown that the decedent's disorientation did in fact persist at the time of the accident.

A similar case, *Bell v. New York City Health & Hospital Corp.,* involved a patient with a history of psychiatric illness, including a mental discharge from the Army, as well as a suicide attempt. He was admitted to the psychiatric unit of the defendant hospital, upon the order of a domestic court. The defendant psychiatrist diagnosed acute psychotic schizophrenia. No attempt was made to ascertain the extent of the hallucinations the patient was experiencing. He was released on the sixth day of his hospitalization even though he was more delusional and resistive. He returned to his home and attempted to kill himself by setting himself on fire. A jury returned an award of over $564,000.

A number of cases have resulted in liability when a dangerous patient was released and then committed random acts of violence. The most famous to date is a jury verdict for *Hicks v. Holder* (there was no appeal and consequently no useful appellate court citation) rendered in Montgomery, Alabama for $25 million on behalf of the estate of a person who was killed by an individual who recently had been released from the state mental hospital. Defendants included psychologists, psychiatrists, and the Commissioner of Mental Health. All were included in the jury's general verdict. The case was later settled without appeal for $900,000.

Failure To Warn

I am sure that very few members of the mental health professions have not heard the name Tarasoff. Tatiana Tarasoff was a California teenager who was killed by a young man (Poddar) who was a patient at Cowell Memorial Hospital at the University of California at Berkeley. The killer was examined prior to the crime by psychologists who decided that he should be committed, by two psychiatrists who concurred with this evaluation and recommendation, and by another psychiatrist, chief of the department, who countermanded the psychologists' decision and directed the staff to take no action to confine him. The man carried out his previously expressed threat and killed the unknowing victim. One other important and discouraging fact is that the psychologists had warned the campus police. Three officers took Poddar into custody but released him because they considered him to be rational.

The importance of the *Tarasoff v. Regents of U. of California* case is in the conclusions made by the Supreme Court of California regarding the liability of the psychologist and the psychiatrist involved. That court held that when a psychologist or psychiatrist determines, or pursuant to the standards of the professions, should determine, that a patient presents a serious danger of violence to another, he or she incurs an obligation to use reasonable care to protect the intended victim from such danger. Furthermore, the discharge of this duty may require that the therapist take one or more various steps, depending on the nature of the case, including warning the intended victim or others who are likely to apprise the victim of the danger, notifying the police, or taking whatever steps are reasonably necessary under the circumstances. You do not need to be in practice long to understand how difficult such decisions can be. Mental health professionals know and recognize that predicting violence is unreliable, but this is rarely understood by lay persons. Moreover, the problems with confidential communications are clear and compelling.

There is no simple solution to the problem, and this theory of liability is not limited to California. For instance, *Davis v. Lhim* is a 1981 case in which a Michigan jury awarded $500,000 to the estate of a middle-aged woman who was shot by her son after he was released from a state psychiatric hospital. The woman's son was originally admitted to that hospital with a diagnosis of paranoid schizophrenia, which followed a suicide attempt. He was in prison when he attempted suicide, and the prison records revealed a history of drug addiction and alcohol abuse. He was admitted to the state hospital five times during the three years prior to the admission that was most closely associated with her death, and each time he was diagnosed as having paranoid or undifferentiated schizophrenia with delusions. On his last admission, he was kept two weeks and then released by a psychiatrist.

The mental hospital's records are replete with references to stressful conditions in his home. Two weeks after he was discharged, he shot his mother, who was apparently trying to prevent him from killing himself. Suit was brought, and among other things, the state alleged failure to warn the mother of the patient's dangerous tendencies. Although the hospital escaped liability under the theory of governmental immunity, the jury found against the defendant psychiatrist.

In Kansas, in the federal court case of *Durflinger v. Artiles,* a jury returned a $92,000 verdict for the estate of a woman who, along with her 12-year-old son, was killed by her other son, a psychiatric patient, shortly after his release from a state hospital. The child who killed his brother and mother had been committed to the state psychiatric hospital after he broke into his grandparent's home and was found holding an axe over his grandmother, shouting that he was going to kill both his grandparents and steal their cars. He was diagnosed as passive-aggressive personality with sociopathic tendencies. Instead of being transferred to another state institution, this patient was discharged on the instructions of the hospital staff.

A critical memo was found during discovery that indicated that it was too time-consuming and expensive to transfer this patient. Less than a week after his release, he killed his mother and brother in order to use the family car, allegedly to visit a friend back at the state hospital. Defendants in the case included physicians, psychiatrists, and a psychologist, and it was alleged that the defendants knew of the individual's potential to harm others and had failed to warn these victims of the danger posed by his release. The psychologist settled for $25,000 prior to trial, and the jury returned a verdict in excess of $92,000 against the other defendants.

Inadequate Or Improper Prescribing

Most psychologists will look at this subheading and say, "I can't prescribe; how can I be liable?" Most would also admit that they know a good deal about narcotics that are used in patient therapy and that they have witnessed cases in which patients were the victims of improper prescribing by an attending physician. The types of cases adjudicated by the courts include the following:

1. inadequate antipsychotic medication involving patients who could have been restrained, who were not restrained, and who caused injury to themselves;
2. prescriptions for overdoses that resulted in death or serious injury;
3. negligent overprescriptions to patients who were abusing such drugs;
4. overmedication to the point of dependency;
5. improper use of tranquilizing medications, leading to side effects such as tardive dyskinesia.

People can be held liable for what they do not do as well as for what they do. Psychologists on staff in hospitals or in mixed practices who ignore improper prescribing cases are vulnerable targets for litigation.

Public Disclosure Of Confidential Information

Although the principles of confidentiality have been eroded somewhat, I think it is still fair to say that communications between psychologists and clients should be kept confidential absent a release from the patient, a court order, the presence of child abuse, or in a situation similar to that described in the Tarasoff case. The intentional or negligent release of such information can surely lead to litigation and to liability. In order to prevail in such a case, the plaintiff would have to prove that (a) a confidential relationship existed, (b) public disclosure occurred, (c) private facts were disclosed, and (d) the substance of the disclosed facts were offensive, objectionable, or harmful to the plaintiff's reputation.

Just such a case is *MacDonald v. Clinger,* in which the New York Supreme Court approved a cause of action on behalf of a patient against his psychiatrist, who had disclosed personal information without the patient's consent. In some jurisdictions a claim for invasion of privacy would also be made. A case recognizing such is *Vassiliades v. Garfinckel's, Brooks Brothers, et al.* Here, the District of Columbia courts held that a surgeon could be held liable for invasion of privacy when photographs of a patient were released without appropriate consent.

CRIMINAL LIABILITY

Most psychologists would never think twice about the possibility that they might be some day brought before a grand jury and accused of a criminal offense. It has been my experience, however, that although the numbers involved are small, the phenomenon does occur, often because of ignorance. I will offer a few examples of how it can occur so that you might be extremely cautious in certain areas.

Child Abuse

One of the most difficult fact situations that calls for competent legal advice involves the matter of child abuse. I would be willing to bet that every state in the United States has a mandatory child abuse reporting act. These acts make it a crime to fail to report knowledge of child abuse.

The problem, however, is one of treatment for the alleged child abuser. For example, while drinking, a father strikes a child in a manner that could be construed, given the appropriate circumstances, to be child abuse. The father recognizes his error and seeks psychological treatment. The psychologist is put in a tremendous bind in a case like this. If the psychologist is required to notify the law enforcement authorities, the client will probably deny the incident and will certainly avoid further counseling. Will this help the child or the parent? Not at all. Should the strict letter of the law be followed?

I cannot count the number of times that I have received calls from professionals who are facing this dilemma. It is in many ways a no-win situation and invariably means a judgment call on the part of the professional. Is the child abuse real? Is it so sufficiently present and dangerous that the child's well-being should be addressed first, rather than the parent's or stepparent's problem?

There are no good answers to these questions. Good judgment is essential. Beyond that, the psychologist can only protect him- or herself. To do so requires a second opinion; at least, I think it is of some use to seek one without revealing confidential information. That way, should the problem ever arise, the mental health professional can at least argue that he or she consulted other professionals and that the consensus was that treatment in that particular case was a better option than notifying the authorities. It never hurts to discuss these facts with a lawyer, although legal advice would not necessarily be a defense.

Third-Party Reimbursement

There are many professionals who consciously and unconsciously abuse third-party reimbursement laws. Many mental health professionals unscrupulously bill for time that they are not entitled to bill for or for tests that are given simply because a third-party payer will pay for them.

This abuse will eventually result in quite a number of criminal prosecutions, which already are occurring at an increasing rate. Some professionals get in trouble with criminal laws regarding fraudulent receipt of governmental or other funds through ignorance or through a desire to help other professionals. A classic case is *Fort v. Board of Medical Quality Assurance*. This was not a criminal case; it involved a license-revocation proceeding. Dr. Fort allowed other individuals to sign his name to third-party reimbursement forms. This practice led the third-party payers to believe that he was rendering the treatment when in fact the other professionals were doing so, even though their lack of appropriate credentials made them ineligible to receive third-party pay.

Sexual Relations With Clients

A time is coming when local district attorneys will become involved in criminal prosecutions, for either assault and battery or sexual misconduct, of mental health professionals who have engaged in sexual activity with their clients. These cases will not be limited to male practitioners and female clients. I can think of no worse problem for a female practitioner than to become involved with another female patient, particularly a minor. I believe that it would result in criminal prosecution and that should a conviction occur, significant incarceration could be the result. In fact, in 1984, the Minnesota Legislature amended its statute on Criminal Sexual Conduct in the Third and Fourth Degrees to provide that a psychotherapist who engages in sexual contact or penetration with a patient under certain circumstances is guilty of criminal sexual conduct. A third-degree conviction carries a penalty of up to 10 years' imprisonment and fines of not more than $20,000.

Inappropriate Use Of Credentials

I was involved in the indictment of an individual who, at the request of certain lawyers, identified himself incorrectly before a jury in a murder case. Although the individual felt authorized to use the title *psychologist* in this case, he was not licensed to do so, and the district attorney knew that he was not. Nevertheless, the individual testified regarding the insanity issue and testified that he was a psychologist, a violation of the Psychology Practice Act in that state. This testimony subjected the individual to criminal prosecution.

This kind of case will occur more frequently as organizations such as Victims of Crime and Leniency (VOCAL) begin to focus on professionals who testify in murder cases and cases involving other heinous crimes. Almost all practice acts now include criminal penalties for misrepresentation of professional credentials, and many include civil injunctive relief. Although the civil injunctive relief may sound like a slap on the wrist, it is not, because a civil trial judge can incarcerate a professional who violates an injunctive order such as this for contempt of court. Each new incident can be construed as an additional violation of the order and can subject the individual to significant jail time.

License-Related Liability

The days of the "good old boys and girls" on licensing and certification boards, cronies who could look after and protect the errant practitioner, are gone. Too much pressure has been exerted during the past 10 years. Some of this pressure is a part of the consumer movement, and some of it stems from efforts to contain health care costs, but most of it can be attributed to the efforts of "sunset" committee legislators. Misguided as the sunset movement has been, it has been a vehicle for public scrutiny of once almost secret license-related proceedings.

Suffice it to say that many boards now look for the chance to discipline mental health practitioners who have gone astray. Be this a result of heightened consciousness or of a desire to satisfy legislative review, it is a fact that is beginning to pervade the mental health professions. Although figures regarding these matters are impossible to obtain, some examples exist. For instance, the January 1985 Disciplinary Data System Report issued by the American Association of State Psychology Boards contained a list of 15 psychologists whose licenses were revoked or suspended as of that date. This is a profession in which hardly a handful of such cases can be found reported in regional reporters for the 20 years prior to the 1980s. Moreover, this system does not report licensees placed on probation.

The basis of the vast majority of licensure cases resulting in disciplinary action against psychologists is sexual relations with clients. Studies on the subject are revealing. In 1977, Holroyd and Brodsky conducted a survey of at least 1,000 licensed psychologists. The survey was done by mail and the response rate was over 70 percent. Of those numbers responding, 6.1 percent admitted having engaged in relations with clients during therapy. Another 2.9 percent admitted having sex with a client within 90 days of terminating therapy. The results reported by these psychologists concur with a similar study conducted by Kardener, Fuller, and Mensh in 1973. The target of this survey was Los Angeles area physicians. There, 7.2 percent admitted having engaged in erotic contact, including intercourse, with female patients.

Why are these behaviors so serious in terms of license liability? There are, in my opinion, several reasons. First, such behaviors are condemned by most codes of ethics. Second, if the behaviors are made public, pressure rapidly mounts to bring the alleged perpetrator before a disciplinary panel. Last, and certainly not least, it has been my experience that the mental health professions have more female practitioners than most other professions. They seem to sympathize more readily with the alleged victim and feel strongly that such behaviors should be severely punished.

Misrepresentation of professional qualifications can sometimes lead to disciplinary action. An example is *Packer v. Board of Medical Examiners,* in which a California Court of Appeals upheld the revocation of a psychologist's license, saying that the misrepresentation that the individual had a doctoral degree, although not in itself grounds, was punishable as a misrepresentation of the professional qualifications of honesty and integrity.

A number of conclusions can be drawn from a review of the legal literature concerning psychology. This profession, as well as all other professions, is facing a new crisis in terms of litigation and the threat of litigation. The various theories or causes of action now recognized by state and federal courts expose all mental health practitioners to serious liability. The impaired professional is at even greater risk. He or she cannot, because of the impairment, function in the same manner as the nonimpaired practitioner. The impairment may result in civil, criminal, or license-related liability. Any one of these could result in the loss of family, home, and professional practice.

References

American Association of State Psychology Boards. (1985, January). *Data report.*

American Psychological Association. (1981). Ethical principles of psychologists. *American Psychologist, 36,* 633–638.

Bell v. New York City Health & Hospital Corp., 456 N.Y.S.2d 787 (App. Div. 1982).

Breitbard v. Leonard, 26 A. of Trial of Lawyers of America L. Rep. 187 (1983, May).

Campbell v. U.S., 23 A. of Trial Lawyers of America L. Rep. 474 (1980, Dec.).

Davis v. Lhim, 335 N.W.2d 481 (Mich. App. 1983).

Dunn v. Washington Hospital Center, 26 A. of Trial Lawyers of America L. Rep. 232 (1983, June).

Durflinger v. Artiles, 673 P.2d 86 (Kan. 1983).

Evelyn Walker v. Zane D. Parzen, 24 A. of Trial Lawyers of America L. Rep. 295 (1981, Sept.).

Fort v. Board of Medical Quality Assurance, 185 Cal. Rptr. 836 (Cal. App.).

Hicks v. Holder, CV-81-1621-T, Circuit Court of Montgomery County, Alabama.

Holroyd, J. C., & Brodsky, A. M. (1977). Psychologists' attitudes and practices regarding erotic and nonerotic physical contact with patients. *American Psychologist, 32,* 843–849.

Kardener, S., Fuller, M., & Mensh, I. (1977). A survey of physicians' attitudes and practices regarding erotic and nonerotic contact with patients. *American Journal of Psychiatry, 32,* 1077–1081.

Kulick v. Gates, 28 A. of Trial Lawyers of America L. Rep. 471 (1985, Dec.).

Martin v. Washington Hospital Center, 423 A.2d 913 (D.C. App. 1980).

Minnesota Statutes, § 609.341, et seq. (1984).

Packer v. Board of Medical Examiners, 112 Cal. Rptr. 76 (1974).

Pisel v. Stamford Hospital, 23 A. of Trial Lawyers of America L. Rep. 138 (1979, April).

Radzikowski v. Metcalfe, 22 A. of Trial Lawyers of America L. Rep. 89 (1979, March).

Roesler v. Menorah Medical Center, 21 A. of Trial Lawyers of America L. Rep. 327 (1978, Sept.).

Smith v. Rush Presbyterian St. Luke's Medical Center, 23 A. of Trial Lawyers of America L. Rep. 44 (1980, Feb.).

Smith v. U.S., 437 F. Supp. 1004 (E.D. Pa. 1977).

Tarasoff v. Regents of U. of California, 17 Cal.3d 425, 551 P.2d 334 (Cal. 1976).

Vassiliades v. Garfinckel's, Brooks Brothers, et al., 492 A.2d 580 (1985).

SECTION III: SOLUTIONS

THERAPY WITH DISTRESSED PSYCHOTHERAPISTS: SPECIAL PROBLEMS AND CHALLENGES

10

Florence W. Kaslow

This chapter combines a consideration of: (a) what constitutes impairment or distress in psychologists and other mental health professionals; (b) what therapists bring with them to the task from their prior and current lives that make them vulnerable to burnout and distress (at times illustrated by clinical vignettes); (c) some of the special problems, even hazards, of devoting one's professional life to being a psychotherapist in a clinical, academic, or other institutional setting; (d) the extra challenges of treating professional colleagues as patients—therapeutically, ethically, morally, and legally (illuminated through summaries of actual cases); and (e) education and preventative strategies to enable therapists to be less prone to impairment. I discuss my own excursion into treating therapists in a somewhat stream-of-consciousness style throughout the chapter. The scant extant literature will be cited where relevant, rather than reviewed as a separate section of this chapter.

For over a decade I have been intrigued with questions such as how does one become identified as a therapist's therapist? Why are some clinicians sought out by their colleagues, while others are not? What are the factors that go into selecting a therapist when the patient is also a professional therapist? In what ways is therapy with a therapist similar to and different from therapy with a nontherapist? And what are the special problems, challenges, and rewards of treating professional colleagues?

I began to speculate about these questions when I was on the faculty at Hahnemann Medical University in Philadelphia from 1973 to 1980—a faculty composed of several hundred psychologists, psychiatrists, psychoanalysts, social workers, and marital and family therapists, most of whom maintained independent practices. In this therapy-conscious microcommunity of an urban medical school and graduate school located in a metropolitan, highly professional city, therapy was not only acceptable, but encouraged for trainees and interns. This attitude also permeated the wider community with the result that practicing professionals did not feel stigmatized by seeking therapy or analysis—even when they had supposedly completed analysis or another form of treatment before. A veritable smorgasbord of fine therapists were available for appointments.

In the Analytic Institutes, the choice of therapist was partially predetermined. Only certain distinguished senior members were (and still are) designated as training analysts who could conduct a didactic analysis. Except for this special, long-standing approach, nonanalytic trainees, faculty, and staff were free to seek therapy from whomever they chose. As in other metropolitan communities with several medical schools and graduate and professional schools, reciprocal arrangements were worked out with other universities for treatment because it was preferred that students not be treated by potential or current professors and supervisors in their own institutions. Nevertheless, when a particular faculty member was well reputed as a therapist, some trainees and staff still preferred treatment with that faculty member to going outside the university system, despite the precarious situations regarding protection of confidentiality, potential dual and conflictual roles, and possible jeopardy to careers, if a faculty member and therapist thought a patient too disturbed or dysfunctional to be in the professional training program.

The ethical issues that surfaced regarding whether to transgress confidentiality and discuss the trainee therapist-patient with a program director in order to protect the trainee's current and future patients were quite serious. Because these problems resemble those that practitioners face when treating severely impaired colleagues, I will discuss the issue and its implications later in the chapter. One would think the same problems must periodically confront the training analyst whose analysand shows severe pathology. Yet, I have rarely if ever heard the matter discussed (or written about) in training forums.

During the last few years that I was at Hahnemann, I had an increasing number of therapists as patients—former students who had graduated (as my personal policy was not to treat students in the programs in which I taught), psychiatric residents, and mental health professionals in the community. Often these individuals had heard me present lectures at professional meetings or had read some of my articles. This became one clue as to whom practicing therapists choose for therapy—someone whose philosophy they have some familiarity with and whose work they respect.

From my own clinical cases its seems that therapists are different in some ways from other patients. They are, for example, apparently more eager for the revelations of the therapeutic adventure, yet more uneasy about seeking help, even if they are primarily motivated by "growth goals" rather than overcoming pathological, dysfunctional thinking and behavior. They are more intellectually resistant against clarification and interpretation and capable of using their knowledge to defend themselves from exploring feared areas. They are more curious about and competitive with their therapists and more likely to identify with, yet want to denigrate, their therapist's knowledge and skill. Conversely, I have found that I worked harder with them than nontherapists to help enhance their self-knowledge and self-esteem, and to improve their overall state of being in the world. My positive countertransference entailed wanting to impress them with my ability to truly help them achieve their goals. Because they were more confrontational and critical, it became a special challenge and responsibility—sometimes even a burden. Because, to some extent, everyone is judged by the lay populace and professionals in other disciplines by the adequacy of colleagues in their personal and professional self-presentation, helping a therapist-patient in treatment overcome deep-seated problems and obstacles to effective functioning is indeed a weighty task.

A summary of a sample case should illuminate the concerns alluded to and begin to amplify therapeutic strategies and management in the treatment of psychologists and other mental health professionals.[1]

The case of Liz—High-anxiety, indecisiveness, and procrastination

Liz had been a patient of mine, first in marital treatment and later in individual treatment during 1976 and 1977. She and her husband, Duke, were good friends but not good lovers. She craved more emotional expressiveness, social expansiveness, and creativity in her life-style. She was an artist and in many ways uninhibited, despite her desire to have emotional interactions very specific. By contrast, Duke was an accountant, quite constrained and quiet, and somewhat obsessive–compulsive. He wanted a contemplative life-style and enjoyed fishing or working in the woods for recreation. The complementarity (Pollack, N. Kaslow, & Harvey, 1982) in their personality patterns that had originally attracted them to each other was no longer satisfying. Liz began to escalate her demands on Duke for more articulation of his caring and for greater displays of affection. Duke responded by withdrawing further until they reached an impasse. When it became clear neither wanted to budge from their positions, Liz decided to divorce and see whether she could find a more affectionate, loquacious, and gregarious partner. I worked with both of them during the divorce process to make it as constructive as possible (Kaslow, 1981). When both felt reasonably reintegrated, treatment was terminated by mutual agreement.

Two years later Liz called and was quite elated. She had met a wonderful man named Jerry and was very much in love. Jerry was sensitive, empathic, expressive, caring, and a superb and giving lover. He was divorced, available, and interested. He was a master's-level psychologist working with a well-respected private-practice group and was being urged to pursue his doctorate. I congratulated her on her good fortune and told her I thought it was kind of her to let me know about this exciting development in her life. She said she would like to come in with him for some couples counseling because of a major problem.

Jerry had been actively bisexual. He said he now wanted to make a commitment to heterosexuality and a straight life, yet neither of them were certain whether this was possible. Liz could accept his prior homosexual liaisons, but could not go along with this in the future. Before they became engaged, they wanted to work on this issue. I agreed to see them.

A 9-month course of intensive treatment ensued, usually weekly but twice weekly when needed. It began as couples therapy, but as Jerry's need to work

---

[1] All identifying case materials have been carefully disguised to protect the identities of the actual therapists. Nonetheless, certain critical features (and the therapeutic process) have been described as they occurred so that the rendition contained herein is accurate.

through some turbulent and troubled aspects from his childhood surfaced, we set a pattern of three individual visits for him followed by one conjoint session so Liz would not feel excluded or uninformed. The Masters and Johnson (1979) report on treating bisexuals who wanted to "go straight" had recently been published. Strengthened by its data that men who had had prior successful heterosexual experiences and sincerely wanted to live heterosexually had a high likelihood of succeeding, we began.

Jerry saw his bisexuality as interfering with (a) his desire to marry, live monogamously, and have a family; (b) his ability to be honest in his relationships with colleagues—he had never "come out of the closet" and did not want to be labeled gay; (c) his ability to feel "whole" and proud; and (d) his ability to get into a clinical psychology doctoral program and achieve career success after graduation. He procrastinated about writing testing reports and used other delaying tactics that always made his job seem precarious. He could not resolve the ambivalence between his conscious desire to succeed and his unconscious ways of sabotaging his achievements.

Therapy was psychodynamically oriented with a great deal of time spent reviewing traumatic childhood and adolescent events. In brief, Jerry was raised by his mother and maternal grandmother. His father had deserted them when Jerry was very young, and both women openly abhorred men and did all that they could to see that Jerry "did not become like that scoundrel, your father." They doted on Jerry, caressed him often to satisfy their emotional needs as much as, if not more than, his, and as he grew, continued to physically fondle him all over, including his genitals. Mother bathed "her darling baby" until he was 8 years old, and he remembered being seductively invited to sleep with her whenever he was upset or mom felt lonesome. Whenever he felt sick, grandma's first remedy was an enema. He recounted the anger and shame at enduring her medicinal intrusions. Both mom and grandmom valued cleanliness and orderliness, and forcefully discouraged Jerry from participating in sports; football was totally forbidden.

As we went through these memories, I encouraged Jerry to verbalize his fury about being sexually exploited and deprived of a good image of his father and other men. He visited his mother and over the course of several months made the "declaration of independence" at age 32 that he had been unable to make as a teenager. He told her that he loved her, yet resented how he had been raised, that in the future she could no longer misuse him or instill him with hatred of men and himself, and that he was going to try to locate his father. He said that henceforth he would make his own decisions without undue influence from her. In addition, he joined a spa so he could work out, develop a more muscular physique, and feel more athletic. Liz went too, making this a new aspect of their shared activities.

In Jerry's early adolescence, a male teacher had befriended him. Eager for a father substitute and male mentor, Jerry responded to the teacher's overtures of friendship and spent a great deal of time with him out of school. When Jerry was about 13 years old, his teacher seduced him physically. Hungry for male acceptance, guidance, and companionship, Jerry succumbed. His teacher was generous, considerate, and attentive, and Jerry was grateful. He led a secret life throughout his teen years with this man and his friends. At the same time, Jerry dated some of his female classmates and found he could "swing both ways," maintaining a facade of respectability and normalcy. He even thought he was in love with a woman when he was 22 years old and they decided to marry.

It lasted 4 years, but after 2 years he found himself in an extramarital gay affair. At the time he entered treatment, his ambivalence was enormous. He thoroughly enjoyed his gay friends and their exciting, partly clandestine life-style. He also craved respectability and "the straight life," detesting what he saw happening in the gay community—the men became older and more desperate for partners and never had the chance to have and raise children. He also viewed some of the gay party scene as sick and weird and felt it was not the right place to be if he wanted to devote his career to the pursuit of mental health.

I did some reframing of his early homosexual encounter as a child, seeking a father and needing to be held, loved, and reassured as a frightened little boy. This fit with how much he had enjoyed being rocked, held on his teacher's lap, and massaged. In this context, he was better able to accept his receptivity to the homosexual involvement as fulfilling a basic infantile need for love and nurturance from a father, and a fundamental adolescent need for a male sex role model to respect and emulate. He decided he could move into nonsexual relationships with male colleagues and teachers that fulfilled healthy longings and did not burden him with the emotional commitment of being a lover.

From this Jerry's anal erotic and retentive tendencies became apparent. By dealing with the sexual content, through abreaction and fantasy, he was able to progress through the phallic to the genital stage of development (Abraham, 1921), thus feeling much more heterosexual. Liz's delight reenforced his determination and pleasure in his clearer heterosexual orientation. The imperative urge to hold onto something that belonged to him, despite enemas and other anal intrusions, led to his withholding in many situations, despite a veneer of generosity in superficial relationships. As we unraveled this, he became able to write his testing reports on time and became productive in other areas of his professional life, including applying to doctoral programs.

On a behavioral level, to enable him to resist the temptations of his earlier dual life-style, I indicated that I could only help him reach his goals if he moved out of the neighborhood where his gay friends lived, discontinued visiting their special clubs, and made a total break from the life-style. To stabilize his heterosexuality, he had to agree to total abstinence. This generated great resistance and a month-long struggle. Finally, with urging from Liz, a nonnegotiable position from me, and reenforcement from his boss, with whom he had finally discussed his situation, he agreed to move in with Liz and to place a 2-year moratorium on homosexual friendships.

When treatment terminated in 1980, Liz and Jerry had married. He was working part-time and going to school part-time. He still wished Liz were thinner (built more like a boy?) and missed the camaraderie of his gay friends, but he felt more content and at peace with his life. Five years later, they have one child and are happily anticipating another. They are well suited in their mutual enjoyment of an artistic and creative life-style, and Jerry is expecting to get his PhD in 1986. He has remained monogamous and affectionate, and his qualities of sensitivity and empathy have made his private practice successful.

[Pennsylvania is one of the states where psychologists can be licensed and practice independently at the master's level.] He feels good about himself and his choice and believes it enables him to guide patients through times of critical decision making.

My impression is that this therapy, which blended individual and marital sessions, psychodynamic, behavioral, and strategic interventions, and occurred within the parameters of the goals set by the therapist-patient, enabled him to become more effective in his work and, in effect, ensured him against future, more severe impairment. No ethical issues surfaced. Jerry had informed his psychologist employer of his problems; he, in turn, carefully supervised Jerry's therapy cases so that personal difficulties did not become blind spots in Jerry's work or become superimposed on his patients.

THERAPY WITH THERAPISTS

After I relocated to Florida in the early 1980s and set up an independent practice in the Palm Beach area, I soon found that about one third of my practice was composed of therapists. No specific or conscious effort made this happen. It occurred as a result of my being contacted by therapists who had heard me present lectures for the local mental health association, do workshops for organizations such as Psychological Seminars, Incorporated, present lectures, appear on radio and television, or serve as a staff trainer or consultant to a local agency. My therapist-patients (TPs) included psychologists, psychiatrists, guidance counselors, social workers, and marriage and family therapists. Treatment modalities included individual, couples, family, sex, divorce, and remarriage therapies.

Presenting problems and symptomatology ranged from desire for growth and greater self-actualization through moderate situational distress and reactive depressions, to phobic anxieties, extreme fears, and severe disorders. On occasion these problems were serious enough to warrant my recommending that a TP request a leave of absence from work or temporarily abstain from private practice to enter voluntarily an in-patient substance abuse program or be in psychotherapy three times a week, plus attend support groups until the crises were averted. When TPs stabilized their functioning at a higher and more suitable level, they were again ready to competently and responsibly treat other distressed individuals.

To ascertain more about psychotherapy with psychotherapists, I decided to study the subject in depth and asked others who I knew were also engaged in this endeavor to collaborate. This resulted in the publication of a multi-authored book on that subject (Kaslow, 1984a). Chapters dealt with TPs who gravitated toward or sought out a variety of different treatment modalities, choosing either the therapist or the approach they thought they would find most beneficial, such as behavioral and multimodal therapy (Fay & Lazarus, 1984), psychoanalytic treatment (Greenberg & F. Kaslow, 1984), hypnotherapy (Churchill, 1984), group psychotherapy (E. Coché, 1984), marital and family therapy (F. Kaslow, 1984b), divorce mediation (Neville, 1984), or therapy that takes into account the special concerns of "women therapists" (J. Coché, 1984). Because we wanted to ascertain more about current expectations regarding therapy for graduate students, interns, and residents, and about how they are personally socialized into the therapeutic culture, one chapter, based partly on a research study, was written about "the interface of personal treatment and clinical training for psychotherapist trainees" (N. Kaslow & Friedman, 1984).

Also, despite the fact that insurance companies will not reimburse for this kind of therapy, I was aware that a certain amount of telephone psychotherapy occurs when trainees or therapists are deeply invested in a therapeutic relationship; and either the TP or the treating therapist goes on a prolonged vacation, sabbatical, or relocates; and they agree that termination or transfer to another therapist would be counterindicated. This was dealt with in a chapter on "long-term telephone psychotherapy," which found it to be efficacious to continue in telephone therapy for reasons such as the following: separation would be considered a harmful abandonment; they were at a critical juncture in therapy and severing the relationship would be injurious; or the transference issues needed resolution before termination was warranted (Padach, 1984).

Several themes emerged across three or more chapters that seem fundamental to therapy with distressed therapists. I shall try to elaborate those that surfaced in the aforementioned volume, those described in a recent article by Fleischer and Wissler (1985); and those raised in workshops I have conducted in the past 18 months on this topic. I shall discuss possible ways of coping appropriately with these. (Greenberg & Stoller [1981] have also addressed therapy for therapists.) I shall use vignettes from cases in my clinical practice illustratively.

Boundary Issues

In other contexts, TPs are also colleagues and may assume an attitude of camaraderie. They utilize the same technical language and concepts and may assume more of a shared identity with the treating therapist. They may expect special consideration regarding fees (and certain therapists comfortably extend professional courtesy in the form of lower fees for colleagues), missed appointments or lateness, and long telephone conversations (for which they assume they will not be billed).

In addition, therapists and trainee TPs are likely to come in contact with one another at professional association meetings, continuing education workshops, and social events such as dinner parties. If a TP and therapist work in the same setting, they may end up in staff meetings together. The trainee-patient may be in the therapist's class or become his or her supervisee (Fay & Lazarus, 1984).

Fleischer and Wissler (1985) have commented that "the choice of therapist should permit the patient a reasonable degree of social life-space anonymity" (p. 588). The same applies to the therapist. In a large, metropolitan area, it is relatively easy to travel a short distance for treatment and find a fine therapist with whom one rarely has outside contact. In smaller towns it is quite another story. There may be only one graduate or professional school, and most of the better practitioners are affiliated as full or adjunct faculty, as clinical or practicum supervisors, or as research advisors. Locating a senior clinician within a reasonable distance may be extremely difficult. The potential patient may decide to seek convenience and expertise, utilizing someone on the faculty or staff and risking loss of anonymity by being seen coming and going to and from their office for regular sessions.

Duplicate roles are much harder to avoid in smaller communities, outside as well as inside academe, and so must be discussed between trainee-patient and therapist at the beginning of the relationship. Consider, for example, the following:

The case of Suzie K—Therapy, supervision, or consultation?

Shortly after my arrival in South Florida, I was invited to serve as a case consultant and staff trainer in family therapy for an agency in the Hollywood area. Several months after this affiliation began, two of the staff members asked if they could come to my office for supervision in tandem. It was acceptable to the agency director and we began.

After a few sessions, the male member of the supervision dyad decided it was too far to travel (about 1 hour and 15 minutes each way). Suzie K decided to continue, and we adjusted the fee per session accordingly. By the second individual session, the content she wanted to discuss became more therapeutic than supervisory. She shifted from a case orientation, regarding her alcoholic clients, to her concerns about her increasing sense of distance from her alcoholic husband. Her own marital turmoil contributed to her often going to work feeling agitated and too preoccupied with her inner turbulence to concentrate on patients' stories and needs. At the end of the session, I sought to clarify whether she wanted supervision or therapy with me, indicating that we might do both sequentially over time but not simultaneously as it would be too confusing. She decided therapy was her more pressing need and that working through her personal dilemmas might serve to enhance her therapeutic capability as much as additional supervision might.

We then set up more frequent sessions and agreed on a therapeutic focus and goals. We discussed whether she wanted her colleagues to know she was in therapy with me and she definitely did not. We agreed that when I did my consultations at the agency we would both act as if we had no special additional relationship. We would avoid any planned social interaction in small groups during the duration of her treatment, which continued for about a year. During that time of combined psychodynamic, family of origin, and existential, humanistic treatment, she became more assertive and comfortable in her abilities as a therapist. She reworked some unfinished childhood issues with her parents on visits home, following through on my coaching interventions (Bowen, 1978). She decided that she and her husband had become irreconcilably incompatible, and that she was strong and independent enough to pursue the divorce she had long wanted. In addition, as alcoholism had become her Achilles' heel, she realized that she should not be treating such substance abusers until and unless she had adequately resolved her own thoughts and emotions about this disease and what was labeled by Al Anon as her co-alcoholic status. During the time she was in treatment, we inevitably saw each other at professional meetings; however, each maintained, by mutual agreement, a posture of casual friendliness and detachment. Now two years post-termination, we have resumed a more collegial, personal, and spontaneous relationship when we meet.

It seems imperative that during the time a therapist is in treatment, if specific problems such as the co-addiction of Suzie K surface, that the person refrain from treating others with similar problems in order to avoid such potential difficulties as loss of objectivity, overidentification, or being unduly harsh because of projective identification or a rejecting negative counter-transference. As Fleischer and Wissler have indicated, "the task of boundary maintenance, even extending beyond the interview segment of psychotherapy, is usually more rigorously tested by TPs than by "patients who are not thera-pists'" (1985, p. 588).

One other aspect of this boundary issue bears mentioning here. The TP, like any other patient, is apt to discuss with friends and associates the therapist as a person. Often this seems to be done without any indication that the TP is in treatment with the person, and it may occur during a particularly traumatic period in the therapeutic process when the transference is negative and the TP is highly critical. If the implication is that the TP has heard from several others that Dr. X is not a very skilled, genuine, or empathic therapist, or that the TP has heard Dr. X lecture or viewed him or her over a one-way mirror and was disappointed with the quality of work, this can be somewhat damaging to the therapist's reputation. However, the treating therapist cannot respond by dis-closing that the critic is a patient, given that the treating therapist is bound by confidentiality.

I know of one extremely well-known psychologist in Florida who also treats many therapists and other prominent professionals in his home com-munity. He has chosen to severely curtail his social life to avoid unwanted contacts outside the sanctuary of his therapy office. My approach is to discuss with each TP I treat how we will handle chance meetings in order not to detract from the potency of the therapeutic relationship. This is the most im-portant aspect of our interaction. Other facets are secondary and may not be permitted to conflict with or overshadow it.

Role Modeling

Many TPs carefully select a therapist, perhaps as a way of seeking a mentor, teacher, or person to emulate as well as a healer. Generally I have found that TPs gravitate toward someone with impeccable credentials and an outstanding reputation. The therapist sought is to be beyond reproach, clinically and ethi-cally, and someone the TP can respect and identify with. J. Coché (1984) found that many women therapists specifically sought treatment with her because, as a woman therapist, she was well known for her clinical skill, her organizational activities in city and state psychological groups, and her ability to successfully combine career, marriage, and family. In individual treatment and in the re-search questionnaire she administered to gather data for her article, she found that the desire to have a competent female psychologist as a therapeutic role model for both the professional and personal life of females TPs was a promi-nent factor in their choice of therapist. My own experience with female TPs duplicates Coché's. This factor seems particularly salient in the case histories of women who have had few, if any, high profile and prestigious women professors in psychology or psychiatry graduate or professional training programs. Female therapists feel a special need in their quest to fashion their own sense of self and to help them resolve critical identity issues.

Some TPs go further, as if in pursuit of a "guru" therapist. Three quarters of a century ago, to have been analyzed by Freud, Adler, or Jung was a mark of great distinction—as if being in the frequent presence of such greatness somehow elevated the patient to the status of greatness by some kind of (mystical) incorporation of the analyst's essence. This phenomenon still seems operative in some quarters. To be treated by the most esteemed therapist in a community, with whom the patient becomes highly, almost symbiotically, identified, is considered by some as an anointment through a variation of a "laying on of hands" by the master therapist. TPs then pattern their own treatment style, personality, and interventions as closely as possible after their sometimes unsuspecting therapist. Any deviation might feel like an unwarranted, nonappreciative disloyalty.

Because of the role-modeling aspect of therapy with TPs, the ethical behavior of the therapist must be beyond reproach. If the therapist lacks honesty, integrity, and authenticity, the TP is likely to become demoralized, even desperate, as he or she sees in the therapist a poor representative of the self-idealized therapist. Throughout the remainder of this section on themes in the treatment of troubled or disturbed TPs, I will discuss the case of Dr. R.

Dr. R—A severe anxiety disorder with borderline features and substance abuse behaviors

Dr. R was referred to me in early 1982 by a psychologist in Orlando who had done a full psychometric assessment of him and believed he needed long-term, intensive treatment with a gentle yet strong female therapist. Dr. R had graduated more than a decade earlier from an APA-approved PhD program in which he had run into interpersonal conflicts with faculty and done marginal academic and clinical work despite an IQ in the superior range. Since then he had "knocked around" professionally, moving from job to job and community to community, working in several residential treatment programs for disturbed male adolescents, and doing some part-time undergraduate college teaching.

At the time of his beginning therapy with me Dr. R was on the periphery of psychology, uncertain whether he wanted to remain in the profession and unhappy, even disgusted, with his life. He was dissatisfied with his lack of achievement, low income, and continuing unsatisfying interpersonal relationships. A man in his late 30s, he had never married, had had a string of short-lived relationships, and still exhibited much adolescent and rebellious behavior toward his parents. His goals in therapy included resolving his hostile dependency toward his parents, resolving his personal and professional identity crisis, getting his passive/aggressive behavior and temper outbursts more under control, gaining more confidence and developing a better self-image, and becoming less anxious and depressed.

During the 3 years of his treatment, he traveled more than 3 hours to and from Orlando for his therapy sessions. He definitely had requested a referral to someone out of town because he did not wish to risk "spilling his guts" and all the "filth inside me" to anyone in his home town, later feeling uncomfortable with that person professionally. He thought that his professional reputation was shaky and that he needed to insulate himself from any possible breach of confidentiality, including gossip among secretaries or from being seen frequenting another therapist's office.

What emerged was a portrait of a disturbed, distressed man. He had periods of heavy drinking and much of his social life revolved around going to the "swinging singles" bars to "pick up broads" and "drown my sorrows." Although he got "smashed" occasionally, he did not appear to be an alcoholic. He was and had been "heavy into pot" for about 20 years, and during the past 10 years "snorted coke" whenever he was offered it free or inexpensively in social situations. He liked feeling high and realized he escaped from internal pressures and external stresses through moderate to heavy substance usage, which had also included quaaludes and amphetamines.

While he was going to college, his younger sister had gotten into drugs. Although his parents had prevailed upon him to "do something to straighten her out," he had ignored their pleas as he was "too wrapped up in my own life as a big-deal college man, the first in my family to go." She ran around with a wild bunch and one day, when "stoned" at a beach party, had gone for a swim and drowned. His parents' shock and grief were overwhelming. Dr. R became numb when he first heard the news. When the numbness subsided, he was devastated with his sense of sorrow and self-reproach. He had not in the 17 years since this traumatic event occurred confronted and dealt with his sense of loss, his anger at what "fate" had dealt out to his little sister, and his whole family, nor his own survivor guilt. He still had nightmares about the drowning and how he might have prevented it. He reproached himself for not trying to intervene and help his sister move off her self-destructive course. His own "drinking and drugging" had escalated following her death, then tapering off before taking on a cyclic pattern, highest during periods of masochistic self-reproach and loneliness. Periodically, he felt it was his fault and that he did not have the right to live. At these times he experienced suicidal ideation.

Like Jerry in the case discussed earlier, Dr. R also had problems with his sexuality. He had had both homosexual and heterosexual relationships and could not chose which he preferred. He was certain he felt more secure and sure of himself with a male lover. A full sex history revealed that he too had been initiated into homosexuality in adolescence and that his pattern with women was often one of impotence during the first few sexual encounters. If they could "hang in" and be patient and encouraging, he could "perform" just fine. His lack of fairly consistent sexual prowess in one-to-one heterosexual relationships troubled him immensely. To compensate and reassure himself of his sexuality, he often spent weekends at nudist camps, went to sex orgies to make sure he could find willing and uninhibited partners, and dated women he saw as intellectually and socially inferior, which made him feel more adequate by comparison. What also emerged was that on several occasions, prior to his move to Orlando, he had exhibited himself. He lived in mortal dread of the urge to do so again, if he treated an attractive female patient, and so had preferred to work with adolescent males or to do group therapy. His fear was of phobic proportions.

In light of these and other related considerations, the following clinical diagnoses were reached and verified through the Millon Clinical Multi-Axial Inventory (Millon, 1976) and checked against the diagnosis included in the testing report that accompanied the original referral:

Axis I Generalized anxiety disorder with alcohol and cocaine abuse

Axis II Dependent personality with borderline and narcissistic features

Axis IV Psychosocial stressors—job dissatisfaction, poor interpersonal relations, family tensions

Given Dr. R's superior intelligence, his frequently articulated desire "to finally understand what's wrong with me," and his ardent wish to find a therapist he could trust in order to explore his murky inner world with a competent and supportive guide, I shared these diagnostic data with him. Together we confronted what these terms and concepts meant to and for him and their implications for his treatment and life outside of therapy. This sharing helped forge a strong therapeutic alliance. Usually he was seen on a regular basis every other week for 1½ to 2 hours because of the distance he had to travel. In between regular sessions, we held prearranged telephone sessions as needed.

Because his parents lived in the same community where I reside, Dr. R often visited them on the days he came for therapy. We would map out the issues he was to delve into with them and how he might approach them to maximize chances of a positive outcome. Initially in the first year of treatment (Phase I), I encouraged him to work with them alone regarding his feelings about his mother's possessiveness and intrusiveness and his father's passivity and acquiescence. I also encouraged him to look for their attributes and assets and to appreciate these.

Also during this period, it seemed imperative to broach his guilt over his sister's demise. Verbal psychotherapy alone was insufficient to "exorcise the monster memory." I then utilized a combination of yoga-style relaxation therapy and guided regressive abreaction so he could relive the weeks preceding and following her death. One day he reenacted the funeral—in my office—sobbing his way through the minister's farewell eulogy and other parts of the burial service that were still vivid in his mind's eye. We again talked about the concept of responsibility and that he could not have taken over as her guardian angel even if he had come home. There was no way he could have watched over her and restrained her all of the time. We discussed guilt, that because she had died so young and so horribly that that did not mean he did not have the right to live a full and satisfying life and that he no longer had to remain in a victim position. When he seemed to digest and incorporate this and seemed ready for closure and release from the nightmare of his sister's drowning, I urged him to go to visit his sister's grave and say a more conclusive and private farewell.

In accordance with the technique described by Williamson (1978) for graveside grief work to facilitate individuation from the dead loved one, a procedure I use occasionally when something drastic is called for, Dr. R was thoroughly prepared for his visit and asked to tape his monologue. He went, "talked to his sister for about 15 minutes," and then brought the tape to the next session. We listened to it together. He was able to detach himself more and be an observer-listener. Following this sequence of sessions, Dr. R reported feeling as if a huge burden had been lifted and experienced a great resurgence of energy, more than he had felt since his sister's death. After this, the content of therapy shifted and he rarely needed to talk about it. When he did, the reminiscence was no longer intense and tortuous. His suicidal ideation diminished, and his morbid preoccupation with death subsided.

Like other TPs who progress well in treatment, Dr. R periodically indicated that he found himself incorporating much that he was receiving and learning in therapy into his own practice. He was more accepting and much less judgmental of the stories he heard about the horrendous escapades and life histories of the delinquents he treated. He could better understand their resistance and defensive maneuvers. Given that his doctoral training had been largely cognitive-behavioral, and that he had looked askance at psychodynamic concepts and interventions, he was surprised at how often he was utilizing this conceptual framework and its accompanying treatment strategies. He also reported the ability to be a much more "nurturing parent surrogate" while still being able to set rational limits to behavior, including his patients' attempts to smuggle in drugs, which he had previously overlooked. He felt that his work had more candor, strength, and integrity, qualities he attributed to his therapist, and he was quite pleased with his progress in these realms of his own "becoming" or "evolving" as a clinician.

Transference and Countertransference

Because of TPs' greater understanding of what it means to be in therapy with its wonderful creative potential, they may well enter therapy with a more show-me-how-good-you-are attitude than other more therapeutically naive patients. Often they (or their families) will compare themselves with their therapist (Charny, 1984) and develop a critical posture. However, if they are in sufficient pain and distress to be highly motivated to alleviate feelings of anxiety, depression, and fear; or the desire to withdraw, commit suicide or homicide; or if they have been directed by an ethics committee or other professional group to seek treatment because a grievance has been filed; or have been placed on supervision or probation until their dysfunctional behavior is alleviated (Abell & Strong, 1983; American Medical Association [AMA], 1973, 1978; Fleischer & Wissler, 1985; Kempthorne, 1979), then they are likely to ambivalently see the therapist as a potential savior or crucifier. This sets the stage for a strong transference to evolve as the TP projects onto the therapist all kinds of expectations, feelings, and longings from the past and endows the therapist with great authority and power. This must be acknowledged and resisted by the treating therapist.

The stage is also set for a complex and intense countertransference to evolve. Because of the motivation to be a rescuer, an exemplary therapist, and a successful colleague, the treating therapist may find that inadvertently he or she is trying to be omniscient and omnipotent and has more invested personally in the outcome with the TP than with any other patient. For this reason, it is particularly important that the treating therapist develop an ongoing arrangement with a respected senior colleague for consultation, as needed, on such cases. This procedure can provide the treating therapist with a trusted and neutral consultant in a safe sanctuary where one's reactions, blind spots, and impasses can be explored (Kaslow, 1986).

I will now resume consideration of the treatment of Dr. R as it highlights the transference and countertransference themes.

Given the fact that during Phase I of treatment Dr. R felt that he had poor control over his sexual impulses and that his judgment was at times fuzzy from alcohol and drugs and from extreme narcissistic involvement, due partially to the intensity of treatment, we agreed he should stay with his job at the residential treatment center because it was a structured and supervised situation that provided the constraints he needed. He wanted very much to please me and sought advice about his professional decisions. Invariably, though in different ways, I encouraged him to get in touch with his own feelings and needs and explore his options and weigh the pros and cons of each. By utilizing a problem-solving approach to increase his self-awareness and faith in his own cognitive capabilities, he could arrive at and implement his own decisions. Frequently, Dr. R. vacillated and then implored me to "tell me what to do," even though at some level he knew I would not. He decided not to claim insurance reimbursement for treatment since he did not want any questions asked by the "nosy employee benefits counselor" who processed these.

By the end of the first year, he began to toy with going into music professionally. He played in a band avocationally and had some talent. He also considered joining a private practice group so he could have more freedom and earn "bigger bucks." We explored this together, as I was concerned that a shift to music as a vocation represented another kind of promiscuity for him and that such job hopping was counterindicated at that time. I also cautioned him to go slowly regarding entering private practice until he felt more confident generally and had less ongoing pangs about his recurrent impotency and fear of wanting to either exhibit himself or become sexually involved with a patient.

By the second half of the first year (Phase I), we had established a strong therapeutic alliance. He was willing to consider his utilization of drugs and alcohol more objectively, conceding it sometimes got out of hand. After accusing me of being a "goody goody" and old fashioned because I was not into drugs and other testing maneuvers, he agreed to go a month without either substance, adopting a one-day-at-a-time philosophy. By the end of the first month, he reported that his thinking was much clearer, his work habits had improved, and he had begun jogging, a sport he had abandoned years before. He decided he would give up cocaine entirely, which he did successfully, and that he would be satisfied with an occasional drink on the weekend. He was able to do this and was quite proud of his ability to control his former cravings. As he mastered the compulsion to drink and use drugs, the kinds of friends he sought out began to shift.

Periodically, I checked with a colleague for a consultation to be certain that (a) Dr. R was really making the progress I was perceiving, which far exceeded the prognosis contained in the original testing report, and that because I had become fond of him and concerned about his welfare, he was not "conning" me or I was not deceiving myself, and that (b) I was not superimposing my value system on him and trying to remake him and that it was primarily his goals that were guiding the focus and direction of treatment, not mine.

At the beginning of his second year of treatment (Phase II), we reevaluated what had been accomplished and formulated his objectives for the year. These included mainly (a) attempting to renegotiate his relationship with his parents so it could become a more adult and satisfying one, (b) working on his "sexual hang-ups," and (c) consolidating his professional identity and making a job change.

I suggested that Dr. R invite his parents to come in with him for several conjoint family sessions. Like many patients, he initially refused. Although he had read about such multigenerational sessions, his ideas about them were vague. I outlined how I conduct such sessions and what I thought might occur. I stated that he had done some excellent work in improving and repairing his relationship with his parents, but that he still seemed very stirred up by his visits with them and unable to proceed further on his own. I conveyed my optimism, based on experiences with other patients, that such sessions could lead to great therapeutic breakthroughs, that he was fortunate that his parents were alive, ambulatory, and geographically accessible, and that the time to do this seemed to be now, while this was still true. Since this was only the second time he found me to be somewhat insistent and persistent as to what should be done (the first was regarding reliving his sister's funeral and the graveside visit), and because he had developed great trust in my therapeutic interventions, he agreed to try one session. I suggested he invite his parents, who knew he was in therapy, to come as consultants to me (Whitaker, personal communication, 1981) to provide me with some missing pieces about Dr. R's childhood. This was a valid and authentic fact. Therefore, this kind of invitation is usually experienced as intriguing and not terribly threatening. Dr. R's parents, who had been curious about their son's treatment and the changes they saw in him, came willingly.

During the next 6 weeks, I saw Dr. R conjointly with his parents three times for a total of about 5 hours. They recounted what an intelligent and attractive child he had been and that they had very high hopes for him. They were so proud when he received his PhD. It was the one bright spot after their daughter's death. His mother presented herself as a warm and caring person, baffled by her son's hostile, dependent, and ambivalent relationship to her. His father was self-effacing and eager to please his son, wife, and me by trying to smooth over any conflict or dissension as soon as it arose. Dr. R told them about his long repressed guilt and self-recriminations over his sister's death and the grieving he had done in therapy. He asked them to talk about how they felt. They described the long process of working through disbelief, anger, and emptiness until after a decade they were resigned to the loss and determined to make the most of their lives. They also were able to articulate their love for him and their desire to see him lead *his* life as they were leading theirs, with an affectional bond between them but with no expectation that he should play a caretaker role with them. They gave him permission to feel free of unhealthy ties, and encouraged him to move on in his career so he could become financially solvent to take some vacations, have fun, and marry. They expressed a wish for a daughter-in-law and grandchildren.

That they cared enough to become involved at his request, to openly express real caring and concern for him, and not to satisfy their needs vicariously through his achievements, helped diminish some of his emptiness and aloneness. With his mother, he was able to work through his concern about being overpowered by a woman. He also was able to view his mother in the present as much less frightening and domineering. Following these "breakthrough" sessions, in which he renegotiated the "intergenerational hierarchical boundary" (Williamson, 1981), his relationship with his parents became a much more constructive adult-child-to-mellowing-parents one. He also began to think of dating "women on my own level."

He had stopped using drugs completely and he was only taking a drink occasionally, perhaps once a week. It seemed time to explore his phobic anxiety about his fears of exhibiting himself in front of a female patient, getting involved sexually with female patients, or having an embarrassing erection during a therapy session if he became stimulated by sexually laden content. He had begun dating two women closer to his own age. One was a teacher, the other a nurse. Earlier, he had been attracted to bar hostesses and salesgirls, 15 to 17 years younger or 5 years older than he.

With the teacher, he had arrived at a fairly good sexual liaison and was rarely impotent. This occurred after the reworking of his relationship with his mother, the diminishing of his castration fears, and his almost concurrent decision that he no longer wanted brief homosexual encounters and could refrain from them. We spent many sessions on his prior sexual exploits (he had a compulsive need to regurgitate these and test out if I was able to accept his fantasies and behaviors), and then shifted to current expectations of himself and the difference in behavior that is appropriate in a personal versus a professional relationship. We discussed that many therapists report being "turned on" by patients, particularly if they are attractive and seductive, but that therapists know that acting on the feeling is ethically taboo and that they can exercise sufficient control not to.

Since Dr. R was applying to join a private practice group, it seemed critical that he feel more in control of his thoughts and fears. After much discussion, we decided he should have a psychopharmacological consultation. I referred him to a psychiatrist who prescribed a trial course of Xanex to help minimize Dr. R's still underlying depression and reduce his fear of a panic seizure. Fortunately, he responded well to the medication and within 1 month reported feeling less anxious. By about 3 months, his previous hovering cloud of panic-laden apprehension about inappropriate sexual acting out was clearly diminishing. As this was occurring, he felt a resurgence of energy and was able to penetrate his long-standing lethargy. By the end of Phase II, he felt confident enough to become associated with a private practice group, although vestiges of his earlier trepidation still surfaced occasionally.

I hope that this illustration indicates some of the transference and countertransference issues involved in such cases.

Didactic Treatment Versus Therapy for Interpersonal and Intrapsychic Difficulties

Since analytic training requires the candidate to have a didactic analysis, there is a built-in expectation by both analyst and analysand that the therapy will contain a teaching-learning component and be beneficial to the analysand and his or her therapeutic endeavors (Greenberg & F. Kaslow, 1984; McLaughlin, 1974; Shapiro, 1976; Silverstone, 1970). TPs entering other treatment modalities seem to hold similar expectations that they will learn how to practice a particular technique by being exposed to it in their own treatment. They may even deceive themselves that the learning aspect is the main reason they are going. Churchill (1984) discusses this as a rationale when interns, residents, and staff enter hypnotherapy.

As indicated earlier, other TPs believe that in therapy they will learn the process experientially from a master and may fantasize a mentor–trainee relationship more than a therapist–patient one (J. Coché, 1984; Fay & Lazarus, 1984; N. Kaslow & Friedman, 1984). As I treat other therapists, it appears that, although most supervisees resent a supervisor attempting to become their therapist or intruding into their personal affairs (Kaslow, 1977), the opposite is not true. Instead, TPs seem to seek some didactic learning from their therapists and at times specifically solicit supervision on a difficult case during their therapy time. This could be an attempt to digress from painful content in the therapy or to deny one's dysfunctional behavior by shifting to a more theoretical plane. It could signify resistance to being in the patient role by attempting to reframe the relationship as a more collegial one (Fleischer & Wissler, 1985). Sometimes it could be an indicator that something happening in a particular case is especially emotionally disturbing and that the TP is bringing it to therapy for help in unraveling its significance as much as for supervision. Another reason could be that the TP values the therapist's knowledge and skill and is soliciting assistance to break an impasse. Several of these factors became operative in Dr. R's treatment during his third and final year with me.

During his third year of treatment (Phase III), Dr. R continued on Xanex. After 6 months, he did well on a rather low dosage. He continued on this without grave concern about his becoming addicted to it. He went for a medication review every 3 months. He became more comfortable in and with his own body and felt, for the first time in his life, that he could make a commitment to enter into a live-in arrangement with the teacher he had been dating. He was able to afford a much nicer apartment than he had ever had before, and the combination of an intelligent and affectionate partner living with him in an attractive environment boosted his ego and contributed to a heightened sense of well-being. He was generally proud of his progress and accomplishments, yet experienced occasional pangs of despair over having given up his earlier, less respectable, more profligate life-style. When he felt trapped, he would arrange to return for several evenings to the bar and orgy scene. He soon realized however, that he no longer "fit" in there and that it was even less satisfying than it had been.

He liked his new position and was pleased with his decision finally to be "a real psychologist." During this year, he enrolled for several workshops I was giving. As he had become licensed, he needed and wanted CEUs and knew "I delivered what I agreed to." He also borrowed books from my well-stocked office library on topics relevant to cases he was handling. Given the absence of a university-based professional library in the community, this was appropriate. He also was able to see valid connections between his therapy and those which he conducted, raising queries about why I used a psychodynamic approach during certain periods of his therapy, more behavioral strategies at other times, and zeroed-in on multigenerational themes sometimes. He wanted to develop a sound foundation from which to select the treatment that would be most efficacious in a given case. As one of his chief foci in therapy had become his professional identity and development, concentration on this theme seemed productive. The problems he confronted served to illuminate his still unresolved issues.

The night before he was scheduled to see alone the pretty wife of a couple he had been seeing conjointly, he called me for reassurance that he would not "feel and act weird." He had scheduled her when other therapists would be on the premises, and we talked about his having the option to excuse himself and go out of the session for a few minutes if he felt overwhelmed. He called the next day to report that he had felt anxious prior to and during the first few minutes of the session, but as soon as he was able to concentrate on her concerns, the fluttering in his stomach stopped and he was able to assume his therapist role. This was another landmark in overcoming his fear of acting out sexually.

As he began to see the complexity of some of his cases, Dr. R asked if he could use some of his therapy time for supervision. I asked about his supervisory arrangements at his practice. They were almost nonexistent. I encouraged him to assertively request supervision or consultation from a senior member of his group and, if that could not be arranged, to contract for this privately with the best person he could find (Kaslow, 1986) in the Orlando area in order not to have to travel. He tried to be persuasive, resorted to flattery ("No one else could be as proficient"), and even played helpless ("This is critical right now and I don't know what to do") to cajole me into supervising him. I felt however, that it was important not to dilute the therapy in this way. I also interpreted his willingness to utilize his expensive therapeutic time for a different purpose as another indicator that he had achieved the goals he had set for himself in treatment, that he was much healthier and more functional, and that he was capable of being an adequate and ethical therapist. He worked out a consultation arrangement before we terminated. We were both comfortable in the knowledge that he had a clinical resource specialist available that he could turn to for external reinforcement of behavioral controls, if his internal restraints felt precarious.

Confidentiality and Other Ethical Issues

Perhaps it is in this realm that the therapist's therapist has the greatest challenge. Therapists are all imbued and indoctrinated with the importance of confidentiality. Until as recently as 10 years ago, this principle was taught as inviolate, even sacrosanct. With court decisions like *Tarasoff v. Regents of University of California* (1974) and *McIntosh v. Milano* (1979), the therapist's "duty to warn" authorities of a patient's potential harm to self or others was established. The 1981 Revision of APA Code of Ethics (Principle 5, Confidentiality, page 5) proclaims as follows:

> Psychologists have a primary obligation to respect the confidentiality of information obtained from persons in the course of their work as psychologists. They reveal such information to others only with the consent of the person or the person's legal representative, except in those unusual circumstances in which not to do so would result in clear danger to the person or to others. Where appropriate, psychologists inform their clients of the legal limits of confidentiality.

Because of these and similar developments, it is wise not only to discuss the principles of confidentiality and privilege with patients in the initial session, but to explain and elucidate the limits of confidentiality. For clarity and the protection of everyone, I find it advisable to have this in written form and included as part of the therapeutic contract entered into by patient and therapist. When the patient is also a therapist, it is incumbent upon the treating therapist to be especially clear in conveying the legal requirements and ethical guidelines of conducting practice.

For example, in most states therapists are requested to report the suspicion of child abuse. If a TP in individual, group, marital, or family therapy discloses that he or she is disturbed about personal destructive behavior which takes the form of incest, other physical child or spouse abuse in the context of the family, or child molestation or other sex crime outside of the family, the treating therapist is enjoined to report this behavior to the designated agency. If the suspicion is confirmed, criminal charges may be pressed. If the TP is adjudicated guilty, he or she may be placed on probation or sentenced to prison. In either event, the TP may be considered to have committed a felony and will therefore lose his or her license to practice. Knowing the effort that goes into professional training and all that is at stake, it may be harder to report a TP, who also is a colleague, than any other patient. No matter who the patient is, however, many therapists shy away from the social-control function of reporting and eschew the violation of confidentiality. They ruminate about their responsibility to the patient and to protect the public. And they agonize over the bad publicity the helping professions receive whenever a mental health practitioner's impaired behavior comes under public scrutiny.

When the TP reveals that his or her pathology has intruded into the therapeutic role, in such forms as (a) coming to work "stoned" or "inebriated" or having to cancel appointments because of hangovers, (b) sexual involvement with patients, (c) overbilling insurance companies, or (d) psychotic decompensation, the treating therapist has no choice but to report it. Physicians are further along (AMA, 1973, 1978; Raskin, 1977) than psychologists in spelling out the treating professional's responsibility to report to an ethics committee (Laliotis & Grayson, 1985). An important first step is to encourage the impaired TP to take a leave of absence from work, if the problem is either chemical addiction, mental illness, sexual involvement with patients, incest, or spouse abuse. The TP should remain in intensive out-patient treatment or enter in-patient treatment voluntarily until the malady or dysfunction is remedied. Only if and when such problems are under control and the TP is well enough to resume the stressful role and responsibility of therapist should he or she return to practice. If the problem is overbilling patients or insurance companies, the TP's poor judgment and unethical behavior must be confronted and the person urged to rectify errors. Cheating and defrauding are serious violations of any professional code of ethics.

I have recently spoken to several nationally prominent psychologists about this dilemma and they have stated that under no circumstances would they report a TP. Is this misguided loyalty? Are we protecting the offending therapist? Others I have queried have been equally adamant in the reverse. By not reporting offenders, therapists inadvertently contribute to some patients being so exploited or shortchanged that they file malpractice suits. We all in turn bear the brunt of our overprotectiveness in the form of our spiraling malpractice costs (from $75 in 1984 to $300 in 1985 and $450 in 1986). Are we naively or deliberately sowing the seeds of our own destruction by not reporting offending TPs?

THE OUTLOOK FOR THE FUTURE

Fortunately, some state associations and the APA, as evidenced by this volume and other recent activities concerned with the distressed therapist, such as a special task force, are now addressing this issue. Out of the current dialogues, research, and reports on clinical experience should come guidelines on how to approach or confront a colleague believed to be experiencing great distress because of physical or emotional impairment, severe family problems, social stresses, substance abuse, severe eating disorders, fears of aging, loss of competence, burnout, or practicing beyond areas of competence (see VandenBos & Duthie, chapter 11).

In addition, I hope a procedure will be developed for reporting a colleague to the designated ethics body, if indeed that colleague is dysfunctional. This must be clearly defined so we do not (a) needlessly disrupt the lives of colleagues who have a less traditional and more innovative approach, but who are not impaired; or (b) permit one mental health practitioner to unjustly accuse another out of jealousy or animosity, because if such accusations are kept secret, this reporting route provides fertile grounds for acting out vendettas.

If the impaired colleague is being seen on a referral from an ethics committee or other similar body, as a condition of nonrevocation of license or during a probationary period, the TP and the therapist should know the following:

- what will be divulged and to whom about the evaluation results and treatment content;
- when such disclosures will be made;
- what records must be kept and for how long;
- to whom the records belong and who will oversee their confidentiality;
- what relationship the ethics committee will have to the state licensing board (Laliotus & Grayson, 1985, p. 93).

If the TP enters treatment of his or her own accord before the dysfunction has come to the attention of others, the treating therapist must be clear about whether

- reporting of incapacitating distress is mandatory;
- there is a penalty for nonreporting;
- the treating therapist is immune from liability if he or she does or does not report;
- the TP meets or does not meet a legal definition of being impaired or distressed.

The support and involvement of family and close friends may be crucial in helping motivate a TP to seek therapy and benefit from it by (a) participating in it and attempting to change their own contributory behavior, and (b) not sabotaging the therapy. Since this has been covered in chapter 12, this aspect of clinical management has not been duplicated here.

In the interim, some preventive measures should be undertaken. Within the legal and ethical sanctions in which universities, medical schools, and institutes operate, selection criteria for trainees should include the difficult task of assessing "emotional fitness" for psychotherapist training. We do have expertise in this area, as evidenced by the work of industrial and organizational psychologists in utilizing selection procedures. This includes generating psychological profiles of candidates, from which they predict, given a solid picture of the firm or corporation's needs, whether a person is likely to "fit" and perform well in a given situation. Certainly, we know enough about the range of attributes and assets that are likely to herald a positive future for someone as a psychologist. Likewise, we know the borderline and addictive-type personalities that are apt to run into difficulty.

All the way through training, from the initial admissions procedure through course work and internship and residency, teachers and supervisors should apprise a program director that they are concerned about a student and the basis of their concern. If this is done, and several faculty express similar concerns, the program director, or whoever is designated, should seek ways either to help the trainee get the therapy needed, perhaps during a leave of absence, or, if it is believed therapy alone would be insufficient, to strongly recommend that the trainee seek another career. Borenstein and Cook (1982) have described an impairment prevention program utilized at UCLA in the training years. Developments such as these should enable the mental health professions to decrease the amount of future disabling distress among its practitioners.

During training and internship, future mental health practitioners, academicians, and researchers should be made aware of the stress inherent in the daily lives of busy professionals. Dealing with the problems, deprivations, violence, anger, and depression of other people can inundate the clinician. The world seen through patients' experience can seem harsh, cruel, and unfair. Years of emergency calls at night and weekends can take their toll. Having patients commit suicide is always tortuous. Competition for promotions and salary increases, professional recognition, sufficient patients, and service contracts can be intense. Today, the fear of malpractice suits is insidious and omnipresent. And the internal and external pressure to be active in professional organizations, to publish and keep up through reading books and journals, and to have a rich and full personal life, which often includes a spouse and children, means there rarely are enough hours in the day. Where is the time to jog, play tennis, and just relax? Perhaps some clinicians may opt for a less demanding life-style.

Sometimes the onset of distress postdates the training years, subsequent to a traumatic occurrence such as a stroke, heart attack, loss of a child or spouse by death or bitter divorce, or the cumulative stress of years of caring for others and the attempt to diminish that stress through drugs and alcohol. If in the training years, at professional conferences, and at the various mental health settings where therapists work, the climate is conducive to encouraging therapists to seek therapeutic consultations when they are troubled and having a rough time, without embedding such a need in stigma or shame, then distressed therapists are more likely to refer themselves. If they have deteriorated to where they completely deny or are unaware of their impairment, then concerned colleagues may have to intervene to protect the distressed professional, their clients and families, and the profession at large. Treating these professionals is a challenge and a responsibility. I hope this chapter illustrates some of the principal issues and difficulties practitioners face.

References

Abell, J. M., & Strong, P. N. (1983, August). The impaired professional: A preliminary survey of six professions. In P. E. Nathan (Chair), *Psychologist heal thyself.* Symposium conducted at the meeting of the American Psychological Association, Anaheim, CA.

Abraham, K. (1921). Contributions to the theory of the anal character. In K. Abraham (Ed.), *Selected papers on psychoanalysis* (pp. 370–392). New York: Brunner/Mazel.

American Medical Association Council on Mental Health. (1973). The sick physician. *Journal of American Medical Association. 223*(6), 684–687.

American Medical Association Disabled Doctor Act. (1978). In J. Robertson (Ed.), *Proceedings of the Third AMA Conference on the Impaired Physician* (pp. 68–72). Chicago: American Medical Association.

American Psychological Association. (1981). *Ethical principles of psychologists* (rev. ed.). Washington, DC: Author.

Borenstein, D. B., & Cook, K. (1982). Impairment prevention in the training years: New mental health program at UCLA. *Journal of the American Medical Association, 247*(19), 2700–2701.

Bowen, M. (1978). *Family therapy in clinical practice.* New York: Aronson.

Charny, I. (1982). The personal and family mental health of family therapists. In F. W. Kaslow (Ed.), *The international book of family therapy* (pp. 41–55). New York: Brunner/Mazel.

Churchill, J. E. (1984). Hypnotherapy with psychotherapists: An "innocuous" means of seeking help. In F. W. Kaslow (Ed.), *Psychotherapy with psychotherapists.* New York: Haworth Press.

Coché, E. (1984). Group psychotherapy for group psychotherapists. In F. W. Kaslow (Ed.), *Psychotherapy with psychotherapists.* New York: Haworth Press.

Coché, J. (1984). Psychotherapy with women therapists. In F. W. Kaslow (Ed.), *Psychotherapy with psychotherapists.* New York: Haworth Press.

Fay, A., & Lazarus, A. A. (1984). The therapist in behavioral and multimodal therapy. In F. W. Kaslow (Ed.), *Psychotherapy with psychotherapists.* New York: Haworth Press.

Fleischer, A., & Wissler, A. (1985). The therapist as patient: Special problems and considerations. *Psychotherapy. 22*(3), 587–594.

Greenberg, R. P., & Stoller, J. (1981). Personal therapy for therapists. *American Journal of Psychiatry. 138*(11), 1467–1471.

Greenberg, S., & Kaslow, F. W. (1984). Psychoanalytic treatment for therapists, residents and other trainees. In F. W. Kaslow (Ed.), *Psychotherapy with psychotherapists.* New York: Haworth Press.

Kaslow, F. W. (Ed.). (1977). *Supervision, consultation and staff training in the helping professions.* San Francisco: Jossey-Bass.

Kaslow, F. W. (1981). Divorce and divorce therapy. In A. S. Gurman & D. P. Kniskern (Eds.), *Handbook of family therapy* (pp. 662–696). New York: Brunner/Mazel.

Kaslow, F. W. (Ed.). (1984a). *Psychotherapy with psychotherapists.* New York: Haworth Press.

Kaslow, F. W. (1984b). Treatment of marital and family therapists. In F. W. Kaslow (Ed.), *Psychotherapy with psychotherapists* (pp. 79–100). New York: Haworth Press.

Kaslow, F. W. (Ed.), (1986). *Supervision and training: Models, dilemmas, and challenges.* New York: Haworth Press.

Kaslow, N. J., & Friedman, D. (1984). The interface of personal treatment and clinical training for psychotherapist trainees. In F. W. Kaslow (Ed.), *Psychotherapy with psychotherapists.* New York: Haworth Press.

Kempthorne, G. C. (1979). The impaired physician: The role of the state medical society. *Wisconsin Medical Journal, 78,* 24–25.

Laliotis, D. A., & Grayson, J. H. (1985). Psychologist heal thyself: What is available for the impaired psychologist? *American Psychologist. 40*(1), 84–96.

Masters, W. H., & Johnson, V. (1979). *Homosexuality in perspective.* Boston: Little, Brown.

McIntosh v. Milano, 403 A.2d 500 (N.J. 1979).

McLaughlin, F. (1974). A discussion of the paper by D. Shapiro on the training analysis: A retrospective view of the evaluative and reporting role of other "hampering factors." *International Journal of Psychoanalysis, 55,* 307–309.

Millon, T. (1976). *Millon Clinical Multi-Axial Inventory (MCMI).* Minneapolis: National Computer Systems.

Neville, W. G. (1984). Divorce mediation for therapists and their spouses. In F. W. Kaslow (Ed.), *Psychotherapy with psychotherapists.* New York: Haworth Press.

Padach, K. M. (1984). Long term telephone psychotherapy. In F. W. Kaslow (Ed.), *Psychotherapy with psychotherapists.* New York: Haworth Press.

Pollack, S. L., Kaslow, N. J., & Harvey, D. M. (1982). Symmetry, complementarity, and depression: The evaluation of an hypothesis. In F. W. Kaslow, (Ed.), *The international book of family therapy* (pp. 170–185). New York: Brunner/Mazel.

Raskin, H. A. (1977). The impaired physician: An overview. In M. B. Hugunen (Ed.), *Helping the impaired physician. Proceedings of the AMA Conference on the Impaired Physician: Answering the Challenge* (pp. 7–12). Chicago: American Medical Association.

Shapiro, D. (1976). The analyst's own analysis. *Journal of the American Psychoanalytic Association, 24*(1), 5–42.

Silverstone, S. (1970). On the mystique of training analysis. *Psychoanalytic Review, 57,* 283–284.

Tarasoff v. Regents of the University of California, et al., 529 P. 2d 55, 118 Cal. Rptr. 129 (1974).

Williamson, D. S. (1979). New life at the graveyard: A method of therapy for individuation from a dead former parent. *Journal of Marriage and Family Counseling, 4,* 93–101.

Williamson, D. S. (1981). Personal authority via termination of the intergenerational hierarchical boundary: A "new" stage in the family life cycle. *Journal of Marital and Family Therapy, 7,* 441–452.

CONFRONTING AND SUPPORTING COLLEAGUES IN DISTRESS

11

Gary R. VandenBos
Rita F. Duthie

Have you known a colleague who was distressed to the point that his or her professional or personal life was impaired? Did you talk with the person about it? The most probable answers to these two questions are, in sequence, "yes" and then "no." According to the survey of APA members taken by the Task Force on Distressed Psychologists, 69 percent of psychologists have known of colleagues whom they believed were experiencing personal or emotional problems, yet only 36 percent reported having approached a colleague with their concerns. Thirty-three percent reported knowing of colleagues experiencing alcohol problems, but only 12 percent reported attempting to help them. One would assume that, as health professionals, when we recognize colleagues in distress, we would confront and support them in facing and solving their problems. Yet, it appears that more often than not, we do not.

Our purpose in this chapter is to discuss the problems and issues surrounding the confrontation and support of colleagues in distress. Some of the reasons we do not approach distressed colleagues more often are examined. We present a simple model for approaching such situations, and we consider how the specifics of a given situation may influence what we do and how we do it. We present some specific examples of the types of responses that can be expected when a confrontation is made, as well as some suggestions for responding to them.

We wish to thank Kenneth S. Pope, David Mills, Donald Bersoff, Torleiv Odland, Christopher Pino, Jane Annunziata, and Richard Kilburg for their constructive feedback and suggestions on earlier drafts of this manuscript. Edward P. Sheridan provided helpful advice and information in the early stages of formulating the manuscript. And, we greatly appreciate the contributions of Brenda K. Bryant, Director of Special Publications, American Psychological Association, in the later stages of manuscript development.

TO ACT OR TO IGNORE

The fact that more than half of us have not confronted distressed colleagues even when we have recognized and acknowledged (at least to ourselves) the existence of their problems is, in part, a reflection of the difficulty in achieving a balance between concerned intervention and intrusiveness. As professionals, we value our own right to practice without interference, so long as we function within the boundaries of our professional expertise, meet professional standards for the provision of services, and behave in an ethical manner. We generally consider such expectations when we consider approaching a distressed colleague. Deciding when and how our concern about the well-being of a colleague (and our ethical obligation) supersedes his or her right to personal privacy and professional autonomy is a ticklish matter.

The simple fact is that most of us would rather avoid having to confront a colleague about our belief that there is a significant personal or emotional problem that he or she must address. This desire to deny or avoid acknowledging a problem that a colleague may have and to avoid addressing that distressed colleague directly is a human and very understandable response. Who needs the hassle? Who wants to face hostility or defensive denial needlessly? Yet, at a minimum, we have a professional and social obligation to act (and, it is hoped, that action will be based in part on our personal concern for our colleague). The ethical principles of the psychological profession, for example, dictate that a psychologist who knows of another psychologist violating the principles must attempt, if feasible, to resolve the problem informally and, then, if the informal process does not work, must report the incident to the appropriate ethics board (as part of his or her own ethical obligation to protect the public). However, the importance of the social obligation to act is only of small reassurance or support to us when we are faced with the dilemma of raising our concerns with a colleague. Arriving at such a conviction must always follow a thoughtful, serious consideration of the information that raised the concern, of the nature of the relationship with the colleague, and of our investment in making (or avoiding) this confrontation. The decision to take on such responsibility is, in itself, of sufficient gravity to make us reluctant to confront a distressed colleague. Yet, it is unethical for us to do nothing when we know of a distressed professional whose functioning is so impaired that he or she is beginning to harm others (even if that harm is relatively minor at that point).

A number of concerns and fears appear even more significantly to discourage many of us from taking action. There is the fear that our colleague (and other colleagues) will not agree that there is a problem, may accuse us of having a problem that prompts us to take this action, or will view our concern as personal or professional intrusiveness. There is the fear that by confronting a colleague with our concerns about his or her problems, we are tacitly inviting that colleague or other colleagues to confront us about their perceptions of our own personal and professional limitations or flaws. There is the fear of personal risk—of a lawsuit, of a counterattack on us as professionals, or of losing a friend (or several friends). There is the fear of compounding the colleague's problems—of his or her being suspended or fired, of precipitating ethical charges against the person, or of causing further difficulties for the person in his or her personal or professional functioning. There is the fear of being impotent—of trying to help and having that help rejected or ignored or of going through considerable personal frustration and conflict only to see our efforts wasted. There may be the thought that the problem was only a temporary one (and that we have no evidence that it is affecting our colleague's professional functioning), so we should not "embarrass" the person (or cause ourselves risk) by broaching the matter. Even our professional training may get in the way of our initiating a reasonable and needed discussion with a distressed colleague, because most of us have been taught that we should work only with those with whom we have no close personal relationship (and we may not feel comfortable discussing such matters with someone who did not initiate the contact as a result of his or her own distress). Moreover, no one will pay us, reimburse us, or give us professional recognition for our time and trouble. Nonetheless, we must overcome such fears of and rationalization against action. It is interesting to note that a single tale of someone unsuccessfully confronting a distressed colleague may be repeated a hundred times, whereas many successful confrontations are, appropriately, never shared once (nor listed on our vitae, reimbursed by insurance carriers, or considered in tenure decisions).

Even after addressing and resolving such fears and concerns, there is the simple and practical question, "How can I most effectively confront a colleague?" There is no simple answer, as each situation is unique, and every such encounter will be distressing for both parties. In light of the difficulties attendant upon intervening with a distressed colleague, its infrequent occurrence is not surprising. Nonetheless, if we subscribe to the highest principles of our profession, we are responsible for prevailing over these difficulties. In this chapter we describe a process and propose a practical approach that we hope will make the experience less intimidating and more satisfying, both personally and professionally.

STEPS IN CONFRONTING AND SUPPORTING DISTRESSED COLLEAGUES

Step 1: Evaluate the Information

The first step you must take toward confronting and supporting a distressed colleague is to collect and systematically evaluate the available data that generates your concerns (in order to make a convincing presentation later to your colleague). This involves considering whether the information that brings you consciously to acknowledge that your colleague's problem (and your tentative commitment to discuss it with him or her) is sufficient to achieve the desired outcome, or whether it is necessary to gather more information. It usually takes less information to become concerned than it takes to be convinced (and convincing). We strongly recommend that, in this initial process, you write a list of the behaviors and events that concern you (being as specific as possible as to time, place, and detail) and make some notes about the meaning and importance you attach to each. If some of the listed behaviors have been reported to you by others, think carefully about the credibility of the source of the information and about whether the source must be protected during the confrontation. It is best to try to identify examples that you have observed personally that parallel reported events, because personal observations are generally more convincing than the possibly distorted reports of others.

In most instances, the outcome of this process will be that you convince yourself that you are concerned, but you acknowledge that you are not convinced that you have enough information to approach your colleague effectively. You may wish to do some reading or have a general consultation with someone who is more expert with the problem situation you think you may be observing. If the colleague is a close personal friend, you may not need more information and you may be able simply to express your concern as a friend. In the majority of situations, however, you will probably need additional information to convince yourself that you should act and that you will be able to act in a humane and successful manner. Thus, you must decide whether simply to watch and listen or to chat informally about your concerns with other respected colleagues (in order to find out whether or not others are concerned and to collect further information and reported observations). If you have such an informal chat with other colleagues, it is important to stress the confidentiality of the conversation and to adhere to that confidentiality so as not to trigger inappropriate rumors—after all, you are seeking information on a very important matter, and you do not want to engage in gossiping or defamation of character. Sometimes it may be appropriate to contact the distressed professional's spouse, but such an action must be carefully considered before it is taken.

Obviously, your position and your relationship to the colleague in question will influence both whether you talk with colleagues and to which colleagues you talk. If you are the director of the clinic or hospital in which the distressed colleague works, you face an array of advantages and disadvantages for engaging in such discussions. If you are a peer on the same staff level, you also have advantages and disadvantages—but a different mix—for obtaining additional perspectives and input. If you are a subordinate of the possibly distressed professional, you will be in a particularly difficult situation.

The experience of attempting to gather additional information may feel like spying and gossiping, but if your motives for taking such action arise out of concern and compassion, then the action is warranted, appropriate, and necessary (and, if there really is a problem, others are probably already considering taking action anyway). The ultimate end desired is to turn unproductive events into positive, constructive action that benefits the colleague, his or her family, and the individuals served by the distressed professional.

Step 2: Decide Who Should Confront the Individual

The second step in confronting and supporting a distressed colleague is to decide who should discuss the matter with the individual. Just because you have observed evidence of a possible problem does not mean that you are the person who should discuss your concern with the distressed professional. However, you should be sure that someone does it (and that someone may very well end up being you). Moreover, it can be helpful for several colleagues who are in different positions and relationships with the distressed professional to discuss their concerns with the person over a span of time, thereby

PROFESSIONALS IN DISTRESS

overcoming the person's possible denial of the problem and letting the individual know that several colleagues not only are aware of the situation and concerned about it but also are supportive.

It can be assumed that the likelihood of success in approaching the distressed colleague will increase according to the strength of the bond between that person and the individual confronting him or her; thus, in many situations the best choice will be the individual who is closest to the distressed person. If the available information suggests that the distressed colleague is having problems in his or her personal life and there is no evidence to suggest major disruption in professional functioning, the best person to discuss the situation with the distressed person probably will be a close personal friend. However, you can still consider having such a conversation with the individual even though you are not among that person's closest friends.

There will be some situations in which the seriousness of the situation, either for the distressed colleague or the persons served by the colleague, requires prompt attention by an authority figure who has power over the distressed professional and who may not be particularly close to him or her. If the professional functioning of the distressed colleague is affecting the individuals served (whether students or patients) or is negatively affecting working relationships with peers or peers' productivity, it may be necessary for a supervisor to discuss the situation with the distressed professional (although more personal discussions can also be held).

Step 3: Prepare Before the Meeting

The third step in confronting and supporting a distressed colleague relates to organizing your thoughts prior to the discussion with the distressed person. You cannot predict how your colleague will respond to your expression of concern and support. Denial and anger, however, may be the initial emotional reaction. If you plan simply to let the conversation evolve and to present your concerns and supporting data as they seem best to fit into the discussion, you may soon find yourself struggling to defend your concerns, prove the accuracy of your data, and justify your interpretation of events. If so, you also may come to feel, and to appear, less supportive of your colleague.

If you organize your thoughts before the meeting, you will be able to make a more effective presentation to your colleague, and you will be better able to respond flexibly and spontaneously to the feelings your colleague expresses. The most effective way to organize is to write notes to yourself. Review your earlier list of notes and add later observations and reports. Examine the lists to see what patterns emerge and how to group different matters most effectively. It may not be most effective to raise first the possibility that you find the most frightening to imagine (e.g., several recent "accidents" reflect self-harming dynamics that could end in suicide), as it probably represents several extrapolations from the observable data. Such an issue generally can be better approached later in the discussion, unless you believe that your colleague is acutely suicidal.

It may be useful to try to identify the two or three issues that you feel are the most critical and to select two or three behavioral observations that you believe best illustrate each concern. Doing this will force you to narrow your focus to what is most important and most convincing. Then practice making your opening comment. You may wish to tape and listen to yourself. If you were in your colleague's position, would you find the presentation supportive? Clear and convincing? How would you respond? We recommend that you continue refining your opening comments until you can make a succinct, effective, and supportive statement in less than two minutes. By forcing yourself to do this, you will know what you want and need to say (and it will not get lost in the midst of heated conversation), so that you will be free to be genuinely responsive to your colleague's feelings and reactions. Also prepare a list of resources and referrals upon which your colleague could realistically draw should he or she so wish.

In preparing to confront a distressed colleague, it is useful to explore how you feel about the process and the individual. If, for example, the colleague's behavior has had a negative effect on your ability to function, you may have feelings of anger and frustration, which, although quite understandable, will interfere with accomplishing your goal if they emerge during the meeting. Or, if on some level you believe that "we" as professionals ought to be above allowing personal distress to interfere with professional performance, this judgment will be subtly communicated. Overt anger and a judgmental attitude generally elicit defensiveness, which is, of course, a response that should be avoided. If you have been "elected" or "volunteered" to talk with the distressed colleague, as the person most likely to be successful, there may be a feeling of being "stuck" with the job. It might be the better part of valor to take the time to ventilate any negative feelings about the process to someone else whom you trust before making the confrontation.

You will want to be clear, to yourself, about actual, potential, and apparent biases you may hold about the person or the behavior. There may be intense countertransference issues, competitive feelings, and conflict of interest problems related to the intervention. These must be explored before the confrontation takes place. There may be features about the situation or your relationship to the distressed professional that give impressions of biases or conflict of interest. One should be prepared to acknowledge them earlier in the discussion or to discuss them later in the conversation, as seems most appropriate.

It is important to acknowledge to yourself that you will be operating in a dual-role relationship with the distressed professional. You are there to confront, support, and help—but, if the situation does not improve, you will also be forced to report the distressed colleague to the ethics board. It is important, from multiple perspectives, that you acknowledge early in the contact with your distressed colleague that such a dual-role relationship exists. Such a psychological "informed consent" statement will be, in some situations, important for both you and the distressed colleague—so that he or she does not feel "psychologically entrapped" (e.g., encouraged to "open up," only to have that information later given to an ethics committee) and so that you do not inadvertently become an accessory to illegal or unethical actions.

Consideration should also be given to how gender, ethnic, and racial differences may affect the process of confronting a colleague. When such differences exist, there likely will be an additional set of expectations, both for you and for your colleague, resulting from a combination of social stereotypes and personal experience. These expectations can either enhance or confound the process, but are more likely to interfere if not attended to in planning the discussion.

Regarding the effect of such differences on the outcome, the nature of your relationship with the colleague will significantly alter the degree to which social attitudes play a part. If you and your colleague share a vital and warm friendship, you will probably have resolved any of the potential stumbling blocks related to social stereotypes. If, however, the relationship is more distant, and especially if there is a disparity in overt power or authority (one-up, one-down), care should be taken to examine how these differences may contribute to "derailing" the intended direction of the meeting or affect your ability to communicate concern and support while remaining firm in your conviction that the problems you are discussing need to be addressed.

As we mentioned, differences in overt levels of power or authority need to be considered in planning an interview to inform a colleague of your concern. When there is a gender, ethnic, or racial difference, whether the overt power or authority is equal, there probably will be different perceptions of covert power that can interfere with or block both your ability to present your concerns in an empathic manner and with your colleague's ability to hear your concerns clearly. Exploring those perceptions in advance should minimize their impact. This exploration will also reduce your vulnerability to being deflected by a defensive maneuver such as, "How could I expect you to understand, you're a man (woman, Black, White, etc.)!" If you have taken the time to sort through your own concerns regarding the difference in experience, you can respond more clearly as a concerned *person*.

It may seem to some readers that our emphasis on preparing for the discussion is excessive, but in every instance that we have discussed with colleagues who have tried to approach distressed professionals with concerns about their emotional well-being only to have the situation blow up, the initiator had not thought through his or her concerns and observations and could not make a meaningful presentation of them in less than 15 or 20 minutes. That is a long time to expect distressed individuals to "sit on their feelings" (both about your "accusations" and about the array of stressors with which they have been trying to cope). Organizing and condensing your thoughts into a concise opening presentation will make you more confident, convincing, and effective, thereby allowing you to be more supportive of and helpful toward your distressed colleague.

Step 4: Consider How You Will Address Your Colleague

The fourth step in confronting and supporting a distressed colleague is to consider how you should speak in the early minutes of the conversation. This is implied in Step 3. Use simple sentences, without numerous and extensive qualifications. Stick to specifics. Describe succinctly the facts of the behavior you have observed and explain why that behavior is important. Avoid being judgmental! Express an understanding of possible feelings. Express your support for and confidence in your colleague's desire to change. And be brief!

By doing all this, you will ensure that the key issues do get stated. The essential points will have been spelled out, so they can be discussed. By expressing empathic understanding of the struggles and feelings the person must be coping with, you will be concretely expressing your supportive understanding of your colleague. By stating the need for and achievability of change, you will be providing hope and additional support.

Step 5: Speak, Listen, and Discuss

Meet with your colleague and express your concerns. Then, you must be prepared to listen attentively, respond empathically, and assist in problem solving. These actions, of course, are a set of skills with which all mental health professionals are familiar, but remember that you are not in a formal psychotherapeutic situation. You are there as a concerned professional and a supportive colleague. Stick to the reality of the distressed individual's feelings and the reality of his or her behavior.

Be prepared for an initial response of denial or anger. If your colleague initially tries to deny that there is a problem, acknowledge that you may be wrong (and remember that you really may be wrong), but go on to say that it is often difficult and embarrassing for a professional to admit that he or she is overwhelmed and is having difficulty coping with emotional conflict. If the person continues to claim that there is no problem, it may be useful to ask him or her to help you understand their behavior and how it relates to what you have observed (and have apparently misunderstood). Repeatedly state that you wish to understand and to help. If your colleague responds initially with anger, acknowledge that you, too, would feel annoyed and angry with a colleague who questioned your functioning, but go on to restate your concern about the person's well-being and your support for him or her as a colleague and friend.

Invite the individual to explain what you have observed, using a supportive tone and nonjudgmental phrasing which are less likely to elicit defensive responses. Some form of self-disclosure on your part may help your distressed colleague to feel comforted and able to discuss self-revealing topics. You may wish to acknowledge the embarrassment and self-anger that your colleague must feel because he or she has been functioning in a manner that led you and others to be concerned enough to approach the individual about it. It may be helpful to acknowledge your own anxiety and doubt about talking about your concerns, and you can use this to restate your support, your wish to be helpful, and your desire to understand. Your approach generally should be one of expressing empathic understanding and taking the discussion back to what is happening in the person's life and how this might be affecting his or her functioning.

If your colleague acknowledges some difficulty, listen attentively with concern and compassion and respond empathically. Encourage the person to talk further and to identify the problems and difficulties. Utilize your active listening skills. Express the unstated feelings. If the person talks only about stress at work, ask how things are going at home. But, remember, as we stated before, this is not a formal therapeutic relationship, so stay with the current reality of feelings and behavior and acknowledge how anyone would feel under the circumstances. There are no clear guidelines regarding how much detail you allow the person to go into or how long you talk. That will depend on what you and the other person feel comfortable with and on the nature of the basic situation and your relationship to each other. Such discussions may be as short as 30 minutes or as long as 3 or 4 hours. Thus, we recommend that you plan to have the conversation with the distressed colleague at a time when both of you are free to talk for as long as necessary.

At some point you will want to turn the conversation to the question, "What next?" What is the person going to do about whatever you have been discussing? You want to consider new ways of coping with or addressing the basic problems. Engage the person in problem solving. What can he or she do for the short term? How can the family help? What support can you and other friends and colleagues provide? Has the person thought about going into therapy? Is professional help needed? Would the person like to discuss possible referrals? Work to get your colleague's input and involvement in identifying possible ways to begin relieving the stress, resolving the conflict, and solving the problems.

After doing this, you should conclude and summarize the conversation. Restate your perception, concern, and support. Summarize the issues, problems, and conflicts that you have discussed. Recap the array of options you have considered for changing the situation, and state your confidence that things can and will improve, if the person takes action. Ask if there is something that you can do to help the person get started. You should state, if appropriate to the situation, what you will have to do if the outcome that is mutually expected does not occur. You may want to agree to talk again in the future to review what has happened and how things are going. Set a time for meeting again to discuss things further, as a friend and concerned colleague (not as a substitute for a therapist), because you are now in a position to make formal your commitment to be a support and to get the person to make a commitment to him- or herself and to you to take action. The length of time between the initial conversation and follow-up is not firm. It will depend on the gravity of the situation, the nature of your relationship, and the ease with which the two of you can meet.

Step 6: Follow Up

The sixth step in confronting and supporting a distressed colleague is to follow up what you have initiated. As soon as possible after the meeting, write some notes about it for yourself. Do this while it is still fresh in your mind. The notes need not be long, but you should have them both to document the meeting and to refresh your memory before the follow-up meeting. Note when the meeting was held, briefly summarize why you met with your colleague and the initial points you made; include your colleague's initial reactions and subsequent comments. Note what agreements for action were made as well as the range of options discussed, and indicate when the two of you plan to meet again. Be sure to put a note on your calendar regarding recontacting and meeting with your colleague for the follow-up meeting.

You may feel uncomfortable documenting such a meeting. However, by drafting such notes to yourself, you will be better able to recapture the discussion and to be more helpful to your distressed colleague in the follow-up meeting. The notes will make it easier to cover the previously discussed issues and problem situations systematically. They will also provide more accurate data in the unfortunate event that you ultimately are forced to file ethical charges or take other action if there is further deterioration in your colleague's professional functioning (and the notes may be useful in the unlikely situation that your colleague takes legal action against you). Providing yourself with documentation of the meeting is a humane, helpful, ethical, and self-protective course of action. But the most important point is that you follow up and continue to be a source of support for your distressed colleague.

*   *   *

The model discussed should be relatively obvious, and it is undoubtedly familiar. In many ways it merely describes what we have all seen or heard reported. Yet, we hope to have made a few points that you might not have considered and to have reinforced others. We think it was important to walk through the process in order to emphasize the balancing act that one professional often experiences when confronting and aiding another. The balance is difficult. On one hand, there is the impulse to bypass certain simple steps, such as expressing empathy and support, as well as to avoid writing notes to yourself, both before and after the discussion. On the other hand, there is the tendency to start to try to do therapy with someone who is not your patient. Such is part of the dilemma of confronting and supporting a distressed colleague, a situation in which you have multiple responsibilities and desired outcomes.

We next consider some of the varying circumstances under which one may find oneself having to approach a colleague about how he or she is handling life (and how it is affecting his or her professional functioning and affecting others).

INTERVENTION FROM DIFFERENT LEVELS OF AUTHORITY AND POWER

A distressed colleague may be a friend or a casual acquaintance, with whom one may have frequent or rare contact. He or she may work in the same or in a different clinic, hospital, school system, corporation, or university. The individual in distress also may be one's boss, a co-worker, or an employee. Of all of these possibilities, the latter set of factors—the relative positions of power or authority—is the most problematic in terms of how it influences the possibilities for and the nature of approaching the distressed colleague with concerns about his or her emotional well-being and professional functioning. As noted earlier, each position has advantages and disadvantages.

Let us begin by considering the situation of an employee who has concerns about the functioning of his or her supervisor. In such a situation the distressed professional is in a position of power or authority over the concerned initiator. This is, obviously, a high-risk situation, and it is one in which many professionals actively avoid expressing their concerns directly to the distressed professional. In our conversations with other colleagues about attempts to confront an impaired professional, more than half of all "failed attempts" have occurred under such conditions. The vast majority of reported attempts at such direct, personal confrontations by persons in a "one-down" position in a power or authority relationship have failed. We are forced to conclude, tentatively, that when a person is in a one-down power position, he or she should not attempt to directly approach the distressed professional; rather, the concerned individual should take such observations and fears to another respected colleague who can approach the distressed individual as an equal.

We suspect that the dynamics that make this situation one with a low probability of success are multifaceted. The potential initiator's motives are likely to be highly mixed. Although he or she may be genuinely concerned about the well-being of the distressed professional, the potential initiator also may be angry about being short-changed in the professional training that he or she should be receiving or angry over what is perceived as an unfair evaluation or as unrealistically high expectations of his or her performance in comparison to the supervisor's own performance. In addition, the potential initiator may be acting out the wish to confront others who earlier in his or her life operated in a manner that differed from what was expected or desired (or who operated on a double standard of "do as I say, not as I do").

In this situation, the distressed professional also may have irrelevant dynamics activated, which are immediately used in a defensive and aggressive manner in order to undermine the concerns and claims of the initiator. Perceiving the initiator as being in a weaker position, the distressed professional may panic, thinking, "If this person knows and feels confident enough to approach me about this, who else knows and how obvious must it be?" Rather than listening rationally to the concerns and taking corrective action, the distressed professional may (in panic) "attack" the initiator in an attempt to deny the reality, undercut the confidence of the initiator, prevent him or her from telling others, and try to define the observations as part of a problem (which may be partially true) that the initiator has with authority figures, with control, or with evaluation of his or her own competence. Whatever the specific dynamics, it appears that the likelihood of anyone being able to succeed in directly and personally approaching a distressed professional from a one-down position is very low. The concerned individual in such a position is advised to take that observation to another professional who might be more successful in approaching the distressed professional.

The clinic director, department chair, or supervisor (who is in a "one-up" position) also has problems related to "power" when approaching a distressed colleague. The person in authority may feel that "if I know, I must take formal action" (which cuts him or her off from the initial step of informally approaching the distressed individual as a concerned colleague). However, the power of the person in authority, as it is perceived by the distressed professional, may be so enormous that the boss or supervisor cannot be viewed as a concerned colleague, and this perception may cut off the distressed professional from a potential source of support and may cause needless panic about the security of his or her employment.

The boss or supervisor can, however, at least verbally define the situation in different terms, so that the distressed individual need not necessarily feel panicked. The personnel procedures in most settings provide that the person in authority should first hold an informal conversation with an employee who is perceived as not functioning up to expectations, that is, if the behaviors that prompted the meeting are not acute and critical. In addition, if the behaviors that prompted the discussion are not related to work performance, the person in the role of authority can state that and indicate that he or she is acting as a friend and concerned colleague rather than as a director, chair, or supervisor. Defining the exchange in such a manner does not guarantee that it will be so perceived by the distressed individual, but at least the attempt has to be made.

In any case, the person who initiates contact with a distressed colleague about his or her emotional well-being and professional functioning should clearly state the role from which he or she is speaking. The person who is operating from a position of power or authority is, moreover, in a position to offer the distressed professional an added measure of support by telling the person that others will not be allowed to take certain types of action against the distressed individual (at least in the short run) if the person promptly seeks help and makes meaningful progress (and does not violate any major rules or legal statutes). Such concrete assurances can provide significant support to the distressed individual, relieving him or her of one source of existing or potential stress.

However, the fact that a person in a position of authority is discussing one's personal or professional functioning can be very threatening and intimidating. The distressed individual may wonder, "If it has gone so far that the boss is talking to me, how bad is it?" Obviously, an array of possible dynamics about relationship to authority figures may be activated. In the face of perceived criticism from a person in authority, the distressed individual may respond in a variety of ways, ranging from apparent meek compliance to fearful and inappropriate denial. The response will be mediated by whatever has proved to be the "safest" and most effective way to respond to the "accusations" of authority figures in the life experiences of the distressed individual. This has the effect of making it more difficult for the person in authority to assess the initial effect and overall effectiveness of the intervention, and it emphasizes the importance of later follow-up with the distressed colleague.

Although the foregoing might seem to imply that someone who is on an equal professional level with a distressed colleague is in the best position to discuss concerns with the colleague about his or her emotional well-being, this relationship also has its advantages and disadvantages. The obvious advantages are that you do not have any immediate power of control over the distressed individual (which should lessen the possible threat) and that you have a greater initial probability of being perceived as a truly concerned friend. Regardless of any negative interpretations that your colleague may consciously or unconsciously place upon you, it is important that you work to reinforce the potentially positive attributions that the colleague may attach to you because of the apparent equality of your relationship. Using phrases such as "I wanted to talk to you as a friend and colleague" and "Because there is no reason for you to worry about me talking with you about this" will be useful in reinforcing positive attributions of your motivation for approaching the person with your concerns.

However, no one is without flaws, and the distressed individual may respond with, "Who are you (with problem X or Y) to tell me about my problems?" The person in a peer relationship with the distressed professional also may have to cope with the distressed person trying to redefine the initiator's concern into a manifestation of the initiator's problems (as when the person responds, "No, you see it wrong; you're just overreacting, because you have problems with . . .). Moreover, friendship (and apparent equality) does not mean that competition is absent. If the distressed individual feels in competition with you for promotion or recognition (which may be at least in part true, even if you, yourself, do not feel in competition), he or she may have a particularly difficult time viewing your intervention as positive and motivated out of concern for his or her well-being. In most situations, you will not have detailed information about the relationship between your colleague and his or her brothers and sisters, so you will be encountering such dynamics "in the dark." If you are anticipating such possibilities, however, you may quickly recognize them and work to minimize them verbally.

We are aware that we have not mentioned every possible reaction and dynamic that may be manifested in the various types of relationships. However, our goal has been to draw your attention to the numerous potential factors that may operate when you approach a distressed colleague. Some factors may be related to the structure of the power relationship between the two of you, which may take on dynamic implications. Others are more related to typical defensive styles that each of us utilizes in varying ways and to differing extents. What we have tried to emphasize is that any number of reactions may be manifested by the distressed professionals whom you approach. Being aware of the range of possibilities, you will be in a better position to respond to them positively and constructively. We are *not* trying to give the impression that it is impossible (or an absolutely awful experience) to confront and support a distressed colleague. It can be done, and it can be effective. We know that, because we have done it and have talked with others who have successfully done it. Knowing and considering the possibilities will help you to be more effective when you find yourself in a position in which you must confront a distressed colleague.

A CLINICALLY-BASED DISCUSSION

It is all well and good to discuss what one should do and how one should do it, but a sense of what actually occurs during attempts to intervene often brings a richer understanding of the process, its problems, and the ultimate success or failure of the intervention. To provide such illustrations, we will discuss three cases, selected because they varied in the success or failure of the treatment initiative and in the nature of the problems experienced by the distressed professionals.

Case Example 1: Substance Abuse and the Process of Denial

The first case involves alcohol abuse and addiction. The situation was identified and handled within the work setting and its administrative structure. The case illustrates the extent to which some distressed professionals will deny that they have a problem, and the nature of that problem, in this case for a period probably exceeding 5 years. The intervention in this case probably should be considered a failure, despite the fact that the situation did ultimately resolve itself.

Miss Jones was the clinical supervisor for an off-site social work follow-up counseling service of a large public hospital. She was 61 years old, and she had recurring mild back pain resulting from a herniated disk, a problem that could be managed without surgery through diet control, exercise, and correct posture. She had worked for the agency for approximately 8 years, serving for the last 2 as supervisor of the off-site outpatient counseling and guidance service. She supervised a clinical staff of four social workers, one psychologist, and three counselors, all of whom were between 25 and 45 years old. Miss Jones had gradually become the agency's resident "alcohol expert" because she had been sent to a number of seminars and workshops on alcohol-related problems during the last 5 years.

The latter fact is worth a brief comment. We have noted with surprising regularity that when a clinical staff member in a "general service" community mental health clinic, family and child guidance clinic, and other such counseling services evolves, through recurring but informal training, into a so-called specialist in alcohol abuse or drug abuse, it is often the case that the individual has selected his- or herself because of personal problems in that area or that the agency has pushed that individual toward such undertakings as an indirect attempt to force him or her to see his or her own emerging problem. This type of indirect, dare we say nonspecific, intervention is never successful, at least in those instances that we have had an opportunity to observe or later consult on.

Some months after Miss Jones had transferred to the off-site office, individual staff members began to note an apparent deterioration in her work performance. She became less available for supervision of and consultation with staff members, less systematic in the review of cases, and erratic in keeping supervision appointments, and she began to end supervision sessions abruptly after only 10 to 15 minutes. Moreover, clinical staff also was beginning to hear complaints from clients who had direct clinical contact with Miss Jones. Furthermore, Miss Jones's administrative functioning seemed to be deteriorating; she seemed unable to produce needed administrative reports, was erratic and inconsistent in administrative decision making, and was unable to systematically follow through on administrative details.

Concurrently, her co-workers noted an apparent change in personality and behavior. She seemed to have withdrawn and become aloof. She spent less time informally chatting with staff, and she stopped sharing lunch hours with her co-workers. Her absences from work increased, and it became more and more frequent that she would arrive at work late or leave work early because of "not feeling up to par." Clinical and clerical staff began to note a pattern of Miss Jones's having alcohol on her breath during the afternoon and to appear more frequently to be behaviorally "under the influence of alcohol."

It is often the case that only when one looks at all of the areas of functioning of a distressed professional does one see a pattern about which concern and action is appropriate. The casual observer or a colleague visiting the office for an hour or two probably would not become alarmed if the individual's behavior appeared to be different from his or her usual behavior. A colleague who only knew of one or two aspects of the individual's functioning easily could perceive the less than effective functioning as merely the result of a busy schedule, personal distraction, or similar "realistic" causes. At worst, a colleague might view individual behaviors as reflecting slightly inadequate professional functioning or a mild example of poor professional judgment.

> Initially individual staff members commented in private to Miss Jones about one or another concern about her behavior. Her response to such comments or expressions of concern was defensive. She attributed all of her present difficulty to her "back problems," subtly suggested a lack of empathy on the part of the given staff member, and intimated that the staff member's "concern" was placing more pressure on her.
>
> As the situation continued to deteriorate and individual staff members' concern continued to increase, they began to share their concerns with each other. They found that many of them had attempted individually to confront and support Miss Jones, without any apparent result. Finally, the clinical staff jointly confronted her about their observations— the nonproductivity (both administratively and clinically), the withdrawal from co-workers, and the evidence of drinking. She responded to the group in the same manner that she had responded to them as individuals—criticizing them for not understanding, attacking them for making matters worse, and asking them to "back off" for a short time while she attended to her health problem. For a short time after the group confrontation, Miss Jones's functioning improved, but quickly began to deteriorate again. The clinical staff confronted Miss Jones a second time; her response was identical to that in the earlier confrontation. After the second unsuccessful group confrontation, the staff decided to inform the program director at the hospital about the situation.

The intensity and the extent of the denial in this example is not atypical in situations of substance abuse, particularly when the substance is alcohol. Undoubtedly, the inability to confront and support this individual successfully was complicated by her intense and persistent denial combined with confrontations by "subordinates" who were significantly younger than the distressed professional, as well as by the public nature of the group confrontations during the latter stages of the attempted intervention. As noted earlier, we have found that it is difficult, if not impossible, for subordinates in a work setting to successfully confront and assist their "boss," particularly when the confrontation occurs within the work context and draws heavily on work performance. Moreover, the "boss" is generally older than his or her subordinates and may view them, because of their relative youth, as personal and professional threats.

After being informed about the continuing deterioration of Miss Jones's behavior, the program director investigated the problem and obtained collaborating evidence from clerical, administrative, and clinical staff. Despite Miss Jones's continued denials, countercharges, and explanations, the program director concluded that there was a problem and that Miss Jones's functioning had deteriorated, was below an acceptable level, and had to improve. She was given the choice of "doing something" to remedy the situation or being placed on indefinite leave (with a possibility of termination of employment). Miss Jones was told to work out the plan to "do something" about the situation with an agency staff member who was the formally designated alcoholism treatment specialist and to report on follow through on such a plan to that staff member.

A flaw in the administrative action taken is readily apparent. The program director, while firmly taking a stand in confronting the problem, fell into the trap of establishing neither a clear and detailed plan for correcting the situation nor a clear set of procedures for approving the plan, monitoring it, or taking further administrative action. The staff member to whom Miss Jones was to report had no explicit authority to approve or disapprove the treatment plan for "doing something." This type of ill-defined follow-up appears, in our opinion, to be all too common. It may be that as we confront the distressed colleague, our guilt and doubt too often manifest themselves in our failing to develop a systematic and coherent set of expectations in a monitoring plan. It almost appears as if we unconsciously, or at least unintentionally, undermine our own attempt at confrontation as well as the likelihood of helping our colleague.

Miss Jones concluded that her drinking behavior was secondary to her health problem and that stress at work and in her personal life was a further "cause" of the drinking problem. Her self-developed plan to "do something" was to seek stress management counseling. The staff member who was responsible supposedly for monitoring the plan suggested that it did not seem likely that it would ameliorate the situation and recommended that Miss Jones at least simultaneously attend Alcoholics Anonymous (especially since the proposed stress management counseling was not going to focus on the alcohol use). Miss Jones rejected the suggestions, stating that she was in compliance with the agreement she made with the program director to "do something" by seeking the therapy of her choice. After a brief improvement, which lasted for about a month, Miss Jones's performance, behavior, and drinking returned to the previous levels.

After administrative staff found liquor bottles in her desk and filing cabinets, the program director placed Miss Jones on indefinite administrative leave with the option that if she sought "appropriate help" (still undefined) and adequately demonstrated a return to "normal functioning," she could return to her previous position. Miss Jones decided to seek voluntary hospitalization in a facility specializing in the treatment of stress disorders. While in the facility, she ultimately decided to seek early retirement for "health reasons."

This case highlights the extent of the process of denial in cases of alcoholism. Denial is similarly present in drug abuse and addiction cases. However, the most striking matter that this case illustrates is the way in which ill-defined, nonspecific treatment and follow-up plans contribute to the denial process and fail to help a distressed colleague get past this self-destructive attempt at coping.

Case Example 2: Depression and Personal Identity

The second case involves depression. The pattern was identified across a variety of work and quasi-social situations, and the professional in distress was approached on an informal, colleague-to-colleague basis.

> Mr. Brown was the director of a community-based county work release/rehabilitation program in a medium-sized town. He was 34 years old. Mr. Brown was noted for his friendliness, his openness with colleagues and community leaders, his dedication to making the program work for the community and those enrolled, and his well-balanced approach in solving problems and in instructing others about how best to approach the participants in the program. Due to a cut in state funding to be made available to the county, the county board of administration found it necessary to reallocate funds for the next year's budget in such a way that several programs, including the program directed by Mr. Brown, would have to be redefined or possibly even eliminated. Mr. Brown prepared extensive documentation on the success of his program and presented it to the board, making an impassioned plea for its continuation. The board began its deliberations.
>
> Although not directly involved in the decision-making process, Mr. Brown was well known to many of the board members and, as the board's deliberations progressed, some board members formed factions representing a range of opinions about what should happen to the program and shared information on the board's day-to-day deliberations, which were marked by continual changes in opinions, with Mr. Brown. As a result, over a period of six months, Mr. Brown became progressively more frustrated, uncertain, and stressed about the eventual outcome.
>
> Mr. Brown's co-workers began to notice him gradually withdrawing from those around him. Rather than having his lunch in the cafeteria with his colleagues, he began to eat alone in his office, declaring that he was too busy to do otherwise, and he participated less and less in the ordinary social activity of the staff. He also began to limit "business" contact with his colleagues and members of the community to meetings that were as brief as possible. Several of his co-workers as individuals expressed concern about these changes to him. Mr. Brown's explanation was that the uncertainty about the outcome of the board's deliberations was creating a great deal of pressure on him and, as a result, it was difficult for him to concentrate, and he had to focus more intensely on getting his work done.

In this situation, one notes a not infrequent pattern of events that may predate or trigger a depressive episode for a health and human services professional. Professionals, particularly those working in specialized programs dealing with very well-defined populations, often have significant personal commitments and intense identification with their programs and the individuals those programs serve. Although not the case with Mr. Brown, individuals working in such programs may have either personally experienced the problem that the program treats or a close family member who has experienced the difficulty. In short, they have multiple investments in the program, and, when the program is under attack or unappreciated, they may feel (though not be consciously aware of the feeling) that they are personally under attack or that their individual efforts are unappreciated. Memories of other times when they felt the same way may be awakened, or they may choose unconsciously to defend themselves against that reawakening of those feelings and memories. Likewise, what is happening at work may make them feel as other situations in their lives have made them feel, thus magnifying and intensifying their reactions. Being relatively powerless to resolve the overall situation makes them very vulnerable to depression. The withdrawal from social interactions that normally provide outlets for expressing emotions and opportunities for receiving advice and support escalates the situation.

> Others also noted the changes in Mr. Brown. In particular, these changes were noted by an industrial/organizational psychologist working for a large company, which had participated in the work release program for many years, and who considered Mr. Brown to be both a colleague and a friend. His colleague asked Mr. Brown to conduct a training session for several new employees on the staff on how to work effectively with participants in the work release program. On the day following the session, she called Mr. Brown and asked to meet with him in order to share feedback on the session, and they set a meeting time. During the meeting, she expressed concern about the changes she had noted in Mr. Brown's behavior both personally and professionally and her feeling that those changes seemed to represent a pattern of behavior indicating depression. She went on to say that it was apparent that the depression was not being attended to by Mr. Brown.
> As an example of what had caused her to be concerned, she pointed out that during the training session Mr. Brown, who was ordinarily a patient, flexible individual, had responded to members of the group with anger and hostility when they challenged or even questioned elements of his presentation and when they expressed disagreement with his interpretations of material. She noted that this was very inconsistent with his usual behavior. At the same time, she mentioned in passing that she had overheard comments by others—including co-workers and community members—regarding his apparent inaccessibility, both professionally and emotionally. She suggested that Mr. Brown's attempts to control and cope with his distress were not being fully effective and that she and his co-workers wanted to offer whatever support they could. At the same time, she suggested that Mr. Brown might consider entering therapy.
> Initially, Mr. Brown reacted defensively and angrily. He expressed his feeling that his colleague was intruding. However, after continued discussion, it became apparent to him that her concern was genuine and that she expressed the shared caring and frustration of herself, his co-workers,

and others. The effect of her simultaneously confrontational and support-ing approach was to break through Mr. Brown's defensiveness and denial. He began to identify and acknowledge other indications of depressive symptomatology. He also mentioned that his rumination about possible "political outcomes" and his withdrawal from others was further compli-cating the situation for him. Following this confrontation, he went into short-term therapy and his depression was quickly resolved—Mr. Brown again became his friendly, open, effective self.

Although Mr. Brown was certainly a more "open" person than Miss Jones (Case Example 1), the success of the confrontation was greatly facilitated by the organized way in which Mr. Brown's colleague approached and confronted him. The skillful use of data-based and personal observations, combined with a low-key way of noting comments that others were making, was very effective in demonstrating that "something was going on" without condemning the be-havior or Mr. Brown. The genuine concern, caring, and support provided during the confrontation was essential to its success.

Case Example 3: Stress and the Coping Process

The third case involves an individual who, until successful intervention was made, was ineffectively attempting to cope with an incredible number of "life change" stresses. The behavior that raised concern was originally noted in the work situation. The investigation was handled in a relatively informal way on a colleague-to-colleague basis, but not by a close personal friend. This type of case is typical of cumulative life stress. Dewey Jacobs, a PhD psychologist who is a member of the California Psychological Association, reported that when the Association informally polled members about the frequency and causes of impaired functioning by professional psychologists, members attributed the vast majority of such incidences to multiple stresses that introduce reality changes in the professional's life.

> Dr. Smith was a 39-year-old research psychologist at a well-known university. His primary departmental responsibilities were coordinating and supervising graduate students who served as instructors for the intro-ductory psychology courses and coordinating the advisory program for psychology majors (also staffed with graduate students). Early in the fall quarter, several colleagues noted that they had seen relatively little of him so far that fall. Some were aware of rumors about the breakup of Dr. Smith's marriage and began to wonder how severely the stress of the breakup was affecting him. Some weeks later graduate students were overheard commenting on the fact that Dr. Smith had repeatedly missed or cancelled meetings with those graduate students whose activities he was coordinating.
>
> A colleague who happened to live in the same neighborhood as Dr. Smith decided to seek him out one weekend and discuss the growing concern of his colleagues. On arriving at Dr. Smith's home, the colleague was fairly direct about the reason for his visit, stating that he had not seen Dr. Smith on campus, had heard rumors about a marital breakup, and

increasingly had heard others talking about Dr. Smith. The colleague stated that Dr. Smith must be under a great deal of stress and wondered if he wanted to talk about what was going on. Dr. Smith immediately began discussing his "awful summer."

First, his wife had indeed left. One day in June, one of the children had broken an arm while under Dr. Smith's supervision when Mrs. Smith was out shopping. Dr. Smith felt that this was a very minor incident; however, Mrs. Smith reacted more dramatically, moving out and taking the children with her, giving as her reason that Dr. Smith was irresponsible. Dr. Smith was furious over her leaving, especially for what was, in his opinion, a minor accident and for her claim that he was irresponsible. At the same time, however, Dr. Smith acknowledged to his colleague that the marriage had been deteriorating for 3 or 4 years and that many verbal arguments had occurred during the last year (generally around the question of whether his wife could "depend on him" in light of his frequent absences on professional trips, long hours in the research laboratory, and general lack of involvement with his family and home). Dr. Smith now found himself in financial difficulty and in a messy legal situation, primarily related to the divorce settlement and child support payments.

A second cause for Dr. Smith's upset was that in July his mother had a stroke and in August, because his father was also frail from earlier medical problems, he was forced to assist them both in moving into a nursing home. Because his parents lived out of state, the frequent trips to help settle their affairs had placed an additional financial burden on him even though at the moment the cost of the nursing home was not a problem, since his parents had sufficient financial resources to cover the expenses. These two series of events, Dr. Smith acknowledged, had made him feel unsuccessful and inadequate, and, for the first time, he was aware of his own mortality.

In spite of this acknowledgment, however, Dr. Smith was not coping. His absences were related to the fact that he was not going to bed until 4:00 or 5:00 in the morning, either because he had been up all night worrying (and drinking) or because he had been up all night "partying" in a vain attempt to feel better and forget his problems. His partying had begun in the late summer and had continued into the fall. Moreover, he had started dating a young woman, an undergraduate student, during the summer. In the fall, when he started dating another young woman, he tried to break the relationship off with the first woman. She could not accept the breakup and kept turning up at his home at all hours, wanting to talk, make up, and continue the relationship. Both the partying and dating were adding additional stress to his situations.

Dr. Smith's colleague was overwhelmed and certainly had not expected to learn so much or to face such a dilemma. The colleague conceded to Dr. Smith that he doubted that he himself could handle everything Dr. Smith was experiencing while still carrying on his regular activities. He wondered if Dr. Smith needed both more time to get his life in order and an opportunity to temporarily "step outside" of his stressful situations and self-defeating attempt at coping. Dr. Smith and his colleague began problem solving and considering alternative courses of action. Within 2 weeks, Dr. Smith had obtained a 3-month administrative leave from the university, under condition that he enter short-term intensive therapy. He moved out of state temporarily to be near his parents and help stabilize their situation. While out of state, he underwent therapy. At the end of his leave, Dr. Smith returned to the university and his regular duties. He began to deal more effectively with the stresses of his situation, including the finalization of his divorce, stopped dating undergraduates, and returned to productive academic pursuits.

It has been our experience that many of the incidences of distressed behavior by professionals are temporary and that they are often related to the simultaneous occurrence of multiple stressful events (whether "normal" life transitions or major disruptive events that may or may not be the "fault" of the professional). The distressed professional in such instances may or may not be seen as "impaired." Colleagues tend to view the most typical indications of distress as a decline in professional judgment or professional effectiveness rather than as complete and total incompetence. This suggests that for most distressed professionals a fair degree of coping ability still exists, and, therefore, a supportive confrontation frequently may be effective in identifying and preventing major professional difficulties.

CONCLUSION

Acknowledging that a fellow professional has difficulty in facing the same stresses we may face, and that he or she cannot cope without additional support, makes our own vulnerability all too clear to each of us. We find it equally difficult to acknowledge the personal and professional responsibility we have to confront our distressed colleague. We choose to assume that given time he or she will be able to work through the crisis without *our* help. We turn aside or make less of an effort than we might. By taking the same care in preparing for such a confrontation that we would take in preparing for any professional challenge, by having and expressing the patience and understanding for our fellow professionals that we one day may need, we will serve not only our distressed colleagues, but also ourselves, our professions, and our communities.

ADVICE TO FAMILIES AND FRIENDS OF PSYCHOLOGISTS IN DISTRESS

12

Barbara S. McCrady
William Frankenstein

This chapter is directed toward the family and friends of psychologists in distress. If impaired psychologists are to be served effectively, their families and friends are important supports that must be utilized. Because the most immediate indications of impairment emerge in relationships with family and friends, those close to the psychologist are often in the best position to persuade him or her to seek help. Furthermore, once help seeking has been initiated, family members and friends are crucial to the long-lasting restoration of the psychologist's familial, social, and professional functioning. The information in this chapter may be used to advise friends and family members on recognizing, approaching, confronting, and supporting psychologists who are not functioning capably as professionals.

Psychologists are not immune from developing serious problems that may disturb their functioning both as professionals and as friends, spouses, and parents.

The available literature reveals little about how the impaired psychologist affects and is affected by his or her family and friends. We suspect, however, that psychologists do not differ in significant ways from anyone else experiencing substantial distress or dysfunction. Because we believe that the far-reaching effects distressed psychologists have on their family and friends are similar to those of nonpsychologists, we discuss the impact that distress and disturbance can have on any relationship and the importance of family and friends in efforts to resolve dysfunction. Then we provide specific advice on how to help the distressed psychologist. We conclude that family and friends are perhaps the single most important resource in attempts to reach, confront, treat, and restore as functioning professionals those psychologists who are unable to cope with their mental, emotional, behavioral, and health problems.

THE EFFECT OF THE DISTRESSED PROFESSIONAL ON FAMILY AND FRIENDS

When someone experiences emotional distress resulting from illness, maladaptive behavior, or stress, family members and close friends are usually the first to notice. Although a significant other may know that something is wrong, he or she will not at first have a clear sense of the nature or cause of the problem. Family and friends may observe in a person they are close to and concerned about changes in mood (the person may become anxious, depressed, agitated, angry, or emotionally withdrawn); in personal habits, such as eating, sleeping, dress, cleanliness, or adherence to usual routines; in socializing; or in the person's interest in previously enjoyed activities. Parenting practices and attitudes may change, marital intimacy or communication may diminish, or sexual interest may decrease. There may be inexplicable changes in the person's work habits or attitudes toward work.

Observable signs and symptoms of distress vary according to the type of problem an individual is experiencing. For example, increased alcohol use, a shift to activities in which alcohol consumption is sanctioned, denial of drinking, and shifts or swings of mood and behavior may characterize the early abuse of alcohol. Sarcastic and cynical attitudes, anxiety or despair, minor illnesses, and fatigue may signal occupational burnout. The outward signs of distress may vary, but in all cases, the close friend or family member will see that something is different.

Once family members and friends notice signs of distress, their most common and natural reactions are to ignore problems, deny their severity, hope that the distressed individual will change, or hope that the individual will recognize the problem and take steps to get help independently. Family members often feel guilty, as though they are responsible for the person's problems, or they may be afraid of the personal, emotional, or economic consequences if they intervene.

Close others may or may not act on their perceptions of change. In a marriage in which spouses openly communicate their concerns, frank discussion may promote efforts to seek help. In a troubled marriage, however, indications of difficulty, if perceived at all, may alienate spouses even further. It is often difficult for significant others to respond to the distressed person, because they may be confused about whether there is a problem, what the problem is, whose responsibility the problem is, and who should initiate efforts to resolve the problem. Rather than dealing directly with a problem, close others may cope by adapting. For example, a spouse may assume more responsibility for parenting and for decisions about family finances as a way to protect the troubled partner. In this way, family stability is preserved, although often at the expense of the family's long-term adjustment.

Some have claimed that a family's attempts to minimize the effects of distress can protect others from developing problems. For example, Wolin and his colleagues have proposed that children of alcoholics are at less risk to develop the disorder if, while growing up, their family rituals such as regular mealtimes and holiday celebrations are undisturbed by the alcoholic parent's drinking (Wolin, Bennett, & Noonan, 1979). Others, however, have pointed to ways in which the family's natural tendency to adapt may contribute to the development of chronic dysfunction. Steinglass (1980, 1981) has described the process by which the family's adaptation to one person's alcohol abuse masks fundamental unresolved problems within the family while fueling the development of chronic alcoholism.

Researchers have noted the myriad ways that social and family relations both provoke and maintain alcoholism (Paolino & McCrady, 1977); anxiety-based disorders (Emmelkamp, 1981; Goldstein & Chambless, 1978; Vander-eycken, 1982); other substance abuse and habit disorders (Colletti & Brownell, 1982); affective disorders (Davenport, Ebert, Adland, & Goodwin, 1977; Friedman, 1975; Rush, Shaw, & Khatami, 1980); child behavior problems (Emery, 1983); and even medical diseases (Chowanec & Binik, 1982; Steidl et al., 1980). Therefore, spouses, friends, and family members may become inextricably enmeshed in the maintenance of one person's dysfunction. The natural tendencies of close others to adapt to distress can inadvertently compound or obscure family or social instability, discord, or disorganization.

It may be weeks or years before it becomes clear to others that a person's problem is ongoing and not just a transient phenomenon. In fact, one of the most difficult times for family and friends is when the distressed person is diagnosed or confronted by someone outside of the family. By this time it is apparent that attempts to minimize the problem have failed. Invariably, confrontations occur within the family, which can promote resolution by bringing out into the open what family or friends have been going through.

Steps toward recovery may soon follow these open, frank, even conflictual confrontations. Because the problem is now out in the open, those involved can seek help, confer with intimates, and obtain information about treatment. At times, family members may also become involved in treatment. Quite often, it is essential that the family be involved. When help is sought, the family can work to maintain closeness, restore a balance of roles and responsibilities, and openly confront their problems in a context of optimism (Moos, 1982). However, when treatment is not sought or problems are not resolved, distress may become an entrenched aspect of family life, and friendships will dissipate or become mutually unsatisfying.

Researchers have pointed to certain characteristics of families under the chronic stress of mental and emotional disturbance. These families usually lack the ability to solve their problems efficiently and without remorse. Family members may become emotionally uninvolved, or, in contrast, overinvolved. For example, distant spouses may become heavily invested in the welfare of their children but neglect the dissatisfaction they experience in their marriage (Barragan, 1976). Physical health and emotional well-being is usually affected adversely. Members of disturbed families visit their physicians more frequently than do nondisturbed families. Other family members may develop problems—a spouse may become depressed or have an extramarital affair, and children may develop eating disorders, anxiety problems, conduct disturbances, or school problems. In general, the more severe the chronic disorder, the more it strains the family's ability to cope, and the more likely it becomes that other family members will develop problems.

Over time, some families may be able to function with a large degree of stability despite the presence of the impaired adult. Brief periods of instability or crisis may occur, which may counteract the family's efforts at self-preservation and prod renewed efforts to resolve problems. Alternatively, the family can readjust and resume its life without any resolution of problems. Unfortunately, often families do not seek help and are not motivated to change until serious adversity has befallen them.

THE ROLES OF FAMILY AND FRIENDS IN HELPING THOSE IN DISTRESS

From the preceding discussion it is clear that when an individual becomes dysfunctional, family and friends are greatly affected, and they in turn affect the distressed person. Close others influence the evolution of the problem, and they can contribute to resolving the problem. Indeed, close others are critical determinants of eventual outcomes.

Much has been written over the past twenty years on the relevance of social support to the etiology and maintenance of general health and emotional problems (Cobb, 1976; Leavy, 1983; Mueller, 1980). Although social support has many meanings, for our purposes it refers to groups such as family and friends. These groups' interactions with a distressed person provide emotional intimacy, caring, love, and esteem. These groups provide identity, instrumental aid, information, values, and reciprocal support.

People suffer when they have no social supports or when their natural support systems do not function. The mechanisms by which social support groups exert such influence are varied. Social support can promote health by preventing problems from occurring. If problems do occur, a person's supports can insulate or protect the person by facilitating coping. Thus, the overwhelming evidence is that the presence of positively functioning support groups facilitates health. Conversely, the absence of support, or dysfunctional support, increases the likelihood of illness and distress (Syrotiuk & D'Arcy, 1984).

Encouraging Distressed Professionals To Seek Treatment

There is little research on the role of significant others in help seeking. What research there is shows that family and friends are usually the first to recognize and respond to dysfunction (Horwitz, 1978). Close others are also important in providing confidentiality, advice, and referral to professional helpers (Litman, 1974). The family, and to a lesser extent, close friends, also contribute to the pursuit of home remedies before professional contacts are made (Schwenk & Hughes, 1983).

It appears that the process of identifying problems and seeking help involves family and friends differentially. For example, friends are often asked for professional referrals and for advice on decisions to seek help, whereas family members more often provide services such as child care and shelter or instrumental aid such as money (Horwitz, 1978). In addition, certain qualities of family relationships may influence whom a person turns to for help. In a study of first-time applicants to a community mental health center, individuals with healthy, communicative, and satisfying marriages most often initiated help seeking with the aid of their spouses. In contrast, those who considered their relationships to be conflictual and those whose marriages were dissolved were more likely to solicit help from relatives or friends, whereas individuals in aloof, uninvolved, but intact marriages did not solicit anyone's help or advice before seeking professional help (Horwitz, 1978). Alcoholics who are separated or in unstable marriages are among the least likely persons with alcohol problems to seek treatment (Baekeland & Lundwall, 1977). In contrast, in some families, drinking occurs entirely outside the home and interferes little with the maintenance of positive family relations (Kaufman, 1984). In these families, treatment seeking may be delayed simply because the family does not view drinking as a problem.

In general, the evidence appears to support the importance of family and friends in facilitating efforts to identify problems and initiate efforts to seek help. In fact, it is in this domain that friends have a special competency.

Involving Family and Friends in the Treatment of Professionals in Distress

Once a person in distress has been referred for treatment, family and friends may be involved in many different ways. If the person is hospitalized, family and colleagues may have to assume the responsibilities that the professional formerly attended to, as well as answer inquiries about his or her well-being, visit the person, and monitor his or her progress. Family and friends may need to continue providing support as long as the patient remains in treatment.

During treatment, a wide range of approaches have been used to involve close others in treatment. These approaches have ranged from asking a spouse to attend therapy sessions, to using the spouse as a co-therapist, to marital, family, or social network interventions. Although these interventions often are directed at specific psychiatric, medical, or other behaviors (e.g., training the spouse to monitor and selectively reinforce abstinence in a recovering alcoholic), marital and family therapy are also used to rectify problematic relationship issues that may cause or compound maladaptive coping.

The choice between applying a focused marital or family intervention or applying marital or family therapy is partly dictated by the clinician or researcher's theoretical perspective. For example, behavior therapists include the spouse actively in a structured, directive way; family therapists include both the spouse and children because, in their view, an individual's dysfunction occurs in and therefore must be treated in the context of the family system; and psychodynamic psychotherapists might involve the spouse in therapy to provide insight into the relationship between current marital distress and the person's earlier relationships with parents.

In many instances, marital therapy may be employed after more traditional therapies have been tried and found to be unsuccessful. Or, marital therapy may be used to reduce the marital stress that was exacerbated by the individual's psychological disorder. Sometimes, practical considerations necessitate the participation of spouses or friends. For example, the cost-effectiveness and superior outcome for patients that receive kidney dialysis at home rather than in the hospital has led to the development of training programs for spouses as dialysis assistants (Blodgett, 1981–82).

Focused marital interventions vary in the amount of involvement required of spouses. Generally, the least demanding approaches to spouse involvement require that the spouse provide information about the partner's problems or to passively attend psychotherapy sessions. According to these approaches, therapy is focused explicitly on the patient's disorder, but spouses are told that their presence is helpful (e.g., Gallant, Rich, Bey, & Terranova, 1970). In the more active and directive approaches that have been developed for many disorders (cf. Barlow, O'Brien, & Last, 1984), treatment may concentrate only on the identified patient's problem or also on the couple's interactions that are relevant to the maintenance of that problem.

Marital interventions clarify the natural, often counterproductive, ways in which spouses respond counterproductively to a distressed person. Feedback and instruction are used to give the spouse a greater range of options for productively resolving problems (e.g., Brownell, Heckerman, Westlake, Hayes, & Monti, 1978; Pearce, Lebow & Orchard, 1981). In approaches that involve spouses more intensively, the behavior of closest friends, relatives, or the spouse may be examined quite closely, and sometimes detailed manuals are provided to the spouse for support and education (Mathews, Gelder, & Johnston, 1981).

Another intensive approach utilizes conjoint hospitalization for a period of time during the inpatient treatment of alcoholics (Paolino & McCrady, 1976; Steinglass, 1979). In conjoint hospitalization, both members of a couple are observed and involved in therapy while living together in a hospital-based home environment. Examples of how family and friends have been intensively engaged in disorder-specific interventions include home-based treatment in which a couple initiates, plans, and conducts the therapy session from their home (Jannoun, Munby, Catalan, & Gelder, 1980; Mathews, Teasdale, Munby, Johnston, & Shaw, 1977); operant behavioral approaches in which the spouse or close other (Stern & Marks, 1973) administers specific contingencies for desired or undesired behaviors; and conjoint approaches to behavioral exposure therapy in which a spouse or friend accompanies the patient during planned confrontations with the avoided object or situation (Barlow et al., 1984).

In contrast to disorder-focused interventions, marital therapy, and sometimes sex therapy, have also been used to treat disorders directly or to alleviate the stress on relationships that some disorders produce. In most kinds of marital therapy, the focus of treatment is on the couple's relationship per se rather than on the patient's disorder (e.g., Hedberg & Campbell, 1974). Couples examine expectations for marriage, communication patterns, feelings, pleasing and displeasing aspects of the relationship, and goals for their future relationship.

In practical terms, the distinction is blurred between marital therapy and some of the disorder-specific interventions just described. However, as it is used with professionals, marital therapy tends to emphasize sources of marital conflict and emotional distancing as being relevant to the resolution of one person's disorder. Spouse participation has generally been shown to have positive effects on patients' marriages (Cobb, McDonald, Marks, & Stern, 1980), which is significant in view of the claims that for some patients treated individually, improved functioning reduces marital stability (Barlow, Mavissakalian, & Hay, 1982; Milton & Hafner, 1979).

Family members (and sometimes friends) may also participate in their own concurrent therapy for support and aid in coping with stressful times. Family and friends also receive support by attending support groups in the community. Of the most well-known, Al-Anon provides education, assistance, and support to spouses of alcoholics. Ala-Fam provides similar services, but with the family as a whole, thus avoiding the polarization of families that sometimes is a consequence of attending AA or Al-Anon. Other support groups exist for families of persons experiencing a broad spectrum of psychological and health-related disorders. In general, support groups may improve the quality of life for family members of distressed persons by imparting information, support, and instrumental services such as food or shelter.

In family therapy, the family is considered to be the patient, rather than the person with the identifiable problem. This is not to suggest that the person's original problem is ignored; it simply means that the family environment in which the problem exists must be addressed, too. Typically, in family therapy, parents and children participate in therapy together. Adult children and their families, grandparents, or other relatives may be included (Guerin, 1976; Gurman & Kniskern, 1981). Friends of distressed persons may be involved in social network interventions, another broadly based systems approach (Attneave, 1976)

After successful treatment, family and friends also play a major role. Persons who have supportive networks are least likely to have relapses after treatment. People in the distressed psychologist's "support network" will need to learn what he or she has to do to maintain progress, whether it is regular attendance at AA or NA meetings, exercise, or a job change. Supporting these efforts is crucial. Families also need to improve communication and may need to increase the kind and quantity of time spent together. Members of the support network also need to learn to recognize signs of an impending relapse, to realize that relapses are a common part of the recovery from addictive or emotional problems, and to learn how to talk honestly with the psychologist about what they are observing.

To summarize, many different strategies have been used to involve family members, most often the spouse, in treatment, and, to a much lesser extent, friends. Implicit in these varied approaches is a common belief that involving close others in therapy improves the chance of a positive outcome for all involved. The next two sections explore research that addresses this belief.

The Role of Family and Friends in Adherence to Treatment and in Attrition

If the involvement of close others increases the likelihood that a distressed person will attend treatment sessions and not drop out of therapy prematurely, such involvement should also aid treatment outcome because a patient cannot benefit from treatment if he or she is not there to receive it. There is some research that supports this notion. For example, alcoholics who have unstable or dissolved marriages are more likely to drop out of treatment (Baekeland & Lundwall, 1977) or follow-up (Ward, Bendel, & Lange, 1982). Minimal spouse involvement is reported to cause greater attrition than does more active involvement (McCrady et al., in press), a result somewhat in contrast to other reports (e.g., O'Farrell & Cutter, 1982). In addition, short-term follow-up of alcoholics tends to be more difficult if the patients are separated or divorced (Ward et al., 1982). Similarly, if the involvement of close others increases a patient's compliance to psychological or medical prescriptions, then outcome should be enhanced. This presumes that the patient's chance for recovery is enhanced by the correct application of a treatment.

Although obesity is not a problem comparable in seriousness to many of those discussed in this book, the influence that spouses have in treatment outcome for obesity may be relevant. In general, spouse involvement and a positive marital relationship have been shown to improve conformity to dietary and exercise regimens (Brownell et al., 1978; Dubbert & Wilson, 1983, 1984; Rosenthal, Allen, & Winter, 1981; Weisz & Bucher, 1980). Similar results have been found for other habit disorders, such as smoking (Mermelstein, Lichtenstein, & McIntyre, 1984). Active spouse involvement in therapy has also promoted greater adherence in home-based treatment for agoraphobia (Jannoun et al., 1980). Positive family attitudes and interactions were found to predict adherence to dietary and medication regimens and dialysis schedules for end-stage renal patients (Steidl et al., 1980). Thus, the available evidence endorses the importance of family environment and the involvement of close others in promoting a patient's compliance with treatment.

The Effects of Support on Treatment Outcome

When a distressed person concludes treatment and is functioning well, the family environment is critical to ensuring that progress continues (Moos, Bromet, Tsu, & Moos, 1979). A poorly functioning family environment will predispose a person to relapse or failure.

In alcoholism treatment programs, numerous investigations have found that community reinforcement is effective as an adjunct to marital counseling (Hunt & Azrin, 1973), behavioral marital therapy (Hedberg & Campbell, 1974), and spouse-involvement strategies (McCrady et al., in press; O'Farrell & Cutter, 1982). Although the pattern of research results is complex, it appears that many alcoholics achieve positive outcomes when their spouses participate in the therapy.

As has already been mentioned, numerous studies attest to the positive effects of spouse involvement in behavioral treatments for obesity (Brownell et al., 1978; Murphy et al., 1982; Pearce et al., 1981; Saccone & Israel, 1978). Many of the studies report considerable maintenance of weight loss for periods of up to one year or more posttreatment when spouses participate actively in therapy. Although the results are not uniform in their support for spouse involvement (Brownell & Stunkard, 1981), it is clear that many patients are aided by the approach.

Spouse involvement has had wide application in treating anxiety disorders. Agoraphobics treated by home-based methods or by active spouse involvement in an exposure program generally have been found to have better posttreatment and long-term adjustment than those treated without the help of spouses (Barlow et al., 1984; Mathews et al., 1977). Similar results have been achieved for partner-assisted treatment for obsessive-compulsive disorders (Emmelkamp, 1981; Emmelkamp & deLange, 1983).

Marital therapy and spouse involvement have proven useful in the treatment of affective disorders. Marital therapy has been found to improve depressive mood and decrease impairment significantly more than does chemotherapy (Friedman, 1975). When used as an adjunct to lithium carbonate maintenance, marital therapy results in fewer rehospitalizations, suicides, and major life disruptions for patients with bipolar affective disorders (Davenport et al., 1977). Other reports have confirmed these findings (Greene, Lee, & Lustig, 1975; Mayo, O'Connell, & O'Brien, 1979). Marital and family approaches have also been effective with substance abuse and schizophrenic disorders (McGill, Falloon, Boyd, & Wood-Siverio, 1983).

To summarize, both marital therapy and treatments in which the spouse is intensively involved may often lead to better long-term treatment outcomes for many patients suffering a wide range of disorders. Although some research has notably failed to support spouse involvement, none has found marital or family involvement to be a negative influence on treatment outcome. That marital and family intervention invariably improves the family environment strongly favors the use of these strategies. Family environment has repeatedly been cited as a critical determinant of adjustment and functioning in the time period after treatment. Posttreatment relapse and deterioration have been related to conflictual, noncohesive, emotionally unexpressive, or disorganized family environments (Dubbert & Wilson, 1983; Hore, 1971; Marlatt & Gordon, 1980; Moos & Moos, 1984; Rosenthal et al., 1981).

In the first half of the chapter, we have discussed research findings on several roles of family and friends vis a vis the distressed professional: in identification and referral, in treatment, in adherence to treatment, and in treatment outcome. In the second half of the chapter, we turn from the research literature to practical advice to help families and friends be their most effective in assisting the distressed professional.

GENERAL ADVICE TO FAMILIES AND FRIENDS OF DISTRESSED PROFESSIONALS

Because the family is such an important part of the treatment process, this section and the next will detail some of the specific actions and attitudes that can be applied by families or friends of distressed professionals. This section will provide some general guidelines, irrespective of the problem area; the next section will focus on specific syndromes.

The first step that families must take in order to help a distressed psychologist, or other professional, is to recognize that a problem exists. When they notice changes in an individual, family and friends must avoid explaining problems away or simply thinking that the person is under stress. It is also a mistake for family members to assume that the distressed individual can handle his or her problems, because of either personal qualities or professional expertise. Families and friends need to recognize that psychologists are human beings first, subject to the same fears and frailties as the rest of humanity, and are psychologists second.

After realizing that a problem exists, the second step is for the family to gather information, think about what they perceive, and develop a picture of what makes them feel concerned about their family member. Before confronting the psychologist with their concerns, family or friends may need to educate themselves about the problems they are observing. There are many sources of information, including this book. Some are written specifically for families and can be found in the community or university library (e.g., Maxwell, 1976). Talks are given frequently in the community about substance abuse and emotional problems; These are usually listed in the community calendar of the local newspaper. The talks are often excellent introductions to specific syndromes, and lecturers can also be helpful sources of treatment referral information.

There are also many self-help groups, both for families and for persons with problems. The best known groups for distressed people include AA; NA; Widowed-to-Widowed; Recovery, Inc.; Parents Anonymous; and specific groups for many debilitating diseases. Many of these organizations have parallel groups for family members, such as Al-Anon (alcohol), Nar-Anon (drugs), and Reach (mental health). Numbers for all of these can be found in a telephone directory. There are several self-help clearinghouses that can be contacted to get information about self-help groups in a specific area. (Information can be obtained through the New Jersey Self-Help Clearinghouse, 800/452-9790, administered through the St. Clare's Community Mental Health Center in Denville, N.J.) Finally, specific information about impaired psychologists is available through two organizations, Psychologists Helping Psychologists and the Volunteers in Psychology (VIP) network. Information can be obtained through the main offices of the American Psychological Association (202/955-7600).

After family or friends feel that they have enough understanding of the problem and enough concrete information and documentation to support their belief that the psychologist is impaired, the third step is to discuss concerns directly with the psychologist. This may be a difficult undertaking, and the family member embarking on such a confrontation may want professional help either to sort out his or her own feelings about what is happening or to bring about the confrontation. The professional consulted may be, for example, a mental health professional, a family physician, or a member of the clergy. When seeking professional assistance, the family should seek someone who is expert in the problem area of concern and in working with families. In some geographic areas, it may be difficult to find someone with the appropriate expertise, but if the first professional consulted is not able to help, then other options should be pursued.

With or without professional help, confronting a person in distress must have at least three major elements: support and caring, honest information, and hope (Johnson, 1973). Each element is crucial to keep the confrontation from adding to the psychologist's already heavy burden of distress. Family and friends may have to set aside their own anger, fear, and personal distress enough to help the distressed psychologist get into treatment. If they cannot, personal help to deal with these feelings must precede any confrontation.

Care should be taken that time and privacy are sufficient for serious conversation during the confrontation. If the psychologist is abusing alcohol or drugs, the time selected should maximize the chance that he or she will be relatively sober. All of the people who care, who are most affected by the person's problems, who have observed the most, and who can be honest but not cruel, should be involved. Sometimes it is preferable that only one person discuss her or his concerns with the psychologist; sometimes the whole family or a small group of friends is preferable; sometimes the confrontation is best done with an outside professional present, especially if efforts within the family have failed.

The support message to the psychologist should take the form, "I care about you, and I am concerned because you are having problems that seem to be making you unhappy. I have noticed many ways in which you have changed." The spouse, family, or friends should then give honest information—specific feedback about things they have observed that have led them to believe that the person is impaired. It is crucial to stay calm and matter-of-fact, even though the psychologist may become angry or defensive and the family may feel angry as well. Finally, it is helpful to have information about treatment resources available and to communicate a positive sense of hope that these problems will be resolved with appropriate treatment.

It is hoped that the confrontation will lead the psychologist to agree to seek treatment. If he or she does, then the fourth step is participation in treatment. The family may have any of the several roles described earlier, such as providing information to the treatment team, attending educational meetings, participating in therapy concurrent with the psychologist's therapy, participating in couples or family therapy, or participating in conjoint hospitalization. Any of these roles requires the family to be willing to participate and to support efforts involved in the psychologist's treatment (e.g., to make time commitments or financial commitments and to rearrange family schedules). It is also important that each family member define what is and is not his or her responsibility in treatment. It is possible to facilitate and encourage treatment, but it is impossible to make a person stay in treatment. It is possible for a family member to change how she or he reacts to a person's problems, but it is impossible to make a person recover. Recognizing these limits to responsibility is important.

A fifth step is for family members to make their own emotional well-being a priority. Family members may have conflicting emotions when one member is distressed. Concern may be mixed with anger at the person for having problems or for the actions that result from those problems. Guilt and questions of personal responsibility arise, as may doubts about the relationship. Spouses or children may feel less respect for the person than they felt previously and then feel guilty or ashamed about these feelings. Fear about security or about whether the person can recover may also exist. These conflicting emotions are natural reactions to having a distressed family member and should be recognized, accepted as normal, and even discussed among family members. Children in particular are prone to such reactions and may be reluctant to voice their concerns without explicit support from their parents.

A sixth aspect of coping is for family members to help themselves function and have a healthy life. It is essential to remain involved with friends, maintain personal interests, and maintain the usual schedules and rituals of the family (e.g., Wolin, Bennett, & Noonan, 1979). Family members have the right to nurture themselves and each other, in addition to supporting the distressed person. It is also important for families to seek support by talking with friends, family, or clergy, by seeking professional help, or by involving themselves in a self-help group for families. Pride, shame, denial, and embarrassment may make it more difficult to talk about family problems, but support is crucial.

A seventh step is for family members and friends to set personal limits on what they can and cannot tolerate and on what course of action they will pursue. A spouse may decide to separate if alcohol or drug use continues or to obtain a legal restraining order if physical abuse occurs. A friend may decide to discontinue social contact with an alcoholic while active drinking continues. Although setting such limits is painful, family members and friends must, for their own well-being, decide what behaviors they will and will not live with. Setting such limits is often helpful to the distressed psychologist, as the consequences for his or her behavior become clear and unambiguous.

Finally, it is important to acknowledge that friends and family will find coping with the distressed psychologist confusing and upsetting at times. They must realize, however, that they can cope and survive. Advice will often be conflicting, and each person ultimately must sift through the advice to decide what course of action seems best. By dealing with each problem as it occurs, using all the personal and outside resources available, and by recalling that the majority of impaired professionals, with help, will recover from their problems and return to full, productive professional lives (Gualtieri, Cosentino, & Becker, 1983; Herrington, Benzer, Jacobson, & Hawkins, 1982; Morse, Martin, Swenson, & Niven, 1984; Shore, 1982), family members can live through the difficulties of living with an impaired psychologist.

We have outlined eight steps that a family or friends can take when confronted with an impaired psychologist. They are applicable to any of the problems addressed in this volume.

1. recognize that a problem exists
2. gather information about the problem
3. confront the distressed psychologist with their concerns and help the person obtain treatment
4. participate in treatment
5. take care of their own emotional well-being
6. take steps to allow themselves to function and have a healthy lifestyle
7. decide what they can and cannot tolerate
8. remember that they can cope and that the problems will eventually get better.

These steps are general and apply to any of the problem areas addressed in this volume.

ADVICE FOR SPECIFIC SYNDROMES

Substance Abuse

Substance abuse is defined as the use of alcohol or drugs in a way that results in problems in a person's social or family relationships, job functioning, physical health, or emotional well-being. Dependence is diagnosed when a person shows evidence of tolerance (increased dosage needed to obtain the same effect) or of withdrawal symptoms upon cessation of use of the drug (American Psychiatric Association, 1980). Emotional and behavioral changes usually accompany the substance use. The specific signs and symptoms of different types of alcohol and drug abuse are detailed in separate chapters in this volume.

Families usually have a number of reactions to substance abuse (Jackson, 1954; Orford et al., 1975; Stanton, 1979). Denial of problems is common, as are attempts to get the person to stop using the substance. Family members may make increasingly more extreme attempts to control the user's behavior, by controlling the finances of the family, taking car keys, searching the house for and disposing of alcohol or drugs, going to bars to bring the person home, and so on. Families also may attempt to take care of the substance abuser and protect him or her from the painful consequences of the drug-associated behaviors. Families often become disorganized and intensely emotional when substance abuse is present. Children may begin to have school problems or commit delinquent acts, and family members may make many trips to the family doctor or local hospital. All of these reactions are common and are normal reactions of families in distress.

If formally confronting the psychologist with her or his substance abuse does not help, family members can take other actions that may result in the psychologist seeking treatment (Thomas & Santa, 1982). First, the family needs to stop covering up for and protecting the psychologist. If he or she is unable to get to the office, give a lecture, or complete an experiment, the family should not step in and make excuses or find someone else to do the job. Only if the family or friends have strong evidence that the psychologist's state makes him or her dangerous at work should they intervene in the work setting. The sooner the psychologist feels the painful consequences of behavior resulting from drinking or drug use, the sooner he or she will decide to seek treatment. Second, the family should discontinue attempts to make the individual stop using the drug. Such attempts are frustrating and most often are successful only in making the psychologist angry and in provoking more excuses to continue use of the drug. Third, families and friends should give honest feedback about what they observe and experience. Fourth, they should set limits on what they will and will not tolerate. Fifth, they must protect themselves from potential physical harm.

If the psychologist is in treatment, the family should also be actively involved, because family involvement in alcoholism treatment has repeatedly been shown to improve treatment outcomes. Active involvement in Al-Anon, Ala-Teen, or Nar-Anon is also important, as is education about alcohol and alcoholism and about drugs and drug addiction.

During and after an initial period of successful treatment, family and friends can provide concrete support. Supporting attendance at AA or NA meetings is important. The entire family may be involved in changes in lifestyle, activities, and social events. Alcohol may no longer be served, or the recovering psychologist may want to avoid alcohol-related settings. Heavy-drinking friends may need to be avoided, and social activities may shift to those not involving alcohol, such as going to a movie and out for ice cream rather than to a night club.

Decisions about family behavior must be made as a group. For example, a spouse might think that his psychologist wife would like him to remove all the liquor from the house and then proceed to do so. A more helpful approach would be to ask her what would be most helpful to her recovery and to come to a mutual decision about a course of action. This mutual decision making will come up repeatedly with respect to social events and with respect to whether the nondistressed spouse might continue moderate use of the substance of abuse.

Families can also help by reinforcing and supporting the psychologist's abstinence. Families need to recognize that changing a long-standing pattern of drug addiction or abuse is extremely difficult and is much more worth doing if these efforts are appreciated and supported. A helpful message would be, "What you are doing is difficult, and I'm glad that you're doing it."

Families also must learn to deal constructively with problems and feelings. If a family member is angry, anxious, or fearful, he or she may be afraid that expressing such feelings will hurt the psychologist's recovery. Although family cohesion is associated with recovery (e.g., Moos et al., 1979), assertive (not aggressive) expressions of feeling help to develop closeness.

A difficult aspect of substance abuse recovery involves relapses. As many as two thirds of treated substance abusers may have a brief or severe relapse in the first few months after treatment (Hunt, Barnett, & Branch, 1971). In a program for impaired physicians, 67.5 percent remained continuously abstinent after treatment, 15 percent had a brief relapse, and 7.5 percent had a significant relapse (Herrington et al., 1982). Thus, although relapses may be less common among successfully treated impaired professionals than among the general population, they do occur.

Relapse is not always associated with failure, however; a relapse may be used as an opportunity to learn what other personal or life-style changes are needed to maintain abstinence (e.g., Marlatt & Gordon, 1985). Family members can learn to identify early warning signs that a relapse may be approaching and can supportively discuss these observations with the psychologist. These warning signs differ for each person but might include the following: (a) decreasing or discontinuing attendance at self-help group meetings, (b) stopping therapy even though it is apparent to the family that the individual still has significant problems, (c) saying that the substance abuse problem really had not been bad, when it had been, (d) beginning to spend time in activities or with people formerly associated with heavy drinking or drug use, and (e) returning to other patterns that had been associated with drinking or drug use. Family members can also quickly get the psychologist back to a hospital, detoxification center, clinic, or private therapist if a full-blown relapse has occurred.

Friends can do many of the things described in this section. They are in a somewhat different position, however, in not having the same intimate, live-in relationship that family or nonmarried cohabitants have. Friends need to respect a decision for abstinence, even if they are regular alcohol or drug users. Respecting the abstinence decision may result in significant changes in the friendship, such as finding new ways to spend time together that do not involve alcohol or drug use. Friends can also be sure to have attractive nonalcoholic beverages available when socializing with the recovering alcoholic.

Mental and Emotional Disorders

This category includes a broad array of problems. Psychologists are susceptible to any of the myriad of human problems, including psychoses, affective disorders, anxiety disorders, and somatoform disorders (American Psychiatric Association, 1980). In some of these disorders, reality testing is impaired; in others significant mood changes, such as depression or anxiety, are predominant. Millon's chapter (in this volume) describes these disorders in greater detail.

It is impossible to give a general characterization of families' reactions to the diversity of mental and emotional disorders. Instead, two examples will illustrate the effects on families. Emmelkamp and deLange (1983) described the ways that spouses become involved in the compulsive rituals of the partners. Spouses are asked to give repeated reassurance about ritual objects, such as telling their partner that a doorknob is not dirty. They may also take over some of the rituals, by washing things for their partner or by doing ritualistic checking (e.g., going back into the house to be sure that the stove is off). The increasing spouse involvement in obsessive-compulsive rituals may result in significant relationship problems as conflict over the compulsive behaviors escalates.

Coyne (1984) described the effects of depression on a marital relationship. He suggested that the behavior of a depressed person produces negative moods in others. Depressed persons make repeated requests for support and reassurance but are never satisfied when they receive it. The nondepressed partner may begin to expect less of the depressed spouse and demand less in terms of tasks as well as emotional aspects of the relationship. The partner may feel inhibited from expressing anger but then become increasingly impatient, hostile, and withdrawn. Such reactions may exacerbate the depression.

These are but two examples that emotional and mental disorders have a major impact on families and that the family plays a significant role in treatment. In the previous section, we described ways to help a distressed family member seek treatment. Besides observing these general guidelines, families must also recognize that at times they have to take responsibility for the distressed individual and force her or him to obtain treatment. If a person's mental state is so impaired that suicide is possible, if a person is seriously neglecting his or her health, or if he or she is doing things that are dangerous to self or to others, then the family may have to have the individual committed to a period of involuntary treatment. This is an incredibly difficult decision and should be made only when danger is imminent and the person refuses to seek treatment voluntarily. If such action is necessary, the family should call a local mental health center, a psychiatric hospital, a hospital emergency room, or a psychologist or psychiatrist to determine the best course of action. If possible, someone in the family should call the hospital before bringing a family member in for commitment and should be prepared to show clear evidence of the person's dangerous state. If the family member does not believe that he or she can transport the person safely, an ambulance service or the local police can be contacted for assistance. Although the vast majority of mental and emotional problems of psychologists will not require such drastic measures, families need to have such information available to them.

If a family does seek an involuntary commitment, the psychologist may be angry and combative and may resist going to treatment. This anger and resentment will often continue during the first part of the hospitalization, as the family is accused of "not caring" or of "jailing" the individual. These accusations often compound the family's pain in seeing the person so impaired and in having had to seek the involuntary commitment.

During treatment, the family's role will vary dramatically, depending on the nature of the psychologist's problems. In severe problems, such as psychoses, the family should probably be educated about the patient's diagnosis, the nature and phenomenology of psychosis, and research about its etiology and treatment. Family therapy may also be introduced to enhance family communication and problem solving (McGill et al., 1983). Family members may also be asked to help the patient comply with a prescribed medication regimen.

In problems such as obsessive-compulsive disorders or agoraphobia, a spouse may be involved directly in the patient's treatment program. A spouse might help the patient carry out homework assignments and be taught specific ways to coach and support the patient without reinforcing the problem (e.g., Barlow et al., 1984; Emmelkamp & deLange, 1983).

Other problems may be of an individual nature, for which the treatment of choice does not directly involve the spouse or other family members. Even with these problems, the family has the right to communicate with treatment personnel, to clarify what is or is not expected of them. If a person is hospitalized, the family also has the right to inquire about the type of treatment being provided and progress being made. Treatment personnel must protect the confidentiality of the patient, however, and most often will not reveal specific problems being discussed in therapy.

Family members also may want to get involved in support groups themselves. Some treatment programs have such groups available, and self-help groups are also available, such as Reach, the National Alliance of the Mentally Ill, or Parents United (for persons whose partners have been sexually involved with their children).

After treatment, the family behaviors described under "general advice" are appropriate. Support and clear communication are essential to recovery. For most disorders, the family will go through a period during which the psychologist gradually becomes fully functional and begins to resume his or her full role in the family. There are some disorders, however, from which full recovery is not possible (such as Alzheimer's disease), which place the family under long-term stress. Even with full recovery, relapse is always possible after treatment for a mental or emotional disorder. Family members need to recognize that recovery is a gradual process and that a number of setbacks are a normal part of recovery. They also need to learn to recognize early signs that problems are returning and to discuss their observations in ways that help the psychologist. Discussions of relapse and what to do in case of relapse are an important part of treatment.

Stress, Burnout, and Workaholism

Substance abuse and mental or emotional disorders can occur among any occupational group. Stress and burnout are experienced in a unique way in the mental health field. Burnout is characterized by emotional and physical exhaustion related to the stresses of work in clinical settings. Other symptoms include beginning to lose concern for patients, treating patients in a much more detached manner, withdrawing, and spending less time with patients and more on administrative tasks. Eventually, emotional and family problems may result (Farber & Heifetz, 1982; Pines & Maslach, 1978). Burnout may or may not be associated with a "workaholic" pattern, in which the psychologist devotes excessively large amounts of time to work, has little or no time for outside activities or interests, and has little apparent emotional involvement with family or friends.

Little research has been done on family reactions to burnout or workaholics. We can speculate, however, that the family might push the psychologist for more time, attention, and involvement. The family might try to accommodate to the psychologist's schedule, only to find that he or she is still unavailable. Spouse and children alike might feel hurt, angry, and resentful because they perceive the burnout or workaholic pattern as a direct statement that the psychologist's work is more important than they are. The family might, in turn, begin to withdraw emotionally from the psychologist, which would reinforce his or her pattern of emotional distancing.

Because the family has not been studied in relation to burnout and overwork, the following comments about the family's role in treatment and recovery are highly speculative. Prior to treatment, family members should try to give the psychologist clear and specific feedback about the impact of his or her actions on the family or the marriage. Specific attempts to structure positive family time together may be helpful, as well as some limit setting for the workaholic. Limit setting may take the form of specific requests for time together, with treatment being the alternative if such requests cannot be met. Support and nonjudgmental listening may help the psychologist experiencing burnout.

During treatment, the spouse or family may be actively involved in couples or family therapy. The family must be prepared for some excesses on the part of the psychologist, such as passionate commitments to exercise or movies as he or she begins to give up a workaholic pattern. The psychologist also may decide on a job change, which could result in changes in financial status. These major life changes, such as job changes or relocation, should be discussed by the family as a whole. Although the family certainly should not support changes that would be detrimental to them, it is important to recognize and understand the need for change.

Academic and Professional Incompetence

A psychologist may become professionally incompetent for a variety of reasons. He or she may not keep up with current knowledge; may ignore feedback from colleagues, students, or clients; may become isolated professionally; or may be senile or incompetent because of any of the disorders described earlier (Arana, 1982). Similarly, legal problems may arise because of incompetence, unethical behavior, or a lawsuit filed by an unhappy student or client.

Family members are unlikely to be the first to detect these problems, because they do not observe the psychologist at work. When legal problems or incompetence surface, they pose a radical threat to the family. If the psychologist is unable to continue to work, the economic base for the family may be severely threatened. Family members may feel angry or let down, and their respect for the psychologist may be damaged by his or her changed job and professional status. The psychologist will be experiencing similar feelings while at the same time dealing with the enormously complex and expensive issues of a lawsuit, of discontinuing the active practice of psychology, or of changing jobs or job situation to improve his or her level of competency. The combination of personal and practical stressors makes this a particularly difficult time.

It is essential that all family members have good legal and financial planning advice. In addition, they need to find ways to cope with their own feelings about the problems. They must be able to discuss these feelings openly and to provide some emotional support to the psychologist during the crisis. The whole family also may need to constructively problem-solve to generate ways of handling the financial stressors associated with these problems.

Sexual Exploitation

Sexual relationships with clients are unethical, according to the Ethical Principles of Psychologists (APA, 1981). Sexual contact with students is also widely regarded as unethical. A recent survey (Holroyd & Brodsky, 1977) revealed that 5.5 percent of male and 0.6 percent of female licensed psychologists had had sexual intercourse with clients of the opposite sex. Pope, Levenson, and Schover (1979) found that 9.4 percent of the respondents to a survey of 1,000 members of Division 29 (Psychotherapy) of APA had had sexual contact with students. These surveys suggest that sexual contact in the professional lives of psychologists is not common but does exist.

The discovery that a psychologist has had sexual activity within his or her professional role poses two kinds of dilemmas for the spouse. First, the spouse is likely to react as he or she would to any other sexual affair. These reactions could range from casual acceptance to anger, hurt, or even the termination of the relationship. At the same time, however, the spouse is aware that such behavior is unethical and must cope with his or her reactions to perceiving that the spouse is behaving inappropriately as a professional. Reactions to this perception may range from anger to loss of respect to sadness.

Although it is possible that the spouse will become aware of the partner's sexual behavior, at least on some level, spouses are often unaware of their partner's sexual infidelity (Blumstein & Schwartz, 1983) and therefore may be doubly upset if the behavior is detected through another channel. If the partner does become aware of the sexual behavior, he or she needs to decide whether the relationship can continue. If the spouse wants to continue the relationship, therapy might be helpful to allow discussion of the reactions of both partners, identification of and change in relationship problems that might have been associated with the affair, and discussion of the consequences of future sexual transgressions.

Sexual exploitation of clients or students may also lead to lawsuits or criminal charges. Thus, at the same time that the couple is wrestling with difficult problems in their relationship, they also may be facing legal and financial threats, which generate problems of their own, as described in the previous section.

CONCLUSIONS

In this chapter, we have emphasized the difficulties faced by any family that has a distressed member. When that distressed person is a psychologist, the role that family and friends play is even more difficult. Psychologists are experts on human behavior, and to be told that they are not managing their own lives well is particularly threatening because it attacks their professional as well as their personal identities. Because psychologists like to think that they are in control of their lives and that they understand themselves, the idea of seeking professional help may be distressing (Thoreson, Nathan, Skorina, & Kilburg, 1983). Moreover, the nonpsychologist family member or friend may feel presumptuous in commenting on the psychologist's emotional well-being.

Despite these unique problems, the psychological literature and the experience of clinicians who work with distressed professionals suggest that family and friends play a central role in identification, referral to treatment, participation in treatment, and posttreatment support of the impaired psychologist. Families and friends of distressed psychologists can help by recognizing that a problem exists, by learning as much as they can about the problem, by confronting the psychologist and helping him or her to seek professional assistance, by being willing to be involved in treatment if necessary, by attending to their own emotional well-being and that of the rest of the family, by setting personal limits on what they can and cannot tolerate, and by maintaining a sense of realistic hope that the psychologist will be able to deal effectively with his or her personal, family, or professional problems and once again become a fully functional professional and family member or friend.

References

American Psychiatric Association. (1980). *Diagnostic and statistical manual of mental disorders* (3rd ed.). Washington, DC: Author.

American Psychological Association. (1981). Ethical principles of psychologists. *American Psychologist, 36*(6), 633–638.

Arana, G. W. (1982). The impaired physician: A medical and social dilemma. *General Hospital Psychiatry, 4,* 147–153.

Baekeland, F., & Lundwall, L. K. (1977). Engaging the alcoholic in treatment and keeping him there. In B. Kissin & H. Begleiter (Eds.), *The biology of alcoholism: Treatment and rehabilitation of the chronic alcoholic* (pp. 161–196). New York: Plenum Press.

Barlow, D., Mavissakalian, M., & Hay, L. R. (1982). Couples treatment of agoraphobia: Changes in marital satisfaction. *Behaviour Research and Therapy, 19,* 245–255.

Barlow, D. H., O'Brien, G. T., & Last, C. G. (1984). Couples treatment of agoraphobia. *Behavior Therapy, 15,* 41–58.

Barragan, M. (1976). The child-centered family. In P. J. Guerin (Ed.), *Family therapy: Theory and practice* (pp. 234–238). New York: Gardner Press.

Blodgett, C. (1981–82). A selected review of the literature of adjustment to hemodialysis. *International Journal of Psychiatry in Medicine, 11,* 97–124.

Blumstein, P., & Schwartz, P. (1983). *American Couples.* New York: Morrow & Co.

Brownell, K. D., Heckerman, C. L., Westlake, R. J., Hayes, S. C., & Monti, P. M. (1978). The effects of couples training & partner cooperativeness in the behavioral treatment of obesity. *Behaviour Research and Therapy, 16,* 327–334.

Brownell, K. D., & Stunkard, A. J. (1981). Couples training, pharmacotherapy, and behavior therapy in the treatment of obesity. *Archives of General Psychiatry, 38,* 1224–1229.

Chowanec, G. D., & Binik, Y. M. (1982). End stage renal disease and the marital dyad. *Social Science and Medicine, 16,* 1551–1558.

Cobb, S. (1976). Social support as a moderator in life stress. *Psychosomatic Medicine, 38,* 300–314.

Cobb, J., McDonald, R., Marks, I., & Stern, R. (1980). Marital versus exposure therapy: Psychological treatments of co-existing marital and phobic-obsessive problems. *Behaviour Analysis and Modification, 4,* 3–16.

Colletti, G., & Brownell, K. D. (1982). The physical and emotional benefits of social support: Application to obesity, smoking and alcoholism. *Progress in Behavior Modification, 13,* 109–178.

Coyne, J. C. (1984). Strategic therapy with depressed married persons: Initial agenda, themes and interventions. *Journal of Marital and Family Therapy, 10,* 53–62.

Davenport, Y. B., Ebert, M. H., Adland, M. L., & Goodwin, F. K. (1977). Couples group therapy as an adjunct to lithium maintenance of the manic patient. *American Journal of Orthopsychiatry, 47,* 495–502.

Dubbert, P. M., & Wilson, G. T. (1983). Treatment failures in behavior therapy for obesity: Causes, correlates and consequences. In E. Foa & P. M. G. Emmelkamp (Eds.), *Treatment failure in behavior therapy.* New York: Wiley.

Dubbert, P. M., & Wilson, G. T. (1984). Goal-setting and spouse involvement in the treatment of obesity. *Behaviour Research and Therapy, 22,* 227–242.

Emery, R. E. (1983). Interparental conflict and the children of discord and divorce. *Psychological Bulletin, 92,* 310–330.

Emmelkamp, P. M. G. (1981). Recent developments in the behavioral treatment of obsessive-compulsive disorders. In J. C. Boulougaris (Ed.), *Learning theory approaches to psychiatry.* New York: Wiley.

Emmelkamp, P. M. G., & deLange, I. (1983). Spouse involvement in the treatment of obsessive compulsive patients. *Behaviour Research and Therapy, 4,* 341–346.

Farber, B. A., & Heifetz, L. J. (1982). The process and dimensions of burnout in psychotherapists. *Professional Psychology, 13,* 293–301.

Friedman, A. S. (1975). Interaction of drug therapy with marital therapy in depressive patients. *Archives of General Psychiatry, 32,* 619–637.

Gallant, D. M., Rich, A., Bey, E., and Terranova, L. (1970). Group psychotherapy with married couples: A successful technique in New Orleans alcoholism clinic patients. *Journal of the Louisiana Medical Society, 122,* 41–44.

Goldstein, A. J., & Chambless, D. L. (1978). A reanalysis of agoraphobia. *Behavior Therapy, 9,* 47–59.

Greene, B. L., Lee, R. R., & Lustig, N. (1975). Treatment of marital disharmony where one spouse has a primary affective disorder (Manic-depressive illness): I. General overview—100 couples. *Journal of Marriage and Family Counseling, 1,* 82–100.

Gualtieri, A. C., Cosentino, J. P., & Becker, J. S. (1983). The California experience with a diversion program for impaired physicians. *Journal of the American Medical Association, 294,* 226–229.

Guerin, P. (1976). *Family therapy: Theory and practice,* New York: Gardner Press.

Gurman, A. S., & Kniskern, D. P. (1981). *Handbook of family therapy.* New York: Brunner/Mazel.

Hedberg, A. G., & Campbell, L. (1974). A comparison of four behavioral treatments of alcoholism. *Journal of Behavior Therapy and Experimental Psychiatry, 5,* 251–256.

Herrington, R. E., Benzer, D. G., Jacobson, G. R., & Hawkins, M. K. (1982). Treating substance-use disorders among physicians. *Journal of the American Medical Association, 247,* 2253–2257.

Holroyd, J. C., & Brodsky, A. M. (1977). Psychologists' attitudes and practices regarding erotic and non-erotic physical contact with patients. *American Psychologist, 32,* 843–849.

Hore, B. D. (1971). Life events and alcoholic relapse. *British Journal of Addiction, 66,* 83–88.

Horwitz, A. (1978). Family, kin, and friend networks in psychiatric help-seeking. *Social Science and Medicine, 12,* 297–304.

Hunt, G. M., & Azrin, N. H. (1973). A community-reinforcement approach to alcoholism. *Behaviour Research and Therapy, 11,* 91–104.

Hunt, W. A., Barnett, L. W., & Branch, L. G. (1971). Relapse rates in addiction programs. *Journal of Clinical Psychology, 27,* 455–456.

Jackson, J. K. (1954). The adjustment of the family to the crisis of alcoholism. *Quarterly Journal of Studies on Alcohol, 15,* 562–586.

Jannoun, L., Munby, M., Catalan, J., & Gelder, M. (1980). A home-based treatment program for agoraphobia: Replication and controlled evaluation. *Behavior Therapy, 11,* 294–305.

Johnson, V. E. (1973). *I'll quit tomorrow.* New York: Harper & Row.

Kaufman, E. (1984). Family system variables in alcoholism. *Alcoholism: Clinical and Experimental Research, 8,* 4–8.

Leavy, R. L. (1983). Social support and psychological disorder: A review. *Journal of Community Psychology, 10,* 3–21.

Litman, T. J. (1974). The family as a basic unit in health and medical care: A sociobehavioral overview. *Social Science and Medicine, 8,* 495–507.

Marlatt, G. A., & Gordon, J. (1985). *Relapse prevention: Maintenance strategies in the treatment of addictive behaviors.* New York: Guilford Press.

Marlatt, G. A., & Gordon, J. R. (1980). Determinants of relapse: Implications for the maintenance of behavior change. In P. O. Davidson & S. M. Davidson (Eds.), *Behavioral medicine: Changing health lifestyles* (pp. 410–452). New York: Brunner/Mazel.

Mathews, A. M., Gelder, M. G., & Johnston, D. W. (1981). *Agoraphobia: Nature and treatment.* New York: Guilford Press.

Mathews, A. M., Teasdale, J., Munby, M., Johnston, D., & Shaw, P. M. (1977). A home-based treatment program for agoraphobia. *Behavior Therapy, 8,* 915–924.

Maxwell, R. (1976). *The booze bottle.* New York: Praeger.

Mayo, J. A., O'Connell, R. A., & O'Brien, J. (1979). Families of manic-depressive patients: Effect of treatment. *American Journal of Psychiatry, 136,* 1535–1539.

McCrady, B. S., Noel, N. E., Abrams, D. B., Stout, R. L., Fisher-Nelson, H., & Hay, W. (in press). Comparative effectiveness of three types of spouse-involvement in outpatient behavioral alcoholism treatment. *Journal of Studies on Alcohol.*

McGill, C. W., Falloon, I. R. H., Boyd, J. L., & Wood-Siverio, C. (1983). Family educational intervention in the treatment of schizophrenia. *Hospital and Community Psychiatry, 34,* 934–938.

Mermelstein, R., Lichtenstein, E., & McIntyre, K. (1984). Partner support and relapse in smoking cessation programs. *Journal of Consulting and Clinical Psychology, 51,* 465–466.

Milton, F., & Hafner, J. (1979). The outcome of behavior therapy for agoraphobia in relation to marital adjustment. *Archives of General Psychiatry, 36,* 807–811.

Moos, R. (1982). Coping with acute health crises. In T. Millon, C. Green, & R. Meagher (Eds.), *Handbook of clinical health psychology* (pp. 129–152). New York: Plenum Press.

Moos, R. M., Bromet, E., Tsu, V., & Moos, B. (1979). Family characteristics and the outcome of treatment for alcoholism. *Journal of Studies on Alcohol, 40,* 78–88.

Moos, R. H., & Moos, B. S. (1984). The process of recovery from alcoholism: III. Comparing functioning in families of alcoholics and matched control families. *Journal of Studies on Alcohol, 45,* 111–118.

Morse, R. M., Martin, M. A., Swenson, W. M., & Niven, R. G. (1984). Prognosis for physicians treated for alcoholism and drug dependence. *Journal of the American Medical Association, 251,* 743–746.

Mueller, D. P. (1980). Social networks: A promising direction for research on the relationship of the social environment to psychiatric disorder. *Social Science and Medicine, 14,* 147–161.

Murphy, J. K., Williamson, D. A., Buxton, A. E., Moody, S. C., Absher, N., & Warner, M. (1982). The long-term effects of spouse involvement upon weight loss and maintenance. *Behavior Therapy, 13,* 681–693.

O'Farrell, T. J., & Cutter, H. S. G. (1982, November). Effects of adding a behavioral or an interactional couples group to individual outpatient alcoholism counseling. Paper presented at the meeting of the Association for Advancement of Behavior Therapy, Los Angeles, CA.

Orford, J., Guthrie, S., Nicholls, P., Oppenheimer, E., Egert, S., & Hensman, C. (1975). Self-reported coping behavior of wives of alcoholics and its association with drinking outcome. *Journal of Studies on Alcohol, 36,* 1254–1267.

Paolino, T. J., & McCrady, B. S. (1976). Joint admission as a treatment modality for problem drinkers: A case report. *American Journal of Psychiatry, 133,* 222–224.

Paolino, T. J., & McCrady, B. S. (1977). *The alcoholic marriage: Alternative perspectives.* New York: Grune & Stratton.

Pearce, J., Lebow, M., & Orchard, J. (1981). The role of spouse involvement in the behavioral treatment of overweight women. *Journal of Consulting and Clinical Psychology, 49,* 236–244.

Pines, A., & Maslach, C. (1978). Characteristics of staff burnout in mental health settings. *Hospital and Community Psychiatry, 29,* 233–237.

Pope, K. S., Levenson, H., & Schover, L. R. (1979). Sexual intimacy in psychology training. Results and implications of a national survey. *American Psychologist, 34,* 682–689.

Rosenthal, B., Allen, G. J., & Winter, C. (1981). Husband involvement in the behavioral treatment of overweight women: Initial effects and long-term follow-up. *International Journal of Obesity, 4,* 165–173.

Rush, A. J., Shaw, B., & Khatami, M. (1980). Cognitive therapy of depression: Utilizing the couples system. *Cognitive Therapy and Research, 4,* 103–113.

Saccone, A. J., & Israel, A. C. (1978). Effects of experimenter versus significant-other-controlled reinforcement and choice of target behavior on weight loss. *Behavior Therapy, 9,* 271–278.

Schwenk, T. L., & Hughes, C. C. (1983). The family as patient in family medicine: Rhetoric or reality. *Social Science and Medicine, 17,* 1–16.

Shore, J. H. (1982). The impaired physician. Four years after probation. *Journal of the American Medical Association, 248,* 3127–3130.

Stanton, M. D. (1979). Family treatment approaches to drug abuse problems. *Family Process, 18,* 251–280.

Steidl, J. H., Finkelstein, F. O., Wexler, J. P., Feigenbaum, H., Kitsen, J., Kliger, A. S., & Quinland, D. M. (1980). Medical condition, adherence to treatment regimes, and family functioning. *Archives of General Psychiatry, 37,* 1025–1027.

Steinglass, P. (1979). An experimental treatment program for alcoholic couples. *Journal of Studies on Alcohol, 40,* 159–182.

Steinglass, P. (1980). A life history model of the alcoholic family. *Family Process, 19,* 211–226.

Steinglass, P. (1981). The alcoholic family at home. *Archives of General Psychiatry, 38,* 578–584.

Stern, R. S., & Marks, I. M. (1973). Contract therapy in obsessive-compulsive neurosis with marital discord. *British Journal of Psychiatry, 123,* 681–684.

Syrotiuk, J., & D'Arcy, C. (1984). Social support and mental health: Direct, protective, and compensatory effects. *Social Science and Medicine, 18,* 229–236.

Thomas, E. J., & Santa, C. A. (1982). Unilateral family therapy for alcohol abuse: A working conception. *American Journal of Family Therapy, 10,* 49–58.

Thoreson, R. W., Nathan, P. E., Skorina, J. K., & Kilburg, R. R. (1983). The alcoholic psychologist: Issues, problems, and implications for the profession. *Professional Psychology, 14,* 670–684.

Vandereycken, W. (1982). *Agoraphobia and the marital relationship: Theory, treatment and research.* Unpublished manuscript.

Ward, D. A., Bendel, R. B., & Lange, D. (1982). A reconsideration of environmental resources and the posttreatment functioning of alcoholic patients. *Journal of Health and Social Behavior, 23,* 310–317.

Weisz, W., & Bucher, B. (1980). Involving husbands in treatment of obesity—Effects on weight loss, depression and marital satisfaction. *Behavior Therapy, 11,* 643–650.

Wolin, S. J., Bennett, L. A., and Noonan, D. L. (1979). Family rituals and the recurrence of alcoholism over generations. *American Journal of Psychiatry, 136,* 589–593.

PREVENTING AND MANAGING JOB-RELATED STRESS 13

Cary Cherniss
Stephen A. Dantzig

he problem of stress in the work lives of psychologists does not lend itself to easy remedies. Nevertheless, research and practice during the last decade have provided many promising strategies for the prevention and alleviation of stress. In fact, so rich are the possibilities that a chapter such as this one can only describe them in the most general way. But enough can be said to help those who are concerned about distressed psychologists and other professionals.

The stress syndrome has been described in detail in chapter 4 of this volume. In this chapter, we define stress as a feeling of tension, often accompanied by negative emotional or physiological symptoms (e.g., anger, anxiety, depression; elevated heart rate and blood serum cholesterol levels).

Strategies for stress management can be conceptualized in many different ways. First, they can be directed to the *individual* or the *situational* factors that contribute to stress. Second, there are *preventive* interventions as well as *clinical/remedial* ones. Third, there are interventions that reduce the *source of stress* (either situational or individual) and those that support the *coping process*. Finally, a distinction has been made between stress management techniques that involve *active problem-solving* and those that are *palliative*.

These distinctions tend to overlap, yet each contributes a different and potentially useful perspective. For instance, interventions designed to reduce or eliminate environmental (situational) sources of stress usually can be considered preventive. However, preventive interventions can also focus on individual contributors to stress.

Writers on stress management tend to take strong positions on what strategies are best. For instance, some argue that individual strategies are preferable because little can be done about situational sources of stress (e.g., Edelwich & Brodsky, 1980). Others argue that individual strategies are limited in effectiveness and involve blaming the victim; therefore, we should concentrate on group and organizational strategies (e.g., Shinn & Mørch, 1983). As shall be seen, work in the field has been biased toward individual-level interventions; many more published studies have used these strategies than have used organizational ones. Nevertheless, organizational strategies have been articulated and used to combat stress, and we also shall consider these. Rather than argue that one strategy is better than another, we shall consider the relative strengths and weaknesses of each.

In the first part of this chapter we present strategies designed to influence individual factors (individual stress management). These include techniques directed at the somatic level (e.g., relaxation training, biofeedback), cognitive-behavioral interventions, and educative and insight-oriented interventions. In the second part of this chapter we consider group stress management strategies: mutual aid or social support groups. In the last part of the chapter, we turn to a number of promising organizational strategies.

INDIVIDUAL STRESS MANAGEMENT STRATEGIES

Many individual stress management programs combine a variety of techniques. Thus, although one can make a clear conceptual distinction between those that focus on somatic, behavioral, and cognitive aspects of the stress response, in fact many programs include all of these. Nevertheless, we try here to isolate the strategies for purposes of discussion and explication. At the end of this section we discuss some issues to consider in selecting and combining various techniques.

Educative Interventions

A particularly popular form of intervention in the workplace is the educative stress management workshop. These workshops vary greatly in their length and content; they may be as brief as one one-hour session or as long as three full days. They may be purely didactic, using a large group/lecture format; but more often they combine informative lectures with more active, experiential learning segments. (More specific training in relaxation or cognitive-behavioral methods of stress management is not included in this category. This type of training will be discussed in the next section.)

Compared to other types of intervention, the advantages and limitations of the stress management workshop are obvious. On the one hand, workshops are relatively inexpensive, reaching many more people than does clinical stress management with individuals. They are also easier to "sell" to administrators and participants than more intrusive organizational development programs. On the other hand, didactic presentations are so superficial that it is questionable whether they do any more than produce a temporary "workshop high." Yet, one cannot dismiss the possibility that at least a few participants in any given workshop might be inspired to change their life-style, values, and attitudes, and consequently experience less stress.

Two typical stress management workshop programs were described by Sparks and Ingram (1979) and Baron and Cohen (1982). The first was developed for teachers, the second for help-line telephone counselors. Topics covered included (a) the symptoms of burnout, (b) personal and organizational contributions to burnout, (c) analysis of positive aspects of work and the successes that are often minimized, (d) factors that one can and cannot control, and (e) personal and organizational coping methods.

Outcome data on stress management workshops are scarce. Sparks and

Ingram (1979) offered only anecdotal evidence of improvements in job satisfaction and behavior, whereas Baron and Cohen (1982) offered no information on outcome at all. The best controlled evaluation of the educative-workshop approach was done by West (1982), who found that a workshop produced no better results than a no-treatment control. (Other conditions in West's study, such as cognitive-behavioral training, did result in statistically significant improvement.) Even if educative presentations have a minimal impact by themselves, however, they still may have some value as "ports of entry" to other, more effective methods.

Even less is known about the impact of another educative method, the familiar "self-help" article or book. Those works, read by millions of Americans, are disparaged by many psychology professionals and behavioral scientists. Nevertheless, many of these books are written by, and are no doubt also read by, psychologists. Their impact on stress and coping is difficult to assess, but the books probably do help some people. The potential of written material for helping distressed psychologists thus remains unknown.

Relaxation and Related Techniques

Among the most popular stress management techniques in clinical practice and industry are relaxation training, biofeedback, meditation, yoga, and other methods designed to reduce stress by focusing on the somatic manifestations of the stress response. These techniques are clearly palliative: they seek to reduce uncomfortable and potentially harmful reactions to stressful events rather than actively attack the causes of those events.

All of these techniques seek to induce relaxation. Thus, *relaxation training* is the most straightforward of this group of methods. The original form of this training was developed by Jacobson (1938). In his version, the subject is taught to identify, in progressively diminishing intensities, the presence of tension in any of the over 1,000 striated muscles that make up the human body. The Jacobsonian trainee is taught how to recognize and release minute degrees of tension in muscle groups that are not required for the task at hand, thereby shutting off an upcoming attack of detrimental tension.

The major drawback of the original progressive relaxation technique is that it is time consuming. Trainees are taught to recognize and release tensions in particular muscle groups (e.g., left and right arms, the legs, the torso, the head and neck) individually. The trainee is instructed to concentrate on one of these groups, for each hour-long session, and the training for a single region may require up to 19 sessions. The entire practice sequence requires 90 sessions in the prone position. The trainee then may be asked to repeat the sequence in a sitting position.

Modifications of this technique change the focus in order to shorten the amount of time required. Woolfolk and Lehrer (1984, p. 5) stated that "In the abbreviated method, the emphasis tends to be somewhat less on the awareness of tension and more on the active 'production' of relaxation." Much of the work on condensing progressive relaxation training is attributable to Wolpe's concept of reciprocal inhibition, "which suggests that an undesirable emotional response can be suppressed by evoking a stronger incompatible response" (Bernstein & Given, 1984). Condensed progressive relaxation training is a procedure that involves a "tension-release" cycle in which the trainee is taught to progressively create a sensation of tension and subsequent total relaxation of 16 muscle groups. (The 16 groups are outlined in detail in Bernstein & Given, 1984.) The proposed timetable for the condensed version is 10 sessions.

Bernstein and Given (1984) outlined a number of potential problems that may be encountered when the shortened training is used, including muscle cramps, gross motor movements, laughter, talking, muscle spasms, anxiety-producing thoughts, sexual arousal, sleep, and coughing and sneezing. It should be noted that one of the issues that transcends the particular relaxation procedure chosen is the need for practice. In order to master relaxation, the trainee must spend time practicing the technique.

Biofeedback techniques are based on essentially the same principle as the progressive relaxation procedures: identification and ultimate control of bodily reactions to stress. Budzynski and Stoyva (1984) described the biofeedback process as follows:

> In general, biofeedback systems operate by detecting changes in the bio-logical environment and, by means of visual and auditory signals, notifying the patient of these changes. The patient, using this precise and immediate information, engages in trial-and-error strategy testing in order to make the signals change in the desired direction. With the biofeedback as a guide, the patient in relatively short order learns how to control the biological response from whence the biofeedback signals originate. With additional training, the patient is gradually weaned away from the bio-feedback; having now calibrated the subtle internal events corresponding to the biological system in question, he or she can maintain control without the feedback. (p. 188)

The more common forms of biofeedback involve the use of electroencephalo-graphic or electromyographic machines that provide the client with the visual or auditory feedback described by Budzynski and Stoyva.

Several other techniques have been developed for reducing tension, including hypnosis, meditation, autogenic training, and yoga. (Each of these techniques is clearly described in Woolfolk and Lehrer, 1984). Each technique has its adherents, and there do seem to be some differences in their effects. However, no one technique seems to be clearly superior to the others. The most important factor influencing their impact seems to be the clinician's and client's preferences (Woolfolk & Lehrer, 1984).

The question that remains to be answered is, "What are the outcomes of progressive relaxation and related techniques?" Several recent doctoral dissertations have investigated the use of relaxation techniques (in conjunction with other stress management procedures) in the treatment of distress in various human service workers (nurses, teachers, mental health workers, and probate court juvenile case workers). The findings of these studies suggest that relaxation techniques are helpful in alleviating chronic stress (Crook, 1982; Croyle, 1982; Kibler, 1982; Lazar, 1981; Ray, 1982).

In many cases, however, the effect of relaxation techniques depends on how stress is measured. Relaxation and related stress management techniques often reduce some signs and symptoms of stress but not others. For instance, feelings of tension and physiological indicators such as blood pressure may drop as the result of treatment while anxiety and job satisfaction remain unchanged (Forman, 1983). Also, long-term follow-ups rarely have been done in these studies. Nevertheless, relaxation training and related forms of intervention do seem to be beneficial palliatives for some individuals.

Cognitive-Behavioral Methods

In some theoretical models cognitions are causes of stress, whereas in others they are seen as mediators between stressors and stress responses. In either case, techniques designed to change beliefs and thoughts associated with stress have become popular. Several clinician-researchers have developed their own unique yet similar approaches (e.g., Beck, 1984; Ellis, 1962; A. Lazarus, 1976; Meichenbaum, 1977; Novaco, 1983).

The key to cognitive techniques for managing stress lies in reevaluating an individual's disturbance-causing ideations. Often these are irrational distortions and exaggerations—faulty appraisals of essentially benign or only mildly threatening situations. For instance, a psychologist teaching in a university who has not yet received tenure will undoubtedly experience some stress as the time for the tenure decision approaches. But certain cognitions could raise this stress to unnecessarily high and disruptive levels. These cognitions might include beliefs such as "If I don't get tenure, I'll never be able to find another satisfying job"; "Getting tenure will mean that I'm competent; if I don't get tenure it will mean I'm incompetent and thus worthless"; "Many people will stop liking and respecting me if I don't get tenure, and that will be awful"; "This process is sheer torture; I shouldn't have to go through this. It's mean and cruel." This list, of course, could be expanded.

In cognitive methods of stress reduction, specific techniques are used to help distressed individuals to become aware of these disturbing cognitions and to rationally analyze their validity. Beck (1984) refered to this process as one of "collaborative empiricism" (p. 304). The therapist and client "frame" the client's conclusions as "hypotheses which are investigated and tested by increasing both objectivity and perspective."

The outcome research on cognitive-behavioral approaches to stress management still is scant, but the results to date are promising. Cognitive and relaxation methods seem to be most effective when used in combination; but if one must choose, cognitive approaches seem to be slightly more effective (Lehrer & Woolfolk, 1984).

Thurman (1985) offers tentative support for the use of cognitive-behavioral approaches to stress management with professionals. He identified a group of university faculty who were at high risk for "Type A" behaviors and assigned them to one of three groups. A "cognitive behavior modification" group received 8 weekly 2-hour sessions incorporating training in Rational–Emotive Therapy (Ellis, 1962), anger management (Novaco, 1983), and rational–emotive imagery (Maultsby, 1971). The training focused on the anger/hostility, competitive achievement striving, and time urgency/impatience dimensions of the Type A behavior pattern.

A second group received the identical treatment with the addition of two sessions of Lange and Jakubowski's (1979) assertion training program. A third, minimal treatment control group received a one-hour presentation on Type A behavior with suggestions on how to reduce it.

Thurman's treatment groups showed positive change on some but not all outcome measures. Specifically, self-reported levels of Type A behavior, hostility, irrational beliefs, and speed/impatience improved more in the treatment groups. These improvements were maintained at a one-year follow-up, with no significant differences between the two treatment groups. However, these groups did not differ from the control group on measures of hard-driving behavior, state anger, rational behavior, blood pressure, or pulse rate.

Similar results were obtained in Forman's (1981) stress management program for school psychologists. Forman used a mixed approach, combining education, relaxation, and cognitive restructuring. The latter component was based on Meichenbaum's (1977) stress inoculation model. Ten school psychologists were randomly assigned to a treatment group and eight to a control group. Those in the treatment group showed a significant decrease in self-reported anxiety and an increase in job satisfaction compared to the controls.

One other program worth noting was designed to alleviate "reality shock" in new nurses. Kramer's (1974) program not only included cognitive-behavioral components but also taught organizational problem-solving and conflict-resolution skills. She designed the program by collecting vignettes involving typical professional-bureaucratic role conflicts experienced by nurses currently working in the field. She then identified a group of nurses who seemed to be particularly adept at handling these conflicts and asked them how they would deal with each vignette. These examples and solutions formed the basis of the training program, which was successfully used with both students and new nurses. Those exposed to the program experienced less stress and also maintained their idealism and commitment to a greater extent than did a control group (Kramer, 1974).

Thus, cognitive-behavioral approaches to stress management in professionals have shown some promise in the first few studies to appear in the literature. Long-term follow-ups have been rare, and the evaluations have been done by the interventionists themselves rather than by independent evaluators. Nevertheless, the cognitive-behavioral approaches seem to be the most promising of the individual stress management strategies.

Perhaps the greatest danger is that these individual stress management techniques may be used in a mechanical fashion that ignores the subtleties of human behavior. Woolfolk and Lehrer (1984) urged that any program for reducing stress in an individual should include a careful evaluation of the whole person, including goals and aspirations, style of life, and the social context in which the person functions. These authors further noted that certain individuals may not be good candidates for stress management and should be screened out of any program. These persons include psychotics, severe depressives, those whose stress problems are organically based, and those experiencing other "problems in living" that may undermine a program of stress management.

Even if individual stress management techniques are effective in some situations, they are limited in the same way that any clinical intervention is limited: Success requires a client who is willing to work at the techniques offered by the clinician (Woolfolk & Lehrer, 1984). Of course, client compliance

PROFESSIONALS IN DISTRESS

can be influenced to some extent by the therapist's technique. Woolfolk and Lehrer suggested a number of ways in which this can be done, including emphasizing the self-responsibility of the client, giving the client the basic rationale behind the techniques chosen, choosing a technique that is compatible with the client's personality, helping the client to weave practice sessions into the routines of daily life, and providing appropriate expectations.

The problem of individual expectations is particularly important in the use of stress management techniques with psychologists. Psychologists tend to have strong beliefs about the most valid approaches to the study, understanding, and modification of human behavior. They usually are committed to particular theories of behavior to an extent that lay people usually are not. Any approach—whether behavioral, cognitive, somatic, or insight oriented—that is anathema to the psychologist-client probably will not be effective.

GROUP-BASED STRATEGIES

The distinction between individual and group stress management strategies is ambiguous, because many individual techniques, such as relaxation training or rational–emotive restructuring, often are provided in a group setting. For our purposes, we have considered these to be individual strategies whether or not they are provided in a one-to-one setting, because the most direct targets of the intervention are individual-level variables. These individual strategies are contrasted with those that are directed at group variables, such as social support. The distinction still can be obscure, however, because programs may combine the two (e.g., Gray-Toft, 1980).

"Social support" has become a popular topic in the research literature on stress. Some studies have suggested that people who are part of a positive, supportive social network of family, friends, and neighbors often are better able to cope with stress (e.g., Cobb, 1976; Gottlieb, 1981; La Rocco, House, & French, 1980). Cherniss (1980a) found that new professionals working in the public sector experienced less stress and symptoms of "burnout" when they were involved in satisfying social relationships outside of work and when colleagues at work provided practical and emotional support. Similar findings for other professionals have come from the work of Pines (1983). And Farber and Heifetz (1982) found that almost all of the 60 psychotherapists interviewed in their study expressed a desire for more social support from colleagues.

To be sure, all social interaction with others is not always helpful. As Beck (1984) pointed out, interaction with others may reinforce negative cognitions that contribute to stress. But under the right conditions, social support networks can be helpful in alleviating stress. One strategy for expanding social support networks is the social support or *mutual aid group*. Members of such groups help each other by providing information on how to deal with problems, material assistance, corrective feedback, reassurance and confirmation, and a sense of belonging and emotional support (Silverman & Murrow, 1976).

The development of an effective mutual aid group can be a complicated undertaking. Plans for a mutual aid group should be thought out in great detail prior to its introduction to potential participants. Two of the primary considerations are the degree to which the need for a group is felt by potential participants and the degree to which they have a say in its development. Weiner, Caldwell, and Tyson (1983) discussed the development of three support groups among intensive care unit nurses. One of these groups succeeded and the other two failed. In the successful group, the idea had been initiated from within. In the two failures, the idea had been initiated by an outsider (a physician) who noticed stress-related symptoms among the nurses.

Leadership also seems to be a critical factor in the development of a successful mutual aid group. Spicuzza (1982) emphasized that the leader must have the full support of the group. New groups must be wary of the power struggles that may ensue. Each member of the group should have some say in the selection of the group leader, for as Spicuzza stated, "Members assembled to focus on the issue of burnout do not need an additional situation where they feel they have no control or guidelines with which to focus" (p. 98). Weiner et al. (1983) confirmed this suggestion, noting that the leader of their successful group was known to its members, whereas this was not the case with the two failures.

The size and orientation of the group are also important considerations. Spicuzza (1982) proposed that the ideal size of a mutual aid group is between 8 and 12 members. He warned that a smaller group may be dominated by one or two members, and a larger group may inhibit communication. The degree of structure also may be an important issue. Weiner et al. (1983) averred that it is desirable to use a highly structured format in initial meetings. Then, over time, a group may become more informal.

Cherniss (1979) discussed several institutional barriers that may inhibit the development of social support among professional staff in a work setting. These include conflicting theoretical orientations or personal values, competing commitments outside of the job, and differences in perceived power, status, or resources of group members. Other barriers are the role structure of the organization (in settings where individuals work more independently, social support is more difficult to develop), informal norms discouraging meaningful interaction, and high turnover rates. Those who develop mutual aid groups should assess the possible influence of these barriers. If any of these barriers exist, members sometimes can overcome them by developing appropriate facilitating structures and procedures.

Outcome research on "pure" mutual aid groups is virtually nonexistent. One reason is that previous studies have dealt with groups combining individual didactic training delivered by an expert/leader with facilitation of mutual aid among members. The data available, however, suggest that groups in which the encouragement of social support is emphasized are somewhat less effective as stress management aids than are more structured, cognitive-behavioral interventions.

For instance, Weiner et al. (1983) reported on three different social support groups for nurses, only one of which was successful. Amaral, Nehemkis, and Fox (1981) studied the impact of a "mixed" group on staff working in a cancer ward. Their group involved both structured (didactic) and unstructured sessions and went on for 8 months. The 10 participants enjoyed the group, and it may have kept stress levels from increasing during this period. (There was no control group.) But it did not result in a lowering of stress. Finally, Anderson (1982) found that mental health professionals who participated in a peer support group were no different in burnout levels at the end than a control group who did not participate.

Thus, the mutual aid or social support group may not be as effective in reducing stress as more focused and structured cognitive-behavioral interventions. Positive social support can be helpful, however, and mutual aid groups sometimes do succeed in fostering such support among their members. Also, this type of intervention has not yet received an adequate test. Therefore, the mutual aid group cannot be dismissed; in fact, the trend has been to combine it with other interventions.

ORGANIZATIONAL STRATEGIES

Most psychologists work in organizations, and these organizations exert a powerful influence on their numbers. Even those who work alone in private practice are part of an "organization," albeit one of their own making, and how they manage that organization will affect their levels of stress and their abilities to cope with it.

Unfortunately, many psychologists are not "organization minded"; they are accustomed to thinking about behavior in terms of the individual. Thus, they find the prospect of dealing with stress at the organizational level perplexing, if not overwhelming. There often seems to be a sense of resignation and hopelessness when it comes to considering organizational, as opposed to individual, change.

The research literature on planned organizational change is not uniformly positive; nevertheless, there are enough well-documented examples of efforts to promote positive change to suggest that people can change organizations to make them less stressful as work environments. And although a top-level manager certainly has more leverage than staff at lower levels, even those on the lowest levels can effect change in their organizational settings. How to do so is beyond the scope of this chapter, but many excellent guides are available, such as Brager and Holloway's (1978) book, which presents a detailed framework to help lower-level direct service staff in human service programs to induce change. Thus, by working with others and mastering a few basic change skills, psychologists can have an impact on their work settings.

Organizations can reduce stress and facilitate coping in a number of ways. Staff development programs are one obvious vehicle for doing so. Organizations can provide support for continuing education and for inservice training programs. Some organizations even sponsor social support groups, individual "burnout checkups," and counseling for their staff.

There are three other areas in any organization to which stress-prevention efforts could be directed: job structure, the supervisory process, and organizational problem solving.

Reducing Stress by Modifying the Job

Redesigning a worker's job is perhaps the easiest and most powerful way of reducing stress. Ample research has shown that stress in work settings often is caused by role overload, ambiguity, conflict, or "underload" (Chapter 5). Thus, designing jobs to minimize these factors can do much to reduce stress.

Before we consider some specific ways of redesigning jobs, we would like to emphasize that the fit between the worker and the job is of primary importance. Workers (including psychologists) differ in their interests and abilities. A job may be stressful for some workers but not for others. Too often, organizations try to fit the worker to the job rather than the job to the worker.

There are many ways in which jobs can be restructured to reduce stress. Five methods, however, are germane to almost any work situation:

1. *Distribute the "dirty work" evenly.* In any work setting, some duties are more onerous than others. In academia, certain courses or committees may be less desirable than others. In human service settings, certain client groups or programs may be the ones most psychologists try to avoid. If one individual or group of individuals is assigned most of an organization's "dirty work," stress will be particularly high. Thus, a simple solution is to spread out the most unpleasant duties through rotation of assignment or other procedures.

An example of this approach is the Central Connecticut Regional Center's policy of requiring that all staff work in at least two different programs (Sarason, Zitnay, & Grossman, 1971). Thus, even if one program assignment for a staff member in this mental retardation agency were unpleasant, the other might be more appealing.

2. *Arrange the day so that rewarding and unrewarding activities alternate.* This simple idea can be used by almost any individual who has some control over his or her work situation. It is particularly relevant for those who have considerable autonomy, such as psychologists working in private practice or in many academic settings.

3. *Build in "time outs."* A "time out" is time during the day when one removes oneself from the typical duties and demands of the job. It is not necessarily the same as the standard 15-minute "coffee break." An example might be a therapist who sets aside an hour in the middle of every day for reading.

4. *Do not discourage part-time employment.* Many psychologists probably would work less than full time if it were easier to do so. Unfortunately, the personnel policies of many large corporations penalize people for working less than full time. Our culture's strong work ethic also discourages shorter work weeks. Thus, many employees probably are working full time—and experiencing more stress than necessary—simply because of strong cultural norms encouraging this practice and because many important benefits such as sick leave, medical insurance, and retirement programs would be lost if they cut back their time.

5. *Give every staff member the opportunity to develop new programs.* Even the most interesting professional work can become routine and stale. One way a person can avoid this outcome is to spend part of the time experimenting with new approaches. Some organizations make this a standard part of the job. Whether or not the experimental initiatives turn out to be valuable additions to the organization, their positive effect on the professional's motivation and morale probably makes them worth the cost.

These are but a few of the ways in which jobs can be designed to reduce stress and increase fulfillment. Each work setting probably offers many more avenues that are unique to that kind of setting. But these five simple approaches are general enough to be relevant to almost any work situation.

Reducing Stress Through Supervision

Supervision is another aspect of the work setting that can affect the degree of stress experienced by workers. One characteristic of the professional "ideal type" is that supervision is supposed to be of minimal importance. Long years of training and socialization are supposed to enable professionals to work on their own without the close supervision required for other kinds of workers.

This ideal notion of a professional probably is misleading in certain respects. Although it is to be hoped that most professionals do not need close supervision, even good, experienced professionals can benefit from a style of supervision that combines meaningful structure and direction with support and autonomy (Cherniss, 1980b). "Consultative" supervision, as this style sometimes has been labeled, can help reduce stress for many professional workers.

Supervisory training is the most obvious and popular intervention for producing a consultative style of supervision in work settings. Well-designed training can have much value, especially in educational and human service work settings where administrators usually have had no formal training in management prior to assuming their jobs. Department chairs in universities and administrators in human service organizations do not necessarily possess a knowledge base that encourages the development of good supervisory practices.

Even well-designed training, however, may be limited in its impact on on-the-job behavior. An interesting alternative is *survey feedback,* in which subordinates anonymously complete questionnaires evaluating supervisory behavior, and then the results are provided to their supervisor. Some well-designed studies have found that this procedure can be effective in modifying supervisory behavior (e.g., Burns, 1977; Hegarty, 1974). Survey feedback is particularly useful when done on a regular basis.

Survey feedback has limitations, however. Even when supervisors know what they should be doing and have feedback from subordinates encouraging them to do it, political and structural factors in the organization may prevent them from providing optimal supervision. An example of how this can happen occurred in a project conducted by the senior author. A survey feedback intervention with the director of a large children's service agency initially led to positive change in the director's behavior toward subordinates. However, a severe financial crisis occurred about two months later, and the director became preoccupied with the demands associated with the crisis. His subordinates reported that his behavior soon reverted to the old, unsatisfactory pattern.

The ultimate failure of survey feedback in the example just cited might have been averted if the survey feedback process had occurred at regular intervals (e.g., every 6 months). The example also demonstrates, however, that supervisory behavior is strongly influenced by the larger social system in which the supervisor works. Helping supervisors handle the stresses associated with their own work can thus help reduce stress in their subordinates. All of the ideas presented in this chapter are relevant for reducing stress in supervisors as well as in their subordinates.

Organizational Problem-Solving Processes

Even when jobs are well designed and supervision is good, conflicts, problems, and strains will occur in any organization. Unfortunately, organizations usually are designed as though their creators assumed that eventually there would be no internal stress or problems (Sarason, 1972). Consequently, surprisingly few organizations have permanent, formal mechanisms to monitor the internal work climate and deal with problems when they first emerge.

Regularly meeting problem-solving groups, whether they are called quality circles, employee involvement groups, quality-of-work-life committees, or some other name, offer a promising way of minimizing the stresses that are inevitable in any work setting. Participation in such groups can reduce role ambiguity, conflict, and perceived powerlessness in the employee, three major sources of stress (Jackson, 1983). In addition, such structures can improve the communication of information between higher and lower layers of a hierarchical organization. This communication leads to an improvement in the quality and quantity of information available for making decisions, which ultimately leads to better decisions and less stressful work settings.

There are many barriers to the development of effective participatory problem-solving structures in organizations. Managerial resistance to giving up power is but one of them. Group problem solving often requires added time, and groups do not necessarily make higher quality decisions than individuals. Nevertheless, participatory structures and processes in organizations have been shown to be effective in reducing stress.

One recent study by Jackson (1983) provides a particularly good example. In a carefully designed experiment using a Solomon four-group design, some nursing and clerical staff in a large hospital outpatient facility were randomly assigned to an "increased-participation" condition. Participation was increased by the requirement that unit heads hold scheduled staff meetings at least twice a month. Unit heads attended a 2-day training workshop on how to run such meetings in a manner that enhanced participation, and they were given a list of suggested topics to cover at the meetings. Results of the study revealed that workers in the increased-participation condition reported less role conflict and ambiguity and more perceived personal influence. Positive changes in emotional strain, job dissatisfaction, absence frequency, and turnover intention also occurred. And the changes persisted at a 6-month follow-up.

Many other strategies for improving organizational problem-solving processes and increasing employee participation in settings employing professionals can be found in a number of sources (e.g., Coughlan, Cooke, & Safer, 1972; Graham, 1982; Sarason et al., 1971). A careful study of these experiments reveals that establishing participatory structures usually is not sufficient to improve the work climate. There must be strong support and determination to do so from top management. Furthermore, the people who are involved in those programs need well-designed training and socialization experiences to prepare them to function in their new and often demanding roles. If these facilitating preconditions are provided, participatory problem-solving and decision-making mechanisms constitute another strategy for reducing the sources of stress in work organizations.

CONCLUSION

In this chapter we have outlined a variety of strategies that have been used to help individuals cope with occupational stress. Because coping with stress is a complex process involving a transaction between individuals and their environments, effective interventions can occur at different levels and at different points in the process. We have described strategies directed at individual, group, and organizational factors. We also have described preventive interventions and clinical-remedial strategies designed to help those already suffering from prolonged stress.

Controversy over the "best" approach to stress management continues, and this controversy undoubtedly is a useful spur to better research and practice. In advocating our own, preferred approach, we should not lose sight of the obvious fact that individuals, therapists, trainers, and consultants, as well as work settings, differ greatly. The best approach in any situation ultimately depends on the unique preferences, strengths, and constraints involved.

Given the desirability of maintaining an open mind about the best strategy to use in any situation, it is important also to note underlying biases that psychologists typically bring to the study and treatment of stress. As Sarason (1981) has pointed out, psychology as a discipline has tended historically to emphasize individual-based, remedial solutions to problems. Consequently, the potential of preventive interventions and those directed at social systems factors usually is not adequately explored. In this chapter, we have shown that group and organizational strategies are available and have been used successfully in combatting stress. We hope that in programs to help distressed psychologists to manage stress, prevention will receive its due. Also, we hope that systems-level approaches will continue to be used and refined in future work.

EPILOGUE: GETTING HELP

What can distressed professionals—and those who know them—do about stress? The following suggestions are organized in two ways. First, we offer individual, group-based, and organizational strategies. Changes in *individual* attitudes and coping skills can help to alleviate the negative consequences of stress, but *group* and *organizational* action also should be considered. Second, in each section we offer one set of suggestions for the distressed professionals themselves and then another for those who know them (supervisors, co-workers, and friends).

Individual Remedies: Advice for the Distressed Professional

Self-Analysis. The first step is to recognize feelings of distress: Under which circumstances does stress become a problem? Under which circumstances is stress not a problem? What are the thoughts and images that accompany stress? Are there any environmental or internal signals that warn you of the onset of stress? These and other questions can be considered alone or in the company of a trusted confidant. For some people, this kind of evaluation of their work and personal lives is sufficient to reduce stress to a comfortable level. Often a pattern is detected that was previously unknown to the distressed professional. Once the pattern is identified, breaking it is straightforward.

Relaxation. If, however, a thoughtful evaluation of stressful situations does not help enough, other methods can be used. One of the least intrusive methods is the abbreviated relaxation training procedure described above. Within this context there are two options. You may choose to obtain taped lessons and learn them at your leisure. If this proves unsatisfactory, then you can schedule several appointments with a therapist who can devise a personalized relaxation scheme geared toward the precipitants that you have already identified. In deciding whether or not to seek the help of another person, keep in mind that some research suggests that practicing relaxation methods with the guidance and support of someone else is superior to doing it alone. If you are reluctant to seek the help of an unknown professional therapist who charges a fee, consider who in your own social network might be able and willing to provide the additional support.

Once you begin relaxation techniques, remember that setting aside time to practice is essential. Plan daily practice sessions for the most convenient times, given your life-style. If you find it difficult to use relaxation training, try one or more of the related techniques (biofeedback, hypnosis, meditation, autogenic training, or yoga). No one method is superior in general, but many individuals do seem to do better with one particular method. Thus, if one method does not work for you, another one might.

Cognitive-Behavioral Techniques. If you feel that you need a little more structure to handle stress, then you may want to try cognitive-behavioral techniques. There are a number of options to choose from. Although these techniques are generally more effective with the support and guidance of another individual or a small group, self-help materials are available that may be useful by themselves. If you cannot (or do not wish to) find outside help but would like to try this approach, then try to find books, articles, or training tapes produced by reputable individuals or organizations. Again, if you decide that support would be useful, contact someone who can guide you through the principles dictated by cognitive-behavioral techniques. This individual need not be someone with training in cognitive-behavioral stress-reduction techniques, although this may be an option worth considering.

Cognitive-behavioral methods help you to reevaluate the stress-producing situation you identified in your initial self-analysis. Stressful situations (e.g., too much to do and not enough time to do it, interpersonal conflicts, bureaucratic barriers) become particularly distressing because of what we "tell ourselves," often subconsciously. For example, you might find that time stress is heightened because you are saying to yourself, "It will be disastrous if I don't get this project done on time. I'll lose all my credibility. People's lives will suffer horribly."

Once you have identified the cognitions contributing to the stress, the next step is to analyze their validity as objectively as possible. If you see that at least some of them are exaggerations, you can try to replace them with more rational interpretations of the situation.

You probably will find that you need to go over this analytical process each day for a week or two in order to replace the old statements with the new ones and reduce stress. Again, if you find it difficult to do this immediately, don't give up. Try to find other training materials and get someone to help guide you, even if it is not someone with training in cognitive-behavioral stress-reduction techniques.

Individual Remedies: Advice for the Person Who Knows the Distressed Professional

It can be difficult to suggest to someone you know that he or she needs help. One way to introduce the idea is to summarize as concretely as you can the behaviors you have observed, express your concern, and suggest a possible course of action (you might want to leave out the suggestion until you get the person's response to your observation). For example: "You get upset about what's happening at work whenever we discuss it. Many experts believe that this sometimes is a sign of excessive stress and that people in such situations may benefit from stress management techniques such as relaxation training, biofeedback, or cognitive approaches. What do you think about trying something like that?"

If the person expresses interest, try to help the person follow through without becoming "pushy." One helpful method is to develop a concrete action plan right on the spot, specifying what the person will do and when she or he will do it. Arrange a time to check back on whether the plan has led to positive results.

Another way to be helpful is to actively assist the individual to obtain the needed resources. These resources might include the name and phone number of a professional who could provide the training, books or training tapes, and yourself or others who might go through the training with the individual and provide valuable support and guidance.

If the first stress program does not work, remain positive. Do not make the person feel that it is her or his fault. Suggest that the person try another technique that might be more suited to her or his personality and life-style. If you are in a management position, consider developing institutional supports for the stress management activities. Examples of such supports are paid release time and a limited amount of money to reimburse employees for expenses (similar to health insurance). There are reputable professionals who could be hired on a consulting basis to come out to your work setting and provide stress management training to individuals or small groups. Any institutional support, no matter how modest, can make a great difference.

Group-Based Strategies: Advice for the Distressed Professional

Think about your current social support network. Who can you talk to about the stressful things in your life? Are these individuals helpful? Consider ways of strengthening your social support network. For example, try to strengthen your relationships with the potentially most supportive people in your network. This can be done by making an effort to see these people more often socially and by trying to be supportive to them. If you help them, they will be more willing to help you.

Another way to strengthen the network is to expand its size. Look for opportunities to meet new people and develop new, supportive relationships. Think of the time you invest in these "nonproductive" activities as wise investments. Not all personal relationships are supportive. Avoid those people and situations that reinforce negative feelings (e.g., the lunch room at work if co-workers often "gripe" about things and discourage thinking about positive ways of improving the situation). You also might consider starting a mutual aid group using Spicuzza's (1982) article or a similar reading as a manual.

Group-Based Strategies: Advice for the Person Who Knows the Distressed Professional

Help the individual to consider trying the ideas presented in the section on individual strategies. If you are a manager, consider ways that your organization could formally encourage group-based stress management interventions. For instance, you could help staff develop a mutual aid group. Provide release time or an outside facilitator for the group. Contact managers in other, related work settings that might have some candidates for the group, and try to pool resources. A group made up of workers from different agencies might be better because members might feel freer to talk about themselves and less competitive, and there might be more new ideas generated.

Remember that a successful mutual aid group requires a strong sense of ownership by those in the group. Instead of taking the initiative yourself, try to have a staff person who is respected by the other staff do it. Then support and encourage that person as much as possible without "taking over."

Organizational Strategies: Advice for the Distressed Professional

Organizational change is not just for administrators. People at all levels can, and do, make a difference. By working effectively with others who share your concerns, you might be able to change some of the organizational structures and procedures that are so frustrating. Successful organizational change from the bottom up requires effective strategy and change skills. Brager and Holloway's (1978) book is a useful manual, especially when you have a particular change in mind.

In addition to reading about change, consider consulting people who have expertise in this area. Just as we can go to counselors and therapists for help with personal problems, so, too, can we go to organizational consultants for advice on how to tackle organizational problems. If a group of workers pool their resources, the cost for such consultation may be modest.

Organizational Strategies: Advice for the Person Who Knows the Distressed Professional

It is important to avoid the usual practice of seeing the problem as being rooted in the individual. Even if only one of your staff members is visibly reacting to stress, it is possible that many others also are experiencing stress, even if they are not showing it. Look at the situation. Examine the pressures, demands, and conflicts inherent in the stressed person's *role,* and consider what you might do to change it. Are you providing clear enough direction? Are you providing too much direction? Can you help the individual secure feedback on his or her positive accomplishments?

Although you can conduct an informal organizational assessment on your own, consider administering a survey to staff. Securing the help of an outside consultant could help enhance the perceived confidentiality and anonymity of the survey. Experienced, professional management consultants can be quite expensive, but many universities have graduate training programs in administration, management, community psychology, human resource development, and so forth. These programs always need practicum opportunities for students and could be inexpensive resources.

In conducting your assessment, do not overlook the possibility of your own contribution to the problem. Even if you are a sensitive and competent manager whose approach is appropriate for many employees, your approach may not be right for others. Try to arrange regularly occurring ways of receiving honest feedback from your staff on your own supervisory performance.

Once you have completed your assessment, identify the sources of stress and consider possible remedies. The remedies described in this chapter constitute a starting point, but there probably are many others you can think of on your own, and they may be better suited to your situation.

Do not be afraid to share organizational problems with your subordinates. Let them know the sources of the problems and the constraints you face in trying to solve them. Then encourage them to join you in trying to generate potential solutions. This kind of group problem solving in the workplace often leads to creative, unexpected ideas that help alleviate even the most intractable problems. Even if this group problem-solving activity does not lead to a solution, you will experience less stress because you have shared the problem rather than trying to solve it on your own. Your employees also may find it easier to cope, just knowing what is involved. And everyone may benefit because this collaborative process will have improved relationships within the group.

As we noted in the first part of the chapter, reducing stress is often a complex process affected by many individual and environmental factors. Thus, it is difficult in a few pages to provide advice that will be valid for every situation. Nevertheless, we hope that the suggestions offered here may help distressed professionals and concerned others to confront the pressures and frustrations that often are inevitable in the work lives of professionals.

References

Amaral, P., Nehemkis, A. M., & Fox, L. (1981). Staff support group on a cancer ward: A pilot project. *Death Education, 5,* 267–274.

Anderson, C. M. (1982). *The effects of peer support groups on levels of burnout among mental health professionals.* Unpublished dissertation, University of Washington.

Baron, A., & Cohen, R. B. (1982). Helping telephone counselors cope with burnout: A consciousness-raising workshop. *Personnel and Guidance Journal, 60,* 508–510.

Beck, A. T. (1984). Cognitive approaches to stress. In R. L. Woolfolk & P. M. Lehrer (Eds.), *Principles and practices of stress management* (pp. 255–305). New York: Guilford.

Bernstein, D. A., & Given, B. A. (1984). Progressive relaxation: Abbreviated methods. In R. L. Woolfolk & P. M. Lehrer (Eds.), *Principles and practices of stress management* (pp. 43–69). New York: Guilford.

Brager, G., & Holloway, S. (1978). *Changing human service organizations: Politics and practice.* New York: Free Press.

Budzynski, T. H., & Stoyva, J. M. (1984). Biofeedback methods in the treatment of anxiety and stress. In R. L. Woolfolk & P. M. Lehrer (Eds.), *Principles and practices of stress management* (pp. 188–219). New York: Guilford.

Burns, M. L. (1977). The effects of feedback and commitment to change on the behavior of elementary school principals. *Journal of Applied Behavioral Science, 13,* 159–166.

Cherniss, C. (1979). Institutional barriers to social support among human service staff. In K. A. Reid & R. A. Quinlan (Eds.), *Burnout in the helping professions* (pp. 80–92). Kalamazoo, MI: Western Michigan University.

Cherniss, C. (1980a). *Professional burnout in human service organizations.* New York: Praeger.

Cherniss, C. (1980b). *Staff burnout: Job stress in the human services.* Beverly Hills, CA: Sage.

Cobb, S. (1976). Social support as a moderator of life stress. *Psychosomatic Medicine, 38,* 300–314.

Coughlan, R. J., Cooke, R. A., & Safer, L. A., Jr. (1972). *An assessment of a survey feedback-problem-solving-collective decision intervention in schools.* Final report, Office of Education Bureau of Research.

Crook, D. H., Jr. (1982). *Assessment of a stress reduction program with progressive relaxation on nursing services personnel of a general hospital.* Unpublished doctoral dissertation, University of Alabama.

Croyle, G. W. (1982). *The development of a stress management program for teachers.* Unpublished doctoral dissertation, University of Pittsburgh.

Edelwich, J., & Brodsky, A. (1980). *Burn-out.* New York: Human Sciences Press.

Ellis, A. (1962). *Reason and emotion in psychotherapy.* New York: Lyle Stuart.

Farber, B. A., & Heifetz, L. J. (1982). The process and dimensions of burnout in psychotherapists. *Professional Psychology, 13,* 293–301.

Forman, J. S. (1983). *The effects of an aerobic dance program for women teachers on symptoms of burnout.* Unpublished doctoral dissertation, University of Cincinnati.

Forman, S. G. (1981). Stress management training: Evaluation of effects on school psychological services. *Journal of School Psychology, 19,* 233–241.

Gottlieb, B. (1981). *Social networks and social support in community mental health.* Beverly Hills, CA: Sage.

Graham, R. S. (1982). Employee support systems in a psychosocial rehabilitation setting. *Psychosocial Rehabilitation Journal, 6,* 12–19.

Gray-Toft, P. (1980). Effectiveness of a counseling support program for hospice nurses. *Journal of Counseling Psychology, 27,* 346–354.

Hegarty, W. H. (1974). Using subordinate ratings to elicit behavioral changes in supervisors. *Journal of Applied Psychology, 59,* 764–766.

Jackson, S. E. (1983). Participation in decision-making as a strategy for reducing job-related strain. *Journal of Applied Psychology, 68,* 3–19.

Jacobson, E. (1938). *Progressive relaxation* (2nd ed.). Chicago. University of Chicago Press.

Kibler, R. D. (1982). *Burnout intervention with public school teachers.* Unpublished doctoral dissertation, University of Virginia.

Kramer, M. (1974). *Reality shock.* St. Louis, MO: C. V. Moseley.

Lange, A. J., & Jakubowski, P. (1979). *Responsible assertive behaviors: Cognitive/behavioral procedures for trainers.* Champaign, IL: Research Press.

LaRocco, J. M., House, J. S., & French, J. R. P., Jr. (1980). Social support, occupational stress, and health. *Journal of Health and Social Behavior, 21,* 202–218.

Lazar, S. A. (1981). The effects of autogenic training in reducing the occupational stress of probate court juvenile case workers. *Dissertation Abstracts International, 41* (12–B, pt. 1), 4639.

Lazarus, A. A. (1976). *Multi-modal behavior therapy*. New York: Springer.

Lehrer, P. M., & Woolfolk, R. L. (1984). Are stress reduction techniques interchangeable, or do they have specific effects? A review of the comparative empirical literature. In R. L. Woolfolk & P. M. Lehrer (Eds.), *Principles and practices of stress management* (pp. 404–477). New York: Guilford.

Maultsby, M. C. (1971). Rational–emotive imagery. *Rational Living, 3*, 24–26.

Meichenbaum, D. (1977). *Cognitive-behavior modification: An integrative approach*. New York: Plenum Press.

Novaco, R. (1983). *Stress inoculation therapy for anger control: A manual for therapists*. Unpublished manuscript, University of California, Irvine.

Pines, A. (1983). On burnout and the buffering effects of social support. In B. A. Farber (Ed.), *Stress and burnout in the human service professions* (pp. 155–174). New York: Pergamon Press.

Ray, C. A. (1982). Holistic stress management training: A burnout strategy for mental health workers. *Dissertation Abstracts International, 42* (7–B), 2972–2973.

Sarason, S. B. (1972). *The creation of settings and the future societies*. San Francisco: Jossey-Bass.

Sarason, S. B. (1981). *Psychology misdirected*. New York: Free Press.

Sarason, S. B., Zitnay, G., & Grossman, F. K. (1971). *The creation of a community setting*. Syracuse, NY: Syracuse University Press.

Shinn, M., & Mørch, H. A. (1983). A tripartite model of coping with burnout. In B. A. Farber (Ed.), *Stress and burnout in the human service professions* (pp. 227–240). New York: Pergamon Press.

Silverman, P. R., & Murrow, H. G. (1976). Mutual help during critical role transitions. *Journal of Applied Behavioral Science, 12*, 410–418.

Sparks, D., & Ingram, M. J. (1979). Stress prevention and management: A workshop approach. *Personnel and Guidance Journal, 58*, 197–200.

Spicuzza, F. J. (1982). Burnout in the helping professions: Mutual aid groups as self-help. *Personnel & Guidance Journal, 61*, 95–99.

Thurman, C. W. (1985). Effectiveness of cognitive-behavioral treatments in reducing Type A behavior among university faculty. *Journal of Counseling Psychology, 32*, 74–83.

Weiner, M. F., Caldwell, T., & Tyson, J. (1983). Stresses and coping in ICU nursing: Why support groups fail. *General Hospital Psychiatry, 5*, 179–183.

West, D. J., Jr. (1982). *Occupational stress inoculation: An experimental application on registered nurses in an acute care hospital setting*. Unpublished doctoral dissertation, Pennsylvania State University.

Woolfolk, R. L., & Lehrer, P. M. (1984). (Eds.). *Principles and practices of stress management*. New York: Guilford.

ISSUES AND PROCEDURES IN THE DISCIPLINING OF DISTRESSED PSYCHOLOGISTS

14

Judy E. Hall

t is important for any psychologist to understand disciplinary procedures even though he or she is not personally accused of any wrongdoing, because any psychologist may become involved in the disciplinary process if consulted by a colleague who is charged with unethical or unprofessional conduct, if sued for malpractice, or if consulted by a distressed psychologist. This chapter first informs those involved in the disciplinary process what they might expect and what their rights include. This will be done by examining the licensure statutes, rules, and regulations and the American Psychological Association's ethical code (APA, 1981a), by summarizing sections pertaining to discipline and by providing an overview of the disciplinary process for the 50 states, the District of Columbia, the territory of Puerto Rico, and the eight Canadian provinces.[1] Because the disciplinary process might culminate in the revocation of a license to practice, the investigation and hearing must be conducted in a manner in which the licensee's constitutional rights are safeguarded. This is also true of the professional society's disciplinary process, even though those proceedings are less formal and the rules of procedure are less restrictive than in civil or criminal proceedings.

The second objective of this chapter is to focus on those aspects of the disciplinary system that are of particular interest to the distressed psychologist.

---

[1]*State* is used to refer to the jurisdictions in the United States (50 states, District of Columbia, Puerto Rico) and Canada (eight provinces) that regulate the title and practice of psychology. The U.S. territory of Guam, which recently passed legislation regarding the practice of psychology, is not included. The source material came from current licensure statutes, regulations and rules, and the administrative procedures act. Phone calls to the office of the state regulatory board or the administrative agency overseeing the board were often necessary to verify or clarify information. This summary is current as of June 1985.

One definition of a distressed psychologist includes "those suffering from physical, emotional, legal or job related problems adversely affecting professional performance" (Nathan, Thoreson, & Kilburg, 1983). This chapter provides an analysis of the regulatory and ethical provisions addressing the occurrence of alcoholism, drug abuse, sexual intimacies with clients, physical and emotional problems, and incompetence among psychologists. Whereas other chapters in this volume address assessment and treatment of those conditions, this chapter focuses on the jurisdictional variations in the disciplinary process.

OVERVIEW OF DISCIPLINARY PROCESSES

Disciplinary proceedings may center on charges of unethical conduct against a member of a professional society or association. The disciplinary action of the association ranges from censure or a reprimand, which may be confidential, to expulsion from membership, which is usually announced to the membership. Professional societies delegate this disciplinary function typically to an ethics committee, which is bound by the societies' rules and procedures, written or unwritten. The judgment of the committee is paramount in deciding whether the member has violated professional standards or the ethical code, and the judgment is usually reached in closed session without the member present. If the committee recommends expulsion from membership, the recommendation is forwarded to the board of directors for a decision.

Disciplinary proceedings may involve charges brought against a licensed psychologist who is subject to disciplinary action by a state licensing board. The action of the board could range from an administrative warning or a censure or reprimand, which may be confidential, to license revocation, which is never confidential. The board's authority to discipline stems from the state's power to protect the health, safety, and welfare of its citizens. Boards conduct such administrative proceedings in accordance with requirements set by the law and elaborated by rule or by the state's administrative procedures act, a statute designed to standardize procedures for rule making and for contesting cases across agencies in the state. A complaint to the board will initiate formal proceedings only when the complaint concerns (a) someone over whom the board has jurisdiction and (b) a rule, regulation, or statute administered by the board.

The grounds for discipline of a licensee are located in the state statute or the state rules and regulations. Typically, the state may have adopted as a state rule a version of the APA ethics code or a separate professional conduct code. In addition to either the APA ethics code or a professional conduct code, provisions specific to a state are often located in a section in the statute titled "grounds for disciplinary action." Typically, these sections are idiosyncratic statements covering alcohol and drug abuse, incompetency, and sexual abuse of clients. Although the grounds for discipline of a licensee are not identical in the 52 jurisdictions in the United States and the eight Canadian provinces, as of June 1985, the 1981 APA ethics code (APA, 1981a) had been adopted by reference or directly incorporated in regulation to serve as the professional conduct code in 29 states.[2] An additional 13 jurisdictions had adopted as their professional conduct code either the 1977 or the 1979 version of the APA code, sometimes with modifications of certain sections.[3] Instead of adopting the APA ethics code, 15 jurisdictions have developed their own comprehensive codes of conduct. Of those 15, Illinois (which is currently revising its rules), Minnesota, and California are empowered to use the APA ethics code to resolve any ambiguity in interpretation in their own professional conduct codes.[4]

Several states are currently in transition to a new code or a new statute. Washington incorporated in its new statute a number of grounds for discipline but the state is currently attempting to adopt, in addition, the 1981 APA ethics code with modifications. Nevada is revising its statute and has no professional conduct code, but its current law does include grounds for discipline. Nebraska is developing a professional conduct code and currently has no provisions in its statute that specify grounds for discipline of psychologists. Puerto Rico, which has only a few statements in its recent law specifying grounds for discipline, plans the promulgation of rules and a professional conduct code. In addition to these standards for professional conduct, nine jurisdictions currently require adherence to the 1977 revision of the *Standards for Providers of Psychological Services* (APA, 1977).[5] None have adopted the *Specialty Guidelines for the Delivery of Services* (APA, 1981b) as binding policy, although South Carolina has a set of specialty guidelines that define seven different specialties of practice.

In summary, in order to determine the grounds for discipline in the various jurisdictions, the psychologist must examine the statute and accompanying rules and regulations, including any separate codes of conduct. Usually there are rules and regulations (including professional conduct codes) that elaborate the provisions in statute, but in some jurisdictions, the statute is all that exists (e.g., the District of Columbia, Nebraska, Nevada, Puerto Rico, and Washington).

[2]Twenty-nine jurisdictions that have adopted the 1981 APA code of ethics, often with modification of certain sections: Alabama, Alaska, Arkansas, Delaware, District of Columbia, Georgia, Idaho, Indiana, Kentucky, Louisiana, Maine, Maryland, Mississippi, Missouri, Montana (although the 1957 revision is specified in statute), New Hampshire, North Carolina, North Dakota, Oklahoma, Oregon, Pennsylvania, Rhode Island, South Carolina, South Dakota, Texas, Vermont, West Virginia, Wisconsin, Wyoming.

[3]Thirteen jurisdictions that have adopted the 1977 or 1979 APA code of ethics: Iowa, New Mexico, Massachusetts, Tennessee, Utah, West Virginia, and seven of the eight Canadian provinces with registration acts: Alberta, British Columbia, New Brunswick, Manitoba, Nova Scotia, Ontario, and Saskatchewan.

[4]Fourteen jurisdictions with unique professional conduct codes: Arizona, California, Colorado, Connecticut, Florida, Hawaii, Illinois, Kansas, Michigan, Minnesota, New Jersey, New York, Ohio, and Quebec.

[5]Nine jurisdictions that require adherence to the 1977 revision of the *Standards for Providers of Psychological Services:* Alabama, Alaska, Arkansas, Indiana, Maryland, North Dakota, British Columbia, Nova Scotia, and Ontario.

STATE DISCIPLINARY ACTIONS AGAINST PSYCHOLOGISTS

A Question of Moral Character

There are two points in the licensure process at which a psychologist can be charged with a violation of state law, rules, and regulations: (a) prior to licensure, as part of the character and fitness requirement, and (b) after licensure, upon receipt of a complaint. The first type of charge is often called a question of "moral character" and usually concerns an applicant who has previously been convicted of a felony or of "a crime against moral turpitude" (Reaves, 1984, p. 213). It may also affect licensure applicants who have practiced the profession without a license or, in certain states, who have had a history of mental illness, alcoholism, or drug addiction. In 29 of the 52 U.S. jurisdictions under consideration, the statutes specify that the grounds for disciplining a licensee can be used for denial of a license,[6] and Texas and Virginia indicate that violations of the disciplinary code can be used for nonrenewal of a license to practice.

In New York, if a question of moral character is raised regarding an applicant for licensure, either through information supplied by the applicant in the application for licensure or by a complaint, there is a "full and complete investigation of the circumstances surrounding such conviction or act" by the New York State Education Department, Office of Professional Discipline (1985, p. 23). If it is determined that a reasonable question exists regarding the applicant's moral character, the results of the investigation are submitted to a panel of the State Board of Psychology to determine if a substantial question exists. If so, the applicant is given the opportunity for a hearing on the question. Following the hearing and a recommendation by the State Board, there is a review by a subcommittee of the Board of Regents, the Regents Review Committee, followed by a recommendation that is either approved or modified by a vote of the Board of Regents. The purpose of this lengthy process is to remove any question of whether the candidate is able to practice the profession safely.

Elements of Due Process

Substantial justice has been accorded the accused when a state board observes due process requirements before taking an action that could deprive a person of a valuable right. Reaves (1984) outlined the elements of due process:

1. Notice of the time and place of hearing.
2. A hearing before a properly authorized body.

[6]Twenty-nine jurisdictions that can deny a license on grounds of unprofessional conduct: Alabama, California, Colorado, District of Columbia, Florida, Georgia, Hawaii, Idaho, Illinois, Maine, Maryland, Michigan, Mississippi, Missouri, Montana, New Jersey, New Mexico, North Carolina, North Dakota, Ohio, Oregon, Rhode Island, South Carolina, South Dakota, Tennessee, Virginia, Washington, Wisconsin, Wyoming.

3. A reasonably definite statement of the charge or charges preferred against the accused.
4. The right to confront and cross-examine the witnesses who testify against the accused person.
5. The right to produce witnesses in one's own behalf.
6. A full consideration and a fair determination according to the evidence of the controversy by an impartial body before whom the hearing is held.

As Reaves (1984) pointed out, additional rights are accorded the accused, such as the right to appear with counsel and the right to receive a record of the proceedings. In addition, all jurisdictions provide for an appeal to a higher court, typically the county, the district, or another state court, even though there is no constitutional right to an appeal.

Right to a Hearing

The U.S. Constitution provides that no person can be deprived of life, liberty, or property without due process of law. Most courts, including the United States Supreme Court, have interpreted this to require a formal hearing in proceedings that are held to determines a person's rights, duties, or privileges (National Association of Attorneys General, 1978). Therefore, a licensee has the right to a hearing in an action to revoke, refuse to renew, or suspend a license. The state licensing board is authorized to hold a hearing in any contested case, subject to whatever restrictions are imposed by state law or regulation.

The purpose of a disciplinary hearing is to determine contested facts and derive legal conclusions—that is, to determine whether the licensee committed certain acts and, if he or she did, whether those acts violated statutes or rules administered and enforced by the state board; and to determine the appropriate disciplinary action. Often these cases are referred to as "contested cases" in the administrative procedures act. The steps in a disciplinary investigation and prosecution typically follow this sequence (National Association of Attorneys General, 1978):

1. The board or licensure agency receives a complaint. This complaint may be placed over the phone initially, but a written complaint must be signed prior to investigation.
2. The charges are investigated by the state investigators.
3. The board may attempt to resolve the charges informally through correspondence, a conference, or a consent order.
4. Failing an informal resolution, the board initiates formal proceedings.
5. A formal notice of hearing is sent to the accused.
6. The board or the hearing officer (or both) conducts the hearing.
7. The board makes a determination (or recommendation) on the basis of the hearing and, in some jurisdictions, on the basis of the hearing officer's recommendations.
8. Sanctions are determined and imposed or, in certain states, recom-

mended and reviewed by an internal administrative review process and then imposed.

9. Judicial review is available through the county, district, or state courts.

Notice of Hearing

The purpose of notice is to provide sufficient time for the accused to prepare a defense against the charges specified in the notice. The number of days from notice to formal hearing varies from 14 to 30 days among 36 states.[7] In other states, the accused may request a hearing after the notice to revoke a license is served. For instance, in Alaska and Ohio, the licensee has 15 and 30 days, respectively, within which to request a hearing; once the hearing is requested, the person is given at least 10 and 7 days' notice, respectively. The notice requirement in the remaining 22 jurisdictions is not clearly specified in the statutes or rules.

Use of Hearing Officers

The degree to which the quasi-judicial hearing is modeled after a criminal or civil court trial varies. A majority of states, at least 30, rely on administrative hearing officers to conduct the hearings.[8] Depending on the degree to which the state has delegated the authority to regulate to an administrative agency (Roederer & Shimberg, 1980), and depending upon the resources available to the state boards, one of the following patterns is typical: (a) the hearing officer presides over the hearing, acting as a judge, ruling on motions and admissibility of evidence, and the board members form the jury (e.g., New York and Illinois); (b) a hearing officer conducts the hearing independently, and the board reviews the record and determines the sanction (e.g., California); (c) the board delegates the total responsibility for the hearing to a hearing officer (e.g., Indiana and Michigan); or (d) the board acts as judge and jury and conducts all disciplinary hearings (e.g., Alabama, Arkansas, and Louisiana).

This pattern is often a direct result of the degree to which a centralized state administrative agency, rather than the board, has been given the administrative responsibilities. In 1980, Roederer and Shimberg organized the various patterns into five categories, A through E, ranging from completely centralized administrative agencies with full authority (E) to no centralization and a completely autonomous board (A). The type of pattern appears to vary with

[7]Jurisdictions requiring 10 days' notice: Arizona, Illinois, Iowa, Oklahoma, Texas, Wisconsin, Wyoming, and Quebec; jurisdictions requiring 14 days' notice: New Brunswick, New Hampshire, and Vermont; jurisdictions requiring 15 days' notice: Connecticut, Hawaii, and New York; jurisdictions requiring 20 days' notice: Alabama, Arkansas, Kentucky, Michigan, New Jersey, Rhode Island, South Carolina, and Tennessee; jurisdictions requiring 30 days' notice: Delaware, Georgia, Kansas, Louisiana, Maryland, Mississippi, Nebraska, Nevada, North Carolina, North Dakota, West Virginia, Puerto Rico, British Columbia, and Nova Scotia.

[8]Thirty jurisdictions with authority for hearing officers: Alaska, Arizona, California, Colorado, Connecticut, Delaware, District of Columbia, Florida, Georgia, Hawaii, Idaho, Illinois, Iowa, Louisiana, Michigan, Montana, Nevada, New Jersey, New York, North Carolina, Oklahoma, Oregon, Pennsylvania, Rhode Island, Tennessee, Texas, Virginia, Washington, Wisconsin, and Wyoming.

PROFESSIONALS IN DISTRESS

the number of practitioners in the jurisdiction, with larger states typically having some degree of centralization (B–E). Using the categories developed by Roederer and Shimberg (1980), I classified the model in place as of June 1985 in each jurisdiction.[9] Whether the pattern directly relates to the effectiveness of discipline has not been systematically evaluated, although states fitting Model A frequently have never had a formal hearing nor revoked a license to practice. In a 1982 survey of disciplinary activity conducted by Wand (1984), the incidence of complaints against licensees varied from 10 percent of the licensees in a small state to 0.5 percent of the psychologists in another state, with the median incidence of disciplinary activity at 1.5 percent of the psychologists in the states responding to the survey. In attempting to evaluate disciplinary activity in a state, it is important to remember that a formal hearing may last more than one year, whereas administrative warnings or consent orders may be more quickly carried out. In addition, one particular year may not be typical, for example, the 10 percent rate mentioned above. In that same survey, Wand noted that in the United States, 13 percent of the complaints went to formal hearings, whereas in Canada, 23 percent of the complaints went to formal hearings. One third of the states held no hearings at all.

Open Versus Closed Hearings

Whether hearings are open to the public varies. Twenty-one jurisdictions require public access to the hearings;[10] an additional 14 states with public hearing laws make allowances for closing if necessary, usually to protect the psychologist charged or the private life of the person bringing the charge.[11] Fifteen jurisdictions have closed or *in camera* hearings,[12] but six of those jurisdictions provide for opening the hearings to the public.[13] Statutes in ten states appear

[9]The 17 Model A states are Alabama, Arkansas, Kansas, Louisiana, Mississippi, Nevada, New Mexico, North Carolina, North Dakota, Ohio, Oregon, New Hampshire, Puerto Rico, South Carolina, Texas, West Virginia, and Wyoming; the 12 Model B states are Arizona, Georgia, Indiana, Iowa, Kentucky, Maine, Massachusetts, Minnesota, Nebraska, Oklahoma, South Dakota, and Virginia; the 17 Model C states are Alaska, California, Colorado, Delaware, District of Columbia, Hawaii, Idaho, Maryland, Michigan, Missouri, Montana, New Jersey, Pennsylvania, Rhode Island, Tennessee, Vermont, and Wisconsin; the 4 model D states are Connecticut, Florida, Utah, and Washington; 2 states have model E administrative organization: Illinois and New York. Of the eight Canadian provinces, only two have a board separate from the professional association: Nova Scotia and Ontario. Each would probably be classified as model B.

[10]Twenty-one jurisdictions that have open hearings: Arkansas, Connecticut, Delaware, District of Columbia, Florida, Idaho, Kansas, Kentucky, Louisiana, Maine, Michigan, New Hampshire, North Carolina, North Dakota, Ohio, Oklahoma, Pennsylvania, South Carolina, Tennessee, Texas, and Virginia.

[11]Fourteen states that have the power to close their normally open hearings: Alabama, Arizona, California, Colorado, Illinois, Indiana, Iowa, Massachusetts, Mississippi, Missouri, Nebraska, New Jersey, Montana, and Utah.

[12]Fifteen jurisdictions with closed hearings: Alaska, Georgia, Hawaii, Maryland, Minnesota, Nevada, New Mexico, New York, Rhode Island, Vermont, Wisconsin, Wyoming, West Virginia, New Brunswick, and Quebec.

[13]Six jurisdictions with closed hearings that can be opened to the public: Alaska, Georgia, Hawaii, Nevada, New York, and New Mexico.

to be silent on whether the hearings are open or closed.[14]

Proponents of open hearings believe that public access ensures that all parties will be treated fairly and evenhandedly and lessens the likelihood of uninformed public criticism of administrative procedure. Opponents of closed hearings often characterize them as a star-chamber type of proceeding (Naftalison, 1972). Partly as a result of pressure from consumer groups and of increasing recognition of the necessity to make state action public, the administrative procedures acts often require licensure agencies to provide public hearings to those accused. In fact, Reaves stated that, even if not required by law, every psychologist is entitled to a public hearing if she or he wants one (R. Reaves, personal communication, January 1985).

Even in jurisdictions where the hearing is open to the public, in certain circumstances, the hearing can be closed upon appropriate motion. Usually, the reasons include the protection of either the individual's good name because the complaint may not be sustained (as in Alabama) or the prevention of unnecessary disclosure of the personal or family life of the client bringing the charge (Arizona). The decision to close may be made by the board or at the request of the attorney for the respondent, or it may be prescribed narrowly in the statute.

Rules of Privilege

The board must follow the rules of privilege in excluding certain evidence. Privileged communication is defined by state law, and generally communications to an attorney, psychologist, religious advisor, or physician may not be disclosed without the consent of the person who sought the professional's assistance. For example, if the accused psychologist is in therapy with another psychologist, the board cannot require the therapist to testify. However, if the accused psychologist is found guilty of the charges and is required to seek professional help, the board may require as a condition of probation or suspension of the license the submission of periodic reports indicating progress in therapy. In addition, when a client brings a charge of unethical conduct against a licensed psychologist, the client's legal privilege is thereby waived, and the accused is able to present records and testimony and thereby defend against the charges.

Burden of Proof

In a disciplinary action against a licensee, the burden of proof is on the agency bringing the charges. State law determines what degree of proof is required. Some states require clear and convincing proof, others require substantial evidence to support the board's decision, and others use a preponderance of the evidence or a similar test (National Association of Attorneys General, 1978). Reaves has suggested that most jurisdictions employ a substantial evidence test defined as "evidence which is valid, legal and persuasive and such

---

[14]Ten jurisdictions that do not specify whether the hearing is open or closed: Oregon, Puerto Rico, South Dakota, Washington, Alberta, British Columbia, Manitoba, Nova Scotia, Ontario, and Saskatchewan.

relevant evidence as a reasonable mind might accept as adequate to support a conclusion" (Reaves, 1984, p. 196).

Consent Order

After a notice for a formal hearing is sent to the accused psychologist, there is often an opportunity for him or her to plead guilty to all or some of the charges (called stipulating) and to accept sòme form of sanction, without the necessity for a formal hearing. This plea-bargaining agreement is called a consent order. A consent order must be in writing and be accepted and signed by both parties; it is not confidential. Because a stipulation of guilt to some or all of the charges is a major characteristic of a consent order, the consent order is proof of guilt in any subsequent malpractice suit. A consent order may be used by licensure boards for minor violations such as those involving advertisements or fee splitting, or the consent order could actually involve the surrender of a license. Oregon has a specific procedure outlined in regulation for those licensed psychologists who resign while under investigation or while disciplinary proceedings are pending.

Emergency Action

There are certain emergency situations wherein a license might be summarily suspended by a state board prior to a disciplinary hearing in order to protect the public health and safety. However, statutes require that an opportunity for a formal hearing must be accorded within a reasonable time after summary action is taken. Eleven states have explicit provisions for summary suspension or revocation;[15] in Colorado and Nevada emergency action can be taken following an adjudication of mental incompetence. In addition, at least 24 states have the ability to obtain a court order to prevent someone from carrying out a certain action, although this injunctive authority is usually used to prevent someone from illegally practicing psychology.[16] Colorado and Washington have available both injunctive relief and summary proceedings. Nevada has proposed a revision of the current statute that would add injunctive relief to the emergency action already available.

Determining Sanctions

If the licensee is found to have violated the professional conduct code, the board must decide on or recommend the sanctions to be imposed. The sanctions available to a board are always determined by law. These include revocation or cancellation and suspension of the license in all states, with 12 states

[15]Eleven states that specify ability to summarily suspend a license: Alaska, Florida, Georgia, Hawaii, Indiana, Massachusetts, Michigan, New Jersey, New York, Vermont, and Washington.
[16]Twenty-four jurisdictions with injunctive powers: Arizona, California, Colorado, Connecticut, District of Columbia, Georgia, Hawaii, Kansas, Louisiana, Mississippi, Montana, Nebraska, New Jersey, Nevada (proposed), Ohio, Oklahoma, Rhode Island, South Dakota, Texas, Vermont, Washington, West Virginia, Wisconsin, and Nova Scotia.

specifying a time limit on the suspension.[17] Other actions that state boards may take are probation; censure or reprimand; restriction of practice to specific populations, service settings, or techniques; and the requirement of additional education, training, or supervision, as well as psychotherapy. Fines may be imposed in addition to any of the above corrective procedures, including having to pay for the costs of the hearing if found guilty (as in Quebec). California, Michigan, and Virginia provide the hearing officer with disciplinary guidelines (maximum and minimum suggested sanctions) for specified offenses. An example of the sanction for abuse of drugs and alcohol in California follows (California Board of Medical Quality Assurance, n.d.).

> Maximum: Revocation
> Minimum: Stayed revocation with five years' probation
> Conditions of probation:
> 1. Abuse of drugs:
>   a. Successful completion of an educational program on drug abuse prescribed by the Psychology Examining Committee
>   b. Submission to periodic drug testing and compliance with the Board's Probation Surveillance Compliance Program
>   c. Psychotherapeutic treatment as recommended by a psychiatrist or psychologist approved by the Committee
>   d. Successful completion of an oral examination administered by the Committee or its designees.
> 2. Abuse of alcohol:
>   a. Participation in Alcoholics Anonymous or a similar rehabilitation program approved by the Committee
>   b. Abstention from the use of alcohol
>   c. Items 1.b–d., listed previously

The sanctions specified in the Virginia guidelines for these two offenses are the same except that the maximum time period for stayed revocation in Virginia is three years. Virginia has additional guidelines pertaining to those determined to be mentally, emotionally, or physically incompetent to practice the profession.

Rehabilitation Plan

Laws or regulations with specific reference to rehabilitation criteria are rare for licensure boards. At present, only two states provide guidelines for a rehabilitation plan (Texas and Utah). As a result, the guidelines developed by the Texas State Board of Examiners of Psychologists (TSBEP) might be helpful to

---

[17]Twelve states with a time limit on the suspension of a license: Alabama (1 year), District of Columbia (5 years), Florida (5 years), Georgia (1 year), Kansas (1 year), Kentucky (1 year), Louisiana (2 years), Missouri (5 years), New Hampshire (5 years), North Dakota (1 year), Oregon (not less than 1 year), Wisconsin (1 year).

states that are developing their own set of criteria. The Texas guidelines follow (TSBEP, 1983).

§ 465.20 Rehabilitation Guidelines. In the event of revocation, cancellation or suspension of a certificate or license due to non-compliance with the rules of the Board and/or its ethical principles, the psychologist or psychological associate can expect to receive from the Board a plan of rehabilitation at the next regularly scheduled Board meeting following the date of the order. The plan shall outline the steps the person must follow in order to be considered for recertification/relicensure or removal of suspension. Completion of the plan may lead to consideration of (a) submission of an application for recertification and/or relicensure; (b) removal of suspension; (c) removal of supervision requirements. In the event the psychologist or psychological associate has not met the Board's criteria for rehabilitation, the plan may be revised, expanded, and/or continued depending upon the progress of the rehabilitation program. The Board may follow one or more options in devising a rehabilitation plan:

1. The individual may be supervised in all or selected areas of activities related to his/her practice as a psychologist or psychological associate by a licensed psychologist approved by the Board for a specified length of time.
   a. The Board will specify the focus of the supervision.
   b. The Board will specify the number of hours per week required in a face-to-face supervisory contract.
   c. The supervisor will provide periodic and timely reports to the Board concerning the progress of the supervisee.
   d. Any fees for supervision time will be the responsibility of the supervisee.
   e. The supervisor is acting as a "friend" of the Board. Judgments of the supervisor are to be made independently and without reference to Board opinions.

2. The individual may be expected to successfully complete a variety of appropriate educational programs. Appropriate educational formats may include but are not limited to workshops, seminars, courses in regionally accredited universities, or organized pre- or post-doctoral internship settings. Workshops or seminars which are not held in a setting of academic review (approved Continuing Education) need prior approval of the Board. Any course of study must be approved by the board prior to enrollment if it is to meet the criteria of a rehabilitation plan.

3. The Board may require of the individual:
   a. psychodiagnostic evaluations by a psychologist acceptable to the Board and the individual;
   b. psychotherapy on a regular, continuing basis from a psychologist or other professional acceptable to the Board and the individual.

4. The Board may require the individual to:
   a. take or retake the generic licensing examination currently pro-

vided by the American Association of State Psychology Boards;
  b. take or retake the jurisprudence examination.

Restoration of License

For complaints that result in license revocation, state law may specify a minimum time before the reinstatement or restoration of a license is possible. Wyoming sets the minimum at six months. Eleven states specify 1 year,[18] six states specify 2 years,[19] six states specify 3 years,[20] and the District of Columbia requires 5 years. The remaining 35 jurisdictions either have no minimum time period or specify that a decision to restore a license is dependent on a majority vote of the board. Therefore, although a person may lose the right to practice, the opportunity for relicensure exists but is typically dependent upon waiting a minimum time period and demonstrating appropriate behavior following suspension or revocation.

Appeal of the Board's Decision

By statute, the psychologist has the option of appealing an adverse decision of a state board. In all jurisdictions, the psychologist can appeal to a higher body, typically a county, district, or state court. The court may affirm the decision or remand the case for further proceeding. In North Carolina, the court may modify the decision if the findings, inferences, conclusions, or decisions were

  (a) in violation of constitutional provisions,
  (b) in excess of statutory authority or jurisdiction,
  (c) made upon unlawful procedure,
  (d) affected by other error of law,
  (e) unsupported by substantive evidence, or
  (f) arbitrary and capricious (N.C. Gen. Stat., 1983).

In five states such appeals are not on the record but are actually new trials.[21] The term used to describe this type of appeal, in which all the issues are tried as if no administrative hearing had taken place, is *trial de novo*. However, should the licensee request and receive a stay of the enforcement powers of the board, the sanction imposed by the board will not be applied. Individual law determines at what stage a decision of the board is final and enforceable. If a motion for reconsideration or rehearing is denied, the board's decision is final and binding. If the motion is not denied, the order may still be enforced, depending on the jurisdiction in question.

---

[18]Eleven states that restore licenses after 1 year: Alaska, California, Delaware, Kansas, Michigan, Nevada, New Hampshire, New Jersey, New York, Texas, and Wisconsin.

[19]Six states that restore licenses after 2 years: Colorado, Louisiana, Mississippi, New Mexico, North Dakota, and Virginia.

[20]Six states that restore licenses after 3 years: Alabama, Georgia, Kentucky, Massachusetts, South Carolina, and Tennessee.

[21]Five states with appeal via *trial de novo:* Alabama, Alaska, Louisiana, Oklahoma, and Wyoming.

THE AMERICAN PSYCHOLOGICAL ASSOCIATION'S DISCIPLINARY PROCESS

The difference between the due process procedures followed by a state and those of a professional society derives from the fact that, once a state confers a property interest to a professional, the state cannot withdraw that property right without adhering to the elements of due process. Membership in a society is not a property right but rather a privilege that can be taken away without due process. Even so, two points are worth noting: (a) actions taken by the American Psychological Association (APA) with respect to membership are still subject to judicial scrutiny to ensure good-faith use of power in accordance with APA Bylaws and (b) most state psychological associations have modeled their procedures to conform with many of the elements of due process. In fact, 27 of the 44 state associations responding to the survey sent out by the APA Ethics Office (Hall & Hare-Mustin, 1983) have developed a formal set of rules and procedures.[22] Six of those associations have adopted the provisions of the APA Rules and Procedures (APA, 1985).[23]

The APA Ethics Committee attempts to handle most complaints through an informal process and by correspondence. Once a complaint form is received and reviewed by the Chairperson and the Administrative Officer for Ethics, a letter specifying the complaint is sent to the member. With the complaint letter, the member receives a copy of the form signed by the complainant, which releases the accused member from maintaining confidentiality and thereby enables the member to answer specific charges. At that point, a "timely response" to the Ethics Committee is considered to be within 30 days of receiving the letter specifying the charges. However, whenever the Committee finds that a member has been convicted of a felony, has been expelled for unethical conduct from an affiliated state or regional association, or has had a license revoked on ethical grounds, the Committee follows a specified procedure that involves giving the member 60 days in which to show cause why he or she should not be expelled from the Association. Either type of disciplinary action is carried out by correspondence.

If the Committee finds a member guilty of a violation of the APA ethics code, the Committee can issue a censure or reprimand, negotiate a stipulated resignation, or recommend expulsion or dropping from membership. The Committee determines whether or not the member is guilty, primarily on the basis of documentation submitted by correspondence. This decision is a peer judgment, and in some cases the standard of proof may vary from what would exist in a court of law (Hare-Mustin & Hall, 1981). The Committee's rule is similar to a disciplinary hearing in that the "preponderance of the evidence" criterion is typically used (D. Mills, personal communication, December 1984).

[22]Twenty-seven jurisdictions with rules and procedures manuals for their ethics committee: Arizona, Arkansas, California, Colorado, Illinois, Kansas, Maryland, Massachusetts, Michigan, Mississippi, Montana, New Jersey, New York, North Carolina, Ohio, Oklahoma, Oregon, Pennsylvania, Rhode Island, Tennessee, Texas, Virginia, Washington, West Virginia, Wyoming, Puerto Rico, and Ontario.

[23]Six jurisdictions having adopted the APA Ethics Committee Rules and Procedures manual: Arkansas, Mississippi, Montana, New Jersey, Pennsylvania and West Virginia.

Somewhat parallel to the consent order used by licensure boards is the stipulated resignation used by the Ethics Committee. The stipulated resignation is basically a confidential contract that states that the member is allowed to resign for a specified number of years, usually less than 5, contingent upon the member's fulfilling during that period certain requirements regarding restriction of practice, supervision, continuing education, or personal psychotherapy. The stipulation involves an admission of guilt by the member and a willingness to follow a plan outlined by the Committee. At the completion of the contract with the Ethics Committee, the former member is readmitted to membership. Should the ex-member violate the agreement, the disciplinary process will begin anew. The difference between the stipulated resignation and the loss of membership in APA (through expulsion or being dropped from membership) is that the Committee develops a formal plan of rehabilitation. The Committee may also require submission of periodic reports to the Committee by the member's therapist as part of the stipulated agreement. Stipulated resignation has been used with a first and single instance of sexual intimacy with a client (Hall & Hare-Mustin, 1983), and this approach could also be used for rehabilitating those who abuse alcohol and drugs. In recent times, however, the Committee has been using censure rather than a stipulated resignation, because the person retains membership and thus the scrutiny of the Association (D. Mills, personal communication, November 1984).

Hearing Process Within the Ethics Committee

Failure to accept the sanction determined by the Ethics Committee may lead to formal charges being filed against a member. When formal action is taken against a member, the person so charged has 30 days in which to request a hearing before three members of the Standing Hearing Panel. The Hearing Panel receives evidence presented by the member and by the Ethics Committee and renders an opinion, which is sent to all parties concerned and to the Board of Directors of APA. This same Standing Hearing Panel also decides whether or not the failure of a member to accept a sanction or censure, reprimand, or probation through the informal adjudication process of the Ethics Committee has merit. "If a majority decide that there is merit to the nonacceptance, then the case is referred back to the Committee for further investigation or other action" (Mills, 1984, p. 674). If the majority agrees with the Committee's decision, the matter is closed with the censure, reprimand, or expulsion left standing.

An application for readmission to membership in APA by a person who has been expelled can be submitted to the Ethics Committee five years from the date of expulsion. An application for readmission by a member who has been permitted to resign can be considered three years from the date of resignation.

Keeping in mind the framework for investigation, charges, prosecution, and sanction of licensed psychologists and the complaint process for members of professional associations, let us direct our attention to the more specific problem of disciplining the distressed psychologist. Although all of the preceding information in this chapter applies to any psychologist, there may be differences by state in the intervention approach taken and the definition of who is a distressed professional.

GROUNDS FOR DISCIPLINARY ACTION AGAINST PSYCHOLOGISTS

A distressed psychologist is a psychologist who is afflicted by incapacitating physical, emotional, legal, or job-related problems or disorders that adversely affect professional performance. These stressors are thought to be at least partly responsible for alcoholism, drug dependence, burnout, incompetence, emotional disorders, and sexual intimacy with clients. If a psychologist is found guilty of these violations and if there is a demonstrated effect on the practice (or in some states, the teaching) of the psychologist, a sanction or a rehabilitation plan may follow. Let us examine these grounds for disciplinary action as each is described in the statutes or regulations of the 60 jurisdictions under consideration.

Alcoholism

Nineteen jurisdictions specify that a psychologist violates the professional conduct code when he or she "uses any alcoholic beverage to such an extent that practice is impaired or is dangerous to self."[24] Thirteen jurisdictions cite that "habitual intoxication or being a habitual drunkard" is grounds for revocation of a license,[25] whereas nine indicate "habitual intemperance" as a violation of the professional conduct code.[26] Five jurisdictions find a "severe dependency" on alcohol to be unprofessional conduct.[27] Six jurisdictions use unique wording to address the problem (Kansas, Michigan, Minnesota, Florida, Quebec, and Washington). The eight jurisdictions that do not have a specific prohibition against alcoholism are West Virginia and the remaining seven Canadian provinces. Each of these jurisdictions has adopted the APA ethics code, which addresses the problem indirectly. Therefore, even though the wording may vary across jurisdictions, alcoholism as it affects practice is a basis for disciplinary action against psychologists in every jurisdiction.

Drug Abuse

The same descriptive patterns emerge in statutes for drug abuse as for alcohol; the statutes that address "using any alcoholic beverage to such an extent . . ." also include "using any drug to such an extent . . . ." Some of the statutes focus

---

[24]Nineteen jurisdictions specifying "use of alcoholic beverage": Arizona, California, Connecticut, Colorado, Delaware, District of Columbia, Louisiana, Massachusetts, Mississippi, Missouri, Montana, New Mexico, North Dakota, Ohio, South Dakota, Texas, Virginia, Utah, and Wisconsin.
[25]Thirteen jurisdictions specifying "habitual drunkard": Hawaii, Idaho, Illinois, Iowa, Kentucky, Maryland, Nebraska, Nevada, New York, North Carolina, Oklahoma, Oregon, and Pennsylvania.
[26]Nine jurisdictions specifying "habitual intemperance": Alabama, Arkansas, Georgia, Maine, New Jersey, Rhode Island, South Carolina, Tennessee, and Vermont.
[27]Five jurisdictions specifying "severe dependency": Alaska, Indiana, New Hampshire, Wyoming, and Puerto Rico.

on drug abuse, whereas others list all categories of drugs, such as narcotics, stimulants, barbiturates, amphetamines, or chemicals, and use of all of them in excess or in a dependent way is forbidden. Basically the intent of the statutes and description of alcohol abuse and drug abuse are consistent within the jurisdictions.

For some time, alcohol and drug abuse have been recognized as frequently occurring problems among physicians and dentists, especially because those two professions have direct access to drugs, and alcohol dependency is not seen as being very different by many professionals. Also, members of both professional groups have busy practices and are often under great stress. In recent times, attention has shifted to psychologists (Thoreson, Nathan, Skorina, & Kilburg, 1983). As a result, it is likely that reports of alcoholism and drug abuse among psychologists may increase, as have reports of sexual intimacy with clients.

Physical and Mental Disabilities

Ten jurisdictions specifically address the impact of a mental or physical disability on the ability to practice.[28] An additional 11 hold that mental disability or illness as evidenced by involuntary commitment is a basis for revocation of a license.[29] Ten jurisdictions have the option of requiring an examination in order to determine whether the practitioner is practicing safely.[30] Statutes of Minnesota and Washington include a reference to a severe health problem or illness as disciplinary grounds but do not explain whether that includes mental as well as physical illness. California has a provision that introduces the APA Ethical Principle 2F by stating that "a psychologist's effectiveness depends upon his or her ability to maintain sound interpersonal relations and that temporary or more enduring problems in a psychologist's own personality may interfere with this ability and distort his/her appraisal of others" (Calif. Title 16, 1983) Quebec's law states that a psychologist must refrain from practicing while he or she is in a state that could impair quality of services or while his or her health is an obstacle.

Probably the person best qualified to determine if a psychologist is mentally ill is another psychologist. Unfortunately, many have taken the attitude that they are "not their brother's keeper" and they "don't want to get involved," especially given the likelihood of being sued. As mentioned earlier, moral fitness is determined before licensure. In some states, that may include mental fitness, or there may be a statute requiring that the candidate for licensure be mentally fit to practice the profession. Although supervisors are asked these questions routinely about licensure applicants, they may not answer truthfully

[28]Ten jurisdictions specifying "physical or mental disability": Alaska, Arizona, Colorado, Florida, Illinois, Iowa, New Hampshire, New York, North Dakota, and Oregon.
[29]Eleven jurisdictions revoking license with involuntary commitment: District of Columbia, Maine, Mississippi, Missouri, New Mexico, North Dakota, Ohio, Oregon, Pennsylvania, Rhode Island, and Puerto Rico.
[30]Ten jurisdictions with authority to require mental and physical status examination: Connecticut, Indiana, Michigan, Ohio, South Dakota, Texas, Washington, Virginia, New Brunswick, and Quebec.

PROFESSIONALS IN DISTRESS

or they may pass the concern on to the licensure board and when questioned, may refuse to back up what they have said.

A particularly unpleasant example of this occurred recently at the state board level. An applicant who had been licensed in one state applied for licensure in a second. Supervisors who had not seen the candidate in a few years either refused to send in an experience form, that is, would not say anything, or they sent samples of the very disturbed, recent communications from the candidate. The one supervisor who was most qualified to judge the current mental state of the applicant and who was an American Board of Professional Psychology (ABPP) Diplomate in Counseling Psychology was unwilling to do anything other than to submit a sample of the applicant's paranoid ideation to the state licensure board. Those with direct contact who knew the applicant were unwilling to testify as to his possible mental instability. They, too, were Fellows of APA and Diplomates.

This candidate was denied a license in the second state because of insufficient experience. Upon follow-up, the state was able to determine that he had let his first license lapse, lost his job, and became a transient. Although his supervisors may have been properly cautious, they were not considering the necessity of intervening for the candidate's sake or for the protection of the public.

Stress as a Defense

How effective are pleas for mercy when a psychologist has been determined to be chemically dependent or even mentally ill? Most people would probably believe the first problem to be more remediable than the latter, and the presence of alcoholism has been used as a successful defense in disciplinary trials against licensed professionals. Reaves (1984) pointed out that certain criteria must be present in order for the state board or the criminal court to negotiate a successful resolution to the charge of unprofessional conduct or practicing with negligence. The attorney for the accused must demonstrate all of the following: (a) The accused is affected by alcoholism; (b) The alcoholism caused the misconduct; (c) The accused is recovering from the alcoholism; and (d) The misconduct has been arrested and is not likely to occur again.

Presumably this approach would apply to drug abuse also. In cases of mental illness it may be more difficult to convince the board members that the problem is remediable or that it was a temporary aberration that was reversible. However, these three presenting problems (alcoholism, drug abuse, and physical or mental disabilities) have received the most attention in rehabilitation plans set up by professional societies for physicians and dentists and for lawyers. Admittedly, these approaches seem to work best when the professional seeks help rather than being forced into treatment. Following is a description of a program that attempts to maximize the likelihood that an impaired professional will return to practice.

Model Diversion Program

Since January 1980, impaired physicians in California have been given the opportunity to be diverted from possible medical board discipline into a statewide treatment program financed by the Board of Medical Quality Assurance (BMQA). The California Diversion Program for Impaired Physicians (1983) was developed for physicians who are "unable to practice medicine with reasonable skill and safety to patients because of physical or mental illness, including deterioration through the aging process or loss of motor skill, or excessive use or abuse of drugs including alcohol" (p. 226). Any physician so troubled is given the opportunity for diversion from possible medical board discipline by self-referral to a statewide treatment program. The program attributes its success to four key elements: (a) a rapid response mechanism, (b) an individually tailored rehabilitation program, (c) strict confidentiality, and (d) frequent monitoring by involved colleagues and the program's staff (Gualtieri, Cosentino, & Becker, 1983).

This program was modeled after the first program of its kind originally sponsored by the DeKalb County Medical Society and later supported statewide by the Georgia State Medical Society. The diversion program is restricted to physicians who are impaired by virtue of alcohol abuse, self-administration of drugs, mental or physical illness, or emotional disorder affecting competency to practice. It is not designed nor has it expanded to diverting those who have sexually abused their patients. The individually designed treatment program may extend from one to five years. If the BMQA has an investigation pending against the impaired physician, BMQA ceases its investigation when the physician refers him- or herself and is admitted to the diversion program. In cases in which a complaint has been filed, the complaint is withdrawn when the physician has successfully completed the program. Upon completion of the program, the records of the Diversion Evaluation Committee are destroyed. The program was initiated in January 1980, and as of March 1983, a total of 275 physician referrals had been received. As of March 1983, 149 were active in the program. Of those, 73 had clear license status with the BMQA (California Diversion Program, 1983).

To date, no similar state-mandated programs have been set up for psychologists. Many of the state psychological associations are establishing advisory services for psychologists in need, but no board has instituted a diversion-from-discipline program for psychologists.

Sexual Intimacy With Clients

There is a specific prohibition against sexual intimacies with clients in all jurisdictions except Nevada, which has proposed such a provision for a revised statute. As indicated earlier, 42 of the states have adopted the 1977, 1979, or 1981 APA ethics code, which state that "sexual intimacies with clients are unethical." An additional 12, in their own professional conduct code, specifically prohibit sexual intimacies with clients.[31] Three states take disciplinary action for sexual intimacies with clients after reaching a judgment that the psychologist has "acted wrongfully" (Connecticut), "affected the welfare of the client" (Hawaii), or is "incompetent" (Michigan). Puerto Rico has words indi-

[31]Twelve jurisdictions with a professional conduct code prohibiting sexual intimacies with clients: Arizona, California, Colorado, Florida, Illinois, Kansas, Minnesota, New Jersey, New York, Ohio, Washington, and Quebec.

cating "moral depravity" in the statute, which will have to serve until the U.S. territory develops a professional conduct code.

The tougher attitude toward disciplining those who have engaged in sexual intimacies, contact, or a relationship with a client is evidenced by (a) a stricter attitude toward enforcement, (b) an increasing frequency of cases reported and given publicity, and (c) the large malpractice sums and punitive damages being awarded to complainants. Reflecting the attitude of legislatures and the public toward this behavior, some states have introduced legislation that makes the act criminal. In Wisconsin, engaging in sexual intimacies with a client is also grounds for a criminal conviction. In Colorado, the state board may take action by referring a complaint to appropriate authorities for criminal prosecution or to the Office of the Attorney General for injunctive proceedings if (a) the violation resulted in significant damage, (b) the violation represents a threat to the public welfare, or (c) the violation is not likely to be corrected or eliminated by informal disposition of the complaint.

To convince the public that psychologists who engage in sexual intimacies with clients may have had precipitating personal problems (cf. Keith-Spiegel & Koocher, 1985), especially when the action is repeated with several clients or concerns children, is difficult at best. In fact, the recent $1.7 million and $1.5 million awards in two malpractice actions against two psychologists who engaged in sexual intimacies may indicate an escalating public outrage (Kovacs, 1984; N. Cummings, personal communication, April 1985). The increasing recognition of the frequency with which sexual abuse of clients takes place has sensitized the public to the necessity for sanction, not forgiveness.

Incompetence and Burnout

The relationship of stress to professional incompetence is even less understood, especially by the public. Freudenberger and Richelson (1975) described burnout as emotional exhaustion due to excessive demands on energy, time, strength, and personal resources in the work setting. Currently, the statutes do not recognize the concept of burnout, but each does address minimal competence needed to practice safely or incompetence, practicing below acceptable standards, or practicing with negligence. (The legal term for practicing with negligence is malpractice.) All states specify in statute that incompetence, gross or repeated negligence, or engaging in wrongful actions are bases for disciplinary action against a licensee.

Principle 2f of the APA code addresses this first concept indirectly by recognizing that personal problems and conflicts might occur and must be addressed.

> Psychologists recognize that personal problems and conflicts may interfere with professional effectiveness. Accordingly, they refrain from undertaking any activity in which their personal problems are likely to lead to inadequate performance or harm to a client, colleague, student, or research participant. If engaged in such activity when they become aware of their personal problems, they seek competent professional assistance to determine whether they should suspend, terminate, or limit the scope of their professional and/or scientific activities. (APA, 1981a, p. 234)

The second approach to competence derives from the requirement in the APA ethical code that practitioners must function within the areas or boundaries of their competence. Both types of incompetence could result from professional burnout: In addition to failing to recognize excessive demands on ability to practice safely, a psychologist could fail to recognize that a client is not improving and thus must be referred elsewhere. This lack of improvement could be due to the psychologist's working outside established areas of competency.

The 42 states that have adopted the APA ethics code (either 1977, 1979, or 1981) have incorporated Principle 2 as their standard of competence:

> The maintenance of high standards of competence is a responsibility shared by all psychologists in the interest of the public and the profession as a whole. Psychologists recognize the boundaries of their competence and the limitations of their techniques. They only provide services and only use techniques for which they are qualified by training and experience. In those areas in which recognized standards do not yet exist, psychologists take whatever precautions are necessary to protect the welfare of their clients. They maintain knowledge of current scientific and professional information related to the services they render. (APA, 1981a)

Several of those same states recognize that licensees might wish to change their competencies to new areas of specialization and therefore provide guidance by the adoption of Principle 1.7 of the *Standards for Providers of Psychological Services* (APA, 1977), which requires that a psychologist obtain formal education and training in a doctoral program in the new specialty area before attempting practice in that new area (Hall, 1983).

RESPONSES OF DISTRESSED PSYCHOLOGISTS

The psychologists who survive charges of unprofessional or unethical conduct relatively intact are those who admitted their fault early in the investigation or complaint process, made necessary changes in their professional practice and workload, and obtained psychotherapeutic help or supervision. Those who were not guilty responded to the charges in writing with a complete, documented answer.

Some examples of those who did follow that course of action are summarized below.

1. In the settlement stipulation in one state, the licensee admitted that he "was involved with his own personal problems and was providing psychological services to a heavy case load, involving nine hours of work per day, five days a week." Since the events concerning the client with whom he became sexually involved, "licensee has decreased his case load, works approximately five to six hours per day, five days per week, and has attempted to resolve his personal problems."

2. In another case of sexual intimacy with clients, this time with children, the board revoked the psychologist's license and did not require remediation because the board members were familiar with the literature and felt that a

cure was very unlikely. (Although the psychologist did not appeal for the opportunity to follow a rehabilitation plan developed by the board, it would have been wise for him to do so.)

3. A member of an association was found to have plagiarized the dissertation discussion section (the data were presumably not forged) and, when contacted by the committee, immediately asked for a personal appearance, admitted guilt, and indicated his good faith attempt to remediate his error. He indicated that he was under a great deal of stress because of his dominant mother and was under pressure to succeed because he was not a U.S. citizen. He had previously contacted his university, and they were willing to accept a rewritten discussion section. The committee accepted his explanation and remediation and gave him a censure/reprimand.

4. A licensee in a jurisdiction that has a title act, rather than a restricted definition of practice, showed good faith to observe the board's ruling that he not practice for a specific period by obtaining a job in a different field in that interim. (He could have legally practiced psychology under a different title.)

Those psychologists who deny all guilt throughout the whole process, engage in delaying tactics themselves or through their attorneys, file countersuits, or violate the stipulated agreements either with the ethics committee or with the court are most likely to do so at great personal and financial cost. Often these individuals also choose every avenue for appeal, which leads to tremendous costs for the system and for them and ensures that their names will be known both in and out of the state. They end up with no sympathy from anyone except their lawyers, to whom they are indebted.

Assuming that the psychologist seeks help and wants to do everything to reestablish him- or herself in the community and as a psychologist, boards are willing to tailor the rehabilitation plan to the individual needs of the psychologist. Certainly, the focus of the ethics committee is to keep members, not lose them. That is also true of state licensing boards. Now we shall examine their philosophy regarding rehabilitation.

REHABILITATIVE APPROACH

Even though some states have never revoked a psychologist's license (e.g., Alabama, Louisiana, Nevada, and North Dakota), it appears that the rate and the number of disciplinary actions against psychologists have increased, as a result of an increasingly sophisticated public and of the increasing recognition that, in particular, sexual intimacies with clients are unethical and may be damaging to the clients. Even in those states that have revoked a license, however, board members comment that it may be preferable to keep the psychologist, subject to a rehabilitation plan, than to revoke the license to practice, because those that lose their licenses may practice under another title, without being subject to a professional conduct code and thus might cause more public harm. Thus, it may be more desirable for a professional society to sanction and to rehabilitate than simply to expel and thus lose control. The desire to salvage a career and the mandate to protect the public are the goals that the state and the association must weigh.

Others believe that it is preferable to revoke the license first and require rehabilitation prior to relicensure or to expel from the association and demand evidence of acceptable behavior prior to readmission. Often this attitude reflects an awareness of the lax enforcement of professional and statutory standards for many years and the view that the shift to more effective, more swift justice is long overdue.

As indicated earlier, the APA ethics code, unlike state statutes, contains no specific prohibition against alcoholism, drug abuse, or mental and physical impairment. Instead, Principle 2f focuses on the harm that might result from these impairments and requires that the psychologist seek help and refrain from practicing if personal problems are affecting the ability to provide services. In the absence of specific prohibition against alcoholism, drug abuse, and mental illness, these kinds of complaints appear to be referred more often to the state board than to the Ethics Committee. The complaint of sexual intimacy with clients, which the APA ethics code does prohibit, frequently is submitted to both the state and the association (Hall & Hare-Mustin, 1983).

PUBLIC NOTICE AND REPORTING REQUIREMENTS

What are the implications for the distressed psychologist found guilty of violating certain provisions of statute or regulation? The first implication derives from the fact that the licensure bodies are an arm of the state government and thus all final actions are made public. Because all jurisdictions except Guam and Michigan are members of the American Association of State Psychology Boards (AASPB) and because the AASPB has established a Disciplinary Data System to facilitate the communication of formal actions (defined as probation, suspension, and revocation) concerning licensees to all other states, every jurisdiction now receives a list of the names of those licensees who have violated the professional conduct provisions. The AASPB Disciplinary Data Bank is also sent to the APA Ethics Committee, the state ethics committees, and the Council for the National Register of Health Service Providers, because many licensees may be members of the national or state association and may be listed in the National Register. When notified of the final action taken, those organizations can obtain copies of the official record and find against the member or registrant anew. If a psychologist is licensed in additional states, each state must review the disciplinary record and decide whether to take disciplinary action. Therefore, the AASPB Disciplinary Data Bank increases the likelihood that APA, the state associations, and the National Register will follow up on action taken by a state board.

The receipt of the AASPB list of disciplinary charges by the APA Ethics Committee increases the likelihood that APA will take action to drop the person from membership or recommend expulsion to the Board of Directors. The Ethics Committee automatically communicates to the APA membership once a year the names of the members who have been expelled from membership by the APA Board of Directors and the names of the members who were dropped from APA membership upon the recommendation of the Ethics Committee. In turn, although certain sanctions by the Ethics Committee are typically confidential (censure and reprimand, probation, and stipulated resignation), the Committee has the authority to release that information to the state boards if the Committee is convinced that to do otherwise would pose a threat to the public. If a complaint is filed simultaneously with the Ethics Committee and a state board, however, the Committee will typically wait for final action by the board before taking action.

The APA Ethics Committee has developed guidelines for referring a complaint to a state association and referring the complainant to the Ethics Committee. The purpose of these guidelines is to reduce the triple jeopardy that occurs while assuring that the complainant has an avenue of redress. (Those guidelines are available from the Ethics Office of APA.) In addition, in Alabama, Delaware, Montana, and Tennessee, there is a formal relationship between the state ethics committee and the state board.

In addition, if a charge of practicing with negligence had been brought first in civil court and the jury had found the psychologist guilty of malpractice, information on the award or the settlement would eventually reach the licensure boards either through direct referral or by public notice. For example, in the profession of medicine there is a requirement that insurance companies and malpractice arbitration panels make mandatory reports to 16 of the existing medical licensure boards (Federation of State Medical Boards of the United States, Inc., 1984). In the future, states may require the reporting of psychological malpractice, as now occurs in Iowa and Michigan. In Kansas, evidence of wrongful action or lack of good moral character includes failing to report disciplinary action by another licensure authority or professional association or failing to notify the board of violation of state laws or rules by a practitioner or teacher of psychology. In Minnesota a psychologist is required to report when she or he has reason to believe that another psychologist is or has been engaged in sexual contact with a client. In addition, if a psychologist is convicted of a crime such as drunk driving, tax evasion, or perjury, that criminal conviction may be automatically referred to the state licensure board, as it is in New York and Michigan.

RECOMMENDATIONS

Given that these matters constitute a most serious threat to the future professional lives of psychologists in distress, what are the recommendations to those charged with an ethical or disciplinary complaint?

If not guilty:

1. Prepare a complete and full response and ask for an informal hearing to resolve the complaint.

2. If the complaint comes from an ethics committee, take the time to respond completely and submit available documentation. If you need additional time to respond fully, call or write to the ethics office or committee chair for additional time.

If guilty:

1. Engage an experienced trial attorney knowledgeable in administrative law. Use a specialist rather than your family attorney.

2. Admit your guilt and ask for a speedy resolution and for a rehabilitation plan. If you decide to fight, assess the consequences: financial, emotional, familial, and professional. Consider a consent order and balance that with the costs of a trial.

3. If seeking an informal solution does not prevent a formal hearing, discuss with your attorney whether it is best to request a closed hearing (to lessen stress on those involved) or to request a public hearing.

4. If the complaint comes from an ethics committee, you must first decide on a strategy. An attorney with experience in these matters may be helpful for advice but he or she cannot respond for you. Consider admitting guilt and ask for a rehabilitation plan that spells out what you must do to retain or regain membership.

5. If you are unable to clearly understand these issues, seek professional help. Discuss your uncertainties within the context of a confidential relationship.

6. Carefully follow through on any agreement or rehabilitation plan made with a state board or ethics committee. Remember, your professional future depends upon a demonstration of a sincere commitment to change your life. In these situations, half-hearted commitments, casual attitudes, and attempts at manipulation can only lead to more trouble.

In summary, distressed psychologists and other distressed professionals are automatically involved in a system of public and professional regulation. Poor performance and misconduct can lead to the most serious consequences. State boards have police power and in some instances, they punish people severely for their transgressions.

In this chapter, I have attempted to describe how this system works and to provide information about how distressed psychologists may resolve real problems. Failure to understand these complexities or to heed the advice given here can result in even more distress. Remember, in most instances, the professionals who serve on these bodies have some understanding of these problems and will, in most cases, try to assist colleagues who are seriously interested in resolving their difficulties.

References

American Psychological Association. (1977). *Standards for providers of psychological services* (rev. ed.). Washington, DC: Author.

American Psychological Association. (1981a). Ethical principles of psychologists. *American Psychologist, 36*(6), 633–638.

American Psychological Association. (1981b). *Specialty guidelines for the delivery of services.* Washington, DC: Author.

American Psychological Association, Ethics Committee (1985). Rules and procedures. *American Psychologist, 40,* 685–694.

California Diversion Program for Impaired Physicians. (1983, March 29). *The diversion program for physicians: Status report.* (Available from the Diversion Program, P.O. Box 255853, Sacramento, CA 98525).

California Board of Medical Quality Assurance, Psychology Examining Committee. (n.d.). *Disciplinary guidelines.* (Available from Psychology Examining Committee, 1430 Howe Ave., Sacramento, CA 95825)

Calif. Stat. tit. 16, § 1396.1 (1983).

Federation of State Medical Boards of the United States, Inc. (1984, August 30). *Medical examining boards in states having mandatory reporting requirements.* (Available from the Federation, 2630 West Freeway, Suite 138, Fort Worth, TX 76102).

Freudenberger, H. J., & Richelson, G. (1980). *Burnout.* New York: Anchor Press.

Gualtieri, A. C., Cosentino, J. P., & Becker, J. S. (1983). The California experience with a diversion program for impaired physicians. *Journal of the American Medical Association, 249*(2), 226–229.

Hall, J. E. (1983). Respecialization, licensure and conduct. *The Clinical Psychologist, 36*(3), 68–71.

Hall, J. E., & Hare-Mustin, R. T. (1983). Sanctions and the diversity of ethical complaints against psychologists. *American Psychologist, 36,* 714–729.

Hare-Mustin, R. T., & Hall, J. E. (1981). Procedures for responding to ethics complaints against psychologists. *American Psychologist, 36,* 1494–1505.

Keith-Spiegel, P., & Koocher, G. (1985). *Ethics and professional standards.* New York: Random House.

Kovacs, A. L. (1984). Psychology's growing malpractice crisis: APA's response. *The Independent Practitioner, 4*(4), 9–12.

Mills, D. H. (1984). Ethics education and adjudication within psychology. *American Psychologist, 39,* 669–675.

Naftalison, L. J. (1972). *Manual for hearing officers in administrative adjudication in the State of New York.* (Available from the New York State Civil Service Commission, Albany, NY 12201).

Nathan, P. E., Thoreson, R. W., & Kilburg, R. R. (1983). *Board of Professional Affairs, Steering Committee on Distressed Psychologists: Draft report.* (Available from the American Psychological Association, 1200 Seventeenth St. N.W., Washington, DC 20036).

National Association of Attorneys General. (1978). *Disciplinary action manual for occupational licensing boards.* (Available from the Association, 3901 Barrett Drive, Raleigh, NC 27609).

N.C. Gen. Stat. § 150a–51 (1983).

New York State Education Department. (1985, November). *Psychology.* (Available from the Office of the Professions, NYSED, Cultural Education Center, Albany, NY 12230).

Reaves, R. P. (1984). *The law of professional licensing and certification.* (Available from Publications for Professionals, P.O. Box 13579, Charlotte, NC 28211).

Roederer, D., & Shimberg, B. (1980). *Occupational licensing: Centralizing state licensure functions.* Lexington, KY: Council of State Governments.

Texas State Board of Examiners of Psychologists. (1983, September). *General rulings.* (Available from the Texas Board, 1300 E. Anderson Ln., Suite C-270, Austin, TX 78752)

Thoreson, R. W., Nathan, P. E., Skorina, J. K., & Kilburg, R. R. (1983). The alcoholic psychologist: Issues, problems, and implications for the profession. *Professional Psychology: Research and Practice, 14,* 670–684.

Wand, B. (1984). Financial resources and the regulatory activities of professional licensing bodies in psychology. *Professional Practice of Psychology: Legal, Regulatory and Licensure Issues, 5*(1), 41–50.